T0250225

INCORPORATING AI TECHNOLOGY IN THE SERVICE SECTOR

*Innovations in Creating Knowledge,
Improving Efficiency, and Elevating Quality of Life*

AAP Advances in Artificial Intelligence and Robotics

INCORPORATING AI TECHNOLOGY IN THE SERVICE SECTOR

*Innovations in Creating Knowledge,
Improving Efficiency, and Elevating Quality of Life*

Edited by
Maria José Sousa, PhD
Subhendu Kumar Pani, PhD
Francesca Dal Mas, PhD
Sérgio Sousa, PhD

AAP APPLE ACADEMIC PRESS

First edition published 2024

Apple Academic Press Inc.
1265 Goldenrod Circle, NE,
Palm Bay, FL 32905 USA

760 Laurentian Drive, Unit 19,
Burlington, ON L7N 0A4, CANADA

CRC Press
2385 NW Executive Center Drive,
Suite 320, Boca Raton FL 33431

4 Park Square, Milton Park,
Abingdon, Oxon, OX14 4RN UK

© 2024 by Apple Academic Press, Inc.

Apple Academic Press exclusively co-publishes with CRC Press, an imprint of Taylor & Francis Group, LLC

Reasonable efforts have been made to publish reliable data and information, but the authors, editors, and publisher cannot assume responsibility for the validity of all materials or the consequences of their use. The authors, editors, and publishers have attempted to trace the copyright holders of all material reproduced in this publication and apologize to copyright holders if permission to publish in this form has not been obtained. If any copyright material has not been acknowledged, please write and let us know so we may rectify in any future reprint.

Except as permitted under U.S. Copyright Law, no part of this book may be reprinted, reproduced, transmitted, or utilized in any form by any electronic, mechanical, or other means, now known or hereafter invented, including photocopying, microfilming, and recording, or in any information storage or retrieval system, without written permission from the publishers.

For permission to photocopy or use material electronically from this work, access www.copyright.com or contact the Copyright Clearance Center, Inc. (CCC), 222 Rosewood Drive, Danvers, MA 01923, 978-750-8400. For works that are not available on CCC please contact mpkbookspermissions@tandf.co.uk

Trademark notice: Product or corporate names may be trademarks or registered trademarks and are used only for identification and explanation without intent to infringe.

Library and Archives Canada Cataloguing in Publication

Title: Incorporating AI technology in the service sector : innovations in creating knowledge, improving efficiency, and elevating quality of life / edited by Maria José Sousa, PhD, Subhendu Kumar Pani, PhD, Francesca Dal Mas, PhD, Sérgio Sousa, PhD.
Names: Sousa, Maria José, editor. | Pani, Subhendu Kumar, 1980- editor. | Dal Mas, Francesca, editor. | Sousa, Sérgio, editor.
Description: First edition. | Series statement: AAP advances in artificial intelligence and robotics | Includes bibliographical references and index.
Identifiers: Canadiana (print) 20230475078 | Canadiana (ebook) 20230475183 | ISBN 9781774913338 (hardcover) | ISBN 9781774913345 (softcover) | ISBN 9781003378068 (ebook)
Subjects: LCSH: Service industries—Technological innovations. | LCSH: Artificial intelligence.
Classification: LCC HD9980.5 .I53 2024 | DDC 338.40285/63—dc23

Library of Congress Cataloging-in-Publication Data

Names: Sousa, Maria Jose, editor.
Title: Incorporating AI technology in the service sector : innovations in creating knowledge, improving efficiency, and elevating quality of life / edited by Maria José Sousa, PhD, Subhendu Subhendu Pani Kumar Pani, PhD, Francesca Dal Mas, PhD, Sérgio Sousa, PhD.
Description: First edition. | Palm Bay, FL : Apple Academic Press, [2024] | Series: AAP advances in artificial intelligence and robotics | Includes bibliographical references and index. | Summary: "Due to advances in technology, particularly in artificial intelligence and robotics, the service sector is being reshaped, and AI may even be necessary for survival of the service industries. Innovations in digital technology lead to improving processes and, in many situations, are a solution to improving the efficiency and the quality of processes and services. This volume examines in depth how AI innovation is creating knowledge, improving efficiency, and elevating quality of life for millions of people and how it applies to the service industry. This volume addresses advances, issues, and challenges from several points of view from diverse service areas, including healthcare, mental health, finance, management, learning and education, and others. The authors demonstrate how service practices can incorporate the subareas of AI, such as machine learning, deep learning, blockchain, big data, neural networks, etc. The diverse roster of chapter authors includes 48 scholars from different fields, (management, public policies, accounting, information technologies, engineering, medicine) along with executives and managers of private enterprises and public bodies in different sectors, from life sciences to healthcare. Several chapters also evaluate AI's application in service industries during the COVID-19 era. This book, Incorporating AI Technology in the Service Sector: Innovations in Creating Knowledge, Improving Efficiency, and Elevating Quality of Life, provides professionals, administrators, educators, researchers, and students with useful perspectives by introducing new approaches and innovations for identifying future strategies for service sector companies"-- Provided by publisher.
Identifiers: LCCN 2023027574 (print) | LCCN 2023027575 (ebook) | ISBN 9781774913338 (hardcover) | ISBN 9781774913345 (paperback) | ISBN 9781003378068 (ebook)
Subjects: LCSH: Service industries--Technological innovations. | Human services--Technological innovations. | Artificial intelligence--Industrial applications.
Classification: LCC HD9980.5 .I526 2024 (print) | LCC HD9980.5 (ebook) | DDC 338/.064--dc23/eng/20230615
LC record available at https://lccn.loc.gov/2023027574
LC ebook record available at https://lccn.loc.gov/2023027575

ISBN: 978-1-77491-333-8 (hbk)
ISBN: 978-1-77491-334-5 (pbk)
ISBN: 978-1-00337-806-8 (ebk)

AAP ADVANCES IN ARTIFICIAL INTELLIGENCE AND ROBOTICS

The new book series AAP Advances in Artificial Intelligence & Robotics will provide detailed coverage of innovations in artificial life, computational intelligence, evolutionary computing, machine learning, robotics, and applications. The list of topics covers all the application areas of artificial intelligence and robotics such as: computational neuroscience, social intelligence, ambient intelligence, artificial life, virtual worlds and society, cognitive science and systems, computational intelligence, human-centered and human-centric computing, intelligent decision making and support, intelligent network security.

With this innovative era of simulated and artificial intelligence, much research is required in order to advance the field and also to estimate the societal and ethical concerns of the existence robotics and scientific computing. The series also aims that books in this series will be practically relevant, so that the results will be useful for managers in leadership roles related to AI and robotics, researchers, data analysts, project managers, and others. Therefore, both theoretical and managerial implications of the research need to be considered.

The book series will broadly consider the contributions from the following fields:

- Artificial Intelligence Applications in Security
- Artificial Intelligence in Bioinformatics
- Robot Structure Design and Control
- Artificial Intelligence in Biomedical and Healthcare
- Multi-Robot Intelligent Aggregation Mechanisms and Operation Platforms
- Artificial Intelligence and Learning Environments
- Advances in AI-Driven Smart System Designs
- Robot Navigation, Positioning, and Autonomous Control
- Robot Perception and Data Fusion
- Advances in Artificial Intelligence Research
- Advances in AI-Driven Data Analytics and Innovation
- Application of Intelligent Systems for Solving Real-World Problems

- Hybrid Systems Design and Applications Using AI
- Robot Grabbing and Operation
- Robot Behavior Decision and Control
- Robot Motion and Path Planning
- Applications of Intelligent Systems and Computer Vision

For additional information, contact:
Book Series Editor: Subhendu Kumar Pani
Professor & Research Co-ordinator
Dept. of Computer Science and Engineering
Orissa Engineering College, Bhubaneswar, India
Email: pani.subhendu@gmail.com

BOOKS IN THE SERIES

Advancements in Artificial Intelligence, Blockchain Technology, and IoT in Higher Education: Mitigating the Impact of COVID-19
Editors: Subhendu Kumar Pani, PhD, Kamalakanta Muduli, PhD, Sujoy Kumar Jana, PhD, Srikanth Bathula, PhD, and Golam Sarwar Khan, PhD

The Fusion of Artificial Intelligence and Soft Computing Techniques for Cybersecurity
Editors: M. Ajabbar, PhD, Sanju Tiwari, PhD, Subhendu Kumar Pani, PhD, and Stephen Huang, PhD

Incorporating AI Technology in the Service Sector: Innovations in Creating Knowledge, Improving Efficiency, and Elevating Quality of Life
Editors: Maria José Sousa, PhD, Subhendu Pani, PhD, Francesca dal Mas, PhD, and Sérgio Sousa, PhD,

Handbook of Research on Artificial Intelligence and Soft Computing Techniques in Personalized Healthcare Services
Editors: Uma N. Dulhare, PhD, A. V. Senthil Kumar, Amit Dutta, PhD, Seddik Bri, PhD, and Ibrahiem M. M. EI Emary, PhD

Fusion of Artificial Intelligence and Machine Learning in Advanced Image Processing
Editors: Rashmi Gupta, PhD, Sharad Sharma, PhD, Ahmad A. Elngar, PhD, Arun Rana, PhD, and Sachin Dhawan, PhD

Advances in Autonomous Navigation through Intelligent Technologies
Editors: Niharika Singh, PhD, Thipendra Pal Singh, PhD, and Brian Azzopardi, PhD

ABOUT THE EDITORS

Maria José Sousa (PhD in Management) is a Professor with habilitation and a research fellow at ISCTE/Instituto Universitário de Lisboa, Lisbon. Her research interests currently are public policies, information science, innovation and management issues. She is a best seller author in research methods, ICT, and people management and has coauthored over 100 articles and book chapters and published in several scientific journals (i.e., *Journal of Business Research, Information Systems Frontiers, European Planning Studies, Systems Research and Behavioral Science, Computational and Mathematical Organization Theory, Future Generation Computer Systems,* and others). She has also organized and peer-reviewed international conferences and is the guest editor of more than five special issues from Elsevier and Springer. She has coordinated several European projects of innovation and is also external expert of COST Association-European Cooperation in Science and Technology and is former president of the ISO/TC 260—Human Resources Management, representing Portugal in the International Organization for Standardization.

Subhendu Kumar Pani received his PhD from Utkal University, Odisha, India in the year 2013. He is working as Professor at Krupajal Engineering College under BPUT, Odisha, India. He has more than 18 years of teaching and research experience. His research interests include data mining, big data analysis, web data analytics, fuzzy decision making, and computational intelligence. He is the recipient of five researcher awards. In addition to research, he has guided two PhD students and 31 MTech students. He has published 51 international journal papers (25 Scopus indexed). His professional activities include roles as book series editor (CRC Press, Apple Academic Press, Wiley-Scrivener), associate editor, editorial board member and/or reviewer of various international journals. He is associated with a number of conference societies. He has more than 150 international publications, five authored books, 15 edited and upcoming books and 20 book chapters to his credit. He is a fellow in Scientific Society of Advance Research and Social Change and life member in IE, ISTE, ISCA, OBA.OMS, SMIACSIT, SMUACEE, CSI.

Francesca Dal Mas has a bachelor's and a master's degree in Business Administration from the University of Udine, Italy, a bachelor's degree in law from the University of Bologna, Italy, and a PhD in Managerial and Actuarial Sciences from the Universities of Udine and Trieste. She is a senior lecturer in Accounting at the Ca' Foscari University of Venice, Italy. Prior to joining Ca' Foscari, she was a Senior Lecturer in Strategy and Enterprise at the Department of Management, Lincoln International Business School, University of Lincoln. She was a visiting research fellow and guest lecturer at the University of Pavia, Italy, the Sapienza University of Rome, Italy, the Aoyama Gakuin University in Tokyo, Japan, the Hong Kong Polytechnic University, Hong Kong, the IHU—Institute for Image-Guided Surgery in Strasbourg, France, the Sharif University of Technology of Tehran, Iran, among others. Her research interests include healthcare management, intellectual capital, knowledge management, sustainability, digital transformation, and new business models. She has more than 100 publications on the abovementioned topics. She is an international assessor for the MIKE—Most Innovative Knowledge Enterprise for Italy and Iran.

Sérgio Sousa is a Programme Codirector and Visiting Professor in the Human Resource Management (HRM), Business and Psychology domains, with 25 years' experience teaching in higher education, in the United Kingdom and abroad. A Fellow of the Chartered Institute of Personnel and Development (CIPD), and a Fellow of the Higher Education Academy (HEA), he holds a PhD in Management, an MSc in Science and Technology, and a BA (Hons) in HRM and Organizational Psychology, and specialized qualifications from the University of Cambridge, INSEAD, Babson College, and the University of Hertfordshire. Concurrently, he has been working as a senior HR Director, with a robust path working with several FTSE100, FT Global 500 and Fortune 500 companies, with more than 20 years of international exposure at management level in numerous business sectors, in the scope of HRM, talent, and learning.

CONTENTS

CONTRIBUTORS

Andrea Albarelli
Department of Environmental Sciences, Informatics and Statistics, Ca'Foscari University of Venice, Venice, Italy

Dario Ambrosio
Department Neuroscience and Rehabilitation, Institute of Psychiatry, University of Ferrara, Ferrara, Italy

Luca Ansaloni
Department of Clinical, Diagnostic and Pediatric Sciences, University of Pavia, Pavia, Italy

Carlo Bagnoli
Department of Management, Ca'Foscari University of Venice, Ca'Foscari University of Venice, Venice, Italy

Marta Basaldella
Department Neuroscience and Rehabilitation, Institute of Psychiatry, University of Ferrara, Ferrara, Italy

António Pimenta de Brito
BRU-ISCTE/ESCAD—IP Luso, ISCTE-Instituto Universitário de Lisboa/IP Luso—Universidade Lusófona, Lisbon, Portugal

Isabel Sofia Brito
Polytechnic Institute of Beja, Beja, Portugal

Davide Calandra
Department of Management, University of Turin, Turin, Italy

Johnny Camello
School of Sociology and Public Policy (ESPP), ISCTE—University Institute of Lisbon, Lisbon, Portugal

Fausto Catena
General and Emergency Surgery Department, Cesena Bufalini Hospital, Cesena, Italy

Davide Cirimbelli
ASST Franciacorta, Chiari, Italy

Lorenzo Cobianchi
Department of Clinical, Diagnostic and Pediatric Sciences, University of Pavia, Pavia, Italy

Alessandro Cominelli
ATS Valpadana, Mantova, Italy

Marcello Cutroni
Department Neuroscience and Rehabilitation, Institute of Psychiatry, University of Ferrara, Ferrara, Italy

Luigi Faccincani
ASST Franciacorta, Chiari, Italy

Maria Ferrara
Department Neuroscience and Rehabilitation, Institute of Psychiatry, University of Ferrara, Ferrara, Italy
Department of Psychiatry, Yale School of Medicine, New Haven, CT, USA

Cristian Fracassi
Isinnova SRL, Brescia, Italy

Giorgia Franchini
Department of Mathematics and Computer Science, University of Ferrara, Ferrara, Italy

Melissa Funaro
Harvey Cushing/John Hay Whitney Medical Library, Yale University, New Haven, CT, USA

Luigi Grassi
Department Neuroscience and Rehabilitation, Institute of Psychiatry, University of Ferrara, Ferrara, Italy

James Edward Grove
Department of Management, Lincoln International Business School, University of Lincoln, Lincoln, United Kingdom

Munir Hassan
Department of Economics, Kuwait University, Kuwait City, Kuwait

Badar Alam Iqbal
Monarch Business School, Zug, Switzerland

Jacinto Jardim
Social Sciences and Management Department, Universidade Aberta, Lisbon, Portugal

Federico Lanzalonga
Department of Management, University of Turin, Turin, Italy

Andreia de Bem Machado
Universidade Federal de Santa Catarina, Santa Catarina, Florianópolis, Brazil

Federico Marconi
Department Neuroscience and Rehabilitation, Institute of Psychiatry, University of Ferrara, Ferrara, Italy

Francesca Dal Mas
Department of Management, Ca' Foscari University, Venice, Italy

Maurizio Massaro
Department of Management, Ca' Foscari University of Venice, Ca' Foscari University of Venice, Venice, Italy

Roberto Marseglia
Department of Management, University of Venice Ca' Foscari, Venice, Italy

Matilde Messina
Department of Management, Ca' Foscari University of Venice, Ca' Foscari University of Venice, Venice, Italy

Martino Belvederi Murri
Department Neuroscience and Rehabilitation, Institute of Psychiatry, University of Ferrara, Ferrara, Italy

Andrea Pellegrini
ASST Lariana, Como, Italy

Fernanda Maria dos Santos Pereira
Polytechnic Institute of Beja, Beja, Portugal

António Pesqueira
Bavarian Nordic A/S, Zug, Switzerland

Luís Manuel Pica
Polytechnic Institute of Beja, Beja, Portugal
JusGov, Research Centre for Justice and Governance at University of Minho—School of Law, Braga, Portugal

Mohd Nayyer Rahman
Department of Commerce, Aligarh Muslim University, Aligarh, Uttar Pradesh, India

Nida Rahman
Research and Information System for Developing Countries, New Delhi, India

António Sacavém
Universidade Europeia, Lisbon, Portugal

João Rodrigues dos Santos
Universidade Europeia, Lisbon, Portugal

Silvana Secinaro
Department of Management, University of Turin, Turin, Italy

Sebastiano Seno
Department Neuroscience and Rehabilitation, Institute of Psychiatry, University of Ferrara, Ferrara, Italy

Ramesh Chander Sharma
Ambedkar University Delhi, New Delhi, India

Maria José Sousa
ISCTE-Instituto Universitário de Lisboa: Lisboa, Lisboa, Portugal

Sangeeta Tripathi
Mass Communication Department, University of Technology and Applied Sciences Salalah, Dhofar, Sultanate of Oman

Tommaso Toffanin
Department Neuroscience and Rehabilitation, Institute of Psychiatry, University of Ferrara, Ferrara, Italy

Beatrice Valier
Department Neuroscience and Rehabilitation, Institute of Psychiatry, University of Ferrara, Ferrara, Italy

Luigi Zerbinati
Department Neuroscience and Rehabilitation, Institute of Psychiatry, University of Ferrara, Ferrara, Italy

ABBREVIATIONS

AI	artificial intelligence
ANN	artificial neural networks
AUC	area under curve
BD	big data
BD	bipolar disorder
BIM	business information modeling
CDM	clinical decision-making
CHR-P	clinical high risk for psychosis
CORE	Centres of Research Excellence in Artificial Intelligence
DApp	decentralized application
DE	digital economy
DL	deep learning
DLT	distributed ledger technical
DNA	deoxyribonucleic acid
EEG	electroencephalography
EHRs	electronic health records
e-PB	electronic participatory budget
EU	European Union
FEP	first episode psychosis
ICTAI	International Centre for Transformational Artificial Intelligence
ICTs	information and communication technologies
i-PB	intelligent participatory budget
IoT	Internet of Things
IPR	intellectual property right
MAH	marketing authorization holder
ML	machine learning
MMP	multiple multilayer perceptron
MPCs	multiparty computations
MRI	magnetic resonance imaging
NPV	negative predictive value
OECD	Organization for Economic Cooperation and Development
PB	participatory budget
PCA	principal component analysis
PPV	positive predictive value

P2P	peer-to-peer
RBF	radial basis function
RF	random forest
SCM	supply chain management
SCZ	schizophrenia
SMEs	small and medium enterprises
SVM	support vector machine
TAM	Technology Acceptance Model
UAE	United Arab Emirates
UTAUT	Unified Theory of Acceptance and Use of Technology
WSES	World Society of Emergency Surgery

FOREWORD

Artificial intelligence (AI) is here. It is not only our future, it is our present. From "ok Google, take me home," "hey Siri, how is the weather today," "Alexa, play classic music," to self-driving cars and Netflix suggesting "movies you will like," it is all around us. This book, *Advancements on AI in the Services Sector*, is a timely and genuine tour de force of the current uses of AI in different service sectors. With lively examples from all corners of our world, it is showing how AI, especially robotics, is reshaping the service sector. From economical systems to education to life sciences and healthcare, the book examines in depth how AI innovation is creating knowledge, improving efficiency, and elevating quality of life for millions of people.

Let's take healthcare, for example, and medicine in specific. Image recognition has revolutionized the automated reading of radiological images. The ability to train algorithms with thousands of x-ray and computed tomography images so that accurate diagnoses can be automatically read without direct human input is now a reality. Real-time image recognition algorithms during laparoscopic or robotic surgery that alert the surgeon to unusual anatomy to avoid injuring nearby vital structures are being tested and refined to become soon a reality. Machine learning algorithms, such as smartphone-enabled POTTER, the Predictive OpTimal Trees in Emergency Surgery Risk calculator, can accurately and in a nonlinear fashion predict the recovery trajectory of patients, thus facilitating care plans, and counsel patients and their families compassionately.

However, AI has an Achilles' heel. Most of the algorithms have a "black-box" nature. You feed them data, and they provide output. If the data has bias, and most data does unfortunately, the bias can be unintentionally incorporated in its hidden algorithms and go unnoticed by the human user. For example, if our healthcare system has racial disparities of care related to socioeconomic and access to care barriers, these can result in the algorithms predicting different outcome and different recommendations to different people, thus consolidating the bias and disparities in care. Interpretable machine learning and AI methods, in that sense, provide an advantage that should not be sacrificed for slightly more accurate predictions. In fact, with transparent AI methods, one can potentially uncover these biases and even mitigate them.

AI is here. It is our present and our future. Embracing AI in the services sector is exciting and carries lots of premises, but also some caveats that we all need to keep in mind as we move forward. *Advancements on AI in the Services Sector* is a precious read for anyone who is interested in learning the different applications of AI in all domains of our society, and I wholeheartedly recommend it as a must-read for those who want to explore the fascinating and diverse world of AI and machine learning.

Haytham M. A. Kaafarani, MD, MPH, FACS
Associate Professor of Surgery
Harvard Medical School
Director, Center for Outcomes & Patient Safety in Surgery (COMPASS)
Massachusetts General Hospital, Boston, MA, USA

PREFACE

MARIA JOSÉ SOUSA[1], SUBHENDU PANI[2], FRANCESCA DAL MAS[3], and SERGIO SOUSA[4]

[1]*ISCTE/Instituto Universitário de Lisboa, Lisbon, Portugal*

[2]*Department of Computer Science and Engineering, Krupajal Engineering College, Bhubaneswar, Odisha, India*

[3]*Department of Management, Ca' Foscari University of Venice, Venice, Italy*

[4]*Hertfordshire Business School, University of Hertfordshire, UK; Director, Technology Capability Development, Philip Morris International*

In recent years, artificial intelligence (AI) has been able to disrupt several industrial sectors, starting from manufacturing. AI-related applications and technologies have successfully transformed the way organizations work, leading to new business models (Bagnoli et al., 2019).

The AI revolution has encompassed the service field as well, affecting, for instance, the healthcare sector (Briganti and Le Moine, 2020; Guan, 2019; Silvana Secinaro et al., 2021), the finance and banking system (Jakšič and Marinč, 2019; Payne et al., 2018), the public administration (Dwivedi et al., 2019), and higher education (McArthur et al., 2005; Roll and Wylie, 2016; Sousa et al., 2021; Tan, 2020) among others.

The recent COVID-19 pandemic (WHO, 2020) and its related disruptions (Bagnoli et al., 2021) has fostered the use of new technologies in several service sectors, above all, healthcare (Grenda et al., 2020; Miceli et al., 2021; Sorensen et al., 2020; Wang and Wu, 2020) and education (Dwivedi et al., 2020).

This book was designed as an attempt to follow up the rapid transformation and impact of AI in the service sectors, to collect experiences, practical cases, and literature reviews. Sixteen chapters were selected. Forty-eight authors coming from nine countries contributed to the book. Several of them are scholars in different fields (management, public policies, accounting, information technologies, engineering, medicine). Others are executives and managers of private enterprises and public bodies in different sectors, from life sciences to healthcare.

The summary and contributions of all individual chapters are reported below.

In the first chapter, de Bem Machado and colleagues (2022) conduct a literature review to investigate the meaning of the term *Industry 4.0* and the transformations and advances provided by AI in the service sector. Their results underline a profound change in the services field fostered by AI, affecting both private companies (for example, in the banking and finance sector) and the public administration, calling for dedicated policies.

Starting from the need to develop global policies in the field of AI, in the second chapter, Jardim (2022) describes and discusses the relevance of global innovation policies, identifying the implications for sustainable development. Results underline the strong relationship between creativity, innovation, and entrepreneurship and the need for innovation policies to be systematically revised in light of changes in the different innovation ecosystems.

In the third chapter, Sharma and colleagues (2022) critically examine the educational policies and the use of innovations in learning processes using AI-empowered blockchain technologies through a literature review. The results highlight the importance of public policies in shaping the future educational scenario.

In the fourth chapter, Pesqueira and Sousa (2022) deeply analyze the role of blockchain by conducting a survey of 1524 executives. The study investigates the impact, current adoption, and application of blockchain in life sciences fields. Results underline how life science leaders encourage the adoption and implementation of blockchain-based applications despite the related challenges they would bring. More and more companies in the field will adopt such a technology in the years to come.

The fifth chapter by Grove and Dal Mas (2022) investigates universities' role in engaging with companies, especially small and medium enterprises (SMEs), in promoting big data applications and solutions. Results underline how voluntary networks among academic institutions and firms can generate a win-win effect.

In the sixth chapter, Pica (2022) deepens the role of AI in scouting data on social networks to prevent and detect phenomena such as international tax evasion and fraud. The study underlines the limitations in the practical implementation of such analytical measures, seeking to safeguard taxpayers' rights and legally protected interest.

In the seventh chapter, Camello and Sousa (2022) analyze the impact of AI-based applications in the public sector. More specifically, the study investigates the impact of AI in participatory budgeting processes through a literature review. Findings highlight how the Intelligent Participatory Budget will have the ability to integrate multilevel (local, regional, national, and international) and multidimensional (social, economic, political, technological, and environmental) participatory budgeting processes, transforming the world into a global village.

In the eighth chapter, Secinaro and colleagues (2022) propose an experimental research perspective by assessing academic and practictioners' views on AI applied to the healthcare sector. The analysis of 102 peer-reviewed papers from Scopus and 64 articles from blogs, newspapers, and journals from the Europresse database reveals that the debate covers topics such as applications, integration, and challenges. However, differences in the two groups emerge. In particular, professionals underline the need for academics to design technology and develop a theory to apply AI.

In the ninth chapter, Pimenta De Brito (2022) introduces the topic of the COVID-19 pandemic, by analyzing people analytics through a mixed methodology. Results underline how managers' concerns focused on empathy and data privacy was intensified during the pandemic.

In the tenth chapter, Tripathi (2022) explores the status of awareness regarding AI among students and teachers in the COVID era by examining emerging technologies in education that evolve new ways of teaching and learning among Indian and Omani learners.

In the eleventh chapter, Ferrara and colleagues (2022) discuss the most recent applications of machine learning (ML) technology in severe psychotic illnesses (schizophrenia spectrum and bipolar disorders), focusing on the application of ML in early detection, differential diagnosis, treatment management, and response prediction. The study presents pilot attempts to use ML for mental health service design and implementation.

In the twelfth chapter, Nayyer Rahman and colleagues (2022) deepen the topics of AI, digital economy, and education in the Indian emergent scenario, assessing the new policies.

In the thirteenth chapter, Cobianchi and colleagues (2022) investigate the role of AI in supporting clinical decision-making. Within the World Society of Emergency Surgery Team Dynamics II initiative (Cobianchi et al., 2021), the chapter presents a research protocol aiming to deepen the acceptance of AI-related applications and the barriers and ethical concerns in their adoption by clinical users in the context of emergency surgery.

In the fourteenth chapter, Faccincani and colleagues (2022) report the experience of 3D printing technology and the open innovation process which, during the COVID-19 pandemic, allowed Decathlon's Easy Breath snorkeling masks to be converted into ventilation devices for COVID patients (Cobianchi et al., 2020).

In the fifteenth chapter, Bagnoli and colleagues (2022) examine the phenomenon of new servitization business models for manufacturing firms and the role of digital technologies in enabling such business transformation.

In the last and sixteenth chapter, Massaro and colleagues (2022) reflect on the role of AI in supporting accounting firms to create and assess forecasts and business plans for their clients, especially SMEs. The phenomenon underlines the presence of valuable opportunities and challenges to be addressed.

The following Figure 1 presents a word cloud designed starting from the abstract of the sixteen chapters included in the book. Results highlight the importance of topics like innovation, technology, learning, digital, literature, industry, economy, and organizational changes.

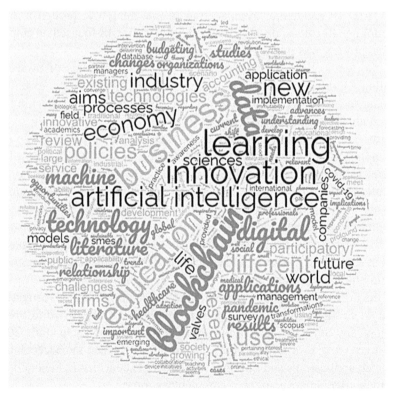

FIGURE 1   Word cloud gathered from the abstracts.

In all, the contributions included in the book underline the tremendous impact of AI and other Industry 4.0 technologies like blockchain, big data analytics, and 3D printing on the service industries, especially in healthcare and life sciences but also in the public sector, education, and business consulting among others. The disruptive effect and the opportunities brought by the new technologies need to be accompanied by dedicated policies that should keep up with the fast technological advances. New educational needs also emerge, and a multistakeholder approach is highly recommended to share the advancements of such technological transformation, its benefits, and practical applications.

We, as the book editors, wish to thank all the authors for their valuable contributions and insights.

REFERENCES

Bagnoli, C.; Dal Mas, F.; Biancuzzi, H.; Massaro, M. Business Models Beyond Covid-19. A Paradoxes Approach. *J. Bus. Models* **2021,** *Online first.* https://doi.org/https://doi.org/10.5278/jbm.v9i3.6419

Bagnoli, C.; Dal Mas, F.; Massaro, M. The 4th Industrial Revolution: Business Models and Evidence From the Field. *Int. J. E-Serv. Mobile Appl.* **2019,** *11*(3), 34–47.

Bagnoli, C.; Massaro, M.; Messina, M. Organizational Change Towards Servitization: Guiding Manufacturing Firms Through the Digital Transformation Process. In *Advancements in Artificial Intelligence in the Service Sector*; Sousa, M. J., Kumar, P. S., Dal Mas, F., Sousa, S., Eds.; Routledge, 2022.

Briganti, G.; Le Moine, O. Artificial Intelligence in Medicine: Today and Tomorrow. *Front. Med.* **2020,** *7*(February), 1–6. https://doi.org/10.3389/fmed.2020.00027

Camello, J.; Sousa, M. J. Is the Intelligent Participatory Budget (i-PB) the Next Generation of Democracy and Governance? In *Advancements in Artificial Intelligence in the Service Sector*; Sousa, M. J., Kumar, P. S., Dal Mas, F., Sousa, S., Eds.; Routledge, 2022.

Cobianchi, L.; Dal Mas, F.; Catena, F.; Ansaloni, A. Artificial Intelligence and Clinical Decision-Making in Emergency Surgery. A Research Protocol. In *Advancements in Artificial Intelligence in the Service Sector*; Sousa, M. J., Kumar, P. S., Dal Mas, F., Sousa, S., Eds.; Routledge, 2022.

Cobianchi, L.; Dal Mas, F.; Massaro, M.; Fugazzola, P.; Coccolini, F.; Kluger, Y.; Leppäniemi, A.; Moore, E. E.; Sartelli, M.; Angelos, P.; Catena, F.; Ansaloni, L. Team Dynamics Study Group. Team Dynamics in Emergency Surgery Teams: Results From a First International Survey. *World J. Emerg. Surg.* **2021,** *16*, 47. https://doi.org/10.1186/s13017-021-00389-6

Cobianchi, L.; Dal Mas, F.; Peloso, A.; Pugliese, L.; Massaro, M.; Bagnoli, C.; Angelos, P. Planning the Full Recovery Phase: An Antifragile Perspective on Surgery after COVID-19. *Ann. Surg.* **2020,** *272*(6), e296–e299. https://doi.org/10.1097/SLA.0000000000004489

de Bem Machado, A.; Rodrigues dos Santos, J.; Sacavém, A.; Sousa, M. J. Digital Transformations: Artificial Intelligence in the Services Sector. In *Advancements in Artificial Intelligence in the Service Sector*; Sousa, M. J., Kumar, P. S., Dal Mas, F., Sousa, S., Eds.; Routledge, 2022.

Dwivedi, Y. K.; Hughes, D. L.; Coombs, C.; Constantiou, I.; Duan, Y.; Edwards, J. S.; Gupta, B.; Lal, B.; Misra, S.; Prashant, P.; Raman, R.; Rana, N. P.; Sharma, S. K.; Upadhyay, N. Impact of COVID-19 Pandemic on Information Management Research and Practice: Transforming Education, Work and Life. *Int. J. Inform. Manag.* **2020,** *55,* 102211. https://doi.org/https://doi.org/10.1016/j.ijinfomgt.2020.102211

Dwivedi, Y. K.; Hughes, L.; Ismagilova, E.; Aarts, G.; Coombs, C.; Crick, T.; Duan, Y.; Dwivedi, R.; Edwards, J.; Eirug, A.; Galanos, V.; Ilavarasan, P. V.; Janssen, M.; Jones, P.; Kar, A. K.; Kizgin, H.; Kronemann, B.; Lal, B.; Lucini, B.; Williams, M. D. Artificial Intelligence (AI): Multidisciplinary Perspectives on Emerging Challenges, Opportunities, and Agenda for Research, Practice and Policy. *Int. J. Inform. Manag.* **2019,** 101994. https://doi.org/https://doi.org/10.1016/j.ijinfomgt.2019.08.002

Faccincani, L.; Cirimbelli, D.; Cominelli, A.; Dal Mas, F.; Fracassi, C.; Pellegrini, A. Open Innovation in Healthcare During the Covid-19 Pandemic: The Case of 3d-Printed Venturi Valves. In *Advancements in Artificial Intelligence in the Service Sector*; Sousa, M. J., Kumar, P. S., Dal Mas, F., Sousa, S., Eds.; Routledge, 2022.

Ferrara, M.; Franchini, G.; Funaro, M.; Belvederi Murri, M.; Toffanin, T.; Zerbinati, L.; Valier, B.; Ambrosio, D.; Marconi, F.; Cutroni, M.; Basaldella, M.; Seno, S.; Grassi, L. Machine Learning for Mental Health. Focus on Affective and Non-Affective Psychosis. In *Advancements in Artificial Intelligence in the Service Sector*; Sousa, M. J., Kumar, P. S., Dal Mas, F., Sousa, S., Eds.; Routledge, 2022.

Grenda, T. R.; Whang, S.; Evans, N. R. Transitioning a Surgery Practice to Telehealth During COVID-19. *Ann. Surg.* **2020,** *272*(2), e168–e169. https://doi.org/10.1097/SLA.0000000000004008

Grove, J. E.; Dal Mas, F. The Commercial Relationship Between Universities and SMEs within the Big Data Sector. A Review of the Literature. In *Advancements in Artificial Intelligence in the Service Sector*; Sousa, M. J., Kumar, P. S., Dal Mas, F., Sousa, S., Eds.; Routledge, 2022.

Guan, J. Artificial Intelligence in Healthcare and Medicine: Promises, Ethical Challenges and Governance. *Chin. Med. Sci. J.* **2019,** *34*(2), 76–83.

Jakšič, M.; Marinč, M. Relationship Banking and Information Technology: The Role of Artificial Intelligence and FinTech. *Risk Manag.* **2019,** *21,* 1–18.

Jardim, J. Global Innovation Policies: Framework for Developing an Innovative Culture Based on Artificial Intelligence. In *Advancements in Artificial Intelligence in the Service Sector*; Sousa, M. J., Kumar, P. S., Dal Mas, F., Sousa, S., Eds.; Routledge, 2022.

Massaro, M.; Bagnoli, C.; Albarelli, A.; Dal Mas, F. Business Planning and Artificial Intelligence. Opportunities and Challenges for Accounting Firms in a Human-Centred Perspective. In *Advancements in Artificial Intelligence in the Service Sector*; Sousa, M. J., Kumar, P. S., Dal Mas, F., Sousa, S., Eds.; Routledge, 2022.

McArthur, D.; Lewis, M.; Bishary, M. The Roles of Artificial Intelligence in Education: Current Progress and Future Prospects. *J. Edu. Technol.* **2005,** *1*(4).

Miceli, L.; Dal Mas, F.; Biancuzzi, H.; Bednarova, R.; Rizzardo, A.; Cobianchi, L.; Holmboe, E. S. Doctor@Home: Through a Telemedicine Co-production and Co-learning Journey. *J. Cancer Edu.* **2021,** *In press.* https://doi.org/10.1007/s13187-020-01945-5

Nayyer Rahman, M.; Alam Iqbal, B.; Rahman, N.; Hassan, M. Artificial Intelligence, Education and Digital Economy in India. In *Advancements in Artificial Intelligence in the Service Sector*; Sousa, M. J., Kumar, P. S., Dal Mas, F., Sousa, S., Eds.; Routledge, 2022.

Payne, M. E.; Peltier, J. W.; Barger, V. A. Mobile Banking and AI-Enabled Mobile Banking: The Differential Effects of Technological and Non-Technological Factors on Digital

Natives' Perceptions and Behavior. *J. Res. Interact. Mark.* **2018,** *12*(3), 328–346. https://doi. org/10.1108/JRIM-07-2018-0087

Pesqueira, A.; Sousa, M. J. Life Sciences Industry Blockchain Value Management, Investments, and Finance Impact Assessment: Global Questionnaire Survey of 1,524 Industry Professionals and Executives. In *Advancements in Artificial Intelligence in the Service Sector*; Sousa, M. J., Kumar, P. S., Dal Mas, F., Sousa, S., Eds.; Routledge, 2022.

Pica, L. M. Social Analytics and Artificial Intelligence in Tax Law. In *Advancements in Artificial Intelligence in the Service Sector*; Sousa, M. J., Kumar, P. S., Dal Mas, F., Sousa, S., Eds.; Routledge, 2022.

Pimenta de Brito, A. People Analytics and the COVID-19 Pandemic: How Empathy and Privacy Turned Out the Hot Topics. In *Advancements in Artificial Intelligence in the Service Sector*; Sousa, M. J., Kumar, P. S., Dal Mas, F., Sousa, S., Eds.; Routledge, 2022.

Roll, I.; Wylie, R. Evolution and Revolution in Artificial Intelligence in Education. *Int. J. Artif. Intell. Educ. 26*, 582–599.

Secinaro, S.; Calandra, D.; Marseglia, G. R.; Lanzalonga, F. Artificial Intelligence and Healthcare Connection: A State-of-the-Art Discussion Among Academics and Practitioners. In *Advancements in Artificial Intelligence in the Service Sector*; Sousa, M. J., Kumar, P. S., Dal Mas, F., Sousa, S., Eds.; Routledge, 2022.

Secinaro; Silvana; Calandra, D.; Secinaro, A.; Muthurangu, V.; Biancone, P. The Role of Artificial Intelligence in Healthcare: A Structured Literature Review. *BMC Med. Inform. Decis. Mak.* **2021,** *21*(1), 1–23. https://doi.org/10.1186/s12911-021-01488-9

Sharma, R. C.; de Bem Machado, A.; Brito, I. S.; dos Santos Pereira, F. M.; Sousa, M. J. Infusing Artificial Intelligence and Blockchain Powers: Knowledge Representation on Innovations in Learning Process and Educational Policies. In *Advancements in Artificial Intelligence in the Service Sector;* Sousa, M. J., Kumar, P. S., Dal Mas, F., Sousa, S., Eds.; Routledge, 2022.

Sorensen, M. J.; Bessen, S.; Danford, J.; Fleischer, C.; Wong, S. L. Telemedicine for Surgical Consultations–Pandemic Response or Here to Stay? *Ann. Surg.* **2020,** *272*(3), e174–e180. https://doi.org/10.1097/sla.0000000000004125

Sousa, M. J.; Dal Mas, F.; Pesqueira, A.; Lemos, C.; Verde, J. M.; Cobianchi, L. The potential of AI in Health Higher Education to Increase the Students' Learning Outcomes. *TEM J.* **2021,** *10*(2), 488–497. https://doi.org/10.18421/TEM102-02

Tan, S. Artificial Intelligence in Education: Rise of the Machines. *J. Appl. Learn. Teach.* **2020,** *3*(1), 129–133. https://doi.org/10.37074/jalt.2020.3.1.17

Tripathi, S. Paradigm Shift in Higher Education Model by using Artificial Intelligence: Challenges and Future Perspectives in India and Oman. In *Advancements in Artificial Intelligence in the Service Sector*; Sousa, M. J., Kumar, P. S., Dal Mas, F., Sousa, S., Eds.; Routledge, 2022.

Wang, W. T.; Wu, S. Y. Knowledge Management Based on Information Technology in Response to COVID-19 Crisis. *Knowl. Manag. Res. Pract.* **2020,** *00*(00), 1–7. https://doi. org/10.1080/14778238.2020.1860665

WHO. *Coronavirus disease (COVID-19) Pandemic.* Health Topics, 2020. https://www.who. int/emergencies/diseases/novel-coronavirus-2019

CHAPTER 1

DIGITAL TRANSFORMATIONS: ARTIFICIAL INTELLIGENCE IN THE SERVICES SECTOR

ANDREIA DE BEM MACHADO[1], JOÃO RODRIGUES DOS SANTOS[2], ANTÓNIO SACAVÉM[2], and MARIA JOSÉ SOUSA[3]

[1]*Universidade Federal de Santa Catarina, Santa Catarina, Florianópolis, Brazil*

[2]*Universidade Europeia, Lisbon, Portugal*

[3]*ISCTE-Instituto Universitário de Lisboa, Lisbon, Portugal*

ABSTRACT

Digital transformations have brought about a profound paradigm shift in society. These changes have been characterized by a new era of automation associated with the conjunction of important changes in different dimensions of society, including the service sector. Changes characterized as industry 4.0, which provides profound advances in the capabilities of robots that perform not only routine activities—but also cognitive ones; associated with advances in the so-called artificial intelligence (AI); the development of the process called machine learning; and to a process of increasing digitization of the economy. Therefore, the objective of this research will be to analyze the digital transformations of industry 4.0 in the advances in AI in the services sector. In order to answer the following questions, a systematic and integrated review will be conducted in the Scopus database: (1) what is industry 4.0? (2) what are the transformations that occurred through AI in the service sector? and, finally, (3) what are the advances provided by AI in the

Incorporating AI Technology in the Service Sector: Innovations in Creating Knowledge, Improving Efficiency, and Elevating Quality of Life. Maria José Sousa, Subhendu Kumar Pani, Francesca Dal Mas, & Sérgio Sousa (Eds.)
© 2024 Apple Academic Press, Inc. Co-published with CRC Press (Taylor & Francis)

services sector? The results converge to a profound change in the services sector caused by AI.

1.1 INTRODUCTION

Thinking about the functioning of machines in a period prior to artificial intelligence (AI), we arrive at the classic bases of computer systems programming. The first pillar that determines the degree of effectiveness of the operations is the quality of the data sets available for processing. Second, there are the raw data and their availability.

To better understand how it works, just think about scientific research. In order to obtain the best results, the researcher needs to proceed with a thematic delimitation and have a certain amount of data. The quality of the initial data is essential to lead the researcher to discover valuable information. However, it is also possible to work with the so-called inaccurate data and still obtain great results.

For this, the researcher must present reasoning above the average. The faster and more accurate it is, the better the conclusions will be regarding that object of study. In a simplified way, the similarity with computers would be the quality of the processing units.

AI starts from the same premise but shows even more relevant results. With cloud computing expanding on a large scale and the exponential increase in the volume of data, the propitious scenario for the improvement of AI was created. In addition to this improvement, a favorable context was also created in economic terms, both for companies and for public administration.

In this scenario, the objective of the research was to analyze the digital transformations of industry 4.0 in the advances of AI in the services sector. A systematic and integrated review will be undertaken in the Scopus database to answer the following questions: (1) what is industry 4.0? (2) what are the transformations that have occurred through AI in the service sector? and, finally, (3) what are the advances provided by AI in the service sector? The following topics will delve deeper in solving the problems of this study.

1.2 ARTIFICIAL INTELLIGENCE

Dartmouth College originated the term AI in 1956, and it encompasses a number of technologies. It is frequently referred as a machine-based system that consists in programming a computer to do activities that are commonly reserved to human intelligence, like comprehending, operating and learning, based on human-developed goals. Machine learning, rule-based programs, natural language processing, and voice recognition are examples of those technologies (Eggers et al., 2017). AI also allows for the development of decisions that may influence different environments and contexts both in the virtual and physical realms (Berryhill et al., 2019).

The capacity to construct programs capable of proving certain mathematical theorems or playing basic games was the beginning of AI science (Russell and Norvig, 2016). Nowadays, people all over the world is interacting with AI technology, from online services, to phones, to chatbots and apps, like Replika, that allows for the conversation with a virtual character. Advances in AI are driving the destiny of businesses and organizations. AI-advanced technology can learn from data collected in real time by virtue of deep learning resources, allowing for the analysis of new knowledge from a variety of sources and adapting accordingly, with a degree of precision that is inestimable to organizations. For example, Google's AI department is creating resources—"Imagination-Augmented Agents"—that are able to anticipate the effects of different scenarios and foresee the implications of the decisions made (Lui and Lamb, 2018). AI's capability to self-learn improves analytics and ensures a new realm of possibilities when interacting with customers. Furthermore, organizations are looking at it to improve client's experiences and develop new products and services. Organizations agree that if AI isn't rapidly scaled, they may risk going out of business. AI can also help companies achieving their growth objectives. Since AI processes information differently than humans, it can bring to light new opportunities and threats much faster, allowing organizations to launch new services, platforms, and business models at a pace and efficiency that was not conceivable until recently. Therefore, AI supports and improves the quality of human decision process by developing a larger set of effective options which are the basis of its transformational power. In this sense, AI is a complement to human skills, not a substitute for, and the collaboration between machines and humans is more important than ever.

Researchers have agreed on two main perspectives that help define how "intelligent" AI can be. General AI is much like what can be seen in science fiction movies, where intelligent robots imitate human intelligence by thinking strategically, abstractly, and creatively, and are capable of handling a wide variety of tasks. Though computers can perform certain activities better than humans (e.g., data processing), a truly realized vision of general AI has yet to emerge outside of the movie industry. Recent developments in neuroscience research, on the other hand, have provided a better under-standing of how our brains work, hinting that general AI could be attained. There are compelling grounds to believe that distinct artificial brain functions could be linked together to execute increasingly complex cognitive tasks (Goodfellow et al., 2016). Nevertheless, there are a number of drawbacks to general AI. According to Anirudh (2019), a few of them are—replicating transfer learning, which refers to the transfer of information from one domain to another. Humans partake in this activity on a daily basis, and it is an integral feature of civilization—enabling common sense and collabora-tion, which refers to partnership on projects with other human beings, as well as common sense, that is essential to human functioning. Due to the limited development of today's algorithms, dependable teamwork has yet to be achieved in general AI, unlike narrow AI, and common sense remains a distant idea, and—determining consciousness and mind, since conscious-ness is an essential aspect of being human, and it is the most reliable way of determining whether or not intelligence exists. Furthermore, the human mind has not been completely decoded. These concerns remain significant impediments to the development and implementation of general AI.

Unlike broad AI, narrow AI acknowledges and uses the fact that people and machines have various relative strengths and skills, rather than focusing on developing a single superintelligence. The vast majority of what can be encountered in modern daily lives is narrow AI, which focuses on a single task or a group of closely connected activities. Narrow AI takes advantage of the fact that computers excel in processing large amounts of data and carrying out activities with logical and concrete rules, whereas people are still superior at dealing with uncertain situations or those requiring imagination, judgment, creativity, and empathy (Berryhill et al., 2019). Apps for weather and data analysis software are examples of narrow AI.

According to Berryhill et al. (2019), the following are some of the most well-known and commonly used subfields within the considerably broader area of AI:

- computer vision, which refers to AI's ability to process and synthesize visual data, perform tasks like facial recognition and scene analysis and the construction of visual information;
- natural language processing, that refers to a computer's capacity to understand and translate human language, as well as perform activities like translation and text processing. Natural language processing implementations may produce new spoken or written language in addition to processing current language;

- speech recognition that refers to computers' ability to analyze audio recordings in order to recognize and understand spoken language;
- systems based on knowledge, which apprehend as well as store information in a "knowledge base," and then utilize an "inference engine" to deduce insights from the "knowledge base" to solve problems, frequently through the use of preprogrammed "if-then" rules, and
- automated planning, which refers to a machine's ability to formulate automatic and autonomous methods of action or techniques to achieve a goal, including anticipating the implications of alternative possibilities.

AI has recently gained traction as a potentially disruptive set of advancements in a variety of areas, including finance, automobiles, media, travel, and retail (Chui, 2017). For example, clothing retailer Levi's developed a personalized solution for customers through the use of AI technology. Clients are helped to find the ideal jeans with the support of an AI chatbot that effectively processes customers' preferences.

On the one hand, AI is likely a source of future business effectiveness and innovation since its resources can bring agility to routine procedures that can be automated and improved over time. Therefore, AI can help overcome resource utilization challenges, reduce logistical pressures, and carry on considerably more complex tasks (Mehr et al., 2017). On the other hand, the launch of AI may be followed by a slew of threats, such as work loss, due to automation, and privacy invasion, due to digital surveillance. The problem of avoiding injustice and unfairness created by AI technologies may be referred to as AI discrimination. According to previous research, AI can lead to prejudice and to violate ethical standards like equity and justice (Thierer et al., 2017). Mapping the difficulties of AI deployment as seen by key stakeholders who use, disperse, and govern AI technologies can aid in moving beyond the realm of uncertainty and developing smarter options to mitigate hazards and capitalize on industrial opportunities (Sun and Medaglia, 2019). For example, with the launch of Webster and Watson (2002)—IBM's AI system—that answers questions asked in natural language and designs customized care plans based on the most up-to-date medical literature, a significant amount of investment and experimentation is taking place in some parts of China. Nevertheless, tension between concerns and opportunities related with AI is shaping businesses and organizations across the world. For instance, the introduction of a system in India that assigns each person a unique identification number and links it to individual health records, and a variety of health-related schemes, poses ethical, legal, and social concerns, as well as the need for an effective ethical structure and data governance

(Gopichandran et al., 2020). AI transparency, fairness, and inclusion remain unanswered questions. AI-based software and services are becoming more widely accessible in high-income countries as the field develops. To help all, stronger tools for benefit-sharing are needed, as well as evidence-based protections and standards for suitable uses and users (Goodman et al., 2020).

Organizations that are interested in diminishing administrative load, reducing costs and leveraging customer experience and engagement may consider implementing AI by using the following strategies:

- make AI part of an objective-oriented culture and a customer-centric program;
- get client feedback;
- develop upon existing resources;
- be prepared and respect privacy issues;
- avoid ethical risks; and
- train people instead of replacing them (Mehr et al., 2017).

Moreover, since AI may be framed as an extension of employees' abilities, human–machine cooperation is relevant and can improve productivity and performance. Teams of humans and machines may be a promising solution. The use of evolutionary and genetic algorithms to generate a number of viable solutions, allowing a person to select the best practicable option among the various answers presented, is a far-reaching technique in human–AI collaboration, particularly in creative work (Berryhill et al., 2019). Professor Sung-Bae Cho, for example, created an AI application that generates many dress designs and allows the user to choose which ones to keep, while these decisions are fed back into the AI, allowing it to learn and improve in order to generate new designs (Berryhill et al., 2019). Since AI is still unable to completely reconstruct brain structure—science is likely to be far away to reach this point, an emphasis on human–machine cooperation, instead of competition, is a good enough solution. To these days, machines and humans complement each other in ways never seen before. The human brain is extremely adaptable and efficiently filters knowledge so that we can make sense of reality without consuming massive quantities of data, while AI systems are notorious for their voracious appetite for data. Humans nourish AI's work with objectives and meaning since machines are still activity-driven, which means they do not do something until they have a specific target. Therefore, more organizations are planning for the implementation of AI systems that allow them to create next-level products, services, and solutions.

Organizations planning to implement AI technology, according to Berryhill et al. (2019), are invited to take into account the following considerations:

- allowing for versatility and innovation while providing guidance and consistent guidance;
- developing teams from varied skill sets, cultures, ages, and genders to promote multidisciplinary, diverse, and multicultural viewpoints;
- establishing legal and ethical mechanisms, focusing on people who may be impacted, explaining the role of humans in AI-driven systems, exploring the explainability of AI results, and implementing transparent accountability protocols, are all ways to create a trustworthy, equitable, and responsible approach to using AI;
- securing ethical data capture, access, and usage, for example, through data management techniques that allow machine readability, foster privacy and protection, and minimize bias across the data lifecycle;
- ensuring that organizations have access to finance, internal and external capability and resources, and technology, as well as training and recruiting to employ AI, external collaboration and partnership, developing AI-friendly procurement processes, and taking infrastructure needs into account; and
- recognizing the opportunity for major future changes brought on by AI, employ an anticipatory innovation strategy to systematically and continuously study and mold AI's potential within the enterprise while it is still feasible.

In the next 15 years, AI has the potential to raise average economic growth rates in the United States, Germany, and Japan by up to 2% (Purdy and Daugherty, 2016). However, organizations are invited to support this potential growth with sustainable and responsible AI. Responsible AI is a new capability aimed at increasing trust in businesses and their workers and customers. To develop trust, confidentiality, openness, and protection should be built into AI systems from the start, and data must be gathered, used, handled, and maintained securely and responsibly. Therefore, organizations should be able to understand how AI programs arrive at a predetermined result as AI becomes more than ever and important support for strategic, tactic, and operational decisions made by humans.

1.3 INDUSTRY 4.0

First, it is important to consider that the word "revolution" characterizes phenomena in which there is a radical transformation in a society. A novelty only in a manufacturer's production process does not trigger an industrial revolution. For a revolution to materialize, it is necessary to have a technological trend with amplitude to impact production around the world. This does not happen overnight. It may take decades to consolidate and to be recognized as a "revolution."

The invention of steam engines and railroads, which replaced the usage of animals to create strength, ushered in the First Industrial Revolution in the mid-18th century.

The Second Industrial Revolution took place between the end of the 19th century and the beginning of the 20th, with the development of electricity and the production line (Henry Ford), which enabled large-scale production.

The Third Industrial Revolution came along with information technology, the internet, personal computers, and the full range of digital platforms that modernized work in factories and offices.

"The first three industrial revolutions happened as a result of mechanization, electricity, and information technology" (Oberer and Erkollar, 2018, p. 1) and in each of these revolutions, machines started to dispute or steal the protagonism of humans in several functions.

According to Kagermann et al. (2013), industry 4.0 is characterized by cyber-physical manufacturing industry systems. These systems (cyber-physical systems) "comprise smart machines, storage systems and production facilities capable of autonomously exchanging information, triggering actions and controlling each other independently" (p. 11).

According to Sarbu (2020), cyber-physical systems "combine physical operations with information technology networks via sensors which are implanted into production facilities and are connected via internet in order to exchange information, communicate, trigger actions, and control each other independently" (p. 5).

Industry 4.0 is driven by innovative technologies that have profound effects on both production systems and business models. "Industry 4.0 depends on a number of innovative technological developments such as information and communication technologies, which are used to [...] integrate systems at all stages of product development" (Oberer and Erkollar, 2018, p. 4).

The Fourth Industrial Revolution, often known as industry 4.0, describes the current state of affairs. "From construction to healthcare, from production to post consumption behavior of consumers, everywhere a new quick and perfect age has started" (Abdin, 2019, p. 2).

Sony and Aithal (2020) call attention, for example, to the positive changes to environmental sustainability and natural resources, underlining that "Industry 4.0 entails better resource efficiency as resources usage is monitored digitally" (p. 4).

Increasingly affordable costs on the one hand, and, on the other, the increase in the capacity of technologies such as smartphones, tablets, and portable computers makes a very wide range of the population live "online." The internet is part of people's daily lives, being the preferred communication channel and the main "reason for being" of all these technologies. From this context, it can be concluded that everything and everyone are interconnected.

One of the main points of reflection associated with the so-called industry 4.0 is that it is considered by many to be incompatible with the idea of manual production. In this regard, Jayatilake and Withanaarachchi (2016) refer that "one of the key features in the fourth industrial revolution is the concept of 'Factory of the Future,' which now is known as 'smart factory'" (p. 2). In fact, manufacturing has long been replaced by machines and the "ability" of these machines to work without any human operator in charge continues to make progress.

Michlits et al. (2019), in a study on structural changes in employment in Austria, conclude that "automation has both reduced demand for routine cognitive tasks, thus the total employment share of medium-skilled occupations has been declining while those of both low and high-skilled occupations that are harder to automate have been rising" (p. 27).

Naudé (2017), in this sense, refers that "the 4IR therefore poses both threats and opportunities. The main threats are job losses of existing low-skilled routine jobs in manufacturing" (p. 18).

Still relevant to this analysis, Michlits et al. (2019) argue that "it is more likely that the task profiles as well as skill requirements are subject to change within occupations due to computerization, rather than the complete wipeout of a considerable amount of occupations" (p. 18).

In the end, it is possible to affirm that industry 4.0 is the reality in which industrial technology is increasingly intelligent, fast, accurate, and efficient.

The basic premise of industry 4.0 is that by connecting machines, production systems, and equipment, companies will be able to create smart grids across the entire value chain, allowing them to control and command production processes independently and more efficiently, as measured by increased consumer satisfaction.

For the effectiveness of the process described in the previous paragraph, Sony and Aithal (2020) underline that "there is a need for highly skilled consultants and employees to make the joint optimization of human and technical systems a success" (p. 6).

Zuehlke (2019), within the scope of industry 4.0 and the methodological and technological transformation of production models in practically all markets, summarizes this process very well, referring that "all those markets will require new solutions for setting up supply chains and manufacturing networks based on knowledge, human resources, and customer needs" (p. 10). As in any transformation process, it is necessary to assess the starting point, define the horizon to be reached and establish the path to be followed.

Companies can be classified into three types (Sierra, 2016), according to their technological maturity: (1) companies in a basic methodological state, (2) companies with a consolidated production model, and (3) companies oriented toward fourth-generation technologies.

These different technological-organizational phases determine various transformation itineraries, such as technological updating, the adoption of 4.0 technology, and accelerated transformation. It is necessary to bear in mind that these innovative technologies not only enable, in many cases, small- and medium-sized companies to be able to move from traditional operating models to advanced technologies, but are now indispensable for the sustainability and economic viability of companies. "Many successful companies like Kodak, Fuji, Blockbuster, went bust due to their inability to innovate or adopt with newer technological advancement" (Abdin, 2019, p. 2).

The process currently underway to digitize the economy on a global scale will result in more efficient processes, reduced energy consumption, minimized waste, with highly customized products and tailored to the customer. Factories will be increasingly automated, with interconnected systems.

Even so, Madsen (2019) states that, in order to boost the so-called industry 4.0's success, it is essential that the suppliers of this cluster to "provide education and training, as well as help establish users group and networks that can foster organizational learning about I4.0 success and failure factors" (p. 16).

For this reason, there is still a long way to go on this route. Medhi (2019), for example, warns that "specialization is yet to emerge and possible in Industry 4.0 and IoT research" (p. 23). In the same vein, Madsen (2019) concludes that, with regard to Industry 4.0. There are "several areas in need of more research and development" (p. 16).

Regardless of the knowledge that is being built about industry 4.0, the reality is that it is here to stay. It is now up to companies and the public administration in general to analyze changes in markets and societies and adapt their strategies in order to take advantage of the new opportunities that it can bring. For this reason, public managers and decision makers must prepare their organizations for the digital transformation currently underway, making use of the best resources and an adequate structure to respond to the challenges of competitiveness that lie ahead.

1.4 METHODOLOGY

In this research, the method of systematic integrative research, with a qualitative nature, will be used. Machado et al. (2019) state that the qualitative approach, as a research practice, does not present itself as a rigidly structured proposal, it allows imagination and creativity to lead researchers to propose works that explore new approaches.

Systematic research is based on studies that present evidence, being a synthesis of primary studies that contain the description of objectives, materials, and methods (Machado et al., 2019). To conduct an integrative literature review study, a systematic search of an online database was used, followed by an integrative analysis of the results. Thus, we sought to work using the five steps of Torraco (2016), elaborated during the integrative literature review phase described in Figure 1.1 (Machado et al., 2019):

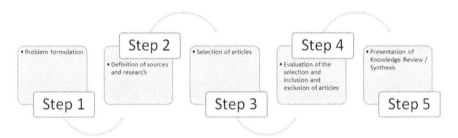

FIGURE 1.1 Steps of the integrative literature review.

In the first stage, the problem that guides this study was formulated. This will answer the question: What are the advances provided by AI in the service sector? In order to answer this question, a search was carried out on the database, which began in March 2021 and ended in April of that year.

In the second stage, called the definition of the research sources, some criteria were defined for the selection of the research, such as the delimitation of the research base. We opted to work with the database Scopus, relevant due to the number of abstracts and references indexed in the space with peer review, as well as its impact in the academic.

Considering the issue of the problem, the third step is the selection of inclusion and exclusion of articles. Considering the research problem, the search terms were delimited, still in the planning phase. Aiming to refine the search in line with the search term to the search problem, we searched using the expression: "AI" "AND" industry 4.0 "AND" service sector, totaling

8 publications. Because a concept depends on the context to which it is related, it is considered that variations of the expressions used for search are presented, in a larger context, within the same proposal, and finally, when planning the search, it was defined by using the terms defined in the fields "title, abstract, and keyword," without making any temporal, language, or other restrictions that may limit the search.

In the fourth step, the selection was evaluated, the research was planned, and the data collection yielded a total of six, indexed works, indicating a record of 2018, initial publication, through 2021.

As a result of this research, it was discovered that these six publications were created by 19 authors who were affiliated with 10 different institutions from 8 different nations. The publications were identified and indexed using 91 keywords spread over 4 fields of knowledge and 5 different types of publications. When mapping the theme of urban gardens, sustainability, and therapy in the Scopus database, Table 1.1 illustrates the results of this data collection in a broad bibliometric analysis.

TABLE 1.1 Bibliometric Data in General.

Database	Scopus
Keywords for your search	"artificial intelligence" AND "industry 4.0" AND "service sector"
Search field	"title," "abstract," "keyword"
Total search	6
Authors	19
Institutions	10
Countries	8
Keywords	91
Areas of expertise	4
Publication style	5

Six researches from the Scopus database were used to create the analyzed publications. These data organized significant information in a bibliometric analysis, such as temporal distribution; main authors, institutions, and countries; kind of publishing in the region; main keywords, and the most referenced works, allowing a more in-depth examination of the results for bibliometric analysis.

The first record is from 2018, with one publication in the area. In 2019, there were no publications. In the year 2020, there were four publications. In 2021, it had a publication, as shown in Graph 1.1:

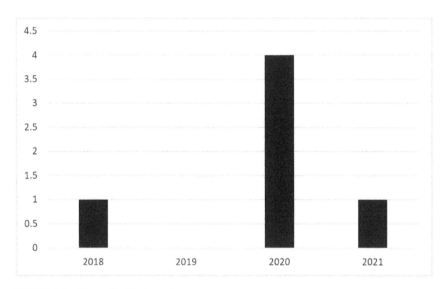

GRAPH 1.1   Time distribution of work.

It was feasible to identify the fields of knowledge of the articles using bibliometric analysis based on the recovered work group in the Scopus database. Engineering has the highest number of publications (39%) followed by Business, Management, and Accounting (23%), and Decision Sciences (23%), as seen in Graph 1.2.

When looking at the nations with the most publications in the area, it can be noted that two significant countries in the field, Italy and Russia, each have 25% of the works published in the area, as shown in Graph 1.3:

It was feasible to assess the type of document the research in the areas of "artificial intelligence," "industry 4.0," and "service sector" based on the results of the general survey. The publications are grouped together in the Conference Document. As illustrated in Graph 1.4, there are five recognized indexing categories and an undefined group that collects the other and probable indexes.

The first article, transforming Indian industries through AI and robotics in industry 4.0 (Dhanabalan and Sathish, 2018), was published in 2018, with the goal of analyzing the relevance of AI in Indian industries now and in the future, as well as addressing the fact that AI-powered technologies were developed with the potential to improve the quality of life in India.

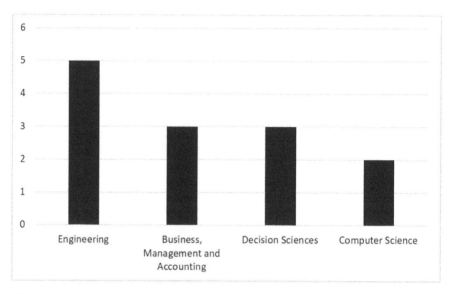

GRAPH 1.2   Areas of publications.

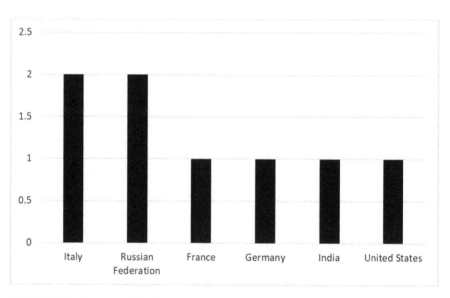

GRAPH 1.3   Country publication.

Of the six articles, five articles were selected to answer the research question as shown in Figure 1.2.

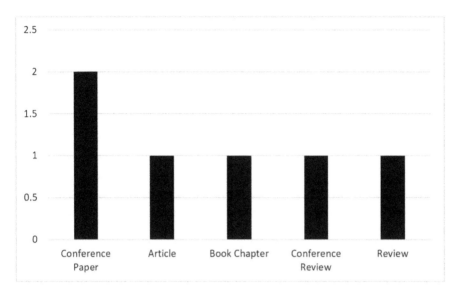

GRAPH 1.4   Distribution by type of publication.

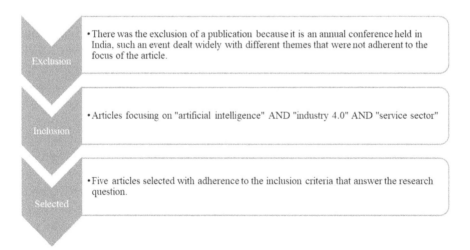

FIGURE 1.2   Criteria for inclusion and exclusion of articles.

In the fifth stage of the research, there is the formulation of the problem that guides this study. This will answer the question: What are the advances provided by AI in the service sector? The five papers were selected for full reading according to the online survey and open-access papers, with the aim of analyzing the digital transformations of industry 4.0 in the advances of AI in the services sector.

As a result of reading the five articles, it has been found that digital transformations powered by AI provide improvements in the economy and in the service sector (Dhanabalan and Sathish, 2018). In the area of civil construction, CAD (vector software) was used as a drawing machine to represent concepts (Dhanabalan et al., 2020). In the service sector, additional arrangements will be required to minimize the social risks related to the transformation of the work area (Putilo et al., 2020). Bataev et al. (2020) explain a model based on the total cost of ownership approach that allows to evaluate the effectiveness of using service robots with AI systems, to guarantee the client's interaction with financial institutions. Ivanov et al. (2021) performed an interdisciplinary and global survey on industry 4.0 subjects to learn about researchers' viewpoints on the topic.

1.5 TRANSFORMATIONS OCCURRED THROUGH AI IN THE SERVICES SECTOR

The public administration has been raising additional reservations regarding the integration of AI in its huge sectors of activity. In this regard, Surya (2019) states that "there is still a need to understand the potential impact generated from AI implementation within the public sector […]. Early studies suggest numerous interdisciplinary challenges that revolve around implementing AI in public" (p. 8).

Still, within the public sector, "policymakers should keep in mind the rich and distinct variety of opportunities presented by artificial intelligence technology" (Thierer et al., 2017, p. 39).

For both companies and public administration, "the option 'cloud computing' is much more cost effective than owning [...] data center since compute and data resources can be purchased on an as-needed basis" (Varian, 2018, p. 7).

Imagine a system created to collect data in the cloud, organize it and make decisions in milliseconds. This is the path of AI. As the years go by, the technology used in AI improves, which produces surprising results in the most different tasks and areas of activity, from the financial area to, for example, Google's Virtual Assistant. For example, Meghani (2020) states that "Artificial Intelligence is the future of banking as it brings the power of advanced data analytics to combat fraudulent transactions and improve compliance" (p. 3). Fernández (2019) points out that the use of "Artificial Intelligence techniques in the provision of financial services can heighten efficiency, reduce costs, enhance quality, raise customer satisfaction levels and boost financial inclusion" (pp. 3–4). "Some of the tasks [developed presently through Artificial Intelligence] are associated with high-wage occupations, such as radiologists, while others are associated with low-wage occupations, such as agricultural workers" (Webb, 2020, p. 2).

Due to this wide range of uses, many put the possibility that AI will have a negative impact on the global level of employment. Alla (2020) states that "this prediction by futurists has been confirmed by the McKinsey Global Institute, which estimates that by 2030, up to 375 million people (14% of the global workforce) will have automatic jobs" (p. 3).

Still, the same author also states that society needs "to look at the positive side of this prediction in order to be able to access machine learning opportunities, make simple changes to professional skills and their acceptance on an individual, institutional, or overseas basis" (Alla, 2020, p. 3).

In fact, the future will depend on how humans will adapt to "cohabit" with AI and, as a result, on how aggregate demand will react. What is certain is that this analysis depends on empirical data, which leaves no doubt as to the extreme importance that research in this area must assume in the future.

For example, Bessen (2018), in this regard, mentions that, if the aggregate demand remains sufficiently elastic, it is quite possible that a "technical change will create jobs rather than destroy them. In this case, a faster rate of technical change will actually create faster employment growth rather than job losses" (p. 16).

In fact, according to Perrault et al. (2019), in the USA, for example, "the share of jobs in AI-related topics increased from 0.26% of total jobs posted in 2010 to 1.32% in October 2019" (p. 7).

In the same sense, Makridis and Mishra (2020), when analyzing the impact of AI on quality of life in the USA, conclude that the "areas with greater increases in the share of AI job postings between 2014 and 2018 also exhibit greater economic growth" (p. 15).

Gries and Naudé (2018), in the same sense, refer to a logical element, which would be a paradox in itself (according to the objectives intended with AI) if it were to materialize. The authors refer that "if labor income does not profit from the economic gains generated by progress in AI, consumption may stagnate and restrict growth" (p. 26).

Pointing out one more danger associated with AI, Aghion et al. (2017) refer that this "may in part discourage future innovation by speeding up imitation; similarly, rapid creative destruction, by limiting the returns to an innovation, may impose its own limit on the growth process" (p. 48).

In fact, despite these "threats," AI is linked to other mechanisms that help to materialize it and establish the calibration between its evolution and the real satisfaction of people, which is, ultimately, what drives the human being toward progress. The Internet of Things, for example, depends on a level of automation provided precisely by AI. According to the system used in a "smart home," the routines of the residents allow to create automatic configurations. Depending on the ambient temperature recorded at each moment, the system can "predict," autonomously, what would be (expectably) the temperature manually adjusted by the user under those conditions. This example perfectly illustrates what is referred to by Varian (2018). For this author, the goal of AI "is to use data to train a computer to learn how to predict" (p. 4).

And how can AI and its virtues be applied in companies and public administration entities, in order to improve their performance and, therefore, to guarantee a better overall quality of life?

To produce positive results, AI projects must be guided by rationality and centered on humans. According to Leslie (2019), three steps (and respective actions) should be considered that should be taken to help ensure the human-centered implementation of your AI project: (1) define roles and evaluate user demands by considering aspects of the application type and domain context; (2) define delivery relations and map delivery procedures by considering aspects of the application type and domain context; and (3) create a platform for ethical implementation (Leslie, 2019).

The use of AI is an excellent way to implant the culture of innovation in companies and public administration services. By innovating, the organization strengthens its structures and learns to cultivate disruptive thinking.

But, in addition to this theoretical dimension, AI already has a strong presence in everyday life today.

Examples of relevant uses of AI in the corporate environment are:

- Image capture and analysis, which, in companies and public administration, can be used in facial recognition systems.
- As applications are increasingly "smarter," AI contributes to free employees from repetitive and tiring activities. Added to this is the reduction or elimination of small faults that, accumulated, become an unnecessary expense for the company or public entity.

- Advances in personalized product recommendations are increasingly impressive. Knowing the profile of people better is essential. A simplified example of this process is the indication of songs and films made by data streaming platforms.
- The adoption of the "cloud" as a destination for data storage is already a reality both for companies and for public administration entities, as well as for individual users. One of the favorable points comes down to the indisputable increase in the security of data that is under the responsibility of a specialized company.
- Before, chatbots and virtual assistants for websites and applications were extremely basic. Currently, attention is drawn to the ease with which human service is confused with that provided by robots.

    Whether more or less basic, the time gain for organizations with bots is undeniable. Often, they are all that the customer or citizen needs to solve a problem. For example, in the critical and important area of financial services, "these enable users to settle common doubts and, in some cases, to secure product recommendations or perform certain transactions (e.g. order transfers, open accounts)" (Fernández, 2019, p. 5).

Meghani (2020), also referring to the banking and financial sector, ends up pointing out the general domains of application of AI to most activities today: fraud detection; customer support and helpdesk (with humanoid chatbot interfaces); management of risk (tailored products can be offered to clients by looking at historical data); security (suspicious behavior, logs analysis, and spurious e-mails), and digitization and automation in back-office processing.

Due to the preponderance that computer activity, especially on the World Wide Web, assumes in the lives of people today, the crucial role that AI plays in cybersecurity stands out. "AI has immensely contributed to cyber security by facilitating user authentication, robust password protection, intercepting phishing and spam attacks, spotting fake news and intensifying war against cybercrime in general" (Mazumdar and Jyoti, 2019, p. 4).

In summary, regarding the impact of AI on employment levels, Thierer et al. (2017) point out that "to remain competitive, those facing unemployment by robot will benefit from remaining flexible and remembering the principle of comparative advantage" (p 26). The principle of comparative advantage states that companies must "specialize in the production and export of the goods they produce at relatively lower costs" (Santos, 2020, p. 56).

1.6   RECOMMENDATIONS FOR MANAGEMENT AND POLICY

Decurrent from the literature review and the policy analysis, it was possible to identify some recommendations regarding AI in services for policymakers:

- Define policies to increase public and private investment in AI and strength the digital infrastructure
- Support public–private partnerships as successful models for the forced financing of AI in services.
- Strengthen collaborative research and innovation projects to facilitate the process of integrating AI in all public services.
- Support the development of new collaborative strategic projects between countries, to improve the knowledge and learning process about AI.
- Implement policies for taking advantage of AI for increasing the quality of life of the citizens.
- Promoting the competitiveness of companies through the adoption of AI.
- Facilitate innovation in start-ups regarding AI projects.
- Promote the use of AI technology, Big Data, and real-time data to conceive, implement, and monitor projects in the service sector.

1.7   FINAL CONCLUSION

Industry 4.0 is a concept that encompasses automation and information technology, including the main technological innovations in these areas, which elevate this automation to maximum power, allowing robots to perform increasingly complex functions. In the context of digital transformation, relevant applications of AI are presented, it can easily be seen that, at present, it presents numerous advantages for companies and public administration.

The advances provided by AI in the services sector verified with this study were as follows: benefits of productivity and results, benefits of risk detection and control, economic benefits, benefits of data and information processing, benefits of service, benefits for society as a whole, benefits of decision-making, benefits of participation and interaction, and benefits of sustainability.

For future work, we recommend the study of digital transformation in knowledge management related to the service sector.

KEYWORDS

- **artificial intelligence**
- **digital**
- **transformations**
- **services sector**
- **Industry 4.0**
- **technology**
- **society**

- **cyber-physical**
- **information technology**
- **systematic integrative**
- **management and policy**
- **policymakers**
- **public services**
- **Big Data**

REFERENCES

Abdin, M. *4th Industrial Revolution and Reality of Industrialisation in Bangladesh*, 2019. Available at SSRN 3319582.

Aghion, P.; Jones, B. F.; Jones, C. I. *Artificial Intelligence and Economic Growth (No. w23928)*; National Bureau of Economic Research, 2017.

Alla, D. *Artificial Intelligence on Information Services*, 2020. Available at SSRN 3737164.

Anirudh, V. K. *What Are the Types of Artificial Intelligence: Narrow, General and Super AI Explained*, 2019. Retrieved April 12, 2021, from https://www.toolbox.com/tech/artificial-intelligence/tech-101/what-are-the-types-of-artificial-intelligence-narrow-general-and-super-ai-explained/

Bataev, A. V.; Dedyukhina, N.; Nasrutdinov, M. N. Innovations in the Financial Sphere: Performance Evaluation of Introducing Service Robots with Artificial Intelligence. In *2020 9th International Conference on Industrial Technology and Management (ICITM)*; IEEE, February 2020; pp 256–260.

Berryhill, J.; Kok Heang, K.; Clogher, R.; McBride, K. Hello, World: Artificial Intelligence and Its Use in the Public Sector. *Working Papers on Public Governance No. 36*; OECD Observatory of Public Service Innovation, 2019.

Chui, M. Artificial Intelligence the Next Digital Frontier. *McKinsey Company Global Inst.* **2017,** *47*, 3–6.

Daniotti, B.; Pavan, A.; Spagnolo, S. L.; Caffi, V.; Pasini, D.; Mirarchi, C. Collaborative Working in a BIM Environment (BIM Platform). *BIM-Based Collaborative Building Process Management*; Springer: Cham, 2020; pp 71–102.

Dhanabalan, T.; Sathish, A. Transforming Indian Industries through Artificial Intelligence and Robotics in Industry 4.0. *Int. J. Mech. Eng. Technol.* **2018,** *9* (10), 835–845.

Eggers, W. D.; Schatsky, D.; Viechnicki, P. *AI-Augmented Government. Using Cognitive Technologies To Redesign Public Sector Work*; Deloitte, 2017. Retrieved April 12, 2021, from https://dupress.deloitte.com/dup-us-en/focus/cognitive-technologies/artificial-intelligence-government.html

Fernández, A. Artificial Intelligence in Financial Services. *Banco Esp. Art.* **2019**, *3*, 19.

Goel, P. M.; Kumar, P.; Johri, P.; Srivastava, S. K.; Suhag, S. *A Comparative Study of Industry 4.0 with Education 4.0*, 2020. Available at SSRN 3553215.

Goodman, K.; Zandi, D.; Reis, A.; Vayena, E. Balancing Risks and Benefits of Artificial Intelligence in the Health Sector. *Bull. World Health Organ.* **2020**, *98* (4), 230.

Goodfellow, I.; Bengio, Y.; Courville, A.; Bengio, Y. *Deep Learning*; MIT Press: Cambridge, 2016; Vol 1, No 2.

Gopichandran, V.; Ganeshkumar, P.; Dash, S.; Ramasamy, A. Ethical Challenges of Digital Health Technologies: Aadhaar, India. *Bull. World Health Organ.* **2020**, *98* (4), 277.

Gries, T.; Naudé, W. Artificial Intelligence, Jobs, Inequality and Productivity: Does Aggregate Demand Matter? *IZA Discussion Paper No. 12005*, 2018.

Ivanov, D.; Tang, C. S.; Dolgui, A.; Battini, D.; Das, A. Researchers' Perspectives on Industry 4.0: Multi-disciplinary Analysis and Opportunities for Operations Management. *Int. J. Prod. Res.* **2021**, *59* (7), 2055–2078.

Jayatilake, H.; Withanaarachchi, A. S. Industry 4.0 in The Apparel-Manufacturing Sector: Opportunities for Sri Lanka. In *1st Interdisciplinary Conference of Management Researchers*, at Sabaragamuwa University of Sri Lanka, August 2016.

Kagermann, H.; Wahlster, W.; Helbig, J. *Recommendations for Implementing the Strategic Initiative Industrie 4.0: Final Report of the Industrie 4.0 Working Group*; Forschungsunion: Berlin, Germany, 2013.

Lui, A.; Lamb, G. W. Artificial Intelligence and Augmented Intelligence Collaboration: Regaining Trust and Confidence in the Financial Sector. *Inform. Commun. Technol. Law* **2018**, *27* (3), 267–283.

Leslie, D. *Understanding Artificial Intelligence Ethics and Safety: A Guide for the Responsible Design and Implementation of AI Systems in the Public Sector*; 2019. Available at SSRN 3403301.

Machado, A. D. B.; Souza, M. J.; Catapan, A. H. Systematic Review: Intersection between Communication and Knowledge. *J. Inf. Syst. Eng. Manage.* **2019**, *4*, 1–9.

Machado, A. D. B.; Sousa, M. J.; Nawaz, F.; Martins, J. M. Impacts of the Integration of Chinese Managers in the Western Economies the Case of Brazil. *Transnatl. Corp. Rev.* **2020**, *12* (3), 319–328.

Madsen, D. Ø. The Emergence and Rise of Industry 4.0 Viewed through the Lens of Management Fashion Theory. *Admin. Sci.* **2019**, *9* (3), 71.

Makridis, C.; Mishra, S. *(How) Does Artificial Intelligence Raise Well-Being? Evidence from Cities in the United States*; 2020. Retrieved April 12, 2021, from http://dx.doi.org/10.2139/ssrn.3669348

Mazumdar, A. C.; Jyoti, A. Automation of Financial Services Using Artificial Intelligence with Human Touch. *Int. J. Modern Eng. Manage. Res.* **2019**. http://dx.doi.org/10.2139/ssrn.3698408

Medhi, D. P. K. *Is Academic Research in Industry 4.0 and IoT Aligned to the Industrial Needs—A Text Analytic Approach*; 2019. Available at SSRN 3450480.

Meghani, K. Use of Artificial Intelligence and Blockchain in Banking Sector: A Study of Scheduled Commercial Banks in India. *Indian J. Appl. Res.* **2020**, *10* (8).

Mehr, H.; Ash, H.; Fellow, D. Artificial Intelligence for Citizen Services and Government. Ash Cent. Democr. Gov. Innov. Harvard Kennedy Sch.; August 2017, pp 1–12.

Michlits, D.; Mahlberg, B.; Haiss, P. R. *Industry 4.0—The Future of Austrian Jobs*, 2019. Available at SSRN 3461525.

Naudé, W. Entrepreneurship, Education and the Fourth Industrial Revolution in Africa; *IZA Discussion Paper No. 10855*; IZA Institute of Labor Economics: Bonn, 2017.

Oberer, B.; Erkollar, A. Leadership 4.0: Digital Leaders in the Age of Industry 4.0. *Int. J. Organ. Leaders.* **2018,** *7* (4), 404–412.

Perrault, R.; Shoham, Y.; Brynjolfsson, E.; Clark, J.; Etchemendy, J.; Grosz, B.; Lyons, T.; Manyika, J.; Mishra, S.; Niebles, J. C. *The AI Index 2019 Annual Report*; AI Index Steering Committee, Human-Centered AI Institute, Stanford University: Stanford, CA, 2019.

Purdy, M.; Daugherty, P. *Why Artificial Intelligence Is the Future of Growth*; Accenture, 2016. Retrieved April 12, 2021, from https://www.accenture.com/ t20170927T080049Z__w__/ us-en/_acnmedia/PDF-33/Accenture-Why-AI-is-the-Future-of-Growth.PDFla=en

Putilo, N. V.; Volkova, N. S.; Antonova, N. V. Robotization in the Area of Labor and Employment: On the Verge of the Fourth Industrial Revolution. In *13th International Scientific and Practical Conference—Artificial Intelligence Anthropogenic nature vs. Social Origin*; Springer: Cham, March 2020; pp 60–75.

Russell, S.; Norvig, P. *Artificial Intelligence: A Modern Approach*, Global Edition. Pearson Higher Ed: Englewood Cliffs, NJ, 2016.

Santos, J. R. *Economia Indispensável*; Lisbon International Press: Lisboa, 2020.

Sarbu, M. *The Impact of Industry 4.0 on Innovation Performance: Insights from German Manufacturing and Service Firms*; 2020. Available at SSRN 3610952.

Sierra, J. Indústria 4.0 e Transformação—Visão Geral. *Vida Econ.* **2016,** *77,* 1–2.

Sony, M.; Aithal, P. S. Developing an Industry 4.0 Readiness Model for Indian Engineering Industries. *Int. J. Manage., Technol., Soc. Sci.* **2020,** *5* (2), 141–153.

Sun, T. Q.; Medaglia, R. Mapping the Challenges of Artificial Intelligence in the Public Sector: Evidence from Public Healthcare. *Govern. Inf. Q.* **2019,** *36* (2), 368–383.

Surya, L. Artificial Intelligence in Public Sector. *Int. J. Innov. Eng. Res. Technol.* **2019,** *6* (8), 7.

Thierer, A. D.; Castillo, O.; A.; Russell, R. Artificial Intelligence and Public Policy. *Mercatus Research Paper*, 2017.

Torraco, R. J. Writing Integrative Literature Reviews: Using the Past and Present to Explore the Future. *Human Resour. Dev. Rev.* **2016,** *15* (4), 404–428.

Webster, J.; Watson, R. T. Analyzing the Past to Prepare for the Future: Writing a Literature Review. *Manage. Inf. Syst. Q.* **2002,** *26* (2), 1–23.

Van de Gevel, A. J.; Noussair, C. N. *The Nexus between Artificial Intelligence and Economics*; Berlin: Springer, 2013.

Varian, H. *Artificial Intelligence, Economics, and Industrial Organization (No. w24839)*; National Bureau of Economic Research, 2018.

Webb, M. *The Impact of Artificial Intelligence on the Labor Market*; 2019. Available at SSRN 3482150.

Zuehlke, D. Industry 4.0: More than a Technological Revolution. *Rev. CEA* **2019,** *5* (10), 9–10.

Zuiderwijk, A.; Chen, Y. C.; Salem, F. Implications of the Use of Artificial Intelligence in Public Governance: A Systematic Literature Review and a Research Agenda. *Govern. Inf. Q.* **2021,** *38* (3), 101577.

CHAPTER 2

GLOBAL INNOVATION POLICIES: FRAMEWORK FOR DEVELOPING AN INNOVATIVE CULTURE BASED ON ARTIFICIAL INTELLIGENCE

JACINTO JARDIM

Social Sciences and Management Department, Universidade Aberta, Lisbon, Portugal

ABSTRACT

Innovation has become a decisive factor for societies and organizations to face the exponential changes seen in today's world. In this sense, this chapter aims to describe and discuss the relevance of global innovation policies and identify the consequent implications for sustainable development, namely in artificial intelligence growth. To this end, we analyzed international studies on innovation policy. The results demonstrated an inextricable relationship between creativity, innovation, and entrepreneurship. We concluded that innovation policy instruments should be systematically revised in light of changes in the different innovation ecosystems. Furthermore, intervention strategies that best promote sustainability, competitiveness, and productivity should be dynamically redefined to integrate local and global policies in a balanced way. In the continuation of this chapter, it is suggested that comparative studies be developed on guidelines developed in different innovative ecosystems.

Incorporating AI Technology in the Service Sector: Innovations in Creating Knowledge, Improving Efficiency, and Elevating Quality of Life. Maria José Sousa, Subhendu Kumar Pani, Francesca Dal Mas, & Sérgio Sousa (Eds.)
© 2024 Apple Academic Press, Inc. Co-published with CRC Press (Taylor & Francis)

2.1 INTRODUCTION

References to innovation policy have grown exponentially since the last decade of the last century (Borrás, 2003; Edler and Fagerberg, 2017; Smits and Kuhlmann, 2004), covering diverse fields of human activity, such as technological, social, industrial, political, educational, and scientific innovation, and referring to both the public and private sectors. This growth is justified because innovative behaviors have been widely promoted to stimulate the development of innovative ecosystems, individuals, organizations, institutions, regions, and society as a whole (Foray, 2015; Jardim, 2010, 2012; Jardim et al., 2019; Nauwelaers and Wintjes, 2003). As a result, one can see the progressive increase in the number of those who distinguish themselves by their originality, thus ceasing to repeat what others have already accomplished simply. To paraphrase Peter Drucker (Drucker, 1985), they have equipped themselves with the tool of innovation and exploited opportunities, solved problems, and created valuable products and services. For example, in Europe, innovation policy has gained particular relevance to the governance and competitiveness of all countries in the scientific field (Borrás, 2003; Powell and Dusdal, 2017). It is also presented as a global concern that requires monitoring by assessing the evolution of global innovation indices (Davis, 2014; Dutta et al., 2020) and its impact on problem areas such as the environment and inclusion (Mavi and Standing, 2016; Sjöström, 2013).

However, the nature of innovation alludes to distinct concepts, theories, and practices that need to be explained and framed (Edler and Fagerberg, 2017; Schot and Steinmueller, 2018). In this sense, it should be noted that Edler and Fagerberg (2017) understand innovation as a phenomenon as old as humanity itself, and from this perspective, policies that affect innovation have always existed in human history. However, if we define innovation policy as a significant impact on innovation, it is already understood as new ways of solving problems, facing challenges, or taking advantage of social and economic opportunities. However, on this subject, Schumpeter (1934) is the classic referred to transversally in the literature when he alludes to innovation due to new combinations of knowledge, capabilities, and resources. Moreover, these combinations give rise to changes in economic and technological activities, in services and industry, in the public and private sectors, in education and research, in politics, and in the media. Therefore, innovation policies are distinguished by the different areas of human activity, as mentioned above. Thus, it can be concluded that innovation policy encompasses other domains and their respective instruments and that there has been an evolution of the concept itself, but which, according to Boekholt (2010), he describes as mainly terminological changes.

In this search for a common understanding, some indicators have been identified that allow the evaluation and comparison of data between countries, such as those used by EUROSTAT, OECD, INE, Community Innovation Survey, and European Innovation Scoreboard. Among them are the input and output verified in areas such as (a) research funding, (b) development and innovation, (c) intellectual property, (d) human resources, (e) excellence and attractiveness of the research and development system, (f) collaborative networks, (g) economic impacts, (h) information society, and (i) innovative companies (Arundel, 2007; Cricelli et al., 2016; Dutta et al., 2020; Evangelista et al., 1998). As a result of this common understanding, it is possible to carry out comparative studies that allow, for example, to define the global ranking of innovation. In this regard, it should be noted that in 2020, in the global innovation ranking, the sequence of the 10 best-performing countries is as follows: Switzerland, Sweden, United States of America, United Kingdom, Netherlands, Denmark, Finland, Singapore, Germany, and Republic of Korea (Dutta et al., 2020). However, it should be borne in mind that the recent COVID-19 crisis will undoubtedly have a substantial impact on innovation, which may change this ranking and require policies accordingly that enable the remarkable recovery from the global economic paralysis (Chaubey and Sahoo, 2021; Lee and Trimi, 2021; Melluso et al., 2020; Piccarozzi et al., 2021), namely, those that facilitate the use of *business intelligence*, the digitalization of the economy, and speed in responding to the needs of society, citizens, and consumers.

In this context, it is necessary to use innovation policy instruments, choosing best-suited to emerging needs and issues (Borrás and Edquist, 2013; Smits and Kuhlmann, 2004). Edler and Georghiou (2007) proposed that the taxonomy has become classic for understanding the multiple instruments and adapting them to specific contexts (Beatriz et al., 2017). Moreover, this usefulness is justified because it presents a relatively comprehensive approach to innovation policy, identifying five types of instruments for the supply of finance (venture capital support, tax incentives, support for research in the public sector, support for training and mobility, grant for research, and development in industry) and two for the supply of services (information and capital market support and networking). In addition, it identifies four types of demand-side instruments for innovation: systemic policies, regulation, public procurement, and private sector demand support.

However, it is necessary to analyze innovation from globalization, taking into account the underlying issues, such as sustainability. In this sense, this chapter aims to describe and discuss the relevance of innovation policy and identify the implications for developing a global culture of innovation. Thus, it seeks to contribute to creation having an even more positive impact on developing multiple areas of human activity, which requires an improvement and refinement of these policies. To this end, relevant research was critically analyzed, elaborating a framework for promoting a culture of innovation. This conceptual approach points to a systematic search for renewal since today, the organizations that do this successfully respond to market changes and competitive demands. However, for innovation to be established in society, creativity must be worked upstream. That consists of operationalizing knowledge, attitudes, and skills to produce new ideas and initial processes (Jardim, 2010). Innovation points more to creating original and valuable products or services (Sarkar, 2014) and is thus associated with entrepreneurship, but the latter is different because it also presupposes an organization that expands its commercialization. Therefore, the triptych' creativity, innovation, and entrepreneurship, considering what is distinctive and complementary in these concepts, constitutes the basis for promoting innovation policy.

Moreover, because this has become imperative to cope with the exponential changes seen in the current global world, this chapter aimed to describe and discuss the impact of global innovation policies and identify the implications for developing a worldwide innovation culture. To this end, the following research questions were posed: What are the main characteristics of the current sociocultural context that justify the development of innovation policies? What are the essential dimensions of innovation policies referred to in the literature? What strategies are appropriate for promoting innovation policies? To answer these questions, we investigated the characteristics of the current sociocultural context that justify the development of innovation policies; their most referred dimensions were highlighted and systematized, and, consequently, strategies were proposed to promote these policies.

2.2   SOCIOCULTURAL CONTEXT THAT JUSTIFIES THE DEVELOPMENT OF INNOVATION POLICIES

The regular and disruptive changes were occurring in society trigger innovation processes. Furthermore, for these to be favorable to citizens, it is necessary to think critically about their development, making choices and planning according to the historical circumstances of each time. In this sense, three characteristics must be considered in developing innovation policies in the current sociocultural context.

The first characteristic of the current conjuncture is that of **exponential changes.** There is a tendency for rapid and intense transformations (Díaz-Piloneta et al., 2021; Link and Scott, 2020; Mastroyiannis, 2018). This phenomenon of change is not new in human history. Heraclitus of Ephesus (c. 540 BC–470 BC), the father of dialectics, already stated: "You cannot enter the same river twice" (Platão, 2015). However, changes have gained another dimension since they affect entire societies and the planet.

Moreover, organizations that are not fast enough to cope with these changes risk disappearing, as Ismail (2014) has shown. Remaining attached to the past, fixating on mental and organizational models that have worked until now, means taking serious risks concerning the future. For example, the transversal use of technologies in all areas of human activity requires adopting new tools, fundamental to the digital disruption of organizations. Examples of business models that are entirely disruptive concerning those in force in the recent past are the case of Microsoft, Apple, Uber, Airbnb, Facebook, WhatsApp, and Amazon.

Thus, it can be concluded that today's remarkable innovations do not follow the classic logic of organizations that slowly and gradually followed a path of gradual and progressive growth and expansion (Jardim, 2020, 2021a). Those societies and organizations that follow business models based on disruptive thinking, managing to order chaos in an innovative logic, can solve large-scale problems, particularly those that arise in times of crisis and emergency. In this sense, education faces the enormous challenge of moving from an obsolete system to an entirely new world, which the new generations will have to build, but which remains unknown (Cardow and Smith, 2015; Cho et al., 2020; Yinfu, 2017). Hence, the imperative for educational communities to invent and reinvent appropriate programs, tools, and strategies for teaching and learning skills will enable them to deal constructively and positively with all the exponential changes and others that will continue to surprise.

A second characteristic is a **digital transformation,** which has occurred in all dimensions of human society and has forced institutions and companies to activate organizational changes and critical adaptations in their business models (Boland and Lyytinen, 2004; Nwaiwu, 2018; Sawyer and Crowston, 2004). According to Yokoi et al. (2019), one-third of the top 10 employees in each sector of an organization will be replaced in the next 5 years due to the introduction of digital. Furthermore, countries are trying to cope with this change. For example, at the European Union level, there is a demand for the spread of digital literacy and the Internet of Things (Bond et al., 2018; Jurčević et al., 2020; Švarc et al., 2021). This demand is undoubtedly a privileged way to increase competitiveness and productivity and overcome the gaps in their digital economy and society index (Castells and Himanen, 2011; Russo, 2020; Sánchez-Serrano et al., 2020). However, it should be taken into account that this transformation requires particular attention to the type of leadership to be promoted, namely the characteristics of the leaders themselves, who should adapt the performance of their functions to the networking context, as shown in a study conducted in the Portuguese context (Porfírio et al., 2021).

The third characteristic is the need to **ensure competitiveness** (Dagilienė et al., 2020; Davis, 2014; Mok, 2015; Mullen, 2019). Only by ensuring competitiveness is it possible to face the challenge of overcoming delays in the regions' innovation capacities. Having a forward-looking agenda aimed at growth presupposes entrepreneurs who design, develop, and expand innovative projects. In this sense, exposure to the political dynamics of innovative countries enables the understanding of contexts and opportunities to be more competitive. To more effectively and efficiently support competitive innovation, stakeholders need to establish partnerships, connect people, and act synergistically to develop differentiated high-quality products and services. In this way, it will be possible to harness the potential of the involvement of private and public stakeholders, thus overcoming the geographic fragmentation that hampers growth and prevents gaining scale. Therefore, it will also be possible to support emerging entirely disruptive innovations but expand and gain global scale. In this sense, innovation policy becomes essential to develop programs that promote data collection that feeds networks of innovation-oriented initiatives. Both the digital transformations and the exponential changes mentioned above support this justification of the need for competitiveness. The changes lead to becoming more competitive, but simultaneously, to cooperate to succeed in innovation.

2.3   INNOVATION POLICIES

Because it is necessary to respond to the gaps and needs of this context, the reflection on innovation policy has presented some essential dimensions, namely sustainability, inclusion, social cohesion, and entrepreneurial skills conducive to proactivity and implementation of worthwhile projects.

Starting with **sustainable development,** we should be noted that it requires creative approaches that link the environment, social cohesion, and entrepreneurship. Although there are diverse understandings of innovation, both in defining its processes and proposing methods and resources for activation, monitoring, and evaluation, innovation is a collective issue that requires a proactive attitude from everyone since it influences the overall sustainable development (Alkemade et al., 2011; Schulz et al., 2021). Therefore, the importance of innovation that respects and cares for ecological environments, the so-called eco-innovation (Mavi and Standing, 2016), is justified. In this sense, UNESCO has carried out at the international level the dissemination to the most diverse populations and institutions the sustainable objectives (Howlett and Saguin, 2018) that will undoubtedly mark the following decades. Moreover, all the reforms that states and nations will implement must also be done sustainably and aiming at the sustainability of the whole planet (Domorenok et al., 2021; Maggetti and Trein, 2021; Trein et al., 2020).

Regarding **social policies conducive to social inclusion and cohesion,** it is essential to mention that these refer to the well-being of the population in general, but paying particular attention to the most disadvantaged groups, who need to be supported in their economic development, so that economic and social inequalities are reduced. Furthermore, they may take on different accents depending on the sociocultural context, for example, the migrations and the naturalization of migrants in the United States of America (Soehl et al., 2020); the social policy of land expropriation in China (Kan, 2020); the colonial policies of sustainable agriculture in India, where the problem of the interests of farmers, subalterns and activists is highlighted (Brown, 2018; Jakobsen, 2020) the need for a broadening of the concept of political competence in Latin America, namely, through the promotion of political knowledge and democratic attitudes (Fuks and Casalecchi, 2018) and, at a global level, the need to define new social policies for the increase of the knowledge-based economy (Choi et al., 2020) and the challenges to gender equality at a time when there are some antigender campaigns (Korolczuk, 2021).

In this sense, it is essential to find innovative social solutions, standing out for originality and persistence in implementing social innovation programs (Gladwell, 2008; Jardim et al., 2019). This creation requires challenging the status quo, critical of possible solutions, resisting hasty conclusions and suspending assumptions, identifying recurring thought patterns, and seeking new frameworks. Moreover, above all, gather the information that validates ideas with facts and evidence. Thus, in addition to convergent thinking, which is linear and objective, divergent thinking is plural in seeking various solutions to a problem (de Bono, 2005; Mumford, 2012), must also be used. Therefore, policymakers need to perform their functions by being clear-headed about the essentials and courageous in defining and implementing innovative policies.

The third dimension of innovation refers to entrepreneurial skills, aiming to promote innovation to favor sustainable growth and solve social problems. In this sense, this has been a constant concern of the European Commission, which, in several documents, reaffirms the idea of prioritizing innovation and promoting an even more entrepreneurial culture since school education (European Commission/EACEA/Eurydice, 2016; European Commission, 2003, 2011). Furthermore, entrepreneurship education objectives indicate thinking creatively, effectively solving problems, objectively analyzing a business idea, developing communication, teamwork, and leadership skills, and evaluating new projects (Comissão Europeia, 2008, 2013). In this sense, it aligns with Peter Drucker's perspective (Drucker, 1985), which alludes to innovation as the specific instrument of entrepreneurship since it confers the ability to create wealth. However, for these skills to be developed, the value of entrepreneurship must become part of the culture of citizens, making them proactive and dynamic (Jardim, 2013, 2019b, 2021b). When an entrepreneurial culture allows innovation to flourish, a virtuous circle begins where more innovators develop ideas and realize valuable projects.

Many biographies about entrepreneurs show how they created and expanded innovative products, services, brands, organizations, or methods. Furthermore, they stood out from the general population by their originality and persistence in bringing their ideas to fruition (Gladwell, 2008; Isaacson, 2015, 2016; Jardim, 2019a). They distinguished themselves by breaking prevailing mental models (Thagard, 2010; Zander and Zander, 2000). It is also notable how entrepreneurial regions encourage creativity and innova-tion, as these are among the priority topics of their educational, economic, and cultural policies. Therefore, creativity and innovation have gained space in the everyday practices of schools, organizations, and academia (Chua and Bedford, 2016; Huggins and Thompson, 2015; Kenney, 2018). It is precisely through the systematic work of helping people think creatively and critically that the conditions will be established for more valuable responses to today's complex problems to emerge. Among these conditions is the promotion of the sharing of bold ideas, feeling comfortable to present new ideas, and carrying out experiments that allow the discovery of the actual context of the exercise of a profession.

2.4   INTERVENTION STRATEGIES FOR THE PROMOTION OF INNOVATION

About the appropriate strategies for promoting innovation policies, those referring to the combination of approaches were identified to guarantee a synergistic performance; the creation of innovative ecosystems, to disseminate this competence to the most significant possible number of individuals; and the development of educational programs on innovation processes, to guarantee their improvement in the long term.

Starting with the **policy mix** strategy, we should be noted that this constitutes a requirement to achieve the objectives set out in promoting the culture of innovation. This strategy provides interdependence between the actors involved in the preparation and implementation of policies, such as political, academic, and social leaders (Borrás and Edquist, 2013; Flanagan et al., 2011). The studies of innovation policy suggest a synergistic performance of the programs, aiming mainly at the long-term gains to be obtained in the future of society. For this reason, political leaders promoting social innovation place concerted plans for local, regional, or national action on their agendas (Eizaguirre and Parés, 2019; Liggett, 2020; Szeto, 2020) but are also able to achieve global leadership aimed at the responsible involvement of all citizens, organizations, and institutions (Cavey, 2020; Likhotal, 2020; Rosser et al., 2020). This point is in line with the proposal previously mentioned when discussing connectivity, which points to the need to create databases and networks that allow a transparent and collaborative performance by all. Furthermore, it corroborates the importance of the innovation policy instruments being designed, considering the multiple ways of solving problems by the innovation systems, which allows having a synergistic performance since it is based on systemic instruments.

Regarding the **creation of innovative ecosystems,** it should be noted that these refer to those regions or places that, by concentrating a series of resources and characteristics, become true "granaries" of new businesses. Moreover, they are defined as those contexts that meet specific conditions, such as good universities, government incentives, business incubators, or the presence of innovative professionals who favor the creation of products or services (Jardim, 2020). For this purpose, the "local actors" of the "triple helix" innovation model (Carayannis et al., 2018; Etzkowitz and Zhou, 2017; Galvao et al., 2019) are habitually combined, a construct that is composed of the interconnection between universities, industry, and governments, having been widely used as a conceptual model for the analysis of entrepreneurial ecosystems, business clusters, and entrepreneurial regions (Bikse et al., 2016; Cvijanović et al., 2020; Etzkowitz and Klofsten, 2005; Etzkowitz and Zhou, 2017; Galvao et al., 2019). In this synergistic interaction, universities, industry, and governments intervene with their knowledge, skills, and resources, implementing projects on a growth trajectory as a way of responding to challenges and pressures, both local and external, and carrying out properly planned and coordinated activities. In this process, universities play a central role, as, as regional organizers of innovation, they are directly involved in local economic growth (Etzkowitz and Zhou, 2017).

Finally, **educational programs on innovation** are the third strategy of this proposal. Furthermore, this is justified because, in a global, technological, and complex society, it is crucial to develop the imagination and, consequently, innovate, creating and recreating from the constant creation and recreation of products and services that satisfy the real needs of contemporary life. This development is not completed quickly, but over the long term and for decades (Borchers and Park, 2011; Ribeiro et al., 2018). The school, the family, and the media can contribute so that the culture of innovation is permanently installed in the thinking, acting, and living of the new generations. The positive correlation between innovation efforts and the formation of innovative minds shows how education for innovation represents an added value for a renewal of the educational system. To this end, educators must encourage the development of creative teams, mobilizing the imagination of young people to disseminate habits and routines favorable to innovation. Moreover, there are already some educational programs that promote innovation at different levels of education. Here are some examples of intervention programs that work with the competence of innovation: for preschool students—*Piratas dos Sonhos* (Jardim et al., 2019a, 2019b); for primary school students—*Youth-Start Entrepreneurial Challenges Program* (Bisanz et al., 2020) *La Fabrica de Sueños* (Vega, 2015), *Brincadores de Sonhos* (Jardim et al., 2015a, 2015b), *Ukids* (Hercz et al., 2021; Pinho et al., 2019) and *School Shop Project* (Pepin, 2018); for high school students—*Emprender en mi Escuela, Empresa Joven Europea*, and *ÍCARO* (Bernal Guerrero and Cárdenas Gutiérrez, 2017), *A Rota das Emoções* (Jardim et al., 2019d), *Inovadores em Ação* (Jardim et al., 2019e); for secondary school students—*Young Achievement Australia* (Peterman and Kennedy, 2003), *Next 36* (Lyons and Zhang, 2018), *Os Originais* (Jardim et al., 2019c); for students in higher education—*Programa de Formation de Competencias en Emprendimiento e Innovación* (Hebles et al., 2019), *Projeto Começar* (Dominguinhos and Carvalho, 2009), and *Programme d'Enseignement en Entrepreneuriat* (Fayolle and Gailly, 2009).

2.5 INNOVATION TRENDS BASED ON ARTIFICIAL INTELLIGENCE

Artificial intelligence (AI) is a transversal innovation trend nowadays (Kuziemski and Misuraca, 2020). Furthermore, governments seek novelty as a powerful motivator for their citizens, adopting technological solutions. In a global and digital world, political leaders compare their country's performance with the socioeconomic performance of their partners. Thus, the current relevance of AI in the public sector is evident. In this sense, Kuziemski and Misuraca (2020) analyzed AI and the strengthening of border control, service provision improvement, and user experience. To do so, they carried out a case study of countries with a medium to high ranking on the Government's IA Readiness Index, such as the immigration control system in Canada; the optimization of employment services in Poland; and meeting the needs of citizens through "AuroraAI" in Finland.

Nevertheless, innovation policies go beyond these domains, influencing citizens' daily lives. Robotics and AI tend to have an increasing impact on industry, transport, health, and work in the agri-food, logistics, security, retail, and construction domain (Huang and Rust, 2018; Perez et al., 2018; Silva, 2019; Yu et al., 2018). Given this growing presence in today's society, research in this field is challenged to deepen this theme and assess the socioeconomic impact and discuss the legal and ethical issues associated with it (Jardim, 2021a). Thus, it will be possible to maximize its benefits and mitigate the adverse effects. Like the science and engineering of building intelligent machines, AI allows developing software that thinks intelligently, similar to intelligent humans (Russell and Norvig, 2010). Consequently, the question remains: Can a machine think and behave like humans?

Regardless of the issues raised, there is a trend toward developing innovation policies that apply human intelligence to machines, creating systems that understand, think, learn, and behave like human beings. According to Beard (2018), it is essential to take creativity seriously in this field of AI as well, on this threshold of the revolution that is taking place in education. Among the educational strategies for education within the scope of AI, those that allow us to understand how the algorithms that shape daily human life stand out. Teaching robotics and programming in schools also contributes to the development of skills associated with computational thinking. Furthermore, learning the basics of mechanics and electronics favors this literacy. These learnings gain even more relevance when they allow the elaboration of projects that are then applied to satisfy the concrete needs of specific populations (Jardim, 2021a; Jardim et al., 2021).

2.6 CONCLUSION

The realization of this chapter allows us to conclude that, among the characteristics of the current sociocultural context that justify the development of innovation policies, the following stand out: exponential and rapid changes, the digital transformation that has reached all societies, and the search for ways of ensuring the competitiveness of people, organizations, and communities. In addition, the innovation policies highlighted the dimensions of sustainability, inclusion, social cohesion, and entrepreneurial skills leading to the proactivity and implementation of worthwhile projects. Regarding the strategies that promote innovation policies, the combination of approaches was identified to guarantee a synergistic performance, the creation of innovative ecosystems, and the development of educational programs on innovation processes.

In addition, it is concluded that **scientific production** constitutes a challenge for an excellent approach to this theme since it allows a critical observation of the phenomenon while at the same time validating and perfecting the indicators used in the measurement of innovation. It is necessary to resort to both quantitative and qualitative studies since they complement each other in the possibilities of methodological rigor and critical reflection. It was also concluded that it is vital to invest in the training of the **younger generations** to properly develop the attitudes and predispositions for innovation to solve the unforeseen problems that will undoubtedly arise. Finally, it is concluded that it is crucial to **promote an innovative pedagogy** that leads to the development of creative teams, enabling them to discover new methods, processes, models, and tools for innovation in this global world and this digital age.

In summary, and based on the review carried out, a flowchart was drawn up with the main conclusions (cf. Figure 2.1), highlighting the problems emerging in the current sociocultural context, the predominant dimensions in the innovation policy, the strategies to be used to promote, and the challenges and opportunities that this theme raises.

It remains to be said that the instruments of innovation policy may benefit from the integration of these concepts significantly when revising them, which is intended to be systematic and taking into account the changes observed in the different innovative ecosystems, particularly innovation in the field of AI. This dynamic redefinition effectively guarantees sustainability, competitiveness, and productivity, resulting from the synergistic complementarity of local and global innovation policies. In the continuation of this chapter, it is suggested that comparative studies be developed on the innovation policy set in different regions or ecosystems based on this frame of reference.

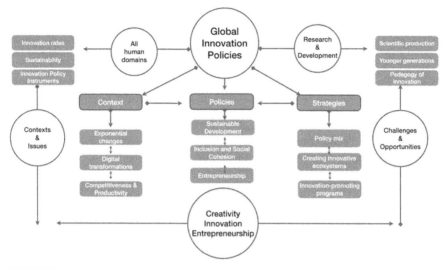

FIGURE 2.1   A flowchart that summarizes the main conclusions of this chapter and guidelines for the definition of innovation policies.

KEYWORDS

- **innovation**
- **innovation policy**
- **competitiveness**
- **innovation culture**
- **policy mix**
- **artificial intelligence**

REFERENCES

Alkemade, F.; Hekkert, M. P.; Negro, S. O. Transition policy and innovation policy: Friends or foes? *Environmental Innovation and Societal Transitions* **2011**, *1* (1), 125–129.

Arundel, A. Innovation Survey Indicators—What Impact on Innovation Policy. In *Science, Technology and Innovation Indicators in a Changing World: Responding to Policy Needs* OECD, Ed.; OECD Publishing, 2007; pp 49–64.

Beard, A. *Natural Born Learners: Inside the Global Learning Revolution*; Orion Publishing, 2018.

Beatriz, M.; Bonacelli, M.; Foss, M. C. Políticas de estímulo à demanda por inovação e o Marco Legal de CT&I. In *Inovação no Brasil: avanços e desafios jurídicos e institucionais*; Coutinho, D. R., Foss, M. C., Mouallem, P. S. B., Eds.; Blucher, 2017; pp 213–239.

Bernal Guerrero, A.; Cárdenas Gutiérrez, A. R. Evaluación del potencial emprendedor en escolares. Una investigación longitudinal. *Educ. XXI* **2017**, *20* (2), 73–94.

Bikse, V.; Lusena-Ezera, I.; Rivza, B.; Volkova, T. The Transformation of Traditional Universities into Entrepreneurial Universities to Ensure Sustainable Higher Education. *J. Teach. Educ. Sustain.* **2016**, *18* (2), 75–88.

Bisanz, A.; Hueber, S.; Lindner, J.; Jambor, E. Social Entrepreneurship Education in Primary School: Empowering Each Child with the YouthStart Entrepreneurial Challenges Programme. *Discour. Commun. Sustain. Educ.* **2020**, *10* (2), 142–156.

Boekholt, P. The Evolution of Innovation Paradigms and their Influence on Research, Technological Development and Innovation Policy Instruments. In *The Theory and Practice of Innovation Policy—An International Research Handbook*; Smits, R., Kuhlmann, S., Shapira, P., Eds.; Edward Elgar, 2010; pp 333–359.

Boland, R. J.; Lyytinen, K. Information Systems Research as Design: Identity, Process, and Narrative. *IFIP Adv. Inform. Commun. Technol.* **2004**, *143*, 53–70.

Bond, M.; Marín, V. I.; Dolch, C.; Bedenlier, S.; Zawacki-Richter, O. Digital Transformation in German Higher Education: Student and Teacher Perceptions and Usage of Digital Media. *Int. J. Educ. Technol. High. Educ.* **2018**, *15* (48). https://doi.org/10.1186/s41239-018-0130-1.

Borchers, A.; Park, S. H. Assessing the Effectiveness of Entrepreneurial Education Programs from a Multi-level Multi-dimensional Perspective with Mental Models. *ASEE Annu. Conf. Expos. Proc.* **2011**, *2011*, 1–9.

Borrás, S. *The Innovation Policy of the European Union: From Government to Governance*; Edward Elgar Publishing, 2003.

Borrás, S.; Edquist, C. The Choice of Innovation Policy Instruments. *Technol. Forecast. Soc. Change* **2013**, *80*, 1513–1522.

Brown, T. *Farmers, Subalterns, and Activists*; Cambridge University Press, 2018. https://doi.org/10.1017/9781108590112

Carayannis, E. G.; Grigoroudis, E.; Campbell, D. F. J.; Meissner, D.; Stamati, D. The Ecosystem as Helix: An Exploratory Theory-Building Study of Regional Co-opetitive Entrepreneurial Ecosystems as Quadruple/Quintuple Helix Innovation Models. *R&D Manage.* **2018**, *48* (1), 148–162.

Cardow, A.; Smith, R. Using Innovative Pedagogies in the Classroom: Re-storying Gothic Tales as Entrepreneur Stories. *Ind. High. Educ.* **2015**, *29* (5), 361–374.

Castells, M.; Himanen, P. The Information Society and the Welfare State. In *The Information Society and the Welfare State*; Oxford University Press, 2011.

Cavey, R. Global Leadership in the 21st Century: A Micro-perspective. *Cadmus* **2020**, *4* (2), 301–307.

Chaubey, A.; Sahoo, C. K. Assimilation of Business Intelligence: The Effect of External Pressures and Top Leaders Commitment during Pandemic Crisis. *Int. J. Inf. Manage.* **2021**, *59*, 102344.

Cho, V.; Mansfield, K. C.; Claughton, J. The Past and Future Technology in Classroom Management and School Discipline: A Systematic Review. *Teach. Teacher Educ.* **2020**, *90*, 103037.

Choi, Y. J.; Huber, E.; Kim, W. S.; Kwon, H. Y.; Shi, S.-J. Social Investment in the Knowledge-Based Economy: New Politics and Policies. *Policy Soc.* **2020**, *39* (2), 147–170.

Chua, H. S.; Bedford, O. A Qualitative Exploration of Fear of Failure and Entrepreneurial Intent in Singapore. *J. Career Dev.* **2016,** *43* (4), 319–334.

Comissão Europeia. *Novas Competências para Novos Empregos: Antecipar e adequar as necessidades do mercado de trabalho e as competências*, 2008.

Comissão Europeia. *Plano de ação "Empreendedorismo 2020" Relançar o espírito empresarial na Europa*, 2013.

Cricelli, L.; Greco, M.; Grimaldi, M. Assessing the Open Innovation Trends by Means of the Eurostat Community Innovation Survey. *Int. J. Innov. Manage.* **2016,** *20* (3), 1–30.

Cvijanović, V.; Griniece, E.; Gulyás, O.; Reid, A.; Varga, H. Stakeholder Engagement through Entrepreneurial Discovery? Lessons from Countries and Regions in Central and Eastern Europe. *Cog. Soc. Sci.* **2020,** *6* (1). doi:10.1080/23311886.2020.1794273.

Dagilienė, L.; Bruneckienė, J.; Jucevičius, R.; Lukauskas, M. Exploring Smart Economic Development and Competitiveness in Central and Eastern European Countries. *Compet. Rev.* **2020,** *30* (5), 485–505.

Davis, N. *Enhancing Europe's Competitiveness Fostering Innovation-Driven Entrepreneurship in Europe*; World Economic Forum, Issue January, 2014.

de Bono, E. *O Pensamento Lateral. Um Manual de Criatividade*; Pergaminho, 2005.

Díaz-Piloneta, M.; Ortega-Fernández, F.; Morán-Palacios, H.; Rodríguez-Montequín, V. Monitoring the Implementation of Exponential Organizations through the Assessment of Their Project Portfolio: Case Study. *Sustainability (Switzerland)* **2021,** *13* (2), 1–20.

Dominguinhos, P. M. C.; Carvalho, L. M. C. Promoting Business Creation through Real World Experience: Projecto Começar. *Educ. Train.* **2009,** *51* (2), 150–169.

Domorenok, E.; Graziano, P.; Polverari, L. Introduction: Policy Integration and Institutional Capacity: Theoretical, Conceptual and Empirical Challenges. *Policy Soc.* **2021,** *40* (1), 1–18.

Drucker, P. F. *Innovation and Entrepreneurship: Practices and Principles*; Harper & Row, 1985.

Dutta, S.; Lanvin, B.; Wunsch-Vincent, S. *Global Innovation Index 2020: Who Will Finance Innovation?* Cornell University, INSEAD, and the World Intellectual Property Organization (WIPO), 2020.

Edler, J.; Fagerberg, J. Innovation Policy: What, Why, and How. *Oxford Rev. Econ. Policy* **2017,** *33* (1), 2–23.

Edler, J.; Georghiou, L. Public Procurement and Innovation—Resurrecting the Demand Side. *Res. Policy* **2007,** *36* (7), 949–963.

Eizaguirre, S.; Parés, M. Communities Making Social Change from Below. Social Innovation and Democratic Leadership in Two Disenfranchised Neighbourhoods in Barcelona. *Urban Res. Pract.* **2019,** *12* (2), 173–191.

Etzkowitz, H.; Klofsten, M. The Innovating Region: Toward a Theory of Knowledge-Based Regional Development. *R&D Manage.* **2005,** *35* (3), 243–255.

Etzkowitz, H.; Zhou, C. *The Triple Helix: University-Industry-Government Innovation and Entrepreneurship*; Taylor and Francis, 2017.

European Commission/EACEA/Eurydice. *Entrepreneurship Education at School in Europe. Eurydice Report*; Publications Office of the European Union, 2016.

European Commission. *Green Paper Entrepreneurship in Europe*; Directorate-General for Enterprise and Industry, 2003.

European Commission. *Entrepreneurship Education: Enabling Teachers as a Critical Success Factor*; Directorate-General for Enterprise and Industry, 2011.

Evangelista, R.; Sirilli, G.; Smith, K. *Measuring Innovation in Services*; STEP Group, 1998.

Fayolle, A.; Gailly, B. Évaluation d'une formation en entrepreneuriat: Prédispositions et impact sur l'intention d'entreprendre. *Management* **2009**, *12* (3), 175–203. https://doi.org/10.3917/mana.123.0176

Flanagan, K.; Uyarra, E.; Laranja, M. Reconceptualising the 'Policy Mix' for Innovation. *Res. Policy* **2011**, *40* (5), 702–713.

Foray, D. *Smart Specialisation: Opportunities and Challenges for Regional Innovation Policy*; Routledge/Regional Studies Association, 2015.

Fuks, M.; Casalecchi, G. A. Expandindo o conceito de competência política: conhecimento político e atitudes democráticas na América Latina. *Rev. Sociol. Pol.* **2018**, *26* (68), 61–74.

Galvao, A.; Mascarenhas, C.; Marques, C.; Ferreira, J.; Ratten, V. Triple Helix and Its Evolution: A Systematic Literature Review. *J. Sci. Technol. Policy Manage.* **2019**, *10* (3), 812–833. https://doi.org/10.1108/JSTPM-10-2018-0103

Gladwell, M. *Outliers: A História do Sucesso*; Dom Quixote, 2008.

Hebles, M.; Llanos-Contreras, O.; Yániz-Álvarez-De-Eulate, C. Perceived Evolution of the Entrepreneurial Competence Based on the Implementation of a Training Program in Entrepreneurship and Innovation. *Rev. Esp. Orient. Psicoped.* **2019**, *30* (1), 9–26.

Hercz, M.; Pozsonyi, F.; Flick-Takács, N. Supporting a Sustainable Way of Life-Long Learning in the Frame of Challenge-Based Learning. *Discour. Commun. Sustain. Educ.* **2021**, *11* (2), 45–64. https://doi.org/10.2478/dcse-2020-0018

Howlett, M. P.; Saguin, K. Policy Capacity for Policy Integration: Implications for the Sustainable Development Goals. *SSRN Electr. J.* **2018**. http://dx.doi.org/10.2139/ssrn.3157448

Huang, M.-H.; Rust, R. T. Artificial Intelligence in Service. *J. Serv. Res.* **2018**, *21* (2), 155–172. https://doi.org/10.1177/1094670517752459

Huggins, R.; Thompson, P. Entrepreneurship, Innovation and Regional Growth: A Network Theory. *Small Bus. Econ.* **2015**, *41* (2015), 103–128. https://doi.org/10.1007/s11187-015-9643-3

Isaacson, W. *Steve Jobs*; Objectiva, 2015.

Isaacson, W. *Os inovadores*; Porto Editora, 2016.

Ismail, S. *Exponential Organizations*; Diversion Books, 2014.

Jakobsen, J. Farmers, Subalterns, and Activists: Social Politics of Sustainable Agriculture in India, by Trent Brown. *J. Agr. Change* **2020**, *20* (2), 338–341.

Jardim, J. *Programa de Desenvolvimento de Competências Pessoais e Sociais: Estudo para a Promoção do Sucesso Académico*; Edições Piaget, 2010.

Jardim, J. *10 Competências Rumo à Felicidade: Guia Prático para Pessoas, Equipas e Organizações Empreendedoras* (2.ª); Instituto Piaget, 2012.

Jardim, J. Competências empreendedoras. In *Portugal Empreendedor: Trinta Figuras Empreendedoras da Cultura Portuguesa—Relevância dos Modelos para a Promoção do Empreendedorismo*; Jardim, J., Franco, J. E., Eds.; Imprensa Nacional Casa da Moeda, 2013; pp 69–79.

Jardim, J. Biografias empreendedoras. In *Empreendipédia—Dicionário de Educação para o Empreendedorismo*; Jardim, J., Franco, J. E., Eds.; Gradiva, 2019a, pp 85–87.

Jardim, J. Competências empreendedoras. In *Empreendipédia—Dicionário de Educação para o Empreendedorismo*; Jardim, J., Franco, J. E., Eds.; Gradiva, 2019b, pp 136–141.

Jardim, J. Regiões Empreendedoras: Descrição e avaliação dos contextos, determinantes e políticas favoráveis à sua evolução. *Rev. Divulg. Cien. AICA* **2020**, *12* (1), 197–212.

Jardim, J. *Empreende: Manual Global de Educação para o Empreendedorismo [Empreende: Global Entrepreneurship Education Handbook]*; Mais Leituras, 2021a.

Jardim, J. Entrepreneurial Skills to Be Successful in the Global and Digital World: Proposal for a Frame of Reference for Entrepreneurial Education. *Educ. Sci.* **2021b**, *11*, 1–13.

Jardim, J.; Pinho, R. B.; Rodrigues, R. *Piratas dos Sonhos*; Theya, 2019a.

Jardim, J.; Pinho, R. B.; Rodrigues, R. *Piratas dos Sonhos—Roteiro para Monitores e Educadores*. Theya, 2019b.

Jardim, J.; Lima, J.; Grilo, C. *Os Originais: Programa de Empreendedorismo Social com Jovens [The Originals: Program of Social Entreprenaruship with Youth]*; Theya, 2019c.

Jardim, J.; Moutinho, A.; Pinho, R. B. *A Rota das Emoções*; Theya, 2019d.

Jardim, J.; Serpa, J.; Figueiredo, V.; Grilo, C. *Inovadores em Ação*; Theya, 2019e.

Jardim, J.; Soares, J. H.; Moutinho, A.; Calheiros, C.; Cardoso, P.; Cardoso, M. S.; Franco, F. A.; Pinho, R. B.; Vargas, A. e P. *Brincadores de Sonhos*; Theya, 2015a.

Jardim, J.; Soares, J. H.; Moutinho, A.; Calheiros, C.; Cardoso, P.; Cardoso, M. S.; Franco, F. A.; Pinho, R. B.; Vargas, A. e P. *Brincadores de Sonhos—Roteiro para Docentes e Formadores*; Theya, 2015b.

Jardim, J.; Bártolo, A.; Pinho, A. Towards a Global Entrepreneurial Culture: A Systematic Review of the Effectiveness of Entrepreneurship Education Programs. *Educ. Sci.* **2021**, *11*, 1–22. https://doi.org/doi.org/10.3390/educsci11080398

Jurčević, M.; Lulić, L.; Mostarac, V. The Digital Transformation of Croatian Economy Compared with EU Member States. *Ekon. Vjesnik: Rev. Contemp. Entrepreneursh., Bus., Econ. Issues* **2020**, *33* (1), 151–164.

Kan, K. The Social Politics of Dispossession: Informal Institutions and Land Expropriation in China. *Urban Stud.* **2020**, *57* (16), 3331–3346.

Kenney, M. Silicon Valley: The DNA of an Entrepreneurial Region. In *Accelerators in Silicon Valley*; Amsterdam University Press, 2018; pp 21–36.

Korolczuk, E. Counteracting Challenges to Gender Equality in the Era of Anti-gender Campaigns: Competing Gender Knowledges and Affective Solidarity. *Social Politics: International Studies in Gender, State & Society* **2021**, *27* (4), 694–717. https://doi.org/ 10.1093/sp/jxaa021

Kuziemski, M.; Misuraca, G. AI Governance in the Public Sector: Three Tales from the Frontiers of Automated Decision-Making in Democratic Settings. *Telecommun. Policy* **2020**, *44* (6), 101976. https://doi.org/10.1016/j.telpol.2020.101976

Lee, S. M.; Trimi, S. Convergence Innovation in the Digital Age and in the COVID-19 Pandemic Crisis. *J. Bus. Res.* **2021**, *123*, 14–22.

Liggett, R. Toward A Conceptualization of Democratic Leadership in a Professional Context. *Can. J. Educ. Adm. Policy* **2020**, *193*, 115–127.

Likhotal, A. Global Leadership in the 21st Century. *Cadmus* **2020**, *4* (2), 134–140.

Link, A. N.; Scott, J. T. Creativity-Enhancing Technological Change in the Production of Scientific Knowledge. *Econ. Innov. New Technol.* **2020**, *29* (5), 489–500.

Lyons, E.; Zhang, L. Who Does (Not) Benefit from Entrepreneurship Programs? *Strat. Manage. J.* **2018**, *39* (1), 85–112.

Maggetti, M.; Trein, P. More Is Less: Partisan Ideology, Changes of Government, and Policy Integration Reforms in the UK. *Policy Soc.* **2021**, 40 (1), 79–98.

Mastroyiannis, M. *Exponential Growth: Do You Know the Exponential Growth Secrets?* Kindle, 2018.

Mavi, R.; Standing, C. Evaluating Eco-innovation of OECD Countries with Data Envelopment Analysis. In *International Conferences ITS, ICEduTech and STE* 2016, 237–244.

Melluso, N.; Bonaccorsi, A.; Chiarello, F.; Fantoni, G. Rapid Detection of Fast Innovation under the Pressure of COVID-19. *PLoS One* **2020**, *15* (12), 1–26.

Mok, K. H. The Quest for Global Competitiveness: Promotion of Innovation and Entrepreneurial Universities in Singapore. *High. Educ. Policy* **2015**, *28* (1), 91–106.

Mullen, C. A. Global Leadership: Competitiveness, Tolerance, and Creativity—A Canadian Provincial Example. *Int. J. Leadersh. Educ.* **2019**, *22* (5), 629–643.

Mumford, M. D. *Handbook of Organizational Creativity*; Academic Press—Elsevier, 2012.

Nauwelaers, C.; Wintjes, R. Regional Innovation Policy for Small-Medium Enterprises. In *Regional Innovation Policy for Small-Medium Enterprises*; Asheim, B., Isaksen, A., Nauwelaers, C., Tödtling, F., Eds.; Edward Elgar Publishing, 2003; pp 193–220.

Nwaiwu, F. Review and Comparison of Conceptual Frameworks on Digital Business Transformation. *Journal of Competitiveness* **2018**, *10* (3), 86–100.

Pepin, M. Learning to Be Enterprising in School through an Inquiry-Based Pedagogy. *Ind. High. Educ.* **2018**, *32* (6), 418–429.

Perez, J. A.; Deligianni, F.; Ravi, D.; Yang, G.-Z. Artificial Intelligence and Robotic Assembly. In *Engineering with Computers*; Ukras.org, 2018. https://doi.org/10.1007/BF01201262

Peterman, N. E.; Kennedy, J. Enterprise Education: Influencing Students' Perceptions of Entrepreneurship. *Entrepreneursh. Theor. Pract.* **2003**, *28* (2), 129–144.

Piccarozzi, M.; Silvestri, C.; Morganti, P. COVID-19 in Management Studies: A Systematic Literature Review. *Sustainability (Switzerland)* **2021**, *13* (7), 1–28.

Pinho, M. I.; Fernandes, D.; Serrão, C.; Mascarenhas, D. Youth Start Social Entrepreneurship Program for Kids: Portuguese UKIDS-Case Study. *Discour. Commun. Sustain. Educ.* **2019**, *10* (2), 33–48.

Platão. *Crátilo*; Paulus, 2015.

Porfírio, J. A.; Carrilho, T.; Felício, J. A.; Jardim, J. Leadership Characteristics and Digital Transformation. *J. Bus. Res.* **2021**, *124*, 610–619.

Powell, J. J. W.; Dusdal, J. Science Production in Germany, France, Belgium, and Luxembourg: Comparing the Contributions of Research Universities and Institutes to Science, Technology, Engineering, Mathematics, and Health. *Minerva* **2017**, *55* (4), 413–434.

Ribeiro, A. T. V. B.; Uechi, J. N.; Plonski, G. A. Building Builders: Entrepreneurship Education from an Ecosystem Perspective at MIT. *Triple Helix* **2018**, *5* (1). https://doi.org/10.1186/s40604-018-0051-y

Rosser, E.; Buckner, E.; Avedissian, T.; Cheung, D. S. K.; Eviza, K.; Hafsteinsdóttir, T. B.; Hsu, M. Y.; Kirshbaum, M. N.; Lai, C.; Ng, Y. C.; Ramsbotham, J.; Waweru, S. The Global Leadership Mentoring Community: Building Capacity across Seven Global Regions. *International Nursing Review* **2020**, *67*, 484–494.

Russell, S.; Norvig, P. *Artificial Intelligence: A Modern Approach*, 3rd ed.; Prentice Hall, 2010.

Russo, V. Digital Economy and Society Index (DESI). European Guidelines and Empirical Applications on the Territory. *Studies in Systems, Decision and Control*; Springer International Publishing, 2020; Vol 208, pp 427–442.

Sánchez-Serrano, J. L. S.; Maturo, F.; Hošková-Mayerová, Š., Eds. Qualitative and Quantitative Models in Socio-economic Systems and Social Work. *Studies in Systems, Decision and Control*; Springer, 2020.

Sarkar, S. *Empreendedorismo e Inovação*; Escolar Editora, 2014.

Sawyer, S.; Crowston, K. Information Systems in Organizations and Society: Speculating on the Next 25 Years of Research. *IFIP Adv. Inform. Commun. Technol.* **2004**, *143*, 35–51.

Schot, J.; Steinmueller, W. Three Frames for Innovation Policy: R&D, Systems of Innovation and Transformative Change. *Res. Policy* **2018**, *47*, 1554–1567.

Schulz, K. P.; Mnisri, K.; Shrivastava, P.; Sroufe, R. Facilitating, Envisioning and Implementing Sustainable Development with Creative Approaches. *J. Clean. Prod.* **2021,** *278,* 123762.

Schumpeter, J. *The Theory of Economic Development*; Harvard Business Review Press, 1934.

Silva, V. V. Identificação Digital. In *Empreendipédia—Dicionário de Educação para o Empreendedorismo*; Jardim, J., Franco, J. E., Eds.; Gradiva, 2019; pp 397–398.

Sjöström, J. Eco-driven Chemical Research in the Boundary between Academia and Industry: PhD Students' Views on Science and Society. *Sci. Educ.* **2013,** *22* (10), 2427–2441.

Smits, R.; Kuhlmann, S. The Rise of Systemic Instruments in Innovation Policy. *Int. J. Foresight Innov. Policy* **2004,** *1* (1–2), 4–32.

Soehl, T.; Waldinger, R.; Luthra, R. Social Politics: The Importance of the Family for Naturalisation Decisions of the 1.5 Generation. *J. Ethn. Migr. Stud.* **2020,** *46* (7), 1240–1260.

Švarc, J.; Lažnjak, J.; Dabić, M. The Role of National Intellectual Capital in the Digital Transformation of EU Countries. Another Digital Divide? *J. Intell. Cap.* **2021,** *22* (4), 768–791.

Szeto, E. How Do Principals' Practices Reflect Democratic Leadership for Inclusion in Diverse School Settings? A Hong Kong Case Study. *Educ. Manage. Adm. Leadersh.* **2020,** *49* (3), 471–492.

Thagard, P. How Brains Make Mental Models. In *Studies in Computational Intelligence*; Springer, 2010; pp 447–461.

Trein, P.; Maggetti, M.; Meyer, I. Necessary Conditions for Policy Integration and Administrative Coordination Reforms: An Exploratory Analysis. *J. Eur. Publ. Policy* **2020,** *28* (9), 1410–1431.

Vega, M. P. "La fábrica de sueños": Programa de Educación Emprendedora para alumnos de la escuela primaria y media. *Ingen. Solidar.* **2015,** *11* (18), 35–39. https://doi.org/10.16925/in.v11i18.989

Yinfu, Y. Concepts and Policy Innovations in the National Education Plan. *Chin. Educ. Soc.* **2017,** *50* (3), 142–161.

Yokoi, T.; Shan, J.; Wade, M. R.; Macaulay, J. *Digital Vortex 2019: Continuous and Connected Change*; Global Center for Digital Business Transformation, 2019.

Yu, K.-H.; Beam, A. L.; Kohane, I. S. Artificial Intelligence in Healthcare. *Nat. Biomed. Eng.* **2018,** *2* (10), 719–731. https://doi.org/10.1038/s41551-018-0305-z

Zander, B.; Zander, R. S. *Art of Possibility: Transforming Professional and Personal Life*; Harvard Business Review Press, 2000.

CHAPTER 3

KNOWLEDGE REPRESENTATION ON INNOVATIONS IN LEARNING PROCESSES AND EDUCATIONAL POLICIES: INFUSING ARTIFICIAL INTELLIGENCE AND BLOCKCHAIN POWERS

RAMESH CHANDER SHARMA[1], ANDREIA DE BEM MACHADO[2], ISABEL SOFIA BRITO[3], FERNANDA MARIA DOS SANTOS PEREIRA[3], and MARIA JOSÉ SOUSA[4]

[1]*Ambedkar University Delhi, New Delhi, India*

[2]*Universidade Federal de Santa Catarina, Florianópolis, SC, Brazil*

[3]*Polytechnic Institute of Beja, Beja, Portugal*

[4]*ISCTE—Instituto Universitário de Lisboa, Lisbon, Portugal*

ABSTRACT

Large amounts of data are generated as a result of educational innovations, and securing its storage with security, availability, and immutability is a significant concern. Artificial intelligence (AI) and blockchain-based applications are examples of technology that are dominated by the Fourth Industrial Revolution. Through data decentralization, the use of computer-oriented blockchain in education may provide security and immutability. Governments and organizations have put policies in place to encourage the

Incorporating AI Technology in the Service Sector: Innovations in Creating Knowledge, Improving Efficiency, and Elevating Quality of Life. Maria José Sousa, Subhendu Kumar Pani, Francesca Dal Mas, & Sérgio Sousa (Eds.)
© 2024 Apple Academic Press, Inc. Co-published with CRC Press (Taylor & Francis)

use of blockchain and AI technologies. The goal of this chapter is to look at educational policy and the usage of innovations in learning processes to see if blockchain infused with AI can be used. In order to answer the following questions, a comprehensive and integrative review was conducted in the Scopus database: (1) What is the difference between AI and blockchain? (2) How are AI and BC being adopted in educational innovation policies? (3) What role might innovation play in the learning process? (4) What are the educational policies on the use of innovations in learning processes in order to apply blockchain? The findings bring together public policies on blockchain and technical innovation in the teaching–learning process, with important implications for the operation and comprehension of open-innovation systems in a globalized environment.

3.1   INTRODUCTION

Today's world is constantly changing and innovation has become a necessary capability in life. The goal of this chapter is to look at educational policy and the usage of innovations in learning processes to see if blockchain infused with artificial intelligence (AI) can be used. We undertook a systematic review to attain this purpose. Initially, each article was analyzed for blockchain applications and, in this way, 31 articles provided different results. Section 3.5 shows the authors of the articles, as well as the 14 categories that were able to be retrieved through the analyses. We conclude that blockchain and AI are unique opportunities to transform teaching and learning process. The authors believe that the immutability of the blockchain in relation to the behavior of students and teachers could promote innovation policies.

3.2   ARTIFICIAL INTELLIGENCE

AI is not a new notion; it was conceived in 1956 at a Dartmouth College workshop. "To proceed on the basis of the premise that any facet of learning or any other trait of intelligence can in principle be so clearly characterized that a computer can be constructed to replicate it," the workshop's purpose said (McCarthy et al., 2006). AI is based on the principle that human intelligence can be specified in a way that a machine can interpret the specification and execute the tasks.

During these years and until now, several definitions have emerged according to the field of application. For example, Kaplan and Haenlein (2019) describe AI as "as a system's ability to correctly understand external data, learn from it, and apply what it has learned to accomplish specific goals and tasks through flexible adaptation." Therefore, AI is able to deal with data in different ways it has the potential to take data exploitation to new heights. AI allows us to complete jobs more quickly and efficiently.

In today's technologically advanced world, AI is one of the most disruptive computer science concepts for improving the learning process of various groups, including teachers, tutors, and students. One of the major issues in education, according to Roll and Wylie (2016), is "personalization," which is described as "the process of adapting anything to meet the requirements of a specific group of people a certain person" (Cambridge Dictionary). In this context, AI can provide a personalized learning experience (https://elearningindustry.com/5-main-roles-artificial-intelligence-in-education). As a result, AI enriches and supports deeper learning while also redefining the classroom experience for each student, creating a unique study timetable for each learner based on their knowledge gaps. In this approach, AI tailors education to the individual needs of students, enhancing their efficiency. Advancements in AI have led to the development of human-like intelligence, which is impacting living standards and restructuring culture. The work on human-like form or semihuman semirobot has opened up a new domain of transhumanism (Uğur and Kurubacak, 2019). AI's key value is its capacity to handle the individual demands of learners and instructors in order to optimize their routine, increase efficiency, improve accessibility, and scale operations.

On the other hand, there are some ethical implications of AI, for example, students' and teachers' privacy and security concerns. In this context, blockchain technology should be applied in order to secure student data and improve the acquisition process.

3.3 BLOCKCHAIN

Since the emergence of the blockchain concept in 2008, as proposed by Satoshi Nakamoto in an article about Bitcoin (Nakamoto, 2008), diverse experts have been placing their stakes on its disruptive potential. Much more than a digital currency infrastructure, this technology is seen as a revolution in centralized transactions and has applicability in a variety of areas such as, for instance, public administration, health, logistics, creative rights, and system audit.

Blockchain is a data structure very similar to a linked list, working as a ledger, but in a shared, public, and decentralized manner. New entries are input to it only following consensus between the network nodes. The entire transaction backtrack is stored on blockchain, and once a block has been saved, it is very hard to alter or remove it. The financial market has been the heaviest investor in this technology. Despite a lot of money having been invested in studies on this technology and its development, few end-user applications are available on the market. On the other hand, several ways of modeling blockchains have been developed and the complexity of identifying which concepts need to be applied for each scenario has increased.

Another conception of blockchain is that it is a transaction database distributed over and shared by the nodes of a distributed system organized as a peer-to-peer (P2P) network. The records held on the database are decentralized and are called blocks (Zielińska et al., 2019). Each block has a unique identification generated from a cryptographic hash function and is referenced to its predecessor, so that it is possible to establish a link between blocks (Chicarin, 2017). In this structure, the database only accepts inclusion of new blocks, and it is not possible to modify or remove existing blocks, in which the collection of blocks grows and stores information from its creation up until its final update. AI's key value is its capacity to handle the individual demands of learners and instructors in order to optimize their routine, increase efficiency, improve accessibility, and scale operations (Chicarin, 2017). Within this context, one of its main characteristics relates to capacity of unchangeability, which derives from it working as a ledger that is public to everyone in the network. It stores detailed information about all transactions that have been performed, which can be linked to their address of origin through to the destination block address (Chicarin, 2017), enabling the genesis of the transaction to be found (Hîrtan and Dobr, 2018). Within this scenario, blockchain emerges as a potential technology for developing new solutions capable of changing many of the systems we deal with daily, such as those intended for education, contract management and smart contracts, payment and currency processing, supply chain management (SCM), asset protection, as well as in personal information record systems (Sharma et al., 2020).

The main applications of blockchain are as follows: notary public, music industry, decentralized storage, IoT (Internet of Things), antifake solutions, bitcoin applications, smart contracts, decentralized autonomous organization, application prototype definition, supply chains, smart city, property rights, hyperledger, as well as in the world of education.

3.4 EDUCATIONAL INNOVATION POLICIES: AI AND BLOCKCHAIN

AI, as one of the technologies of the Fourth Industrial Revolution (Schwab, 2017), has emerged as a killer application making machines think like human being (HfS Research Ltd. and IBM, 2018). AI applications have resulted in increased productivity. Machine reasoning, chatbots, deep learning, speech recognition, computer vision, neural networks, autonomics, virtual agents, machine learning, image recognition, knowledge representation, and natural language processing are some of the AI building blocks (HfS Research Ltd. and IBM, 2018). AI supremacy through the use of chatbots, recommender systems, machine translation, and face and emotion recognition, and so on will fundamentally transform education. Seldon and Abidoye (2018) identified the role of AI in transforming teaching in various ways, like curation specialists would author and identify content suiting to particular student profile using AI, emergence of learning pods, and wide-open and flexible spaces instead of traditional classrooms where psychological and physiological state of students can be monitored using sensors, visual representation of materials, real-time assessment with appropriate feedback for the learning, and enabling students for learning autonomously and identifying their own deficiencies. Students would have the option of studying at a physical campus as well as at a cloud campus. AI and machine learning can create a well-designed tutoring program (e.g., Jill Watson created by Prof Ashok Goel of Georgia Tech, USA) for clarity on the fundamentals of a topic.

Similar to AI as a technology of Fourth Industrial Revolution, blockchain is distributed and decentralized technology which due to being immutable, transparent, and trustworthy has great value in educational policies (Sharma et al., 2020). Predictions are that on a global scale, the blockchain technology revenues will be in excess of 39 billion US dollars by 2025 (Liu, 2020), most common usage being for digital currency and payments, SCM, and IoT, while its global spending is reaching 6.6 billion US dollars in April 2021 (Liu, 2021). UNESCO (2019) realized the potential of blockchain toward building inclusive knowledge societies, disrupting existing economic power structures, and bringing drastic changes in governance. To allow interdisciplinary discussions between researchers and practitioners, the UNESCO hold a high-level conference titled, "Blockchain: practices and perspectives" in May 2019. Governments have identified the benefits blockchain can bring to social and economic development and thus have developed policies about integrating blockchain into their systems. The Government of India's

Ministry of Electronics and Information Technology (MeitY) has recognized the potential of blockchain technology in areas, such as governance, banking and finance, and cybersecurity, and has established a Distributed Centre of Excellence in Blockchain Technology to conduct research in this area (MeitY, 2021). NITI Aayog, Govt. of India also has implemented it as use cases for land records, pharmaceutical supply chain, fertilizer subsidy disbursement, and educational certificates. The Reserve Bank of India anticipates its application in the banking industry, although cryptocurrency transactions in India are prohibited currently. One of the prominent integration of a national-level service with the Unified Blockchain Framework is "DigiLocker" which is an online service where a citizen can save and access their documents/certificates for example, certificates, marksheets, driving license, vehicle registration, and so on.

Gabison (2016) pointed out about implementation of a regulatory framework for registering cryptocurrency exchanges by the Govt. of Isle of Man, in Great Britain. Freedom of expression with the right of privacy is a big challenge for policy makers. In the blockchain domain, deleting information is complicated. This also has implications for copyrighted content. Due to the decentralized nature of blockchain, once such content is added to a blockchain ledger, it cannot be erased. Some Acts, such as the Digital Millennium Copyright Act (DMCA) and the Online Copyright Infringement Liability Limitation Act in the United States of America, are effective tools for copyright protection. Similarly, the EU Copyright Directive in Europe protects the rights of copyright holders. Blockchain technology has its impact on the way such Acts (DMCA) and the EU directives can be used. A challenge of blockchain is the difficulty in identifying the copyright infringer as it masks the IP addresses and identities (Reid and Harrigan, 2011). The applications of blockchain in education were examined by Grech and Camilleri (2017, p. 10) who identified its role for qualifications awards, licensing and accreditation, student record management, intellectual property management, and payment processing.

Prominent institutions like MIT, Open University of UK, University of Nicosia, and Govt. of Malta have also carried out projects of implementing blockchain. The United Arab Emirates is working on "Emirates Blockchain Strategy 2021" where nearly half of the applicable government transactions would be transitioned to the blockchain. Govt. of Malta has established the Malta Digital Innovation Authority whose object is to provide quality assurance solutions in the form of regulation through certification. In case of Liechtenstein, the blockchain act deals regulating the token economy by creating, storing, and transferring tokens with security enforcement in place.

The Blockchain Technology Act in the United States allows businesses to use blockchain and relaxes limits on blockchain or smart contracts. In a similar vein, Wyoming has enacted 13 blockchain and cryptocurrency laws. BitLicence is used by the New York State Department of Financial Services to allow enterprises to operate in the virtual asset field after receiving license approval. Other institutions, including the European Commission, have advocated for it adoption of blockchain and Distributed Ledger Technical (DLT) in the European Union, emphasizing an innovation-friendly regulatory approach to DLT and upholding the principles of technology neutrality and business model neutrality (PwC, 2019).

Because both AI and blockchain have great power, we can create revolutionary business models by merging the two technologies. Some recent developments include Microsoft's integration of Lition Blockchain into Azure, allowing clients to develop, test, and deploy Lition side chains and applications; IBM and Digital Asset Holdings releasing Hyperledger Fabric for writing Ethereum smart contracts; and blockchain-based games (like Age of Rust based on its own Rustbits cryptocurrency, Blankos Block Party, Crypto Space Commander, CryptoWars, etc.). Modern games use digital tokens, based on Ethereum blockchain. Xaya.io has brought open-source (MIT License) games which use the power of blockchain with cryptographic security. Not only for entertainment, these have educational values too. One of the most interesting examples of integration of AI and blockchain is AIDOC (AI Doctor on the Blockchain). It uses medical data and smart doctor AI technology to offer us regular health and wellness insights (http://aidoc.me/). This platform uses deep learning as AI-based decision support system (AI-DSS) for radiology. This system is able to point out acute abnormalities across body so that health professionals can offer targeted patient care. Blockchain, AI, IoT, and other technologies are all on the rise behind AIDOC medical platform. It uses three core modules: Bitdata person, LifeBank, and life data mining.

There are ways in which AI can affect blockchain (Corea, 2019):

- *Optimizing energy consumption:* One of the challenges of dealing with cryptocurrencies is the consumption of lot of energy. AI can play a great role here in optimizing energy consumption for hardware mining.
- *Scalability:* AI can assist in offering federated learning. Federated learning is a form of collaborative learning without the use of centralized training data (McMahan and Ramage, 2017) in mobile learning environments.
- *Security:* Although blockchain has high-security levels, its layers (like DAO, Mt Gox, etc.) may not be that secure. AI can add to extra-security to the blockchain modules.

- *Privacy:* Homomorphic encryption allows us to perform transactions directly on the encrypted data without needing access to the secret key. They are considered to be more secure than factorization and discrete logarithm-based systems such as RSA and other protocols.
- *Efficiency:* AI allows for faster transactions on specific nodes.
- *Data gates:* AI can handle data usage tracking more efficiently in intelligent ways.

Some of the examples of integration of blockchain and AI are:

- *TraneAI:* It uses Transaction Protocol for Artificial Intelligence token, which is an open-source protocol and enhances the efficiency of AI training. This system utilizes Ethereum blockchain.
- Neureal (https://neureal.net/#/) is a P2P AI-supercomputing model which can efficiently predit heart attacks or hurricane so that population can move out from that place.
- Talla (https://talla.com/) a conversational platform to provide quick resolutions and workflows across connected systems can be streamlined and automated.
- Augur (https://augur.net/) is a blockchain-based prediction system to tackle the dissemination of false information via social media.
- *CoiningAI:* Machine learning, natural language processing, and neural networks are used to analyze data and information about coins on social media, assisting users with portfolio building, and providing advice on when to buy and sell bitcoin.

The above discussion indicates that intelligent systems will play a major role in decision-making which can be accurate and faster. An integration of AI and blockchain would assist us in creating data-driven systems, which can be scalable, distributed, collaborative, transparent, real-time, insightful, and self-learning.

3.4.1 INNOVATION LEARNING PROCESSES

This section presents researches that showcase the applications of AI and blockchain technologies to improve learning processes. The study in Ocheja et al. (2019) shows how a new learning platform can be used to maintain track of learning successes beyond transcripts and certificates. Students might be able to migrate their learning records from one institution to another in a secure and verified way if they use blockchain. This is accomplished by using smart contracts on the blockchain to manage access privileges. On the other hand, by adding data analysis techniques (AI) to the platform is possible to offer personalized experience to students. This is achieved when we apply AI techniques to the data collected during the learning process.

Blockchain can be utilized to build a balance to monitor-learning process and outcomes, according to Chen et al. (2018). As a result, blockchain technology has a lot of promise for students and teachers in terms of evaluation, learning activity design and implementation, and keeping track of learning processes.

It is possible to track all aspects of teaching and learning using blockchain and smart contracts. As previously said, one of the blockchain's benefits is its potential to be irreversible; as a result, students' and teachers' actions will be recorded in the blockchain ledger, which will track everything children learn and protect both parties' interests.

However, because of the immutability of blockchain and the purpose of AI personalization, the data recorded on blockchain is more particular, authentic, and antitheft. For example, students can submit their work to an AI-powered learning platform, and the smart contract will evaluate the students' performance and record the results in blocks. From the standpoint of teachers and during the educational process, all activities will be recorded in the blockchain. The smart contract will ensure consistency in teaching design and practice, which will be a key teaching assessment indicator (Mahankali and Chaudhary, 2020).

Finally, a smart contract between instructors and schools, as well as a smart contract between teachers and students, maybe cross-verified. Employers can use these data to match students with employment that are a good fit. It will reduce the likelihood of failure. In conclusion, blockchain serves the best interests of all parties involved.

3.5 METHODOLOGY

Systematic searching of an online database was used as the research method, followed by integrative analysis of the findings. At the outset, we sought to use the five steps proposed by Torraco (2016), as stages of integrative literature reviews described as follows (Machado et al., 2019):

First stage: The first stage is the formulation of research problems to critically examine education policies and use of innovations in learning processes for the applicability of blockchain combined with AI. It is the formulation of research problems to critically examine education policies and the use of innovations in learning processes for the applicability of the blockchain combined with AI. The questions that guided this chapter are:

1. What is AI and blockchain?
2. What policies do educational institutions have in place to promote AI and BC adoption?
3. How can innovation be applied to learning processes?
4. What are the educational policies with the use of innovations in learning processes for the applicability of the blockchain?

In order to answer this question, a search was made on the database, beginning in October 2020 and ending in December 2020.

Second stage: In the second stage, referred to as the definition of the search sources, we defined criteria for selecting the search, such as delimiting the database to be searched. We opted to use the Scopus electronic database (www.scopus.com).

Third stage: selection of papers and/or conferences related to the problem of research.

Fourth stage: establish the inclusion and exclusion criteria for articles to answer the research question.

Fifth stage: conclusive result of the integrative review.

The following filtering process was adopted for each Scopus record found, as shown in Figure 3.1:

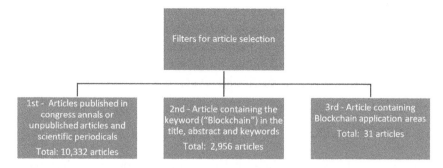

FIGURE 3.1   Article filtering process.

Initially, each article was analyzed for Blockchain applications and, in this way, 31 articles provided different results. Table 3.1 shows the authors of the articles, as well as the 14 categories that were able to be retrieved through the analyses.

TABLE 3.1 Blockchain-Related Applications and Authors.

Notary public	Crosby et al. (2016), Matilla (2016), Shrier et al. (2016), Guo and Liang (2016)
Music industry	Crosby et al. (2016), Huckle et al. (2016)
Decentralized storage	Crosby et al. (2016)
IoT (Internet of Things)	Crosby et al. (2016), Yli-Huumo et al. (2016), Matilla (2016), Huckle et al. (2016), Sun et al. (2016), Bahga and Madisetti (2016), Zhang and Wen (2017), Lee and Lee (2017), Ouaddah et al. (2016)
Antifake solutions	Crosby et al. (2016)
Bitcoin applications	Wright and De Filippi (2015)
Smart contracts	Matilla (2016), Sun et al. (2016), Lin and Liao (2017), Knirisch et al. (2018)
Decentralized autonomous organization	Matilla (2016)
Application prototype definition	Yli-Huumo et al. (2016)
Supply chains	Matilla (2016), Apte and Petrovsky (2016)
Smart city	Sun et al. (2016)
Property rights	Shrier et al. (2016)
Hyperledger	Lin and Liao (2017)
World of education	Hillman and Ganesh (2019), Filvà et al. (2018)

Below we present the characteristics and analyses of each of the 14 categories found:

Notary public: Crosby et al. (2016) report use of the blockchain technology for verifying and analyzing the authenticity of documents. For the author, this reduces costs, eliminates the requirement for a centralized authority, and optimizes processes. Crosby et al. (2016) use the following organizations as examples: Stampery, Viacoin, Block Notary, Crypto Public Notary, and Proof of Existence. According to the author, if each individual used blockchain, they could provide their own Big Data with cryptography, which will guarantee the veracity of information, creating an important credit and personal property resource.

Music industry: Crosby et al. (2016) report that the music industry has undergone great changes in the last decade. The demand for openness in royalty payments has continuously increased since the internet's inception. The author suggests that blockchain technology can help to maintain a comprehensive and up-to-date copyright database serving as a public book.

The author cites the example of a possible solution for this trust in third parties, namely Storj, a platform based on P2P blockchain. As there is no central control, this eliminates errors arising from in-service data and interruptions, providing a considerable increase in security, privacy of use, and control of data.

IoT: Crosby et al. (2016) report that IoT is the basis of a centralized model that depends on an intermediary or a central point to control interaction between devices. According to the author, this centralized model makes the practice of autonomous operations between IoT devices infeasible. The author cites as an example applications on IoT using this currency in the areas of smart property, paid data, and digitally controlled energy.

Smart contracts: Matilla (2016) explains the idea of a smart contract stored in a blockchain, making it fakeproof, self-executing, and automatically applicable, thus reducing human intervention and becoming less risky and more economical. The author states that the possibilities for using smart contracts are virtually infinite. Lin and Liao (2017) explain that a smart contract is a digital contract controlling user assets, formulating the rights and obligations of the parties, as users able to receive and store data, as well as to send data when automatically requested to do so.

Decentralized autonomous organization: Matilla (2016) presents the idea of creating a so-called decentralized autonomous organization, combining cryptocurrency and smart contracts. This organization would be self-executing with a network in which the automated nodes operate in conjunction with a system without any external human guidance. The author presents the case of Neureal, an AI platform that uses blockchain technology to create an open-distributed platform for AI algorithms.

Application prototype development: Yli-Huumo et al. (2016) identified the use of blockchain in the development of application prototypes, with greater security and reliability in their processes. These prototypes are used as a means for smart property contracts, digital content distribution, groups of connected and integrated computers, the so-called botnets, and P2P transmission protocols.

SCM-related activities: Matilla (2016) presents the use of blockchain in operations relating to SCM, where suppliers and consumers have access to all detailed records, which are also unchangeable. The authors present the case of the Everledger, a distributed database, applied in the certification of diamonds. In this case, the use of blockchain ensures the verification of the source of the product, including its transportation, thus increasing security and trust in the process.

Smart cities: Sun et al. (2016) state that for a city to be called "Smart," the smart elements need to be horizontally integrated. According to the authors, this condition would arise from smart government, including smart mobility, smart living, smart use of natural resources, smart citizens and a smart economy, all functioning as one system.

Property rights: Shrier et al. (2016) highlight the strong security of blockchain and its characteristic of decentralization, which make its application adequate for property rights. The authors present the example of the Ascribe startup, the services of which provide the possibility of blocking information, secure sharing, and tracking of digital property.

Hyperledger: Lin and Liao (2017) report the use of an open-code platform called Hyperledger. The name arises from the possibility of a very large number of processes migrating to the digital public records model by means of a global platform. This platform was developed by the Linux Foundation, for development support for distributed blockchain-based ledgers.

World of Education: Smart contracts being implanted in an education audience via blockchain (such as Ethereum or Bitcoin) to recognize and record the time at which Kratos users can have various interactions with data. Use of blockchain technology to preserve students' identity and protect their data.

The fifth step answered the question: What are the educational policies with the use of innovations in learning processes for the applicability of the blockchain? Two articles were chosen as finalists. The first of its kind is Kratos: a secure, authenticated, and publicly verifiable system for educational data using blockchain (Hillman and Ganesh, 2019). It describes an immutable data management system, in which an underlying set of system rules is established in a collection of smart contracts, which are coded in accordance with nonvirtual agreements between schools and educational technology suppliers (Edutech). In order to recognize and record when Kratos users can have various interactions with the data, the article recommends that smart contracts be put on a public blockchain (such as Ethereum or Bitcoin). People can request access to school data through a blockchain-based virtual token that is unique to them, allowing for more control over data access and use. The second study, privacy and identity management in learning analytics processes with blockchain (Filvà et al., 2018), offers a blockchain solution based on automating rules and restrictions with the purpose of providing students with data governance, privacy, and security.

3.6   EDUCATIONAL INNOVATION POLICIES: LEARNING PROCESSES FOR THE APPLICABILITY OF BLOCKCHAIN

Blockchain has tremendous potential for the education sector. With e-learning industry as being one of the fastest-growing sectors in educational field, there are unique possibilities for blockchain and AI to transform teaching and learning. There are good use cases available which have proved the potential of these to the education sector, albeit there are challenges. Verified certification of the learner's achievement addresses the issue of fraud certificates and fake diploma mills. The anonymous ledger technology allows students to participate in providing their independent and honest feedback about quality teaching. Through an open and distributed ledger, the absenteeism can be controlled. This allows the teachers and subject-matter experts to safeguard their intellectual property right (IPR) from any misuse. The University of Melbourne has already successfully tried using blockchain to issue digital credentials in 2017. A verifiable lifetime transcript tackles fraud, reduces overhead, and time in processing cases (Moore, 2019). Approval of the use of cryptocurrencies by governments would bring a new change in the way finances are managed in educational institutions. The King's College in New York City started accepting bitcoin as payment in 2014 as a way to create and trade digital assets. This technology further helps in creating new disruptive business models. The Woolf University (https://woolf.university/) using blockchain technology offers online, mixing synchronous meetings with peer and teacher, and asynchronous course material to the students. Another example is "Education Blockchain Initiative" launched in 2020 by the American Council on Education in partnership with the Office of Educational Technology, Department of Education, USA, uses blockchain for secure, traceable, and verifiable exchange of educational data (https://tech.ed.gov/blockchain/).

3.6.1   *DApp FOR LEARNING PROCESSES*

There are applications which run on a distributed computing system, mostly Ethereum Blockchain. These are called as Decentralized Application (DApp). DApp application is open source in nature, run decentralized, and cryptographically highly secure. We propose below a model case for adopting some DApp tools for the learning process. In the context of online learning and teaching, we use different browsers, operating systems, storage systems, synchronous and asynchronous messaging systems, web or video call systems, social media, and payment gateways. Below, Table 3.2, are some of the popular and effective tools which teachers and students can make use of as DApp.

TABLE 3.2 Examples of Decentralized Application (DApp) for Learning Process (Icon Source: flaticon.com).

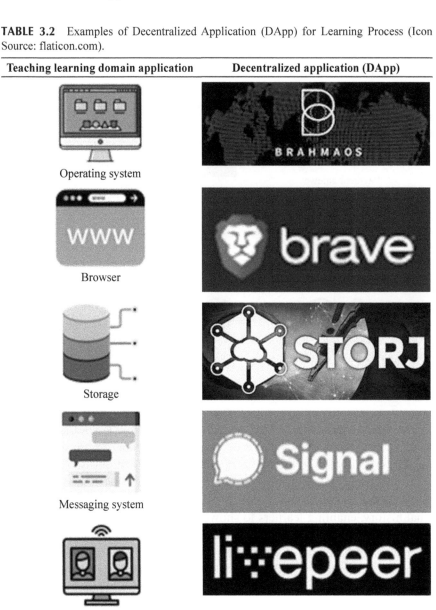

Teaching learning domain application	Decentralized application (DApp)
Operating system	BRAHMAOS
Browser	brave
Storage	STORJ
Messaging system	Signal
Video calling system	li∵epeer

TABLE 3.2   *(Continued)*

Teaching learning domain application	Decentralized application (DApp)

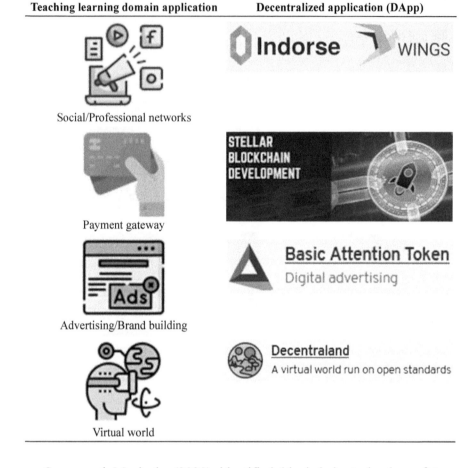

Social/Professional networks

Payment gateway

Advertising/Brand building

Virtual world

Sousa and Machado (2020) identified blockchain technology future trends in education, like the use of public blockchain for storing digital signatures for digital certifications resulting in verification, issuing appropriate credential to an institution, automatic recognition and transfer of credits, wider and verifiable visibility of students' profiles and their educational history, enabling learners to showcase evidence of their learning as a lifelong learning passport, tracking intellectual property, receiving payments via blockchain-based cryptocurrencies, and verifiable student identification. Sousa and Machado propose that suitable policies would define regulations and standards to measure learning outcomes leading to enhanced trust in certification and proof of learning. Our lives have been turned upside down by the pandemic. Educational institutions and other offices and industries have suffered a huge loss in terms of productivity. This is the right time now that we focus on integration and implementation of blockchain and AI to create systems which respond to the crisis situations. Such systems can allow us to monitor and manage our humanitarian efforts in a better way, like tracking of funds received, verification of distribution channels where that help is being directed to, taking care of fake news, better governance of network nodes, transparency of the system providing public visibility, and tracking of operations.

3.7 CONCLUSIONS

We arrive at the conclusion that AI is characterized as a system's ability to accurately perceive external input, learn from it, and apply that learning to specific goals and activities through flexible adaptation. Similar to a linked list, blockchain is a data system that functions as a shared, public, and decentralized ledger.

The educational sector has a lot of opportunity with blockchain. With the e-learning industry being one of the most rapidly expanding sectors in the educational world, blockchain and AI have unique opportunities to transform teaching and learning. While there are obstacles, there are some good use cases that have proved their promise for the education sector. The problem of fraudulent certificates and bogus degree factories is addressed by validated certification of the student's achievements. Students will engage in anonymous reason technology, offering truthful and independent input on quality teaching. Absenteeism can be managed using a transparent and distributed ledger. This helps teachers and subject-matter experts to defend their IPRs from unauthorized use. Blockchain and smart contracts can be used to track all elements of education and learning. The immutability of the blockchain in relation to the behavior of students and teachers registered in the blockchain ledger is the aim of the innovation policies, so that it can track what students have learned while protecting both parties' interests.

The blockchain can be used to create a balance that can be used to monitor the learning process and results. As a result, when it comes to analyzing, planning, and implementing learning activities, as well as tracking learning processes, blockchain technology has a lot of promise for students and teachers. In addition, such policies must take into account the immutability of the blockchain, as well as the goal of personalization of AI and more specific, legitimate, and antitheft data recorded on the blockchain. The development of an AI learning platform and a smart contract will assess student success and record results in blocks that has been discovered as an example of educational innovation.

For future research, we propose the study of blockchain and the innovations brought about by digital transformation in higher education institutions. It would be interesting to examine the potential of AI-based blockchain applications like Learning Experience Platforms where the course content in a secure way. Other areas to investigate would be to achieving personalization of learning and how blockchain applications can assist for self-directed learning.

All the product names, brands, and software applications/platforms, and so on mentioned in this chapter are the trademarks/copyright of their respective owners/companies.

KEYWORDS

- blockchain
- artificial intelligence
- educational policies
- innovation
- teaching and learning
- credentials

REFERENCES

Apte, S.; Petrovsky, N. Will Blockchain Technology Revolutionize Excipient Supply Chain Management? *J. Excip. Food Chem.* **2016,** *7* (3), 76–78.

Bahga, A.; Madissetti, V. K. Blockchain Platform for Industrial Internet of Things. *J. Softw. Eng. Appl.* **2016,** *9* (10), 533–546.

Beck, R.; Avital, M.; Rossi, M.; Thatcher, J. B. Blockchain Technology in Business and Information Systems Research. *Bus. Inform. Syst. Eng.* **2017,** *59* (6), 381–384. https://doi.org/10.1007/s12599-017-0505-1

Biswas, K.; Muthukkumarasamy, V. Securing Smart Cities Using Blockchain Technology. In *Proc. 2016 IEEE 18th International Conference on High Performance Computing and Communications; IEEE 14th International Conference on Smart City; IEEE 2nd International Conference on Data Science and Systems (HPCC/SmartCity/DSS),* 2016; pp 1392–1393.

Chen, G.; Xu, B.; Lu, M.; Chen, N.-S. Exploring Blockchain Technology and Its Potential Applications for Education. *Smart Learn. Environ.* **2018,** *5,* 2196–7091. doi:10.1186/s40561-017-0050-x.

Chicarino, V. R. L.; Jesus, E. F.; de Albuquerque, C. V. N.; Rocha, A. A. A. Uso de blockchain para privacidade e segurança em internet das coisas. In *Minicursos do VII Simpósio Brasileiro de Segurança da Informação e de Sistemas Computacionais (SBSeg 2017),* 2017; pp 149–199.

Corea, F. The Convergence of AI and Blockchain: What's the Deal?: Why a Decentralized Intelligence May Affect Our Future. Blogpost dated Dec. 2, 2017. Available at https://francesco-ai.medium.com/the-convergence-of-ai-and-blockchain-whats-the-deal-60c618e3accc

Corea, F. The Convergence of AI and Blockchain, Applied Artificial Intelligence: Where AI Can Be Used in Business. *Springer Briefs Complex.* **2019,** 19–26. https://doi.org/10.1007/978-3-319-77252-3_4

Crosby, M.; Pattanayak, P.; Verma, S.; Kalyanaraman, V. Blockchain Technology: Beyond Bitcoin. *Appl. Innov.* **2016,** *2* (junho), 6–10.

Endenich, C.; Trapp, R. Ethical Implications of Management Accounting and Control: A Systematic Review of the Contributions from the *Journal of Business Ethics*. *J. Bus. Ethics* **2020,** *163,* 309–328.

Guo, Y.; Liang, C. Blockchain Application and Outlook in the Banking Industry. *Finan. Innov.* **2016,** *2* (1), 2–24.

Filvà, D. A.; García-Peñalvo, F. J.; Forment, M. A.; Escudero, D. F.; Casañ, M. J. Privacy and Identity Management in Learning Analytics Processes with Blockchain. In *Proceedings of the Sixth International Conference on Technological Ecosystems for Enhancing Multiculturality* [S.L.], ACM, 2018; pp 37–47. http://dx.doi.org/10.1145/3284179.3284354

Gabison, G. Policy Considerations for the Blockchain Technology Public and Private Applications. *Science and Technology Law Review* **2016,** *19* (3), 327–350. Retrieved from https://scholar.smu.edu/scitech/vol19/iss3/4

Government Office for Science. *Distributed Ledger Technology: Beyond Block Chain,* 2016. Retrieved from https://assets.publishing.service.gov.uk/government/uploads/system/uploads/attachment_data/file/492972/gs-16-1-distributed-ledger-technology.pdfHan

Grech, A.; Camilleri, A. F. Blockchain in Education. *EUR 28778 EN,* 2017. doi:10.2760/60649.

Haber, S.; Stornetta, S. W. How to Time-Stamp a Digital Document. In *Conference on the Theory and Application of Cryptography,* Springer, Berlin, Heidelberg, 1990; pp 437–455.

Han, G. E. Blockchain: The Promise of Smart Contracts. *Juris Illumin.* **2017,** *8,* 1–4. Retrieved from https://static1.squarespace.com/static/55c714fbe4b0f0d634b061b5/t/58922c3b1b631b5940ff0b4e/1485974587997/Goh+Eng+Han+-+Blockchain+the+promise+of+smart+contracts.pdf

HfS Research Ltd.; IBM. *Making AI the Killer App for Your Data*; HfS Research Ltd, 2018; p 23.

Hillman, V.; Ganesh, V. Kratos: A Secure, Authenticated and Publicly Verifiable System for Educational Data Using the Blockchain. In *2019 IEEE International Conference on Big Data (Big Data)* [S.L.]; IEEE, 2019; pp 238–280. http://dx.doi.org/10.1109/bigdata47090.2019.9006190

Hîrtan, L. A.; Dobre, C. Blockchain Privacy-Preservation in Intelligent Transportation Systems. In *Proc. 2018 IEEE International Conference,* 2018.

Huckle, S.; Bhattachraya, R.; White, M.; Beloff, N. Internet of Things, Blockchain and Shared Economy Applications. *Proc. Comput. Sci.* **2016,** *98* (1), 461–466.

Iasinti, M.; Lakhani, K. R. The Blockchain Revolution. *Harv. Bus. Rev.* **2017,** *95* (2), 20–20.

Jacsó, P. Google Scholar: The Pros and the Cons. *Online Inform. Rev.* **2005,** *29* (2), 208–214.

Kaplan, A.; Haenlein, M. Siri, Siri, in My Hand: Who's the Fairest in the Land? On the Interpretations, Illustrations, and Implications of Artificial Intelligence. *Bus. Horizons* **2019,** *62* (1), 15–25. doi:10.1016/j.bushor.2018.08.004.

Khan, M. A.; Salah, K. IoT Security: Review, Blockchain Solutions, and Open Challenges. *Fut. Gener. Comput. Syst.* **2018,** *82,* 395–411.

Knirisch, F.; Unterweger, A.; Engel, D. Privacy-Preserving Blockchain-Based Electric Vehicle Charging with Dynamic Tariff Decisions. *Comput. Sci.—Res. Dev.* **2018,** *33* (1–2), 71–79.

Lee, B.; Lee, J. Blockchain-Based Secure Firmware Update for Embedded Devices in an Internet of Things Environment. *J. Supercomput.* **2017,** *73* (3), 1152–1167.

Lin, I.; Liao, T. A Survey of Blockchain Security Issues and Challenges. *IJ Network Secur.* **2017,** *19* (5), 653–659.

Liu, S. *Blockchain Technology Market Size Worldwide 2018–2025,* 2020. Blogpost dated June 9, 2020. Retrieved from https://www.statista.com/statistics/647231/worldwide-blockchain-technology-market-size/

Liu, S. *Global Blockchain Solutions Spending 2017–2024,* 2021. Blogpost dated April 22, 2021. Retrieved from https://www.statista.com/statistics/800426/worldwide-blockchain-solutions-spending/

Machado, A. D.; et al. Impacts of the Integration of Chinese Managers in the Western Economies the Case of Brazil. *Transnatl. Corp. Rev.* **2019,** *1* (1), 25. Retrieved June 28, 2020. Accessed from https://www.tandfonline.com/doi/abs/10.1080/19186444.2019.16932 03?journalCode=rncr20

Mahankali, S.; Chaudhary, S. Blockchain in Education: A Comprehensive Approach—Utility, Use Cases, and Implementation in a University. In *Blockchain Technology Applications in Education*; Sharma, R. C., Yildirim, H., Kurubacak, G., Eds.; IGI Global: Hershey, PA, 2020; pp 267–293. http://doi:10.4018/978-1-5225-9478-9.ch014

Matilla, J. The Blockchain Phenomenon—The Disruptive Potential of Distributed Consensus Architectures. *Res. Inst. Finnish Econ.* **2016,** *38,* 1–24.

McCarthy, J.; Minsky, M.; Rochester, N.; Shannon, C. A Proposal for the Dartmouth Summer Research Project on Artificial Intelligence. *AI Mag.* **2006,** *27* (4), 12–14.

McMahan, B.; Ramage, D. *Federated Learning: Collaborative Machine Learning without Centralized Training Data,* 2017. Blogpost dated April 6, 2017. Available at https://ai.googleblog.com/2017/04/federated-learning-collaborative.html

MeitY, Government of India. *National Strategy on Blockchain*; Government of India, Ministry of Electronics and Information Technology (MeitY), 2021. Available at https://www.meity.gov.in/content/draft-national-strategy-blockchain

Mendes-da-Silva, W. Contribuições e Limitações de Revisões Narrativas e Revisões Sistemáticas na Área de Negócios. *Rev. Admin. Contemp.* **2019,** *23* (2), 1–11.

Moore, S. *4 Ways Blockchain Will Transform Higher Education,* 2019. Blogpost dated October 16, 2019. Available at https://www.gartner.com/smarterwithgartner/4-ways-blockchain-will-transform-higher-education/

Mougayar, W. *Blockchain Para Negócios: Promessa, Prática e Aplicações da nova Tecnologia da Internet,* 1st ed.; Atlas Book Editora: Rio de Janeiro, 2017.

Nakamoto, S. *Bitcoin: A Peer-to-Peer Electronic Cash System,* 2008.

Noruzi, A. Google Scholar: The New Generation of Citation Indexes. *Libri* **2005,** *55* (4), 170–180.

Ouaddah, A.; Abou Elkalam, A.; Ait Ouahman, A. FairAccess: A New Blockchain-based Access Control Framework for the Internet of Things. *Secur. Commun. Networks* **2016,** *18* (9), 5943–5964.

Ocheja, P.; Flanagan, B.; Ueda, H.; Ogata, H. Managing Lifelong Learning Records through Blockchain. *Research and Practice in Technology Enhanced Learning;* Springer: New York, 2019; pp 1793–7078. doi:10.1186/s41039-019-0097-0.

PwC. *Establishing Blockchain Policy: Strategies for the Governance of Distributed Ledger Technology Ecosystems,* 2019. Available at https://www.pwc.com/m1/en/publications/establishing-blockchain-policy.html

Reid, F.; Harrigan, M. *An Analysis of Anonymity in the Bitcoin System, Security and Privacy in Social Networks*; Springer-Verlag: Berlin, Germany, 2011. Available from https://arxiv.org/abs/1107.4524

Repanovici, A. Measuring the Visibility of the University's Scientific Production Using Google Scholar, Publish or Perish Software and Scientometrics. In *World Library and Information Congress: 76th IFLA General Conference and Assembly*, Gothenburg, 2010, pp 10–15.

Roll, I.; Wylie, R. Evolution and Revolution in Artificial Intelligence in Education. *Int. J. Artif. Intell. Educ.* **2016,** *26* (2), 582–599. Retrieved from https://doi.org/10.1007/s40593-016-0110-3

Schwab, K. *The Fourth Industrial Revolution*; Penguin Books: London, 2017.

Seldon, A.; Abidoye, O. *The Fourth Education Revolution: Will Artificial Intelligence Liberate or Infantilise Humanity*; University of Buckingham Press: London, 2018.

Sharma, R. C.; Yildirim, H.; Kurubacak, G. *Blockchain Technology Applications in Education*; IGI Global: Hershey, PA, 2020. http://doi:10.4018/978-1-5225-9478-9

Shrier, D.; Wu, W.; Pentland, A. Blockchain & Infrastructure (Identity, Data Security). *MIT Connect. Sci.* **2016,** *3* (1), 1–18.

Sousa, M. J.; Machado, A. D. Blockchain Technology Reshaping Education: Contributions for Policy. In *Blockchain Technology Applications in Education*; Sharma, R. C., Yildirim, H., Kurubacak, G., Eds.; IGI Global: Hershey, PA, 2020; pp 113–125. http://doi:10.4018/978-1-5225-9478-9.ch006

Sun, J.; Yan, J.; Zhang, K. Z. K. Blockchain-Based Sharing Services: What Blockchain Technology Can Contribute to Smart Cities. *Finan. Innov.* **2016,** *1* (2), 26.

Swan, M. *Blockchain: Blueprint for a New Economy*, 1st ed.; O'reilly: Sebastopol, 2015.

UNESCO. *Blockchain: Practices and Perspectives*, 2019. Blogpost retrieved from https://en.unesco.org/blockchain-practices-and-perspectives

Uğur, S.; Kurubacak, G. Artificial Intelligence to Super Artificial Intelligence, Cyber Culture to Transhumanist Culture: Change of the Age and Human. In *Handbook of Research on Learning in the Age of Transhumanism*; Uğur, S., Kurubacak, G., Eds.; IGI Global: Hershey, PA, 2019; pp 1–16. http://doi:10.4018/978-1-5225-8431-5.ch001

Whittemore, R.; Knafl, K. The Integrative Review: Updated Methodology. *J. Adv. Nurs.* **2005,** *52* (5), 546–553.

Wood, G. *Ethereum: A Secure Decentralised Generalised Transaction Ledger*; Ethereum Foundation, 2014. Retrieved from https://github.com/ethereum/wiki/wiki/White-Paper

Wright, A.; De Fillipi, P. *Decentralized Blockchain Technology and the Rise of Lex Cryptographia*; SSRN, 2015.

Yermack, D. Corporate Governance and Blockchains. *Rev. Finan.* **2017,** *21* (1), 7–31.

Ying, W.; Jia, S.; Du, W. Digital Enablement of Blockchain: Evidence from HNA Group. *International Journal of Information Management* **2018,** *39,* 1–4.

Yli-Huuno, J.; Ko, D.; Choi, S.; Park, S.; Smolander, K. Where Is Current Research on Blockchain Technology? A Systematic Review. *PLoS One* **2016,** *11* (10), 1–14.

Zachariadis, M.; Hileman, G.; Scott, S. V. Governance and Control in Distributed Ledgers: Understanding the Challenges Facing Blockchain Technology in Financial Services. *Inf. Organ.* **2019,** *29* (2), 105–117. https://doi.org/10.1016/j.infoandorg.2019.03.001

Zhang, Y.; Wen, J. The IoT Electric Business Model: Using Blockchain Technology for the Internet of Things. *Peer-to-Peer Network. Appl.* **2017,** *10* (4), 983–994.

Zielińska, A.; Skowron, M.; Bień, A. The Concept of the Blockchain Technology Model Use to Settle the Charging Process of an Electric Vehicle. In *Proc. 2019 Applications of Electromagnetics in Modern Engineering and Medicine (PTZE)*, 2019; pp 271–274.

CHAPTER 4

LIFE SCIENCES INDUSTRY BLOCKCHAIN VALUE MANAGEMENT, INVESTMENTS, AND FINANCE IMPACT ASSESSMENT: GLOBAL QUESTIONNAIRE SURVEY OF 1524 INDUSTRY PROFESSIONALS AND EXECUTIVES

ANTÓNIO PESQUEIRA[1] and MARIA JOSÉ SOUSA[2]

[1]*Bavarian Nordic A/S, Zug, Switzerland*

[2]*ISCTE Instituto Universitário de Lisboa, Lisbon, Portugal*

ABSTRACT

Blockchain is a relatively new technology, and its implementation in the life sciences industry is no different. Some of these cases are still in the piloting program stages, but others have already been adopted by life sciences organizations, justifying the emerging need in the field, which is still in its infancy. Blockchain is becoming more important in many different fields and organizations, with a growing influence on pharmaceuticals, biotechnology, and medical device companies. Through this chapter, we will gain a greater understanding of the current applications, future trends, investment areas, and key characteristics of existing life sciences use cases, as well as existing models and platforms of blockchain. About 1524 industry professionals and leaders from relevant functions participated in the survey,

Incorporating AI Technology in the Service Sector: Innovations in Creating Knowledge, Improving Efficiency, and Elevating Quality of Life. Maria José Sousa, Subhendu Kumar Pani, Francesca Dal Mas, & Sérgio Sousa (Eds.)

© 2024 Apple Academic Press, Inc. Co-published with CRC Press (Taylor & Francis)

which was designed as a global survey. Whether companies already run processes using blockchain technology or not, the chapter examines the impact of these changes on companies with or without blockchain strategies. A study supported by an online survey analyzing the current adoption and application of blockchain will provide key conclusions on how the technology is becoming more prevalent in many life sciences fields despite the challenges it faces. Using the data collected to support the conclusions of this study, the analysis found that a substantial percentage of life sciences leaders and professionals are already aware of blockchain and considering implementing it in the next years. Furthermore, it allowed us to understand that the industry is already comfortable with blockchain, and the mentioned use cases and opportunities gave us very reliable research regarding the most relevant application areas and key considerations for the future. By analyzing the survey results and understanding all the connections and relationships collected from respondents, the interconnectedness between blockchain and the industry is revealed.

4.1   INTRODUCTION

In the life sciences industry, blockchain is a relatively new concept. Blockchain's potential use cases for life sciences associations are demonstrated by a portion of these cases that are in the guiding stage and others that have been adopted by organizations. In the pharmaceutical, biotechnology, and medical devices sectors, blockchain solutions fill specific functional areas and can have hierarchical extensions.

Life science has emerged as a potentially transformative force in multiple aspects of operations and support for a variety of strategic functions, including commercial, medical affairs, supply chain, and many others.

Globally, its application had been recognized as effective in reducing organizational costs and ensuring regulatory compliance, while also improving efficiency, as highlighted by a variety of international organizations (Shah and Schulman, 2021).

Despite its technical underpinnings, blockchain technology can enable a variety of life technology organizations to work together more easily, enhance process efficiency, and increase transparency by bringing in security, agility, and transparency across the entire business department and organizational function. Blockchain technology is still in the embryonic stages of development and adoption, but life sciences stakeholders such as policymakers, regulators, industry, and organizational leaders should be aware of the full spectrum of blockchain technologies in addition to legal, regulatory, and privacy concerns.

Additionally, blockchain may not be universally more efficient, which is why we need to identify specific use cases in which it adds value and those where it does not, which will be clarified in this chapter. In just a decade, blockchain technology has the potential to revolutionize interactions between life sciences organizations, healthcare stakeholders, regulators, and regulatory authorities (Jabbar et al., 2021).

Blockchain technology differs from other technologies in the fact that it does not seek to deliver completely new solutions and services to the life sciences industry or other stakeholders alike but rather rework or improve existing processes in a way that unlocks efficiencies and new opportunities. We will elaborate more in this chapter about how blockchain offers unique possibilities to address governance or process issues related to supply chain management or to clinical trial data management, for example.

Different businesses can be made more efficient by allowing their processes to run smoothly, moving in a direction that makes it easier for internal functions to interact with each other using trusted media, and a reduction of regulatory oversight and compliance burdens.

Integrating features of transparency, decentralization, and accountability into internal functions increasing the easiness of insights generation and results-driven operations with blockchain would generate greater internal satisfaction due to improved accountability and efficiency. As part of blockchain technology, every transaction is signed by a unique digital signature to prove who made the transaction by leveraging techniques from the field of mathematics and computer science called cryptography. Public verification of these signatures is possible, yet they are held privately (Bittins et al., 2021).

In this chapter, we will analyze the current applications, future opportunities, key characteristics of existing use cases, key challenges, and the frameworks that exist as of now for life science companies to use blockchain.

An online study will provide insights into the current reception and uses of blockchain that will be supported by information collection. These insights will demonstrate that despite the current challenges, blockchain is becoming a reality in numerous life sciences organizations. Furthermore, considering both current applications and future applications will permit us to comprehend that there is a high blockchain awareness and understanding level inside of this industry where the referenced uses case studies will give us further access to explore the most important application areas and key considerations for the future.

Considering new occasions in which blockchain innovation changes are as of now a developing reality, this chapter examines organizations with or without blockchain systems or existing cycles.

This chapter will thus provide a more in-depth look at the current applications, future trends, potential investment areas, and key characteristics of existing life science use cases, along with the existing blockchain platforms and models.

The study, designed as a global survey, included 1524 participants from industry and relevant functions. We examine the implications of these changes regardless of whether companies are using blockchain technology or not. Based on a survey looking at the current adoption and application of blockchain technology, the research will provide key insights into how the technology is becoming more prevalent across a wide range of life sciences.

Data collected in this survey is the result of an online survey conducted between February 8 and May 4, 2021, focusing on getting a better understanding of general attitudes toward blockchain technology within the life sciences industry. A total of 1524 senior executives were surveyed across all global regions but they all worked in the life sciences sector.

Additionally, one survey was administered to a group of external consultants and experts to gauge their attitudes toward blockchain technology.

The remaining parts of this chapter are organized as follows. The background is presented in Section 4.2 along with a literature review showing how it relates to the topic. Afterward, a methodology for assessing blockchain-based solutions for life science is presented. Afterward, a discussion of data analysis and key observations comes next, followed by a summary of the findings in the last section.

4.2   LITERATURE REVIEW

4.2.1   STATE OF THE ART

Blockchain technology is based on a distributed ledger distributed across multiple users, which is validated by a group of people or a community.

Satoshi Nakamoto introduced blockchain technology through his whitepaper on the cryptocurrency Bitcoin. Among its characteristics are decentralization, transparency, and anonymity. The peers in the network of bitcoins and blockchains validate the transactions. These peers can be individuals or other agents. Whenever a valid transaction is conducted, it is timestamped chronologically and broadcast to all the participants in the network. Then the data are encrypted and stored in blocks (Antal et al., 2021).

Recent years have seen its widespread application in various areas, including supply chain, logistics, transportation, and public administration, because of its many advantages.

Despite national blockchain initiatives, life sciences are not a priority unless there are some minor exceptions. This is due, among other things, to the fact that many stakeholders have yet to learn about the benefits and potential of blockchain technology (Ahmad et al., 2020).

A decentralized consensus enables blockchain to validate transactions requested, executed, and created. By following a consensus protocol, peer nodes in the network are added to the shared digital ledger in the proper order, resulting in transparent and traceable records.

To create an immutable and secure blockchain ledger, cryptographic hash functions are used in an irreversible one-way fashion. Trust in the system is generated because of this consensus. An attacker may be unable to tamper with this record due to this (Puthal et al., 2018).

Blockchains are public ledgers that record digital records of all transactions of all participants in the transaction or event. Almost all participants in the system agree on the validity of every transaction in the public ledger. Information can never be deleted once it is entered. In the blockchain, every single transaction is recorded in a certain way and can be verified. Blockchain technology is most synonymous with Bitcoin, the most popular digital currency. Moreover, it has the most controversy since it enables an anonymous global market without governmental regulation, enabling a multibillion-dollar business. In addition to dealing with national governments and financial institutions, it must also deal with several regulatory issues (Wang et al., 2019).

A distributed consensus could allow for future verification of past and present online transactions involving digital assets. Enabling safe and efficient transactions could revolutionize the digital world. Anonymity and distributed consensus are two of the key characteristics of blockchain technology. Regulation concerns and technical challenges do not outweigh the benefits of blockchain technology.

Even though technologies are evolving rapidly, they are having an increasing impact on how pharmaceutical, biotechnology, and medical device companies acquire and develop skills. Therefore, skill updates are increasingly necessary, which also requires new learning approaches (Cachin and Vukolić, 2017).

Unfortunately, it can be difficult and time-consuming to verify all internal potential use cases across different departments and functions. It is crucial to have instant verification systems for authenticating documents of all types in the life sciences. Blockchain technology offers high security and can integrate data from multiple sources, such as wholesalers, distributors, and manufacturers (Pfleeger and Pfleeger, 2012).

Blockchain technology is a useful tool for solving scalability, privacy, and reliability issues across multiple domains. Blockchain is nothing more than a distributed digital ledger in which members share copies of information and verify any changes collectively. Furthermore, blockchain does not require a human to perform calculations because it is tamper-proof, auditable, and self-governing. This encrypted database provides an irreversible and incorruptible means for unrelated parties to reach a consensus without having to rely on a central authority. One of the fastest-growing applications of blockchain technology is smart contracts, which can be defined as software components that automate the execution of a contract. A smart contract between participating entities can be configured to automatically notify the parties to a contract when one specified condition is met (Aste et al., 2017).

In the past decade, the life sciences industry has experienced a big transformation due to the growth of the Internet and the development of several new processes and capabilities, such as multichannel, digital, or even more agile supply chain management. The topic of using technology cannot be discussed without addressing the issue of security (Pfleeger and Pfleeger, 2012).

When security procedures are not adhered to, the cost of financial and human resources may be increased. Various guidelines, policies, and approaches have been developed to help decision-makers in the field of life sciences make informed decisions regarding security measures to be implemented since the early adoption of technology.

Recently, blockchain technology has been gaining traction thanks to its powerful security capabilities. As evidenced by the exponential success of cryptocurrencies, identity protocols, and smart contracts, there is increased interest in this concept in recent years. Many life sciences leaders, departments, and business leaders are interested in the diverse ways that blockchain can be applied.

4.2.2 BLOCKCHAIN-BASED SOLUTIONS FOR LIFE SCIENCES

To ensure compliance in highly regulated environments that ultimately aim to protect patients, the life sciences industry relies on the cooperation of multiple stakeholders. A lack of transparency, coordination, and trust in this context, as well as this complexity, pose significant challenges to any blockchain implementation (Reyna et al., 2018).

Science papers and reports published to date assert that blockchains could be a transformative technology with enormous potential for the life sciences industry.

In the world of life sciences, blockchain scenarios include certificate issuing, verification of accreditation pathways, supply chain management, intellectual property management, document release and filing to authorities, patient management for clinical trials, and much more, applicable to regulatory, commercial, and research and development operations.

By using blockchain technology, healthcare experts and the overall life sciences industry will be able to improve performance, transparency, accountability, and tracking, while also reducing costs.

Blockchain solutions are being developed and customized at an incredible rate due to increased acceptance by stakeholders, a progressive regulatory environment, and advances in technologies like augmented reality and virtual reality.

Furthermore, blockchain applications are also being explored within commercial and medical affairs activities, including the management of approvals and documents from publications, the secure management of electronic medical records, drug traceability, data security in clinical trials, and document exchanges among healthcare stakeholders.

In addition to full agility and lean management within the pharmaceutical supply chain, the industry and several other firms are also developing other multiple blockchain solutions. Traceability ranks high on the priority list for the supply chain for counterfeit drugs and medicine recalls in the European market.

As we move forward in this section, we will lay out the key areas of blockchain implementation across industries and different organizational functions.

4.2.2.1 PATIENTS DATA MANAGEMENT

Clinical trial management systems and claims management backends are typically slow, complex, and expensive. In an ideal world, the back-end systems would be able to track a patient through the continuum of care and access needed information when needed, but this would require easy access to the medical records of patients, which could be a significant obstacle.

To achieve this goal, a blockchain system that successfully tracks where a patient is, and what procedures and tests they have had, could eliminate a lot of duplication of effort (Drummond et al., 2008).

Patient data are paramount to life sciences researchers, biotech companies, and pharmaceutical companies, where new solutions are needed in getting patients to better log their data and make it easier to give researchers access to it would make the data more widely available and enable better collaboration between research institutions. It is possible to create incentive systems based on patient demand for data that can be monetized as well as using blockchain to secure, manage, and control patient access to data by putting data access rights in patients' hands (Ding, 2018).

Currently, big and medium-sized pharmaceutical companies are evaluating decentralized databases that allow medical professionals to share structured and secure data.

As a result of these structures, a variety of stakeholders will be able to view medical history and have control over data, allowing researchers to leverage shared data to advance scientific research.

These innovations and business cases are closely connected to regulations and data privacy requirements. Hence blockchain technologies can be used to unlock patient consent management with privacy and permission layers, enabling the development of structured data ownership. Patients will be able to control and control their data or change or delete specific medical information on their profiles, and they can also control what data are visible to certain stakeholders in the healthcare ecosystem (Bittins et al., 2021).

Patients may, for instance, choose to share their full medical records with a specialist, but they may choose to share only nonidentifiable data with scientific research firms or other large healthcare organizations.

Therefore, blockchain algorithms can play a key role in ensuring compliance without sharing any data since they provide proof of zero knowledge. In the future, decentralized patient records will make it easier to develop decentralized applications (dApp), since it will be much easier to access data. To verify every transaction in these ecosystems, as well as the exchange of services for currency and data, groups of miners would be required. With the help of new cryptography techniques such as zero-knowledge proofs, homomorphic encryption, and secure multiparty computations (MPCs), encrypted data can be processed. By monetizing digital assets, patients and hospitals can still maintain their confidentiality and be able to use sensitive information without actual exposure of the information themselves (Mangla et al., 2019).

The properties of blockchain, such as transparency, immutability, and auditability, have the potential to enhance the security and integrity of data, as well as the functionality of supply chains for life science companies (including pharmaceuticals).

4.2.2.2   SUPPLY CHAIN MANAGEMENT

Today, different blockchain technologies lead to an increasingly secure and accountable supply chain for life sciences products. These technologies offer transparency, immutability, and interoperability. Through networking, different blockchain applications and supply chain systems can interact coherently, where life sciences manufacturers can use blockchain to register their products and track the movement of products starting from the source point to the end consumer (Escamilla-Ambrosio et al., 2018).

However, it is extremely challenging to manage supply chains in this industry, as they are costly and there is a concern about the lack of transparency in transactions and data exchanges, which ultimately hinders agility.

As a result of the literature review, we understand that supply chain management in life sciences encompasses the overall process of providing pharmaceutical, biological, or medical device products to healthcare systems, hospitals, patients, and pharmacies, as well as private and public clinics in some countries. Although the supply chain network may appear simple, several steps must be taken to make sure that patients can access medications. Currently, manufacturers and buyers of products have no way of knowing where their products are sourced, how much storage and supply they will need due to the lack of transparency in the supply chain (Casino et al., 2019).

Blockchain has immense potential to provide real-time data access and total visibility throughout the entire pharmaceutical supply chain, including wholesalers, suppliers' product codes and labels (decentralized and with little-to-no security systems), and then go to local pharmacies for dispensing prescriptions.

Additionally, life science companies and pharmacy retailers are key players in the promotion of products and the implementation of price change processes, which often result in a technological disconnect.

One of the main benefits of blockchain in pharmaceutical manufacturing is that it is cost-efficient in bringing together data from different third-party systems, which is typically extremely expensive and unable to be harmonized with each other. Several recent studies on the pharmaceutical supply chain and blockchain applications have highlighted the high importance of tracking systems which can be a great help in reducing supply, distribution, and logistic costs. Blockchain-based systems could also be used to create an efficient flow of products and to generate financial gains by allowing manufacturers to efficiently manage inventory levels and prepare for spikes in demand (Rejeb et al., 2019).

Large pharmaceutical corporations such as Abbvie, Genentech, Roche, Novartis, and Pfizer have already participated in a series of blockchain pilot studies to test and qualify the use of closed blockchain systems to track who interacted with which pharmaceutical product when.

Furthermore, some companies are currently considering more advanced supply chain and logistics solutions to prevent counterfeit products from entering the chain by tracking serial numbers and tagging unique identifiers to products, making it more difficult for counterfeit products to enter the system (Yao et al., 2012).

Pharmaceutical manufacturer Roche is collaborating with other manufacturers including Pfizer and Abbvie to test different supply chain management and logistics innovations using blockchain technology through its Genentech division. Additionally, Roche's diagnostics division in Asia has indicated they intend to collaborate as part of an initiative to send heart patient blood data in real time, working with external partners to create solutions that may help clinicians access more up-to-date results instead of waiting weeks or months between appointments. In the next few years, the Drug Supply Chain Security Act (DSCSA) will require pharmaceutical supply chain players to join interoperable electronic systems that will help them track each drug throughout the entire supply chain (Maesa and Mori, 2020).

As part of their environmental management procedures, a blockchain-based supply chain system can also connect to RFID tags and temperature logging mechanisms. By clearly defining the rules, this system can work mostly automatically using smart contracts. At the same time, the system will begin exploring ways to share and store patient data efficiently (Gaukler and Seifert, 2007).

4.2.2.3   PAYERS CONTRACTS MANAGEMENT AND VALUE-BASED OUTCOMES

Blockchain systems can be used to store transactions, emergency data, and more, although private repositories and on-chain and off-chain solutions can meet larger data storage needs, addressing issues of security, scalability, and sensitivity (Tönnissen and Teuteberg, 2020).

Blockchain solutions could be a solution, in which a group of industry professionals and consortiums are supporting already several large pharmaceutical companies and supply chain giants in optimizing results and investments. Different international projects and research programs are assessing processes for tracking who interacted or received which drugs at what time using closed blockchain systems. Since these projects require collaboration among more parties and the risks of accidentally exposing patient data to the public are high, they may take longer to implement (Fennessey et al., 2017).

Decentralization, transparency, and immutability are the three key pillars of any blockchain generic solution. With this set of solutions, the industry can ensure regulatory, legal, and data privacy compliance and validate them through use cases like supply chains, clinical trials, and health data.

In the past decade, cloud storage has gained popularity as an alternative to local storage. However, cloud storage has many disadvantages, since data are stored centralized and are usually owned by large corporations. They are thus susceptible to cyberattacks and local censorship. Additionally, technical problems and downtime can lead to a loss of service and the inability to access their data for the duration of the problem for many users.

Several platforms offer decentralized storage networks, where data are stored across multiple locations and the servers are hosted by independent operators instead of large companies.

A major focus of this initiative will be on evaluating and choosing meaningful outcome standards that are accepted by a wide range of stakeholders (Sunny et al., 2020).

By implementing a state-of-the-art governance model, the European observatory will enable patients to be in control of their data flows, allow ethical data sharing, enable value-based care, and improve patient outcomes.

Many organizations publish standards for outcomes measurement, including the International Consortium for Health Outcomes Measurement (ICHOM), which collaborates with the OECD to analyze patient-centered value assessments and US Standards for Health Outcomes Measurement. PROMIS (Professional Outcomes Measurement and Information System) is a tool developed by the National Institutes of Health to provide validated instruments that can offer computer adaptive testing and scores that can be compared with normative samples. As a result, 2021 has proven to be an extraordinary year for organizations in the life sciences to take their first steps into blockchain-based projects by joining small, closed consortia that use distributed ledger systems or permission blockchains to store and share data (Attaran, 2020).

Life science companies also have relationships with payers, who need to know where a patient has been treated and what the patient's specific plan is.

As an example, medical doctors want to know how much to charge their patients, and everyone wants to know where their claims are in their lifecycles.

A blockchain solution can meet the needs of high-volume applications and be regarded as a standard requirement, allowing millions of transactions a day to be processed (Attaran, 2020).

In the health and pharmaceutical ecosystem, new business and value-based healthcare models are created, and new ways to support the management of new laws, regulations, and governance are developed which will result in significant changes in workflows, processes, roles, and responsibilities through improved traceability and transparency. Additionally, decentralized validation will protect businesses and service providers from fraud or counterfeits, while transparent validation and management will reduce manual error costs.

4.2.2.4   CLAIMS MANAGEMENT AND CLINICAL OR SCIENTIFIC-RELATED PAYMENTS

Data have become more and more valuable, whether for training algorithms, finding better therapies, or figuring out where clinical trials should be conducted. We currently require third parties to de-identify data, but as these become more common, blockchain-based systems may become a practical method for exchanging data. As a result of new regulations, such as GDPR or Consumer Privacy Acts related to data use by third parties, companies will have to create auditing and consent trails for where customer data goes. The first place where we may see this is in genomics, where rare variants are valuable and people are deeply concerned that third parties could get their data or profit from it, like life insurance companies (Chen et al., 2021).

Claims management, payments, and any other clinical trials or posttrial engagement activities requiring internal or external authorizations are other areas of blockchain development within the industry. A blockchain that is aligned with data standards can improve these processes and reduce costs in some cases, as in claims management, where several third parties parse data and follow complex procedures.

It tracks every transaction mentioned above such as data submitted for review, the review itself, approval, or denial, and so on.

The industry is also looking at blockchain solutions to improve the speed and scalability of processing transactions in the pharmaceutical and biotechnology fields, which is a bottleneck for many.

One of the pilots has consistently suggested that rules-based smart contracts run automatically if certain requirements are met or to authenticate and pay providers based on the rules in a smart contract that automatically awards the payments. A similar approach can also be used for prior authorizations for drugs conducted by insurance companies to make sure all other options have been explored before expensive drugs are approved (Shah and Schulman, 2021).

Managing massive amounts of sensitive data from various sources is challenging for researchers and clinical trial participants, who are tasked with coordinating the efforts of several sites and stakeholders.

It is also possible for blockchain to provide a way to link disparate data from a study, which is commonly conducted in different research facilities by different researchers. A traceable record of what each participant did would no longer be necessary by reconciling separate databases together.

After a study is complete, regulatory parties, auditors, or other researchers would have access to an audit trail that can be submitted, since currently, a trial master file is usually used for this purpose. By capturing more granular data via wearables and supply chains, it will be easier to determine how the study may fail. Long-term, blockchain-based ledgers will serve the purpose of decentralizing patient records, enabling patients to access their health records easily, as well as providing healthcare providers with full access to patient information (Cui et al., 2021).

In healthcare and life sciences, the lack of interoperability creates duplication of work, a bad patient experience, and medical errors at worst.

4.2.2.5   *LIFE SCIENCES CYBERSECURITY AND SMART CONTRACTS*

The topic of cybersecurity is also extremely relevant to be discussed, especially since breaches of healthcare information can be costly. It is usually someone delivering information to the wrong place or someone accessing records that they are not authorized to access that results in a breach of health records.

Data can be captured more effectively, and patients can have better access to their data if a decentralized system is used. It would be possible for patients to give keys to their data to whoever they wish. Any business model that depends on hoarding data as a moat would be threatened by this shift, and companies would have to demonstrate what kind of value they would provide to patients directly in exchange for their data, rather than by purchasing it from third parties that collect and de-identify the data (Pólvora et al., 2020).

However, regulations about patient privacy make it difficult to get stakeholders on board or provide third parties with access to relevant but aggregated information, where GDPR in the European market also potentially conflicts with blockchain initiatives, yet it can also be a catalyst for improved compliance solutions.

Because blockchain projects lack data standards, they are often developed in silos, but there are also issues of scalability and the cost of storing data on a blockchain. Some organizations are already adopting models like Faster Healthcare Interoperability Resources to support building out a third-party developer ecosystem and defining shared data standards that will make technology critical areas, such as smart contracts, possible (Ziegler et al., 2021).

Finally, to solve for scalability and sensitivity, blockchain projects are examining ways to combine on-chain solutions, such as those recorded on a distributed ledger, with off-chain solutions, such as actions that are not recorded on the ledger. Generally speaking, blockchain technology and distributed ledgers have real potential for the life sciences industry, and as our literature review demonstrated, blockchains could bring patients into the center of the healthcare ecosystem as they would have access to one of their most valuable resources: data.

Another example is smart contracts, which can be programmed to reward or incentivize specific patient behavior, for example, following a particular treatment plan and/or sharing their data with researchers.

Due to the high cost and the difficulty of accepting the changes involved, blockchain adoption poses a challenge for several different traditional industries. It is also necessary to consider the cost of the time required to define clear and precise processes and more practical smart contracts when calculating the final cost of deploying a blockchain.

Smart contracts could speed up some of these steps by codifying the rules of a payer around a drug, verifying whether all options have been explored, and checking whether previous drugs or tests caused adverse reactions.

Programs like PharmaLedger, for example, are developing a blockchain-based platform enabling trusted and privacy-enabled digital collaboration through knowledge sharing among healthcare stakeholders, involving highly compliant and interoperable data exchange between pharmaceutical and healthcare value chain members (Ziegler et al., 2021).

PharmaLedger is a project recently launched that includes 12 global pharmaceutical companies, as well as 17 public and private entities from academia, legal, regulatory, and research organizations as well as patient representative organizations.

The data records must be immutable as this will ensure transparency and traceability, as well as other valuable results, such as enabling healthcare stakeholders, and patients, in particular, to know what, by whom, and when, their data are used for.

Some options are being explored to provide an industry-wide, blockchain-based platform that is highly scalable, enabling use cases and operational workflows using blockchain technology. The objective here is to provide some benefits to the classical transaction history processes by enabling this highly innovative architecture to provide advantages in terms of performance and the protection of confidential data. As a result, some pharmaceutical companies are already evaluating the hierarchical architecture of blockchains (Jabbar et al., 2021).

Furthermore, the platform underpinning the reference implementations offers many horizontal services, including the management of data and identity, and privacy management. By leveraging an integrated collaboration platform and flexible business processes, all participants in the healthcare value chain ecosystem can communicate seamlessly with each other, exchange data, and enter contractual relationships.

Unlike the traditional collaborative environment, there are no secrets or trade secrets that need to be managed and can be stolen. Some large pharmaceutical companies use MPC and execute smart contracts using encrypted choreographies in a multiparty environment. Smart contracts or immutable transactions generated by ecosystem participants will commit the new data to the blockchain. Governance should integrate elements such as authority, membership, legal structure, and organization, as well as operational models, including the role of stakeholders such as application developers, network operators, and so on.

Patients' engagement and a standardized collection of patient outcomes are critical levers for providing sustainable health-care systems rather than reimbursing for the services provided. The Innovative Medicines Initiative project, a public–private partnership in the European Union, has promoted a multijurisdictional ecosystem called Health Outcomes Observatory (H2O) that is designed to incorporate patient-reported and other health outcomes into health-care decision-making across Europe (Stengel and Post, 2017).

A more detailed understanding of how blockchain technology, cryptocurrencies, and digital tokens will shape our increasingly digital societies and economies becomes clearer as the technology matures. As illustrated in this chapter, blockchain advancements that exploit its strengths are exhibiting the way the industry is likely to evolve in the coming years (Jabbar et al., 2021).

4.2.2.6 RESEARCH AND CLINICAL TRIALS DESIGN

Finally, we will need to discuss the current research and clinical trial designs to determine the use of blockchain in research and clinical trials. This can make it possible to improve healthcare before treatment begins as in clinical trials and research.

Eventually, we will see new systems where patients can offer their data for sale, and entities can bid on the right to access it, where a group of other network participants can verify and process the transaction, adding the block of transactions to the chain and receiving tokens for completing that verification task (Ziegler et al., 2021).

A third party is no longer required to manage the exchange of data and currency through this method.

An integrated blockchain can be used to improve medical consent, trial design, and the evaluation of efficacy, as well as structuring protocols for document exchange. In determining the study design early on, third parties can quickly verify that the original design was followed, and timestamps and smart contracts can ensure researchers stick to the original design and do not change the criteria or analysis midstream.

By removing biases from studies and clinical trials, increases reproducibility and encourages the publication of negative findings, which often do not occur (Shah and Schulman, 2021).

By creating consent forms, each vetted entity could provide access to new data as it is added. This information becomes readily available to everyone on the ledger, rather than having to reconcile separate datasets together, which would ensure no information is lost or manipulated.

Due to the shared database, all study participants have access to a timestamped, real-time list of all data and transactions that are occurring in real-time in a clinical trial or study. A study can be easily walked through end-to-end without the need for data reconciliation, which is helpful for auditors and people who would like to replicate it.

Despite their potential to ease study conduct, they do not address one of the biggest issues: recruiting patients who fit the right criteria for studies.

More readily accessible records could resolve this problem, but before reaching this goal, we still need to overcome many obstacles. In addition to clearer regulations, more ways to create and capture data outside of the current electronic healthcare records system and finding more secure methods to store massive amounts of data, several other issues will need to be addressed.

It would facilitate more accountability if blockchain ledgers could track access to health records. Additionally, there is not any third-party platforms for life sciences that are as user-friendly as the ones built for many other industries. To create a patient-owned personal health record, data generated by consumer diagnostics, wearables, and genomics would have to be structured and gathered. Pharma companies, for instance, rely on such information to determine the areas they should focus on for clinical trials and better inform their marketing campaigns (Jabbar et al., 2021).

Despite being time-consuming and costly, clinical trials are necessary for finding new and effective treatments. With several players involved, there is a need for a high level of security and transparency throughout the process. Tracking clinical trial data using blockchain technology improves efficiency while ensuring that the collected data are authentic. By doing so, all aspects of clinical trial processes conducted by various stakeholders, such as patients and regulators, can be transparent, auditable, traceable, and subject to fine-grain access control.

Health providers and patient associations are enabling the collection of data in the blockchain to support evolutional digitization and straightforward integration of clinical trial data.

As a result of blockchain's consensus mechanism and decentralized structure, which guards against hack or manipulation, where documents may be verified for validity and provenance, data fraud is reduced.

When nodes reach consensus, the integrity of the data is protected, trustworthy results are promoted, and collaboration within the research community is inspired.

Using blockchain technology as a tool to address different life sciences challenges will allow the industry the reach of ensuring that transactions cannot be altered as this emerging technology allows distributed public ledgers to hold immutable data in a secure and encrypted manner.

Blockchain's inherent properties can bring significant benefits to the life sciences sector. With decentralization, for example, life sciences applications can be distributed without relying on centralized authorities to validate the transactions. It means that multiple servers house each data record or "block," allowing stakeholders access to health records without the need for centralized management of health data on behalf of any entity or organization (Attaran, 2020).

4.3   METHODOLOGICAL APPROACH

In this section, we go over the methodology we used in addition to other key metrics that helped us draw meaningful conclusions and better understand the relationship between key variables during our questionnaire data analysis.

Since the purpose of the study is to compare data, the quantitative method was deemed appropriate for the study. According to the findings, the questionnaire method was the most appropriate strategy for the investigation mainly due to its ability to assess and understand different blockchain characteristics as well as to have a more detailed understanding of different influencing factors of blockchain in the life sciences industry. From the questionnaire collected data, we will be able to better understand the dependent and independent variables, summarize key statistics parameters, and understand correlations, associations, and principal components of data associations from this quantitative study (Ibarra et al., 2018).

A questionnaire that was designed and distributed to 1524 life sciences leaders and professionals was utilized as a method for the study.

In addition to the 2021 lockdown restrictions that prevented face-to-face interviews from being conducted, measurement instruments like the questionnaire enable the definition of study objectives with measurable variables and assist in organizing, normalizing, and controlling data collection to gather the information rigorously.

The questionnaire can therefore be used to find out whether the research hypotheses are confirmed or not (Ibarra et al., 2018).

With the assistance of a literature review, we identified key research objectives and defined research questions to help us in designing the questionnaire and understanding how the key research objectives can be validated.

Figure 4.1 outlines the steps involved in defining a methodological approach and in executing it and then applying the questionnaire.

As part of the sample definition, we selected an objective sampling based on the specific objectives in mind, the characteristics of the respondents, and the inclusion criteria. We selected a representative population sample using this sampling technique, which allowed us to divide the samples into well-defined subgroups identified as being more suitable for the study objectives as well as having the necessary experience and expertise for blockchain (Ibarra et al., 2018).

To be included in this sample, several criteria elements were required. The population was eligible due to the above inclusion criteria, as well as proximity and industry expertise from the researchers. Here are the factors considered for inclusion:

- Professionals with more than 3 years of experience in the life sciences industry.
- Professionals with familiarity or basic knowledge of blockchain and key technology concepts as decentralized databases and systems.
- Valid e-mail contact and contact information.

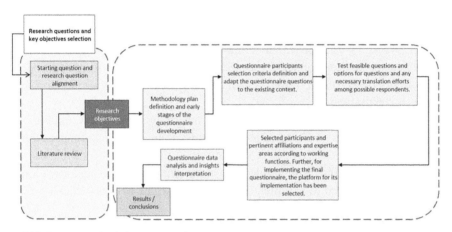

FIGURE 4.1   Methodology approach.

4.3.1   QUESTIONNAIRE DESIGN AND VARIABLE SELECTION

After the literature review, we created a structured questionnaire that was formulated by the defined methodology approach process that was already explained.

An online survey was conducted worldwide among 1524 industry and relevant function participants. Regardless of whether a company uses blockchain technology or not, these changes will impact the company. The research, which is based on a survey to analyze the current adoption and application of blockchain technology, will shed light on how the technology is becoming more widespread in life sciences.

From February 8 to May 4, 2021, researchers conducted an online survey to better understand general attitudes toward blockchain technology within the life sciences sector. The total number of respondents across all global regions was 1524, but all were working in the life sciences sector.

In addition, one survey was administered to external consultants and experts to gauge their views on blockchain technology.

Based on previous studies that were translated and validated by an expert committee consisting of two specialists, a statistician, and the authors, the study used a self-administered survey developed by the authors using Google Forms (Google LLC, Mountain View, CA, USA). The questionnaire was administered in English and included demographic questions like gender and age, as well as questions about blockchain's financial impact, investments, current applications, and future applications. The Google Forms settings were changed to limit the number of responses per person.

Our strategy was to distribute a link to the questionnaire using e-mail and phone messages, describing the purpose of the study, and inviting additional respondents based on the initial respondents identified and their network of contacts to participate.

Respondents were asked to complete an anonymous questionnaire to respect their right to privacy and to not identify their affiliated organizations in the database.

An open-ended and closed-ended questionnaire was used. These questions were mostly designed to complement closed questions in cases when one or more possible answers do not fit respondents.

We conducted a preliminary pilot testing among 10 respondents (all industry professionals), in which they were asked to elaborate on their answers regarding the questions.

To validate the consistency of the questionnaire, 10 respondents, a representative sample of the study population, were analyzed before the distribution of the survey.

We selected individuals from companies around the globe with a confidence level of 95% (and $p = q = 0.5$) who have an interest in blockchain, relevant experience or knowledge of transformative technologies such as blockchain or artificial intelligence, and a focus on the life sciences industry.

As part of the questionnaire invitation e-mail, blockchain was defined as a new emerging technology having significant implications for the life sciences, including supply chain management, clinical trial data management, among other things.

Due to the reminders sent to nonrespondents in April and May 2021, we had an increase in answers collected. A total of 12 qualitative variables were included in the study, as well as two quantitative variables.

Table 4.1 provides an overview of variables, codes, types of data, and related questions.

The questionnaire was divided into three major groups, with the first group representing all demographical questions and variables.

TABLE 4.1 Variables Description, Data Types, and Questions.

Variable code	Data type	Data subtype	Questions
GEN	Qualitative	Nominal	Which gender are you?
AGE	Quantitative	Discrete	Your age, please?
TYOR	Qualitative	Categorical	What kind of organization do you work for?
TIT	Qualitative	Categorical	According to your job focus, which of the following is most relevant?
DEP	Qualitative	Categorical	What department are you in?
BCPRE	Qualitative	Categorical	Is your company currently utilizing any blockchain solutions, technologies, or pilot programs?
INVEST	Qualitative	Categorical	The total investment in Blockchain by your organization to date is approximately how much?
APPLC	Qualitative	Categorical	Could you please describe the current blockchain applications in your company and what you know about them?
FAPPLC	Qualitative	Categorical	Is your organization considering adopting a blockchain-based solution soon?
FINVEST	Qualitative	Categorical	How do you see blockchain's main future applications in life sciences?
BADV	Qualitative	Categorical	Indicate the possible business advantages of blockchain solutions to your organization in the future.
IMPCT	Quantitative	Categorical	What is your organization's assessment of the benefits blockchain brings?
PRLOC	Qualitative	Categorical	Which location is your organization's preferred location for implementing blockchain initiatives and considering future applications?

As a second group, we focused on profiling and sample characterization, and the last group covered the variables and dimensions indicators for a successful explanation and discovery analysis of the study.

Additionally, we sought to assess how the different variables interact with one another, such as investment and value generation, as well as the demographic indications that influence blockchain presence. Our main concern was to understand if an organization was building blockchain processes or implementing projects.

After the end date to all study participants, we then entered the data into an excel spreadsheet to start with the all statistical analysis in SPSS.

TABLE 4.2   Variables Description, Data Types.

Variable code	Group
GEN	Group 1: Demographics
AGE	Group 1: Demographics
TYOR	Group 2: Sample characterization
TIT	Group 2: Sample characterization
DEP	Group 2: Sample characterization
BCPRE	Group 3: Explanatory and discovery
INVEST	Group 3: Explanatory and discovery
APPLC	Group 3: Explanatory and discovery
FAPPLC	Group 3: Explanatory and discovery
FINVEST	Group 3: Explanatory and discovery
BADV	Group 3: Explanatory and discovery
IMPCT	Group 3: Explanatory and discovery
PRLOC	Group 3: Explanatory and discovery

In terms of grouping all dimensions for the study and all composed variables, the questionnaire design followed a systematic logic in providing a clear understanding of data in addressing the objectives and questions of the research.

The following image helps us to understand the followed logic in terms of grouping the dimensions of the key variable. Furthermore, it provides an overview of all variables, independent and dependent, so that data analysis, correlations, and hypothesis testing can be performed as needed.

For a better understanding of the questionnaire, a short fact sheet summarizing the information regarding data collection and technical matters is provided in Table 4.3.

TABLE 4.3   Questionnaire Fact Table.

Fieldwork	February through May 2021
Sample size	1524 surveyed
Survey type	Structured online questionnaire
Geographical area	582 from Europe, 388 North America, 240 Asia Pacific, 146 the Middle East, 130 Central America and the Caribbean, 20 South America, and 18 from Africa

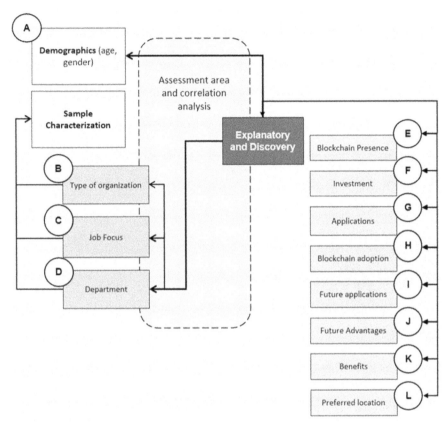

FIGURE 4.2 Variables associations and correlations overview.

4.4 DATA ANALYSIS AND DISCUSSION

Based on the results of the questionnaire, this section summarizes all the important topics. We used SPSS and Microsoft Excel to complete the data analysis part of this study.

During our surveys, 27 questionnaires were returned because the industry professionals were not available for personal reasons. The remaining 2003 questionnaires were responded to by 1524 people (76%).

A generic overview of the above process is shown in Figure 4.1, as well as a graphic representation of how questionnaires were sent out and how many responses were received.

We will also describe some statistical hypotheses in this chapter as well as interpret some correlations or connections.

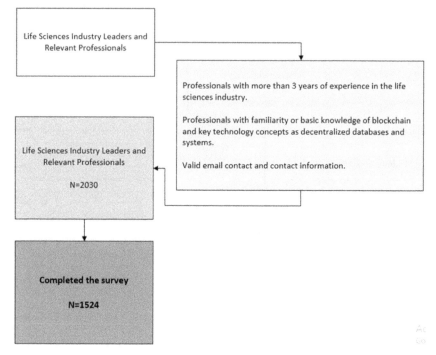

FIGURE 4.3   Flow of questionnaire participants.

Additionally, we assessed whether the sample of industry professionals and decision-makers was representative of the overall population during our statistical and descriptive analyses. The data classification activities required the team to be very careful in terms of understanding which tests would be preferred for categorical and numerical variables.

In Table 4.4, we can find more details about the questions, objectives, and hypotheses selected for this study.

4.4.1   DESCRIPTIVE ANALYSIS

Within this section, we will understand the key descriptive observations and an analysis of the major differences from the selected questionnaire variables will be conducted with 1524 observations, as described previously, and without duplicate data.

A descriptive summary table like the one below can help us understand all relevant statistical indicators, and before we present the comparative data observations (Montgomery, 2019).

TABLE 4.4 Research Questions and Objectives.

Research objective	Research questions	Research hypothesis
Examine the differences between companies that have already implemented a blockchain strategy and the variables that can help us to understand the impact of blockchain applications and strategy on life science companies. In addition, we are also interested in identifying the differences between companies employing blockchain strategies and companies without such strategies.	Question 1: What are some of the current applications, challenges, and future opportunities of blockchain in the life sciences industry? Question 2: In what ways do current blockchain applications influence companies' use of blockchain?	As companies adopt blockchain processes, blockchain applications will create new business processes and technology opportunities.
Learn what proportion of our selected sample of industry professionals has invested in blockchain? Moreover, we would like to know how the different variables interact in terms of investment and value generation as well as the distribution of companies involved, and the investments made in the blockchain.	Question 1: In what ways have blockchain investments and blockchain presence been perceived by various companies? Question 2: How does the life sciences industry plan to invest in blockchain in the future and how are they making investment decisions regarding blockchain projects or processes? Question 3: Is blockchain adoption being influenced or accelerated by the areas of investment made in it? Question 4: Is there a connection between investment in blockchain and value creation and management, as well as a clear distribution of investments across regions?	Can a company have more financial impact with a bigger blockchain investment? Investments in blockchain are generating more value as more is invested in it.
Identify which type of life science companies are implementing blockchain applications and which case studies have been done between them, as well as what types of future applications are currently being researched.	Question 1: In terms of case studies and opportunities, how is blockchain being assessed in the current times and how will it evolve in the future? Question 2: How does blockchain penetration compare to the definition of the population of respondents to the survey and to the affiliated companies who answered the survey?	Companies are becoming more aware of the value and impact of blockchain on the overall business operations and strategy as future applications and opportunities in blockchain expand.

TABLE 4.4 *(Continued)*

Research objective	Research questions	Research hypothesis
Through this study, we aim to identify with a 0–5 scale how blockchain is currently affecting the financial processes and operations of the industry.	Question 1: In terms of blockchain applications, what is perceived and distributed as the financial impact across the companies studied? Question 2: Do blockchain present in the various organizations already generate value or do they have an impact on the finance departments and business strategy?	As blockchain investment and its adoption grow, so do its financial impacts and characteristics.
Identify how life sciences companies and their job foci are distributed in terms of demographic characteristics and whether they tend to understand blockchain applications and implementations differently.	Question 1: Do geography, age, and gender affect blockchain investments and implementation? Question 1: Are there any correlations between the presence of blockchain and investments made by various organizations?	Companies with blockchain presence and the perception of blockchain's financial impact are affected by gender distribution.

Analyzing the collected data was done with SPSS, version 24.0 (SPSS Inc., Chicago, IL, USA). All variables were analyzed using descriptive statistics with frequencies and percentages.

The questionnaire respondents, 57.7% of them belonging to the masculine gender, and 42% to the feminine gender, were analyzed based on a descriptive analysis.

We also learned through the descriptive analysis and understanding of the types of organizations from the respondents that 40% were from large pharmaceutical companies or large biotechnology companies, 29% from mid-sized pharmaceutical companies or biotech companies, and 15% from small pharmaceutical or biotech companies.

Here are percentages and totals for the rest of the provided answers: small medical devices or technology (5%), large medical devices or technology (4.98%), mid-sized medical devices or technology (3.8%), healthcare services (1%), and then contract manufacturing organization, healthcare services and life sciences consultant company with less than 1% of the answers.

To categorize the job position and area of work of respondents, we also collected information on their Job Levels. Director (13%) and department head (17%) accounted for most job levels.

Other relevant job levels include senior director, senior manager, and department or function head.

When we look to the respondent's department, we register that 17% of the sample population were from sales departments, where 16% were from commercial functions that can include marketing, market access, sales, and other departments like commercial operations. The other relevant departments are expressed in Table 4.6.

Our purpose was to develop a consistent and meaningful data analysis by selecting the questions that offered valid conclusions based on the results of the data analysis.

Answering the question "Approximately how much has your organization invested cumulatively to date in Blockchain?" 39% of respondents have not invested, 28% have invested between €1000,000 and €5000,000, 13% are considering investing in the next 2–5 years, 8% have invested less than €1000,000, and 7% have invested above 10 million euros.

In terms of the types of blockchain applications, 17% of respondents said blockchain has not been implemented or is not being considered. In contrast, 25% of the respondents mentioned that blockchain might be used for clinical trials within the next 2–5 years, and 17% noted that blockchain is currently being used for consent data management within clinical trials. Interestingly,

11% of respondents reported that they were implementing digital identity for patients as part of their blockchain strategy during Phase II or III.

TABLE 4.5   Frequencies for Job Focus and Position.

Title	Frequency	Percent	Cumulative percent
Analyst	4	0.262	0.2
Associate Director	51	3.346	3
Associate Manager	79	5.184	8
Business Unit Head	78	5.118	13
Chief Commercial Officer	20	1.312	15
Chief Executive Officer	26	1.706	16
Chief Financial Officer	1	0.066	16
Chief Human Resources Officer	1	0.066	17
Chief Information Officer	26	1.706	18
Chief Technology Officer	4	0.262	19
Coordinator	28	1.837	20
Data Analyst	11	0.722	21
Department Lead	265	17.388	38
Director	204	13.386	52
Executive Director	74	4.856	57
Executive Management	3	0.197	57
Executive Vice President	21	1.378	58
Functional Lead	10	0.656	59
Global Head	76	4.987	64
Head	146	9.580	74
Laboratory Expert	3	0.197	74
Manager	52	3.412	77
Program Manager	6	0.394	78
Project Coordinator	6	0.394	78
R&D Researcher	3	0.197	78
Senior Director	154	10.105	88
Senior Manager	92	6.037	94
Specialist	25	1.640	96
Team Leader	3	0.197	96
Technician	2	0.131	96
Vice President	50	3.281	100
Total	1524	100.000	

TABLE 4.6 Frequencies for Respondent's Department.

Department	Frequency	Percent	Cumulative percent
Advanced Analytics and Insights	142	9.318	9
Business Development	3	0.197	9
Clinical Operations	109	7.152	16
Commercial	248	16.273	32
Commercial Excellence	38	2.493	35
Contract Manufacturing	10	0.656	36
Data Privacy	1	0.066	36
Data Science	35	2.297	38
Development	1	0.066	38
Digital Strategy/Transformation	12	0.787	39
Drug Product Manufacturing	3	0.197	39
Drug Substance Manufacturing	12	0.787	40
Executive Management	159	10.433	50
Finance	1	0.066	50
Finance Controlling Unit	11	0.722	51
HR	1	0.066	51
IT	112	7.349	58
Legal	1	0.066	58
Market Access	8	0.525	59
Marketing	6	0.394	59
Marketing Operations	116	7.612	67
Medical Affairs	9	0.591	68
Procurement	5	0.328	68
Quality	10	0.656	69
Quality and Compliance	5	0.328	69
Quality Control and Assurance	5	0.328	69
R&D	40	2.625	72
Regulatory Affairs	8	0.525	72
Research	1	0.066	72
Sales	261	17.126	90
Supply Chain Management	151	9.908	100
Total	1524	100.000	

TABLE 4.7   Frequencies for the Blockchain Applications.

Applications	Frequency	Percent	Cumulative percent
Being considered for the next 2–5 years	386	25.328	25
Clinical trials and consent data management	273	17.913	43
Commercial and medical affairs speaker programs	22	1.444	44
Continuous medical education certificates	6	0.394	45
Data governance and decentralization storage	118	7.743	52
Digital identity for patients during Phase II or III	169	11.089	63
Drugs safety and manufacturing	10	0.656	64
Intellectual property rights	96	6.299	70
KOLs data management and classification	5	0.328	71
Market sales processing and transactions	3	0.197	71
Medical devices and hardware manufacturing	2	0.131	71
Medical data sharing (e.g., publications, RWE studies)	6	0.394	71
Not being considered or deployed	266	17.454	89
Pricing, tenders, and contracts	20	1.312	90
Product distribution and logistics	1	0.066	90
Product quality control, PV, and safety	4	0.262	91
Product shipping and storage	5	0.328	91
Regulatory/Compliance documents and procedures control	14	0.919	92
Sales and marketing data segmentation	5	0.328	92
Serialization counterfeit tracking and monitoring	19	1.247	93
Serialization tracking and monitoring	7	0.459	94
Smart contracts for patient data management	5	0.328	94
Vaccination certificates management	82	5.381	100
Total	1524	100.000	

In terms of future investments, we can understand that 11% referred that digital tech solutions will be future investments, 10% replied that clinical trials and supply chain services, and then 9% replied serialization and packaging monitoring techniques.

The remaining answers were distributed as follows: electronic data capture (9.9%), project and operations management (7.7%), and supply chain management with 3.6%. Other answers were not representative or expressive.

In the most relevant questionnaire question, where the question about the benefits blockchain brings to your organization was asked, "How do you assess the benefits blockchain brings to your organization?" This allowed us to understand that clearly, the impact is already seen with 15.7% responding with the highest score for the impact blockchain brings to life sciences finance and 26.7% replied with a score of 4.

TABLE 4.8 Financial Impact Scoring.

Impact score	Frequency	Percent	Cumulative percent
1	87	5.709	5.7
2	270	17.717	23
3	520	34.121	57
4	407	26.706	84
5	240	15.748	100
Total	1524	100.000	

Table 4.9 will now provide a compressive overview of all collected observations to the descriptive questions and key variables in terms of the key figures and descriptive descriptions. Additionally, we added additional descriptive parameters from the organizations with blockchain processes (implemented) to better understand how the variable blockchain presence differs among demographic variables and other factors.

A selection of the most relevant data analysis and analysis questions presented valid conclusions that supported the conclusions and discussion.

TABLE 4.9 Descriptive Statistics for Future Investments, Potential Business Features, and Future Applications.

Future investments	Frequency	Percent
Digital tech solutions	173	11.4
Clinical trials supply chain services	153	10.0
Electronic data capture	151	9.9
Forecasting and planning	150	9.8
Artificial intelligence	131	8.6
Project and operations management	118	7.7
Big data and analytics	101	6.6

TABLE 4.9 *(Continued)*

Future investments	Frequency	Percent
Supply chain management	55	3.6
Logistics solutions	42	2.8
Commercial segmentation and targeting	41	2.7
Supply chain and products tracking	32	2.1
Cybersecurity	31	2.0
Patient-centric supply chains	31	2.0
Digital lighthouses/programs	24	1.6
Global storage and distribution and logistics	22	1.4
Quality process and risk management	22	1.4
Virtual events and more digital applications	18	1.2
Information and communication	17	1.1
Master data management	17	1.1
Regulatory support	17	1.1
Clinical returns, reconciliation, and destruction	16	1.1
Retains storage and testing	15	1.0
Tenders and contracts management	15	1.0
Drug development	13	0.9
Data governance framework	10	0.7
HCPs portals	10	0.7
Virtual reality	10	0.7
Content and web filtering	9	0.6
People learning and development	8	0.5
Product portfolio expansion	8	0.5
Backup and archive	7	0.5
Manufacturing	4	0.3
Patient support programs	3	0.2
Protocol analysis and planning	3	0.2
Serialization and traceability	2	0.1
Other	45	3.1
Potential business features of blockchain solutions		
Supply chain innovations and performance increase	383	25.131
Clinical trials data management and patient data consent	198	12.992
Enhanced security by encryption of data at the stage of dissemination	151	9.908
Counterfeit and drugs illegal trading	136	8.924

TABLE 4.9 *(Continued)*

Future investments	Frequency	Percent
Processes through a decentralized model	135	8.858
Patient-centric supply chain	101	6.627
Traceability of all historical transactions	73	4.79
Complete provenance trail of every asset, drug, or medical device	71	4.659
Permanent and authoritative proof of record	71	4.659
Digital assets	43	2.822
Automation using smart contracts/algorithms	41	2.69
Visibility into process flow and claim data	40	2.625
Transparent and predefined rules which facilitate the creation of new products	26	1.706
I have no opinion	25	1.64
Availability of multiple copies of the shared data	16	1.05
Speed and efficiency of transactions by eliminating intermediaries	14	0.919
Future applications		
Securing and improve drug supply chains	423	27.756
Enhancing patient consent and identity management in clinical trials	201	13.189
Enhancing monetization of patient data	195	12.795
Legal and contracts document verifications	181	11.877
Enhancing secure sharing of patient data	177	11.614
Enable patient value outcomes contracts	144	9.449
Consent management	85	5.577
Documents review and data sharing	85	5.577
Not sure	33	2.165

4.4.2 STATISTICAL ANALYSIS

In this chapter, we will describe a few statistical hypotheses and analyze the most relevant correlations and connections.

First, we performed several calculations in terms of univariate statistics, to determine if there is a significant difference between our second and third group and the controls or between totally different treatments.

A classical hypothesis test is performed when only one effect (treatment group) is considered as the main cause of effects. In this study, we aimed to prove that both of our dependent variables are BCPRE and IMPCT and connected with the independent variables like TIT, APPLC, FAPPLC, GEN, AGE, FINVEST, to which we performed the analysis of some of the statistical data from those variables (Montgomery, 2019).

Based on the analysis of BCPRE, the sample respondents have on average more than 50% of the blockchain presence in the related organizations (mean = 0.572), meaning more than 50% of the sample has blockchain present.

In terms of the IMPCT, it was possible to conclude that on average the financial impact from blockchain has an average of 3.2 on a scale of 1–5, where we can conclude the financial impact is significant and shows that we have a sample of respondents that consider the blockchain as influencing the financial impact to the related organizations.

When we performed the testing of internal consistency through Cronbach's alpha, the reliability coefficient scale was a positive value in both dependent variables BCPRE (alpha score = 0.671) and IMPCT (alpha score = 0.825).

Both dependent variables evaluate positively on the internal consistency scale, as indicated by the high score level obtained. Since this value is higher than 0.60, which is the most common value in exploratory cases, it is often considered to be a good internal consistency measurement when this indicator is equal or superior to 0.80, which was the case for the case in question—IMPCT variable.

Categorical data can be analyzed with two-way tables (also called contingency tables) when more than one variable is involved. This type of test was used in our study to determine whether there were significant relationships between different groups of nominal variables (categorical variables).

The first group was the APPLC (blockchain applications) and BCPRE (blockchain presence indicator), wherein the second group we wanted to test APPLC and IMPCT (finance impact).

In terms of the most complex group to perform the hypothesis testing and according to the already presented research hypothesis for this study where we computed and compared the critical value for the chi-square statistic determined by the level of significance (typically 0.05) and the degrees of freedom. Therefore to provide clarity and deep analysis to understand the distribution of responses follows a known distribution we added in the second group the necessary tests for the following variables and providing all necessary details for the proposed research objectives proposed (Objective 3, 4, and 5).

Rows: Gender (GEN), preferred location (PRLOC), future applications (FAPPLC), business Solutions (BADV), and future investments (FINVEST).

For the first group, we failed to reject our hypothesis allowing us to conclude that APPLC and BCPRE are independent and therefore not associated (degree of freedom = 22 and $p < 0.001$).

For the second group, we also failed to reject the hypothesis, meaning that APPLC and IMPCT are independent and not associated (degree of freedom = 88 and $p < 0.001$).

In terms of the third group, we added five nominal (categorical) variables to perform the test with BCPRE and to understand if there are any associations and dependency relations between our different sets of variables.

According to our chi-square distribution table and hypothesis testing for the third group, we only have a significance level with the hypotheses of association between FINVEST and BCPRE ($p = 0.241$), and IMPCT and BCPRE ($p = 0.147$) where we were able to reject the null hypothesis and reject the hypothesis of independence. These results mean that both subgroups of tested variables allow us to understand that we have statistically significant evidence to show that there is a statistically significant association of dependency.

Third, we blended the analysis of variance (ANOVA) with regression to perform an ANCOVA, which is known as the analysis of covariance. Having a very similar effect to the factorial ANOVA, this method allowed us to analyze one independent variable (factor) at a time, without determining the influence of the other variables. Also, allowed for analyzing the difference in means between multiple groups, considering the effects of variables influencing the dependent variable, but that were not controlled in the experiment (covariates).

With the following assumptions in mind that we when we have a variance equal to 0 or the number of observations is <2, then the ANCOVA test will not be able to perform the necessary analysis. Therefore, we were able to select the following fixed factors with the dependent variable of the blockchain presence (BCPRE) and then with the impact score (IMPCT): GEN, FAPPLC, BADV, and PRLOC.

Only for BADV with BCPRE ($p = 0.18$) and FAPPLC also with BCPRE (0.245), the p-value was more than 0.05.

This means that there was no statistically significant difference between groups or levels of the variable. When the covariate and predictor variable were both significant, we would have evidence that there was a statistically significant difference between the groups when controlling for the covariate.

These results confirm that business features solutions have a significant relationship with blockchain presence indicators as well as with future investments. As such, blockchain will be able to influence and impact future investments in the blockchain space as well as business solutions. Hence, it is believed that companies that already have blockchain processes and projects will have a more substantial positive impact on the outcome of the independent variables and we can conclude that companies which already have blockchain processes and projects will be more likely to achieve new future investments and solutions. Moreover, it has been verified that organizations with blockchain strategies perform better when developing new business features or applications, and they are more likely to invest in blockchain in the future. Due to the practical implications of a blockchain strategy, an organization with a blockchain strategy will have better direction and management practices, since the decision-making process is based on valid and accurate data.

Kolmogorov–Smirnov was also used to test for normality, and the multivariate design with covariates is meant to reduce the damage caused by other covariant variables, such as those independently related to innovation, such as the blockchain presence. Using the regression method between the dependent variable and covariable, we can estimate the variance due to individual differences. In statistical analysis, the dependent variable is indexed to the covariable.

4.5 CONCLUSIONS

4.5.1 LIMITATIONS AND FUTURE RESEARCH

Due to the lack of existing literature on blockchain technology, this study has a major limitation. The life sciences industry is beginning to see more and more information about blockchain applications and opportunities, though the information is still quite volatile and subject to frequent changes, due to the novelty of the topic.

After analyzing the data, it became apparent that in the future, it would be useful to have the ability to look at more case studies and blockchain applications to investigate how they contribute to innovation and new technologies. Moreover, it may still be relevant to study the leadership changes when moving through a blockchain project and to consider how the entire company will be affected.

As a result, we believe that our findings are relevant for all industry sectors, providing insight into the existing blockchain presence, but also allow us to identify future investment opportunities, blockchain benefits, and the current adoption of blockchain in our industry. By the time this chapter is published, there will likely be more studies available regarding the topic, since reality is evolving so rapidly. It is necessary to carry out further research into investments, applications, leadership support, and other factors related to new technologies like blockchain.

4.5.2   CONCLUSIONS

In this chapter, all stakeholders involved in the blockchain-based life sciences ecosystem provided very clear examples and details.

Due to a lack of skills and understanding of blockchain, new technologies like blockchain contribute to greater scalability, traceability, integration, and innovation capacity.

Those who evaluate blockchain technology solutions should consider many factors, including implementation challenges, a need for a change in processes, internal skills, and the possibility of developing blockchain applications.

Different hypotheses based on the research questions were tested with Cronbach's alpha, ANCOVA's, and chi-square's hypothesis tests. Future research can benefit from the presented results.

After reflecting on and evaluating the results achieved through these efforts (through the questionnaires and interviews conducted) on the discussions set out in the prompts, where it was proposed to present the research theme and methodology, the following conclusion can be drawn:

As the first research objective, we examined the differences between firms with a blockchain strategy and variables that can help determine the impact of blockchain applications and strategies on life sciences firms. We found that companies employing blockchain strategies performed better than those without such strategies, and using statistical analysis, we were able to determine to better understand that having blockchain implemented there are associations with future investments and new business applications. Blockchain applications will indeed create new technology opportunities and business processes as companies adopt blockchain processes.

In addition, we wanted to learn what proportion of our sample of industry professionals invested in blockchain technology as well as how various variables interact in terms of investment and value generation, as well as the distribution of companies involved and the investments in blockchain technology. Four hundred and twenty-seven respondents said they had invested between 1 and 5 million euros, while 155 said they had not invested at all. A relation and association have also been established between the investments made and the blockchain presence.

In our study, we also identified which types of life science companies are using blockchain applications and what case studies have been done between them. Additionally, we identified the types of future applications currently being studied. Twenty-seven percent of the companies will use blockchain solutions to secure and improve drug supply chains, but also to improve patient value outcome contracts, monetize patient data, improve patient consent and identity management, and enhance data sharing security with patients.

We understood that the presence of blockchain in the investigated organizations has indeed had an influence on their financial operations and processes on a 0–5 scale, thereby answering the research objective to identify how blockchain currently affects financial processes and operations. The adoption and investment in blockchain technology are growing, along with its financial impacts.

Identifying how life science companies are distributed in terms of demographics and how they are utilizing blockchain applications, we found it to be an interesting conclusion. Approximately 58% of the respondents were male. The most prevalent age range was 26–35 years old, followed by 61–66 years old. To answer the research question, "Are there any correlations between the presence of blockchain and investments made by various organizations?" Our analysis revealed that our investments in companies with blockchain do have clear correlations and associations, but not only that, the impact on the financial departments and processes of the investigated companies was also discussed.

Various studies have demonstrated the importance of this work to the blockchain and life sciences communities since blockchain technology is considered a relevant innovation technology, which can provide decision-makers with entirely new sources of value generation and organizational impact.

Blockchain has applications in several different fields, including tissues, pharmaceuticals, biotechnology, and medical devices. Based on this study, we were able to identify the current application, future opportunities, investment areas, existing use cases, major barriers, and existing models, and blockchain platforms in existing models and life sciences. In addition, an in-depth analysis was provided of the industry's interest in and the use of blockchain technology in these changing times.

This empirical research supported by online surveys delivered important conclusions on the recruitment and application of blockchain in the life sciences, and the problems growing in many areas.

Blockchain technology was found to improve the reliability, transparency, and efficiency of transactions in the heavily regulated pharmaceutical industry. The use of blockchain enables life science companies to gain real-time access to data and greater visibility across critical processes and organizational capabilities.

KEYWORDS

- **blockchain**
- **life sciences**
- **online questionnaire**
- **industry professionals**
- **investments**
- **blockchain applications**
- **innovation**
- **financial impact**
- **technology**
- **patients**
- **challenges**
- **opportunities**

REFERENCES

Agarwal, S.; Punn, N. S.; Sonbhadra, S. K.; Tanveer, M.; Nagabhushan, P.; Pandian, K. K.; Saxena, P. Unleashing the Power of Disruptive and Emerging Technologies amid COVID-19: A Detailed Review. *arXiv Preprint* **2020**. arXiv:2005.11507.

Ahmad, R. W.; Salah, K.; Jayaraman, R.; Yaqoob, I.; Ellahham, S.; Omar, M. Blockchain and COVID-19 Pandemic: Applications and Challenges. *IEEE TechRxiv* **2020**.

Antal, C.; Cioara, T.; Anghel, I.; Antal, M.; Salomie, I. Distributed Ledger Technology Review and Decentralized Applications Development Guidelines. *Fut. Intern.* **2021**, *13* (3), 62.

Aste, T.; Tasca, P.; Di Matteo, T. Blockchain Technologies: The Foreseeable Impact on Society and Industry. *Computer* **2017**, *50* (9), 18–28.

Attaran, M. Blockchain Technology in Healthcare: Challenges and Opportunities. *Int. J. Healthcare Manage.* **2020**, *15* (1), 70–83.

Bittins, S.; Kober, G.; Margheri, A.; Masi, M.; Miladi, A.; Sassone, V. Healthcare Data Management by Using Blockchain Technology. *Applications of Blockchain in Healthcare*; Springer: Singapore, 2021; pp 1–27.

Cachin, C.; Vukolić, M. Blockchain Consensus Protocols in the Wild. *arXiv Preprint* **2017**, arXiv:1707.01873.

Casino, F.; Dasaklis, T. K.; Patsakis, C. A Systematic Literature Review of Blockchain-Based Applications: Current Status, Classification and Open Issues. *Telemat. Inform.* **2019,** *36,* 55–81.

Chen, A.; Väyrynen, K.; Leskelä, R. L.; Heinonen, S.; Lillrank, P.; Tekay, A.; Torkki, P. A Qualitative Study on Professionals' Attitudes and Views towards the Introduction of Patient Reported Measures into Public Maternity Care Pathway. *BMC Health Serv. Res.* **2021,** *21* (1), 1–15.

Cui, T. H.; Ghose, A.; Halaburda, H.; Iyengar, R.; Pauwels, K.; Sriram, S.; et al. Informational Challenges in Omnichannel Marketing: Remedies and Future Research. *J. Mark.* **2021,** *85* (1), 103–120.

Ding, B. Pharma Industry 4.0: Literature Review and Research Opportunities in Sustainable Pharmaceutical Supply Chains. *Process Saf. Environ. Protect.* **2018,** *119,* 115–130.

Drummond, M. F.; Schwartz, J. S.; Jönsson, B.; Luce, B. R.; Neumann, P. J.; Siebert, U.; Sullivan, S. D. Key Principles for the Improved Conduct of Health Technology Assessments for Resource Allocation Decisions. *Int. J. Technol. Assess. Health Care* **2008,** *24* (3), 244–258.

Escamilla-Ambrosio, P. J.; Rodríguez-Mota, A.; Aguirre-Anaya, E.; Acosta-Bermejo, R.; Salinas-Rosales, M. Distributing Computing in the Internet of Things: Cloud, Fog and Edge Computing Overview. *NEO 2016*; Springer: Cham, 2018; pp 87–115.

Fennessey, C.; Pinkevych, M.; Immonen, T.; Camus, C.; Del Prete, G.; Estes, J.; et al. Assessing Individual Viral Reactivations of the Latent Reservoir Using a Novel Barcoded Virus. *J. Int. AIDS Soc.* **2017,** *20,* 5.

Gaukler, G. M.; Seifert, R. W. Applications of RFID in Supply Chains. *Trends in Supply Chain Design and Management; Springer Series in Advanced Manufacturing*; Springer: London, 2007, pp 29–48.

Gillenwater, M.; Seres, S. The Clean Development Mechanism: A Review of the First International Offset Programme. *Greenhouse Gas Measure. Manage.* **2011,** *1* (3–4), 179–203.

Ibarra, J. L.; Agas, J. M.; Lee, M.; Pan, J. L.; Buttenheim, A. M. Comparison of Online Survey Recruitment Platforms for Hard-to-Reach Pregnant Smoking Populations: Feasibility Study. *JMIR Res. Protoc.* **2018,** *7* (4), e8071.

Jabbar, S.; Lloyd, H.; Hammoudeh, M.; Adebisi, B.; Raza, U. Blockchain-Enabled Supply Chain: Analysis, Challenges, and Future Directions. *Multimed. Syst.* **2021,** *27,* 787–806.

Maesa, D. D. F.; Mori, P. Blockchain 3.0 Applications Survey. *J. Parallel Distrib. Comput.* **2020,** *138,* 99–114.

Mangla, S. K.; Sharma, Y. K.; Patil, P. P.; Yadav, G.; Xu, J. Logistics and Distribution Challenges to Managing Operations for Corporate Sustainability: Study on Leading Indian Diary Organizations. *J. Clean. Prod.* **2019,** *238,* 117620.

Montgomery Jr, E. B. *Reproducibility in Biomedical Research: Epistemological and Statistical Problems*; Academic Press: Cambridge, MA, 2019.

Pargeter, J.; Khreisheh, N.; Stout, D. Understanding Stone Tool-Making Skill Acquisition: Experimental Methods and Evolutionary Implications. *J. Human Evol.* **2019,** *133,* 146–166.

Pfleeger, C. P.; Pfleeger, S. L. *Analyzing Computer Security: A Threat/Vulnerability/Countermeasure Approach*; Prentice Hall Professional: Hoboken, NJ, 2012.

Pólvora, A.; Nascimento, S.; Lourenço, J. S.; Scapolo, F. Blockchain for Industrial Transformations: A Forward-Looking Approach with Multi-stakeholder Engagement for Policy Advice. *Technol. Forecast. Soc. Change* **2020,** *157,* 120091.

Puthal, D.; Malik, N.; Mohanty, S. P.; Kougianos, E.; Das, G. Everything You Wanted to Know about the Blockchain: Its Promise, Components, Processes, and Problems. *IEEE Consum. Electron. Mag.* **2018,** *7* (4), 6–14.

Rejeb, A.; Keogh, J. G.; Treiblmaier, H. Leveraging the Internet of Things and Blockchain Technology in Supply Chain Management. *Fut. Intern.* **2019,** *11* (7), 161.

Reyna, A.; Martín, C.; Chen, J.; Soler, E.; Díaz, M. On Blockchain and Its Integration with IoT. Challenges and Opportunities. *Fut. Gener. Comput. Syst.* **2018,** *88,* 173–190.

Shah, B. R.; Schulman, K. Do Not Let a Good Crisis Go to Waste: Health Care's Path Forward with Virtual Care. *NEJM Catal. Innov. Care Deliv.* **2021,** *2* (2). doi:10.1056/CAT.20.0693.

Stengel, J.; Post, T. *Unleashing the Innovators: How Mature Companies Find New Life with Startups*; Currency: Redfern, Sydney, 2017.

Sunny, J.; Undralla, N.; Pillai, V. M. Supply Chain Transparency through Blockchain-Based Traceability: An Overview with Demonstration. *Comput. Ind. Eng.* **2020,** *150,* 106895.

Tönnissen, S.; Teuteberg, F. Analysing the Impact of Blockchain-Technology for Operations and Supply Chain Management: An Explanatory Model Drawn from Multiple Case Studies. *Int. J. Inf. Manage.* **2020,** *52,* 101953.

Wang, Y.; Singgih, M.; Wang, J.; Rit, M. Making Sense of Blockchain Technology: How Will It Transform Supply Chains?. *Int. J. Prod. Econ.* **2019,** *211,* 221–236.

Yao, W.; Chu, C. H.; Li, Z. The Adoption and Implementation of RFID Technologies in Healthcare: A Literature Review. *J. Med. Syst.* **2012,** *36* (6), 3507–3525.

Ziegler, Y.; Uli, V.; Wortmann, J. Blockchain Innovation in Pharmaceutical Use Cases: PharmaLedger and Mytigate. *J. Supply Chain Manage., Logist. Procure.* **2021,** *3* (4), 312–325.

CHAPTER 5

THE COMMERCIAL RELATIONSHIP BETWEEN UNIVERSITIES AND SMALL AND MEDIUM ENTERPRISES WITHIN THE BIG DATA SECTOR: A REVIEW OF THE LITERATURE

JAMES EDWARD GROVE[1] and FRANCESCA DAL MAS[2]

[1]Department of Management, Lincoln International Business School, University of Lincoln, Lincoln, United Kingdom

[2]Department of Management, Ca' Foscari University, Venice, Italy

ABSTRACT

Big data (BD) is a complex phenomenon that is only now being incorporated into business models, disrupting the business environment. While the interest from academics and organizations is rising toward such technologies, there seems to be a disconnection between theory and practice. This chapter aims to solve such a gap by inquiring into whether a common methodology for BD implementation for small and medium enterprises (SMEs) can be established. This research aims to examine the BD systematic-wide relationship between SMEs and universities through a literature review. Results underline how SMEs can mobilize and seize opportunities when presented to them, and they are keen to partner with stakeholders that are deemed credible or when they have an existing informal relationship. Interfunctional cooperation and culture represent key elements, as SMEs and academic institutions look different and need to meet in between for a mutual win–win. Voluntary

Incorporating AI Technology in the Service Sector: Innovations in Creating Knowledge, Improving Efficiency, and Elevating Quality of Life. Maria José Sousa, Subhendu Kumar Pani, Francesca Dal Mas, & Sérgio Sousa (Eds.)
© 2024 Apple Academic Press, Inc. Co-published with CRC Press (Taylor & Francis)

networks on the topic between firms and universities work better than those forced by extensive governmental funds. New research avenues can contribute to closing the literature gap.

5.1   INTRODUCTION AND BACKGROUND

Big data (BD) is a complex phenomenon that is only now being incorporated into business models. The researchers de Mauro et al. (2016) defined and classified the innovation as the following:

"Big Data is the information asset characterized by such a High Volume, Velocity and Variety to require specific Technology and Analytical Methods for its transformation into Value."

In the study, there was a fixation on economic value, the ability to transform and transcribe information into insights that create value for companies and society—information is considered an asset, not too dissimilar to traditional financial investments. As a result, the value of BD has been heavily speculated as it could unlock the next phase of economic development.

The Centre for Economics and Business Research Ltd. (2016) fore-casted that between the periods of 2016 and 2020, BD and the Internet of Things would have been responsible for £322 billion worth of economic growth, increasing the value of the sector by 4.5 times. However, due to the COVID-19 outbreak (Cobianchi et al., 2020a, 2020b), it is hard to gauge whether this has been achieved. But, the importance of small and medium enterprises (SMEs) in achieving these targets cannot be understated; in 2019, SMEs contributed £2.1 trillion to the economy, a total of 52% of all revenue generations in the United Kingdom alone. Therefore, their ability to remain competitive and successful is pivotal to the health and stability of the UK economy (UK Government, 2019).

Consequently, the transformation of BD into value is the most pressing concern as Barnard et al. (2017) express that SMEs were struggling to implement BD solutions in their business models or to realize the benefits of a data-driven strategy as a result of a lack of willingness or knowledge to invest into the correct ICT infrastructure. Traditionally, ICT infrastructure concerned itself with the implementation of technologies ranging from cloud-based solutions to brand-new desktop computers. However, Katal et al. (2013) reject the sole notion that business innovation is entirely dependent on access to technological resources. Alternatively, business and IT leaders need to work together to extract value from data and improve data quality to reduce processing time and produce tangible results, indicating that there is a clear disconnect between theoretical solutions and real-world implementation.

Accordingly, this chapter has aimed to solve the disconnect between theory and practical implementation by inquiring into whether a common methodology for SME BD implementation can be established. The aim of this research is to examine the BD systematic-wide relationship between SMEs and Universities. Thereupon, a literature review methodology has been used to establish the feasibility of this objective and to identify inconsistencies within existing academic literature.

5.2 METHODOLOGY

Scopus was used to survey academic databases (Massaro et al., 2016). The identified sources have then been compounded into a table which included the title of work, author, date retrieved, and brief analysis of bias per source to identify further literary gaps. The researchers identified the records using a Scopus query between February 15, 2017 to February 15, 2021; the query included "sme" and "universities" and "technology" and "business and management," or "bd" or "systematic" or "big data" or "cooperation." As seen in Table 5.1, this accounted for 79 documents across a 10-year period, 53% of the total population. Across this period, there has been a growth in literature, particularly between 2014 and 2015 whereby the number of published documents quadrupled. From 2017 onward, the analyzed period, there has been a consistent increase and presence of documentation in this field. Therefore, this query has provided an adequate sample to be analyzed. The number of scientific documents is reported in Table 5.1.

Lastly, the PRISMA methodology has been used to screen the results (Moher et al., 2009; PRISMA Statement, 2021), enabling the research to be repeated in the future as the same query may be used and refined into relevant sources.

After screening the documentation, there were no records that were duplicated. A total of 79 were screened, with 50 of them being excluded from the analysis, often this was due to a document lacking relevance to the topic or contained a weak connection to the subject. Alternatively, papers that were not available were excluded from the analysis, and those that lacked sufficient quality were omitted.

Although conference papers can be considered easier to publish, still they may often share early stage pioneering ideas (Massaro et al., 2015). Therefore, the investigators decided to include them in this analysis, due to the subject being so new and unestablished, as a total of 9. Predominantly, this has meant that emerging case studies have been able to be explored and analyzed which has embedded theory into practice. The PRISMA flow is reported in Figure 5.1.

TABLE 5.1   Number of Scientific Documents.

Year	No. of documents	Percentage
2021	1	1
2020	26	18
2019	31	21
2018	21	14
2017	12	8
2016	17	11
2015	18	12
2014	5	3
2013	6	4
2012	7	5
2011	4	3
Total	**148**	100

Source: Authors' elaboration from Scopus.

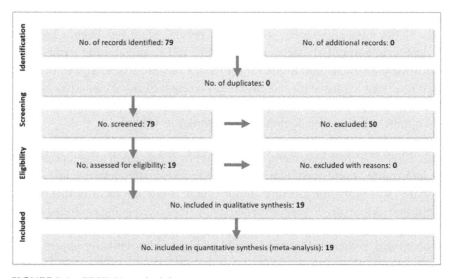

FIGURE 5.1   PRISMA methodology.

The final list of sources is included in Table 5.2.

TABLE 5.2 Table of Sources.

No.	Title	Author(s)	Journal/Conference
1	Knowledge transfer from universities to low- and medium-technology industries: evidence from Italian winemakers	Abbate, T., Cesaroni, F., and Presenza, A. (2020) (Abbate et al., 2020)	*Journal of Technology Transfer*
2	Introduction of medical device development through industry–academia collaboration by the Hamamatsu method	Amano-Ito, Y. (2020) (Amano-Ito, 2020)	*Advanced Biomedical Engineering*
3	New frontiers in computing and data analysis—the European perspectives	Becciani, U. and Petta, C. (2019) (Becciani and Petta, 2019)	*Radiation Effects & Defects in Solids*
4	Industrial case studies for digital transformation of engineering processes using the virtual reality technology	Bellalouna, F. (2020) (Bellalouna, 2020)	*Procedia CIRP*
5	Emergent technologies for inter-enterprises collaboration and business evaluation	Benali, I., Dafflon, B., Bentaha, L., and Moalla, N. (2017) (Benali et al., 2017)	*International Conference on Software, Knowledge, Information Management and Applications*
6	Development strategy analysis of technology business incubator in small medium enterprises accompaniment	Bismala, L., Adriany, D., and Siregar, G. (2020) (Bismala et al., 2020)	*Journal of Critical Reviews*
7	Smart retrofitting by design thinking applied to an industry 4.0 migration process in a steel mill plant	Burresi, G., Ermini, S., Bernabini, D., Lorussu, M. Gelli, F., Frustace, D., and Rizzo, A. (2020) (Burresi et al., 2020)	*Mediterranean Conference on Embedded Computing*
8	Models of innovation development in small and median-sized enterprises of the aeronautical sector in Brazil and in Canada	de Moraes, M., Campos, T., and Lima, E. (2019) (de Moraes et al., 2019)	*Gestão & Produção*
9	Does provision of smart services depend on cooperation flexibility, innovation flexibility, innovation performance or business performance in SMEs?	Kanovska, L. and Doubravsky, K. (2021) (Kanovska and Doubravsky, 2021)	*Periodica Polytechnica Social and Management Sciences*
10	Implementing BIM to streamline a design, manufacture, and fitting workflow: a case study on a fit-out SME in the United Kingdom	Machado, M., Underwood, J., and Fleming, A. J. (2017) (Machado et al., 2017)	*International Journal of 3-D Information Modelling*

TABLE 5.2 *(Continued)*

No.	Title	Author(s)	Journal/Conference
11	Trends of digitalization and adoption of big data & analytics among UK SMEs: Analysis and lessons drawn from a case study of 53 SMEs	Mohamed, M. and Weber, P. (2020) (Mohamed and Weber, 2020)	IEEE International Conference on Engineering, Technology and Innovation
12	African water services sector: a case study for Johannesburg water	Nthutang, P. and Telukdarie, A. (2018) (Nthutang and Telukdarie, 2018)	IEEE International Conference on Industrial Engineering and Engineering Management
13	The oxymoron of digitalization: a resource-based perspective	Osarenkhoe, A. and Fjellström, D. (2021) (Osarenkhoe and Fjellström, 2021)	Journal of Information Technology Research
14	Cooperation between universities and SMEs: a systematic literature review	Pereira, R. and Franco, M. (2021) (Pereira and Franco, 2021)	Industry and Higher Education
15	Application and adoption of big data technologies in SMEs	Rajabion, L. (2018) (Rajabion, 2018)	International Conference on Computational Science and Computational Intelligence
16	An improved solution for partner selection of industry–university cooperation	Ran, C., Song, K., and Yang, L. (2020) (Ran et al., 2020)	Technology Analysis & Strategic Management
17	University-SME relations: needs assessment and feasibility analysis of crowd-sourcing practices implementation	Shaytan, D. and Laptev, G. (2019) (Shaytan and Laptev, 2019)	European Conference on Innovation and Entrepreneurship, ECIE
18	Expertise, leadership style and communication in interfunctional coordination	Tomášková, E. (2018) (Tomášková, 2018)	Periodica Polytechnica Social and Management Sciences
19	Digital transformation process and SMEs	ULAS, D. (2019) (Ulas, 2019)	World Conference on Technology, Innovation and Entrepreneurship

Source: The authors.

5.3   RESULTS

Upon the initial screening and eligibility of the records, it became apparent that 19 sources could be used for both the quantitative and qualitative synthesis.

To understand how the refined results, relate to one another the researcher used the open-source software VOSviewer (Au-Yong-Oliveira et al., 2021; Sousa et al., 2021) to visualize the bibliometric network between the sources. This visualization includes both title and abstract of each document with a minimum of three links per theme and then compounded into three clusters. The software identified that the most relevant theme was "hypothesis" scoring it at 2.41 with only a minimum of three occurrences. Largely, this is because the theme is almost an entirely different cluster, bridging the gap between "sme," "knowledge," and "cooperation" suggesting that research which delivered practical experiments were the most valuable, that is, case studies. In tandem with the predominant themes of "big data," "research," "sme," and "cooperation," each scored above 6+ occurrences indicating that current literature is exploring the relationship between these themes, otherwise known as the relationship between BD, SMEs, and research with the latter representing universities.

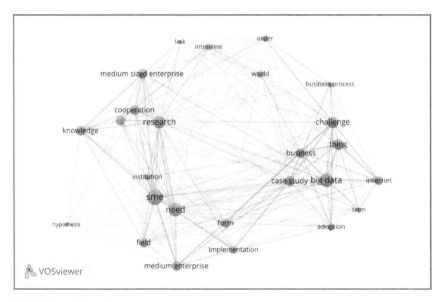

FIGURE 5.2   Key themes.

When analyzing the top four subject areas, it presented interesting results, engineering was represented 10 times, business, management, and accounting, 9; computer science, 8; and decision sciences, 6. Generally, these are practical fields that are involved and concerned with product lifecycles from inception, development, and deployment, demonstrating that there have been key interests generated across relevant research departments, journals, and conferences around this subject. Importantly, these fields make up the core technical skills required behind BD and it is promising to see that research could be conducted to analyze to what extent there has been cross-departmental research in this topic.

Regarding methodologies, when analyzing this aspect of the results, it became clear that the majority of research used a mixed research ethos, including quantitative data to back up qualitative claims. Consequently, results were placed into three categories: literature reviews, 1, mixed-research 10, and case studies at 8. These methodologies reveal that research to date is being conducted in the field; researchers are either producing their own studies or working with firms to run experiments. However, there is a distinct lack of literature reviews to bring this information together and to extract meaningful, practical results. To reiterate, many of these case studies are conference papers and this could be the reason why there is a lack of comprehensive literature reviews. In the future, it will be interesting to examine the changes in methodology over time.

TABLE 5.3   Number of Citations.

Year	Total Citations
2021	4
2020	8
2019	2
Total	14

Source: The authors.

According to Scopus metrics across the data set, there were a total of 14 citations, as seen in Table 5.3. At first, this may appear low as the average citation per source stands at 0.74, but in 2020 there was a large growth in this number. Meanwhile by February 2021, there have already been four citations alone which are likely to increase as the number of publications increase; once more this will be addressed later. Although the main reason for this small number is due to conference papers being used in the population, this trend should be explored again in the future as more journal articles become available.

The analysis revealed that research can be placed into broad four categories: identifying opportunity, mobilizing resources and seizing opportunity, interfunctional cooperation, and network creation. These headings are based upon Osarenkhoe and Fjellström (2021) research, who placed these capabilities within the cluster of activities. Consequently, each activity will act as a section of this discussion whereby relevant research and case studies will be introduced.

5.3.1   IDENTIFYING OPPORTUNITY

In an empirical study by Ran et al. (2020), the correlation between industry–university cooperation was explored to demonstrate the complementary advantages created by the publication of patents via SME and university collaboration, coined win–win development. However, it was found that these benefits are not always realized, and that correct partner selection was imperative to success in this field. In tandem with Osarenkhoe and Fjellström (2021), the researchers referred to the 4W questions when considering partner selection:

- "What are the technology domains for cooperation?"
- "Who are the top competitors?"
- "Where are the leading universities?"
- "Which researchers should we collaborate with?"

These questions pose a multitude of geographical, logistical, and financial issues as the ability to find the appropriate partner can be time-consuming and resource intensive. To solve this, the researchers used a K-means algorithm to perform patent clustering; this involved mapping the cooperative topic, technology competitor, cooperative university, and research team data points. In total, this involved 1639 companies and 152 universities with a total of 8799 documents collected. Summarily, the researchers then processed the algorithm and visualized the results onto a heat map of China enabling technological hot spots to be discovered.

This could provide SMEs with an initial starting point when searching for commercial partners, particularly within the technological space and importantly, BD. However, the researchers conceded that to complete this study, it required large amounts of manual modeling and processing inhibiting the speed in which the study was completed.

Although the above study is promising, it does not solve geographical issues entirely, firms cannot simply uproot themselves and move across a country without difficulty and universities are equally as confined—limiting the capacity in which innovation can spread and/or be assisted.

In a study by Shaytan and Laptev (2019), the researchers assessed university–SME relations in Russia, unsurprisingly Russia is a very large country and acts as an interesting example. The researchers conducted a survey and revealed that less than 9% of university research and teaching staff had any business relationships, but more than 74% were willing to engage in the said practice.

Similarly, 81.4% of SME representatives were keen on gaining access to the knowledge and skills for business development, but 91.5% admitted that they did not know how to explore opportunities in research or consulting, and 98.3% were not aware of the procedures. Revealing that despite the creation of business incubators/accelerators, joint projects, knowledge transfer offices, or university workshops knowledge is unable to penetrate the vast majority of SMEs.

Conclusively, the researchers argue that this is because the participants from universities and SMEs lack common competencies or values to share ideas—simply their cultures are too distinct from one another, suggesting that crowdsourcing practices outside of the university could be used to develop a level playing field between researchers and SME business leaders.

As demonstrated, solutions are available to the identification of strategic partnerships, universities, and SMEs are keen on these relationships, but often they are made difficult due to the complexities of business culture. Fortunately, there is an array of literature expanding upon theoretical and practical literature to portray successful methodology, hopefully incentivizing greater interest in this field and perhaps the development of the previously mentioned identified resources.

5.3.2   MOBILIZING RESOURCES AND SEIZING OPPORTUNITY

In a study by Pereira and Franco (2021), a broad analysis of cooperation between universities and SMEs was completed across industries. Similarly, to this research, there has been continued interest in the topic since 2008 and the study focused on the movement of knowledge between the university and SME, rather than the explicit relationship.

Regardless, upon synthesizing the literature, it became apparent that credibility, informal relationships, and practical objectives were the most sought-after factors in creating positive university–SME relationships. The researcher has expanded upon each of these factors below:

- *Credibility:* the reputation of the university and its ability to deliver results, that is, branding.
- *Informal relationships:* managerial connections to the university via business transactions or alumni status.
- *Practical objectives:* a clearly defined objective such as product development, marketing strategy, or process overhaul.

Coincidentally, the first two factors heavily relate to the culture of the SME as portrayed by Shaytan and Laptev (2019). If the SME is successful, it could be attributed to the alumni of a particular university, and thus, the relationship is established, and credibility boosted. However, the researcher argues that the practical objective factor is far more important. Through the ability to quantify a partnership this simplifies an innovation into business terminology, quickly establishing the win–win between the university and the firm.

The boon of this practical target setting for an independent project can be seen in a study completed by Kanovska and Doubravsky (2021). An analysis was completed of 112 electrotechnical SMEs and their products to measure whether product innovation flexibility increased the higher chance of providing smart services to customers. In business terms, by providing a more specialized service to our customers (x) will it boost our sales figures (y)—although crude sales and profits enable innovative success to be compared.

Summarily, the researchers did find that innovative flexibility improved sales, dubbed in the p-value test as statistically significant, concluding that this same experiment should be adjusted and replicated across industries to provide the business incentive.

In reference to target setting, this provides an end goal to all SMEs in that industry, especially as if you fail to meet the targets an SMEs competitor will soon steal its market share. Therefore, this target enables universities to offer this service via their resources and knowledge and strengthen informal relationships even further, especially as a study has been completed in that field. Unfortunately, these types of microeconomic studies are still rare at the time of writing, but case studies with targets, roadmaps, and results are available. Each of these will now be cross-examined to provide further context.

In a study by Bellalouna (2020), the researcher engaged with a German manufacturer for fire trucks and systems for firefighting. Remarkably, it was identified that state-of-the-art virtual reality technology could be used to allow physical examination of their products by the end user. This enabled firefighting accessories, truck model range, layout of accessories, equipment weight, and the center of gravity/axle-load to be analyzed by customers. Upon completion, all these data could be exported into an excel list based on the configuration, providing ID, designation, weight, supplier, and cost of the parts. The information was then forwarded to the purchasing and production departments to begin assembly. Overall, this innovation improved company efficiency, flexibility, time, and cost savings leading to improved business performances. Finally, the researcher concedes that the main difficulty was the preprocessing required to enable computer-aided design data to be translated to virtual reality data, with time and resources this process itself could become automated.

Consequently, this study is an accurate example of the integration of an innovative technology-backed business with BD (x) boosting the performance of a highly specialized SME (y). This may be a win for practical project target setting, but there are identifiable flaws. First, this is an HT industry with the ability to invest in its own research and development due to it competing in a highly specialized low supplier market, as the researcher will soon explore this is a rare circumstance for the majority of SMEs.

Moreover, with HT industries typically managers are acquainted with industry 4.0 skills, when paired with an equally competent researcher there is a high chance that innovative opportunities can be explored and realized into business value.

Comparatively, in a study by Burresi et al. (2020), the researchers explored an LT Italian steel mill plant and intended to retrofit IT systems and innovate mechanical systems to interact with the former. Despite establishing a complete end-to-end data pipeline with dashboards and cameras to output manufacturing processes, a problem soon became clear. Technicians were able to produce highly innovative solutions but lacked an industry 4.0 manager to translate these retrofits into business value; simply the management in this LT industry lacked the knowledge nor understood the benefits of this BD solution.

In hindsight, these systems could have been used to forecast demand to reduce costs, automate regulatory, and financial reporting as well as review overall efficiency. Importantly, researchers did concede that the project would continue and that publication/subscript paradigms would be included to enable the previous examples to become possible. But in an unforgiving business environment, it is likely that this project would have been canceled due to rising costs and late deadlines. Demonstrating that when an innovative project in an SME lacks grounded business knowledge and is not simplified into an X equals Y paradigm, the consequences can be disastrous.

With these two case studies in mind, it explains why SMEs and universities can become disillusioned or invigorated by the thought of commercial relationships. As Shaytan and Laptev (2019) introduced, this can be attributed to cultural clashes and different ways of thinking and planning. As a result, the researcher has established that sound business logic compounded into a correlated paradigm can achieve progress in this field. But it has been revealed that cooperation is equally as important to boost success rates.

5.3.3   INTERFUNCTIONAL COOPERATION

Rajabion (2018) completed a study examining how SMEs are applying and adopting BD technology in the United States. Although the United States is considered to be a leader in BD technology, the researcher conceded that SMEs were struggling with realizing its value due to technology opacity, over-regulation, data diversity, and fear caused by security and privacy compliance. Alongside this, Osarenkhoe and Fjellström (2021) discovered similar factors in Sweden, these issues paralyzed SMEs and consequently the researchers coined the phrase "The Oxymoron of Digitalization."

SMEs are fully aware that they need to digitalize, but in doing so, it generates additional problems and this makes them question its feasibility. Consequently, if an SME is going to seize an opportunity, then its management need to sell the project to its own organization, promote collaboration internally and externally while working within resource constraints. Osarenkhoe and Fjellström (2021) frame this within the theory of the resource-based firm; each business is a unique bundle of resources that can produce a competitive advantage. This competitive advantage is established by transferring knowledge into dynamic capabilities.

Tomášková (2018) explored how interfunctional coordination can be used to promote dynamic capabilities in the Czech Republic's electrical engineering sector, the same sector discussed by Kanovska and Doubravsky (2021). The results were as follows. An educated workforce promotes interfunctionality. Prioritizing teamwork and cooperation were more important than formal or informal hierarchies. Discussions with lower, middle management, and worker sentiment boosted cooperation and teamwork. Summarily, firms that had an educated, transparent, and cooperative culture were able to have an advantage over competitors as business processes were made more efficient. It is no surprise that when Kanovska and Doubravsky later explored that same sector, innovative flexibility stood out as the key advantage.

With these studies, it is established that SMEs are in dire need of educated colleagues who can operate in cooperative cultures. Coincidentally, universities contain this exact resource. Fortunately, this study has access to two case studies that can examine the effect of academics on SMEs culture when attempting to instill BD.

In a case study by Machado et al. (2017), researchers embarked upon a 30-month project to streamline the business information modeling (BIM) workflow, technology used to map and plan construction projects. Individual processes were then analyzed, and the researchers discovered: information was overproduced or duplicated, departments were idle due to inefficiencies, overproduction, and product defects, and a lack of skills and knowledge economy was apparent.

To solve this, the researchers developed a BIM-based collaborative strategy with overhauled processes and practices mapped, up-to-date IT systems and training plans implemented. This was then rolled out and reviewed/evaluated into inefficiencies that had been removed. Consequently, these innovations led to improved business cycle times throughout the manufacturing and fitting process. However, the main conclusion that researchers drew was that the cultural changes introduced needed to remain embedded if the firm was to achieve strategic objectives. In other words, interfunctional cooperation was at the forefront of this change as this pushed the organization in a direction together.

Another study exemplifying interfunctional cooperation was conducted by Mohamed and Weber (2020). The researchers examined and cooperated with 53 public and private organizations in the West Midlands ranging from 1 to 140+ employees or £10,000 to over £5000,000 in revenue. Training and skill-upgrading seminars, workshops in data skills, and IT systems designs were all provided by the researchers to the SMEs, alongside face-to-face technical consulting on identifying data-driven services using their own and external data, enabling further research between the SMEs and researchers.

Through these services, the SMEs identified that they could use customer purchasing patterns to formulate business strategies, summate data to extract insights to improve goods and services, examine the impact of services, for example, education and achieved outcomes, and identify new markets based on relevant open-source data sets. These solutions help to either boost the revenue of firms or aid in the delivery of public services, delivering a competitive advantage. Accordingly, researchers have realized that SMEs had an innate interest in data when understanding its capabilities. Namely, barriers included the recurring issues: fear of disruption to conventional business and lack of financial resources and skills.

However, the main lesson to be learnt from this case study is that SMEs were keen to engage with researchers on a one-to-one basis, developing their interfunctional cooperative skills and then naturally began to build unique competitive advantages grounded with BD technology.

Therefore, from the previous theory and practical examples, it is demonstrated that interfunctional skills are vital for implementing BD. Commercial partnerships between universities and SMEs will fail without the willingness to amend culture and develop a collaborative approach. As seen in the study by Mohamed and Weber, the researchers successfully built a network of 53 organizations in their local area.

5.3.4   NETWORK CREATION

Open innovation is whereby an organization uses both internal and external sources and resources to drive innovation, summarily this information can be both inbound and outbound within network clusters (Chesbrough and Bogers, 2014). Research to date indicates that this can be a viable solution to network creation. In a study by Ulas (2019), the Turkish government established a digitalization roadmap across the country, encouraging SMEs to cooperate closely alongside 15 research institutions that enrolled on the program, prioritizing the establishment of learning cultures in these businesses. Although positive, it cannot be assumed that these institutions have the necessary resources to transform an entire country; in practicality, progress will be slow and macroeconomic effects minimal. Instead, the researcher explains that this campaign will be used to spread the awareness of industry 4.0 technologies, which as discussed is meaningless unless its benefits are realized.

Moreover, Benali et al. (2017) agreed that interenterprise collaboration (open innovation) was the key enabler to modernize conventional manufacturing sectors with BD technologies. Cooperative projects in theory would be established between a consortium of SMEs, using emergent technologies to produce new efficiencies or services, culminating in recommendations across industries or project evaluation. In theory, this seems simple, find organizations with similar objectives, and then watch as they collaborate to deliver tangible results.

Additional research by Becciani and Petta (2019) assumes the same hypothesis. Through the creation of the European Open Science Cloud initiative, it promises to establish a series of data centers across the continent to provide government, institutions, and business with access to open-source data and ability to upload data. Naturally, it follows a similar logic to the previous studies; groups will begin to cooperate without recognizing that different organizations have different demands and interests. Soon, the researcher will discuss that there are many flaws to these models. However, the researcher does concede that these programs are steps in the right direction and thus practical lessons from previous studies need to be implemented to ensure their success. Otherwise, it is possible that the program suffers the same fate as university business incubators, often only available to students whom are confined to a limited number of years of study and constrained by time (Bismala et al., 2020).

Consequently, open innovation is a potential solution for network creation, but in practice, there are few examples of successful results and many more examples of failure or lack of interest. Fortunately, this review sourced practical research that will now be explored and analyzed.

The methodology by Amano-Ito (2020) is a commendable demonstration of a research and development institution implementing open innovation effectively. Education is provided to promote innovative demand by businesses, ideas are funded, developed, and then implemented to the recipient—a closed loop and repeatable cycle that should in theory enable perpetual cooperation and innovation. However, there were several examples of commercialization failure and thus important lessons. First, the marketing authorization holder (MAH), that is, the group responsible for releasing funding, rejected ideas that were not in line with development strategies. Frustratingly, SMEs would file patents and begin development only to have the project canceled. Furthermore, the MAHs had lengthy, inefficient internal review practices that were often extended without contacting the SMEs. Consequently, SMEs became disinterested and canceled their projects.

Largely these issues caused by the MAHs were due to highly specialized medical devices infused with data that may have been deemed to be high of a commercial risk, or lacked profitability despite the possibility of life-changing medical devices. Lastly, during development, it was found that the medical and technical needs for medical equipment were misunderstood. This was because medical needs changed quickly, or development stages were delayed as described by the previous inefficiencies and consequently the final product was obsolete. Hence, Amano-Ito revealed that the total number of projects that created prototypes stood at 19%, meanwhile only 5% of these were commercialized with an average consultation to commercialization time of 3 years.

Unfortunately, the study demonstrates that the success rate for innovative research hubs is low and very expensive based on poor partner identification and internal process. As explored, this justifies why partner selection is so vital and that open innovation cannot be forced between stakeholders. Nthutang and Telukdarie (2018) explored this same phenomenon within the South African Water Services Sector which sought to embed industry 4.0 technologies, particularly BD. Six strategic objectives were established and examined and then used to provide a business case to universities, government, and business. With this slight tweak to the network model, it created a more streamlined network and should accelerate innovation.

Therefore, network creation is complex and choosing the wrong partners can prove to be destructive. Thus, it can be inferred that network creation is most successful when founded upon informal historical relationships that typically share a common interest, namely profit and competitive advantage. Abbate et al. (2020) hypothesized the *knowledge spillover*, the impact of knowledge transfer on low-tech SMEs in proximity to a university. This study focused on the wine-making industry across Italy, alongside France and Spain, Italy is considered as a member of the old world countries that are competing with the emergence of Chile, Australia, South Africa, and China as they increase their market share. Consequently, this competition is incentivizing Italian winemakers to innovate and amend their production methods.

The need and demand for innovation led to the creation of informal relationships between winemakers and researchers, enabling knowledge to be exploited and a total of 93.19% of sample firms introducing at least one innovation. Abbate et al. (2020) conclude that the competitive advantages derived from this knowledge spill over was caused by internal SME desire to innovate—firms themselves recognized they needed to adapt and sought out a service that could deliver this, leading to universities and local SMEs creating a network born out of circumstance. Although the researchers admit that the findings were only applicable to this industry and this country, it is not the only example of this phenomenon.

de Moraes et al. (2019) explored models of innovation in the Brazilian and Canadian aeronautical sectors. The researchers illustrate the fifth-generation systemic model of innovation, arguably an extension of Porter's five forces as it coincides market factors/conditions alongside education and communication infrastructure. Importantly, these factors draw attention to the dissemination and use of knowledge, that is, knowledge that is applied and used in practice. Upon analyzing, the aeronautical sectors in either country, it became clear that the implementation of knowledge grew out of the demand to compete on the international stage and gain a competitive advantage. Consequently, SMEs and research institutions began to grow around these sectors/firms and thus a network grows naturally. With application to other sectors, similar examples include the rise of Silicon Valley through technology companies in the United States; likewise, London and its large financial sector have led to the birth of financial-technology companies.

Therefore, it could be suggested that networks cannot be forcefully created through large investments; instead, they are a result of mutual goals between interested parties. Thus, attempts by government to force a network are misleading, without a clearly defined objective capital is being misallocated as they wait for opportunities to arrive. It will be interesting to examine in the future whether the national digitalization projects discussed have led to real economic development.

Considering this, it is appropriate to examine a particular aspect of these networks often found on university campuses, the business incubator. Perhaps, the business incubator needs to be re-conceptualized as it poses the unique utility to bring interested parties around a new project, ranging from academia to business. Bismala et al. (2020) did just this, analyzing developmental strategies used in practice within the SME sphere.

To begin, Bismala et al. (2020) identified that the role of a business incubator is unique, providing small businesses with access to scientific knowledge and management skills which help to boost survival rates. However, incubators often lack financial sponsorship, production space, advanced technological facilities and are confined to their geographical region. Therefore, this has meant that the business incubator can only provide the most basic support to young businesses.

Consequently, the researchers performed a SWOT analysis to provide solutions to the weaknesses present:

- Collaboration between academia, business, and government to accompany SMEs in the immediate delivery of products.
- Creating work programs supported by private companies to increase funds available and introduce professional talent.
- Strengthening managers, assistants, and experts to navigate regulatory boundaries and encourage the commercialization of results.
- Encouraging competition between different incubators and reexamining regulations to make development easier.

In summary, these ideas produce tangible resources for SMEs to use and intangible resources to provide the drive, motivation, and leadership to start a new business or adapt to an existing one. Ultimately, the findings of the paper suggest that business incubators need to adapt and become similar to management consultancies, providing specialized and agile advice. Securing key clients and delivering practical outcomes. Interestingly in the study by Mohamed and Weber (2020), many of the above ideas were incorporated into their research, particularly when providing technical expertise to assist their network with expertise. Thus, as this is a relatively new phenomenon, academia could be on the verge of reexamining institutional business incubators.

5.4   DISCUSSION AND CONCLUSIONS

To reiterate, the purpose of this study was to examine whether the use and improvement in commercial relationships could boost the implementation of BD technologies in SMEs. Subsequently, this topic contains the expansiveness to be applied to many technological innovations and therefore the knowledge gained should be applied or investigated further.

Identifying opportunities first begin with the 4W exploratory analysis: (1) What are the technology domains for cooperation? (2) Who are the top competitors? (3) Where are the leading universities? (4) Which researchers should we collaborate with? Although this method acts as a means of finding the correct specialist, it predicates on SMEs having the knowledge to answer these questions and then establishing a beneficial relationship. The research examined indicated that the use of a K-means clustering algorithm could be used to map innovation centers to a map enabling interested firms to locate them easier. Meanwhile, it was also discovered that businesses are interested in partnerships but often misunderstand academic processes and culture to access them.

This led to understanding how SMEs can mobilize and seize opportunities when presented to them. It was established that SMEs are keen to partner with stakeholders that are deemed credible or when they have an existing informal relationship with—the notion of faith and trust exemplified how SMEs are innately skeptical to innovation. Once the partnership began, it became clear that projects which used a simplistic X and Y paradigm placed innovation into transferrable business logic and enabled the benefits of an innovation to be realized. Meanwhile, those that ignored this paradigm led to minimal business transformation and a breakdown in cooperation.

Interfunctional cooperation and culture became a key element of the research, recognizing that SMEs and academic institutions are so different that both needed to evolve and meet in the middle. It was found theoretically and in practice that firms with an educated, transparent, and cooperative culture had a competitive advantage and were more innovative. Fortunately, universities have access to this resource, and it was found that researchers with aptitude in fieldwork created an informal network in the community, embedding innovative solutions.

Consequently, it was then important to reexamine how networks are created because this promoted the greatest amount of change and challenged the formalized structure of institutional networks. Networks embedded with open innovation philosophy were at their best when established via demand-driven, mutually interested stakeholders that were keen to gain mutual benefits through a social-driven or profit-driven project. Those that were forced by way of extensive government funding were often inefficient and sustaining a network which did not produce many commercialized results. This indicated that government policy should fixate on sponsoring new ideas or project through the business incubator as this tool naturally brings interested parties together. However, research suggests that the business incubator needs to be re-invented, resembling a management consultancy that competes alongside other incubators. In contrast to a management consultancy, the business incubator would carry a socially driven objective rather than profit driven.

With these four topics and lessons, the researcher is excited to see whether any of them will continue to be applied in case studies, especially as this provided the practical evidence for the lessons gained in this study. Quantitatively, it was revealed that this topic is a growing and emerging field in academia, at the time of writing it can only be assumed that there will be a growth in the number of publications in 2021, especially as many papers are still in construction. On this subject, it can thus be concluded that the amount of literature only indicates the validity of the study.

However, it is important to address the notable issues. With this type of study, academia is required to consistently synthesize literature, else the subject matter becomes increasingly outdated due to the pace of the industry. Additionally, bias is hard to prevent as the qualitative outcomes concluded are based upon the researcher's interpretation, indicating that the establishment of a formalized framework would assist with benchmarking the synthesis and reducing bias.

Moreover, practical case studies were the most impactful solution to bridging the gap between theory and practice. But, many of these were conference papers, and it would be more reliable and sustainable to only include formal journal articles in the future, although this is dependent on the availability of them over the new few years. With this availability within the BD space, academia would then be able to create a comprehensive empirical study to measure the fiscal benefits of these commercial relationships, providing additional legitimacy and growth to the topic.

Finally, the impact of COVID-19 on BD adoption cannot be understated at the time of completing this research. Yet at the time of writing, there was a lack of comprehensive literature that could be used to analyze the effects of it. Therefore, this should be considered a research avenue for the future.

KEYWORDS

- **big data**
- **universities**
- **collaboration**
- **networking**
- **literature review**
- **digital disruption**
- **big data implementation**

REFERENCES

Abbate, T.; Cesaroni, F.; Presenza, A. Knowledge Transfer from Universities to Low- and Medium-Technology Industries: Evidence from Italian Winemakers. *J. Technol. Transf.* **2020**. https://doi.org/10.1007/s10961-020-09800-x

Amano-Ito, Y. Introduction of Medical Device Development through Industry–Academia Collaboration by the Hamamatsu Method. *Adv. Biomed. Eng.* **2020**, *9*, 112–116. https://doi.org/10.14326/abe.9.112

Au-Yong-Oliveira, M.; Pesqueira, A.; Sousa, M. J.; Dal Mas, F.; Soliman, M. The Potential of Big Data Research in HealthCare for Medical Doctors' Learning. *J. Med. Syst.* **2021**, *45*, 13. https://doi.org/10.1007/s10916-020-01691-7

Barnard, C.; Bakkers, J. H.; Wünsche, S. *The Road to the Digital Future of SMEs*; Virgin Media Business, 2017.

Becciani, U.; Petta, C. New Frontiers in Computing and Data Analysis—The European Perspectives. *Radiat. Effects Defects Solids* **2019**, *174* (11–12), 1020–1030. https://doi.org/10.1080/10420150.2019.1683840

Bellalouna, F. Industrial Case Studies for Digital Transformation of Engineering Processes Using the Virtual Reality Technology. *Proc. CIRP* **2020**, *90*, 636–641. https://doi.org/10.1016/j.procir.2020.01.082

Benali, I.; Dafflon, B.; Bentaha, L.; Moalla, N. Emergent Technologies for Inter-enterprises Collaboration and Business Evaluation. In *11th International Conference on Software, Knowledge, Information Management and Applications (SKIMA)*, 2017.

Bismala, L.; Andriany, D.; Siregar, G. Development Strategy Analysis of Technology Business Incubator in Small Medium Enterprises Accompaniment. *J. Crit. Rev.* **2020,** *7* (1), 221–225. https://doi.org/10.31838/jcr.07.01.39

Burresi, G.; Ermini, S.; Bernabini, D.; Lorusso, M.; Gelli, F.; Frustace, D.; Rizzo, A. Smart Retrofitting by Design Thinking Applied to an Industry 4.0 Migration Process in a Steel Mill Plant. In *Mediterranean Conference on Embedded Computing,* 2020.

Centre for Economics and Business Research Ltd. *The Value of Big Data and the Internet of Things to the UK Economy,* 2016.

Chesbrough, H.; Bogers, M. Explicating Open Innovation: Clarifying an Emerging Paradigm for Understanding Innovation. In *New Frontiers in Open Innovation*; Chesbrough, H., Vanhaverbeke, W., West, J., Eds.; Oxford University Press: Oxford, 2014; pp 3–28.

Cobianchi, L.; Dal Mas, F.; Peloso, A.; Pugliese, L.; Massaro, M.; Bagnoli, C.; Angelos, P. Planning the Full Recovery Phase: An Antifragile Perspective on Surgery after COVID-19. *Ann. Surg.* **2020a,** *272* (6), e296–e299. https://doi.org/10.1097/SLA.0000000000004489

Cobianchi, L.; Pugliese, L.; Peloso, A.; Dal Mas, F.; Angelos, P. To a New Normal: Surgery and COVID-19 during the Transition Phase. *Ann. Surg.* **2020b,** *272,* e49–e51. https://doi.org/ 10.1097/SLA.0000000000004083

De Mauro, A.; Greco, M.; Grimaldi, M. A Formal Definition of Big Data Based on Its Essential Features. *Libr. Rev.* **2016,** *65* (3), 122–135. https://doi.org/10.1108/LR-06-2015-0061

de Moraes, M. B.; Campos, T. M.; Lima, E. Models of Innovation Development in Small and Median-Sized Enterprises of the Aeronautical Sector in Brazil and in Canada. *Gest. Prod.* **2019,** *26* (1). https://doi.org/10.1590/0104-530X2002-19

Kanovska, L.; Doubravsky, K. Does Provision of Smart Services Depend on Cooperation Flexibility, Innovation Flexibility, Innovation Performance or Business Performance in SMEs? *Period. Polytechn. Soc. Manage. Sci.* **2021,** *29* (1), 64–69. https://doi.org/10.3311/ PPSO.15709

Katal, A.; Wazid, M.; Goudar, R. H. Big Data: Issues, Challenges, Tools and Good Practices. In *Sixth International Conference on Contemporary Computing (IC3),* 2013.

Machado, M.; Underwood, J.; Fleming, A. Implementing BIM to Streamline a Design, Manufacture, and Fitting Workflow. *Int. J. 3D Inf. Model.* **2017,** *5* (3), 31–46. https://doi. org/10.4018/ij3dim.2016070103

Massaro, M.; Dumay, J.; Garlatti, A. Public Sector Knowledge Management: A Structured Literature Review. *J. Knowl. Manage.* **2015,** *19* (3), 530–558. https://doi.org/10.1108/JKM-11-2014-0466

Massaro, M.; Dumay, J. C.; Guthrie, J. On the Shoulders of giants: Undertaking a Structured Literature Review in Accounting. *Account., Audit. Account. J.* **2016,** *29* (5), 767–901.

Mohamed, M.; Weber, P. Trends of Digitalization and Adoption of Big Data & Analytics among UK SMEs: Analysis and Lessons Drawn from a Case Study of 53 SMEs. In *IEEE International Conference on Engineering, Technology and Innovation,* 2020.

Moher, D.; Liberati, A.; Tetzlaff, J.; Altman, D. G. Preferred Reporting Items for Systematic Reviews and Meta-analyses: the PRISMA Statement. *J. Clin. Epidemiol.* **2009,** *62* (10), 1006–1012. https://doi.org/10.1016/j.jclinepi.2009.06.005

Nthutang, P.; Telukdarie, A. Integration of Small and Medium Enterprises for Industry 4.0 in the South African Water Services Sector: A Case Study for Johannesburg Water. In *Proceedings of the 2018 IEEM* 2018; pp 1206–1210.

Osarenkhoe, A.; Fjellström, D. The Oxymoron of Digitalization. *J. Inf. Technol. Res.* **2021,** *14* (4), 1–17. https://doi.org/10.4018/jitr.20211001.oa1

Pereira, R.; Franco, M. Cooperation between Universities and SMEs: A Systematic Literature Review. *Ind. High. Educ.* **2021**. https://doi.org/10.1177/0950422221995114

PRISMA Statement. *PRISMA Transparent Reporting of Systematic Reviews and Meta Analysis*, 2021. http://www.prisma-statement.org/

Rajabion, L. Application and Adoption of Big Data Technologies in SMEs. In *Proceedings—2018 International Conference on Computational Science and Computational Intelligence, CSCI 2018*, 2018; pp 1133–1135. https://doi.org/10.1109/CSCI46756.2018.00219

Ran, C.; Song, K.; Yang, L. An Improved Solution for Partner Selection of Industry-University Cooperation. *Technol. Anal. Strat. Manage.* **2020,** *32* (12), 1478–1493. https://doi.org/10.1080/09537325.2020.1786044

Shaytan, D. K.; Laptev, G. D. University-SME Relations: Needs Assessment and Feasibility Analysis of Crowd-Sourcing Practices Implementation. *Proc. Eur. Conf. Innov. Entrepreneursh., ECIE* **2019,** *2*, 953–959. https://doi.org/10.34190/ECIE.19.120

Sousa, M. J.; Dal Mas, F.; Pesqueira, A.; Lemos, C.; Verde, J. M.; Cobianchi, L. The Potential of AI in Health Higher Education to Increase the Students' Learning Outcomes. *TEM J.* **2021,** *10* (2), 488–497.

Tomášková, E. Expertise, Leadership Style and Communication in Interfunctional Coordination. *Period. Polytechn. Soc. Manage. Sci.* **2018,** *26* (2), 103–111. https://doi.org/10.3311/PPso.11692

UK Government. *Business Population Estimates for the UK and the Regions 2019*, 2019.

Ulas, D. Digital Transformation Process and SMEs. *Proced. Comput. Sci.* **2019,** *158*, 662–671. https://doi.org/10.1016/j.procs.2019.09.101

CHAPTER 6

SOCIAL ANALYTICS AND ARTIFICIAL INTELLIGENCE IN TAX LAW

LUÍS MANUEL PICA[1,2]

[1]*Polytechnic Institute of Beja, Beja, Portugal*

[2]*JusGov, Research Centre for Justice and Governance at University of Minho—School of Law, Braga, Portugal*

ABSTRACT

The analysis of existing data in social networks is an important instrument that allows obtaining a varied set of benefits in the most varied branches of applicability. Among these fields, the right and management of the tax system is not immune to the coming of society, and the analysis and processing of existing data in the databases allow the realization of interests and desiderates that maximize the control over the actions of private individuals in the acts of fiscal management, combating phenomena such as international tax evasion and fraud, both upstream and downstream at preventive level in the creation of mitigation and intervention measures against the practice of these phenomena. However, legal problems axiologically cannot be overlooked and neglected in a rule of law, calling important limits on the implementation of these analytical measures, attempting to preserve the legal rights and interests of taxpayers.

6.1 INTRODUCTION

We focus our investigation in this chapter on the significance of social networks in the gathering and preservation of personal data. These large

Incorporating AI Technology in the Service Sector: Innovations in Creating Knowledge, Improving Efficiency, and Elevating Quality of Life. Maria José Sousa, Subhendu Kumar Pani, Francesca Dal Mas, & Sérgio Sousa (Eds.)
© 2024 Apple Academic Press, Inc. Co-published with CRC Press (Taylor & Francis)

databases are one of the main sources of data and information that properly used by the competent authorities, allow the implementation of various designs such as the fulfillment of the public interest, social development, and the well-being of the collectivity in which they are territorially circumscribed.

It is imperative to call the centrality and acuity that these personal data stored in social networks take place in the paradigm of existing legal relations, because through this it is possible to purge platonic ideals, doubts, and theses in dialog with reality, departing from secrecy and conspiracies in the activity of public agencies. These personal data are thus an important source that will allow tax agencies to discover existing wealth manifestations and collect data to create risk profiles that allow the negative and pathological effects of the tax legal relationship to be mitigated.

However, it is necessary to bring to the past the fundamental right adverse and that has been ascending in the hierarchy of social importance, as is the right to the protection of personal data. It is that this, as the reality of contemporary states, implements designs that seek the path of the reserve of private and intimate life, however, in a broader context and which appears to be a recent need that needs to be analyzed (Warren and Brandeis, 1890). Understanding personal data as remnants and footprints of the private and reserved life of its holder, it is necessary to convene instruments that reserve this information from the knowledge of third parties who have no interest in their knowledge and that, therefore, should not be placed on the purview of the public sphere.

A necessary introduction in which it is there for necessary to recall the premise underlying this article, which lies in the intention of giving a small contribution on the following question: how should social analytics be articulated when used in tax context? What are the limits and ontological and axiological values that legitimize the instrumentalization of these data for the purpose of realizing public interests, such as the discovery of material truth?

6.2   ARTIFICIAL INTELLIGENCE, BIG DATA ANALYTICS IN THE INVESTIGATION AND ACTIONS OF PROOF OF ACTS OF EVASION AND TAX FRAUD

One of the Tax Administration's strategic objectives is to promote taxpayer compliance with tax duties, as well as to combat tax evasion and fraud by those taxed who do not comply with the tax obligations to which they are tied. An improvement in compliance with the tax obligations of each of the subjects must be obtained through a varied range of essential tasks of the tax administration officials, namely the investigation and proof of tax evasion and fraud. To this end, it is necessary to carry out a thorough analysis of the results of the actions to control the effects they have on the tax behavior of taxpayers, in order to achieve that the ideal of regularizing tax obligations becomes an additional tool when achieving an improvement in voluntary compliance with them.

The digitization of society as a whole and economic activity concretely is making an important change in the way the business sector and large organizations are organized, particularly in an economic and functional context. In order to meet these new needs, the Tax Administration should implement mechanisms that allow structured and information-oriented information systems to facilitate tax data relating to the control and supervision of tax acts relating to income taxes and VAT, in order to allow for a more simplistic management of tax obligations, the restriction of the use of business information processing systems that allow the concealment of sales or activities, giving a special focus on the activity of online platforms dedicated to the intermediation or direct sale of goods or services. The obtaining of information, the systematization and analysis thereof, the implementation of concrete activities, or the impulse of national and international cooperation to act on this digital world in constant development and process of evolution is a necessity that cannot be neglected here.

Thus, the creation of standards enabling a sectoral analysis so that the recipients of these presented obvious discrepancies between their calculated economic capacity and that deriving from a historical series of their income will allow foreseeable control over the activity of these taxpayers. The creation of risk indicators offers the organs of the Tax Administration greater control, both in fostering compliance with tax obligations, as well as in the level of supervision and control over their true ability to contribute to the declared one. It is in this field that big data and artificial intelligence are revealed as a real added value in the management of this data analysis and in the automatic performance of acts that are convenient to the intended purposes, achieving a fast and efficient action against the data processed and the intended results to achieve. Thus, where the intelligence systems find evidence of noncompliance, which is clear clarity, it shall be of every good effect for it to act in accordance with the appropriate, against leaving the harmful effects arising from the noncompliance or omissions committed.

In the context presented, it should be noted that big data and social analytics will seek priority *action* in a set of tasks that will allow improvement in strategic sectors in the fight against tax evasion and fraud, namely:

1. Sources of information and technological advances aimed at risk analysis, which are the basis of any process of selection of taxpayers. For this purpose, planning processes will be required to act on different sources of information, both internal and international in nature, in order to strategically facilitate the models of data selection obtained by the Tax Administration. At the international level, the models of automatic tax information exchange are gaining an increased importance, in view of the new international information exchange system, which is intended to be converted into a reality and consequently leads to greater difficulty in concealing assets and wealth, in order to ensure the correct taxation and declaration of existing and preceding wealth of different financial assets located abroad. The information received by the Tax Administration has been gradually increased due to the presentation of the so-called country-for-country, in order to avoid the erosion of tax bases and the transfer of benefits (BEPS) to states, countries, or territories fiscally more favorable. The models implemented by Council Directive 2016/881 of May 25, 2016, which focused on large multinationals, also collect a large number of activities in relation to the territories in which they operate. Based on these data, it is possible to create profiles and risk-taking systems that systematize and delimit risks and allow a better follow-up of these risk activities.

2. Internal tax controls through automated transfer pricing risk analysis systems based on a whole range of information available on linked transactions with which the Tax Administration currently counts, making effective use of data and information available to inspection media as a consequence of the BEPS project, both within the OECD and the European Union, including the procedures for the exchange of automatic information on various facts.

3. (a) Control of the granting and maintenance of tax benefits, enabling the applications for exemption or tax benefits to be proven, as well as their maintenance. This will seek to intensify control measures to prove adequate compliance with the specific requirements for the correct application of the special tax regime granting these benefits and exemptions.

    (b) Control in the actions of taxpayers and in the analysis of information, because economic activity manifests itself in recent years in a constantly evolving environment, deserving the business models of analysis by the Tax Administration, not being able to neglect the activity of those who have a higher profile of tax risk. The need to consolidate the different ways of obtaining information to provide information on the amounts, nature, and identification of the parties involved in the trade relationship in a wide range of economic activity is shown. The required data are thus necessary for the Tax Administration to carry out a thorough control of the correct taxation of these businesses, avoiding conduct harmful to tax evasion and fraud.

These guidelines or maximum interventional guidelines that the Tax Administration has been revealing from a *big data analytics and* artificial intelligence perspective ends up considerably marking the functional activity of the Tax Administration, revealing a migration to an activity eminently dependent on personal data and the use of computer and automated means, seeking in various subjects a use of these for a better efficiency of the functional activity and the realization of the results to be continued. However, the denominator common to all these concrete guidelines where the analysis of the large volume of information and the automated processing of data allows better performance by the Tax Administration lies in the personal data and the ways of obtaining them, being in *case* the procedure of information exchange one of the most relevant mechanisms and instruments.

6.3   THE (NEW) SOCIAL OBLIGATIONS OF THE STATES: REFORMULATION OF TAX LAW AND SOCIAL ANALYTICS?

The crisis emerged based on a viral outbreak induced by the global ineffectiveness, and shows the undeniable significance that taxes have for state fiscal systems, especially when taxes are a major source of funding of the states. The idea of the human being as *an ex-machina God* is a mere science fiction left uncovered in the current context of social-economic distortion. The reflections brought by the new coronavirus, its reflexes, and its consequences leave unseen the needs that were considered accommodated in life-long quarantine in the drawers of the constituent legislation and in the foundations of the history that has been overlooked.

This is why the negative repercussions that have been unseen in the current frame and the situation are not different, in particular the social needs that stem from the obligations that the welfare states are obliged to. As we have mentioned above, it is axiomatic that in the economic and social context that reigns momentarily in the pandemic landscape, states lack a comprehensive and loose financial resource to address various problems that are brought to the above fore and which are maximized with this health crisis. Thus, we talk about problems related to the large volume of expenditure generated and that is necessary to support the current public health system, because the overcrowding of material, human, and infrastructure resources need to be maintained using a large financial volume; and, also, a problem related to the system of social providence, because in the current context, it is revealed that dependence on the state tends to increase. With the need to respond to these "new" social needs of the state, resources for financial resources become an increasingly pronounced and imperative need. Consequently, and if until the arrival of the pandemic were problems that were sociologically relegated to a background, the current pandemic context brought them into the sociological spotlight. We refer mainly to two problems underlying these already largely idealized routes, namely the maintenance of the public health system and the social security welfare system.

When we talk about the first issue, it is revealed as an undeniable premise that the state has the constitutional task of providing for a public system and tactful free of health, being positive of this axiological value in Article 64 of the Constitution of the Portuguese Republic. However, the maintenance of a service that is tending to be free and public ends up being supported directly by the state, which, indirectly, is supported by the tax revenues collected by the state. In other words, the increase in public health services and the saturation of human, material, and infrastructure resources have brought an exponential increase in the burden to maintain this entire national health system, so it is necessary to use the means of financing to be able to support all the expenditure generated from the existing pandemic.

As far as the social security welfare system is concerned, the issue is axiologically more complex. We are not talking about a pure right to pensions of a different nature, such as pensions because of old age, invalidity, widowing or illness to natural persons who need them and have actually contributed to this. We are talking about a real issue of social support for people of a diverse nature whose desideratum will not only be to fight poverty, but to combat social support for the maintenance of employment, operation of establishment or maintenance of basic services in strategic sectors for the proper functioning of the economy. It is merely an example of how states have allocated support for maintaining jobs through lost funds, or even support for maintaining strategic services such as the maintenance of airlines whose goal is to keep them operational in order to maintain routes and services essential to the functioning of the national economy. Positively, the state is bound ultimately by the duty to provide for a social security system that protects citizens from sickness, old age, disability, widowers and orphaned, as well as unemployment and in all other situations of lack or decrease of means of subsistence or capacity for work (cf. Article 63(3) of the Constitution of the Portuguese Republic).

There is a set of imperative needs that, despite their lack of functional convergence, are of great importance and in which state intervention emerges as undeniable and necessary. Lacking the state's means of complying with these obligations and social security, it is necessary to call financial resources, in particular, through the use of tax law and the power to create taxes that underlies this branch of law and in which the state holds legal exclusivity. Since taxes and other taxes are the main source of revenue for states, they will be tempted to help themselves from the power to create them in order to meet the immediate needs of the treasury in order to meet the social media needs to which they are entrusted.

Understanding the current society and the needs departing from the new social contours that alter social coexistence can only bring the answer that law and, itself, is an active instrument for adjusting social structures and challenges that escape collective self-determination. It is in this understanding of society that necessarily goes through a period of reflection on the adaptive and transformative possibilities of law, particularly through a dual dimension such as the cause and consequence, that is, the negative effects of the pandemic and the catalyzing effect of a model of society that will follow, mirroring collective aspirations that show new priorities of the post-COVID period. It is in this scenario that the need to adapt the functional system of the tax activity aimed at an efficiency that allows the perfect collection of tax revenues due is shown and is framed. The structural reforms that are enunciated undergo a modernization of the functional activity of the Tax Administration, eventually asserting an inevitability of changes that are axiomatically necessary in the face of the existing globalized context and the great complexification of intersubjective bonds created in a business and commercial world.

The reforms proposed and announced essentially include the advent of new forms of action of the Tax Administration, namely the use of new technologies and the new ways of obtaining information that allow this a general coverage on the fulfillment of tax obligations that imposes on the tax obliged. These technological innovations translate into means of monitoring taxpayers' tax obligations through the collection of data and information about taxpayers, identifying potential hubs of noncompliance. Among these sources of information collected for the purposes of treatment by tax administrations and creation of risk profiles that allow upstream prevent the noncompliance with tax obligations and downstream corrective action on unfulfilled tax obligations are artificial intelligence measures and big data analytics. It aims to integrate data collection measures for further treatment and prevention of tax evasion and fraud, with the goal of improving tax management efficiency and, as a result, tax revenue collection for later distribution in essential services that are critical in the exercise of political and social functions.

The change in the fundamental balance between administrative entities and economic operators underlies the need to provide the first means to enable it to manage the tax system efficiently, in particular with the collection of data and proper storage that will have to be handled in order to be able to act effectively, unless the purposes of recourse to this instrument are revealed and frustrated. For this reason, the collection of tax data is an imperative need in today's times, since it allows the mitigation of the imbalance created by the effect of globalization and high complexification of existing economic and commercial relations and, also, through phenomena such as unfair tax competition with the implementation of opaque measures that allow a concealment of wealth that should under normal circumstances be subject to taxation.

Among these instruments of data collection by tax administrations, special emphasis is placed on obtaining data through social networks and social instruments where the holders themselves place, in an accessible and freely public manner, information that may show prominence for the purposes of determining will in tax matters. For this reason, legal systems such as French or Spanish have instituted measures that allow tax administrative bodies to consult and collect data published on social networks (e.g., *Facebook*, *Instagram*, *Twitter*, etc.), with the desideratum of determining possible noncompliances or creating profiles that allow the management of risk analysis on certain matters or taxpayers, allowing them to act in order to combat phenomena such as tax evasion and fraud.

Thus, it cannot be assumed that the state is called for new social needs, it can only be affirmed that they have been emphasized and maximized due to the enteric outbreak and the negative consequences of it, so it becomes even more important to implement fiscal measures that allow mitigating the existing negative effects, through the existing social obligations as a corollary of the duties that on the state is imposed. But in order for the response to be efficient and to allow the correction of inequalities through the fiscal strategy, it is necessary for the state to develop the necessary measures to structure functional development that allows it to respond to new challenges in order to identify situations of noncompliance and act accordingly to obtain the necessary revenues due to the completion of the responses to which it is called to respond.

6.4   SOCIAL ANALYTICS AND ARTIFICIAL INTELLIGENCE IN THE FUNCTIONAL ACTIVITY OF TAX ADMINISTRATION

Social analytics is, together with the use of artificial intelligence, one of the new instruments that allow a restructuring of the functional activity of the Tax Administration. When the questions are raised, the state must provide new approaches that allow the realization of material norms associated with the manifestations of wealth. It should be seen that we do not ignore, nor weaken, matters of a substantive legal nature, particularly when modeling the tax legal relations established between the state and taxpayers, but rather the very qualification rules that allow the functional legal action of the Tax Administration to simultaneously pursue formal and material purposes, depending on the need for urgent response to the threats arising from the strong economic context complexion and often opaque.

Data analytics presupposes here an important solution in times of techno-logical evolution that makes personal data and artificial intelligence fed by them an instrument of undeniable importance. It should be seen that in several contexts, the possibility of collecting and processing taxpayers' data allows timely identification of situations of noncompliance with tax obligations, as well as the creation of risk profiles that allow to control with greater efficiency concrete sectors of the economy that tend to be more conducive to possible situations of tax evasion and fraud. Also, the automated mechanisms using these data can act functionally, either by unity or even *by plurality*, against possible illegal practices and in conformity with the structuring principles of the rule of law.

That said, it should be noted that the state should strategically select the instruments and means by which it should obtain the information considered relevant for tax purposes, under penalty of acting disproportionately in the institution of measures considered harmful to the legal sphere of taxpayers. It is in this dogmatic path that the legislator found as working support for obtaining information, one of the largest databases on the subjects, such as social media and, in particular, social networks. We can therefore with ownership ensure that social networks constitute true online platforms that allow their users to generate a profile in which they can share information and personal data about themselves or about third parties, as well as interact spontaneously with other users in order to communicate and share convergent and common interests. Networks such as Facebook, YouTube, WhatsApp, Twitter, Instagram, or LinkedIn turn out to be real databases that stand up as an important source of information whose potential is incalculable, as it may serve a set of interests, namely interests of a tax nature. It is in this need on the part of the states and in the availability that these large social networks as a database and information converge, that the interests converge that must legitimize access for purposes of a different nature.

In view of the above, several tax systems in order to rationalize the activity of its tax administrative bodies have been implementing true systems based on big data that seek control of possible situations of tax evasion and fraud. Through the use of social media databases, it allows control over various sectors of the economy, in particular those that there is a preponderance for noncompliance with the tax obligations to which the tax obliged are enforced. For this, agents and employees of the Tax Administration can collect data and information existing on social networks, in particular through the qualification that they have regarding the information that the subjects publish on social networks and that are free access. In this way, it is up to us to ascertain whether there is actually conformity with the statements submitted and what they actually expose from their lives on social networks. In a practical context, one might think that if a subject expose on his social network numerous information (graphic or textual) in which he demonstrates a luxurious life without declaring sufficient means to have them, it may mean the admissibility of the existence of discrepancy between the wealth demonstrated and the declared. Also, in terms of determining the household may be valuable for determining the location of the riches demonstrated and which should be subject to taxation.

With the need to implement a new technological system, important projects have been introduced aimed at detecting acts of tax evasion and fraud by economic agents. However, it is an implementation that must show a set of assumptions and steps for a correct and concrete implementation of the processing of the collected data and its application to the concrete facts that are intended to be realized.

First, it must be identified which social databases are configured as obtaining the most reliable data and those whose accuracy is necessary for the purpose desired by the tax agencies. It should be seen that if we talk about data related to philosophical, political, or even health issues, they, still reaching a nature of sensitive data, are not relevant (at first analysis) to the tax purposes pursued by the tax services. On the contrary, if we talk about personal data hosted in databases such as YouTube, Facebook, Instagram, or even pages like Only Fans where it is possible to glimpse manifestations of wealth, even in directly or indirectly. Thus, the first phase consists in the identification of the databases and data that are really necessary in the face of the desiderates pursued, seeking a task of previous prognosis that aims to identify the data and their collection for further treatment compared to the purpose that is intended to be *realized*, concretely the search for material truth in tax matters.

Second, when identifying which databases are to be collected from taxpayers' personal data, a general and objective identification of the criteria that taxpayers will be selected will be identified, and there can be no discretionary, discriminatory, or attentive action here of fundamental principles such as the principle of equality, the dignity of the human person or proportionality. Often, the use of these instruments lacks the use of artificial intelligence and existing information and communication systems, as these allow a maximized processing of data and information almost instantaneously, not being possible by the human resources that the Tax Administration has the treatment and accomplishment of this task in a timely manner, or at least without neglecting other tasks as or more important than this. Thus, it is necessary that intelligent systems that select the databases, the data to be collected and the selection of taxpayers be programmed with algorithms that allow to comply with the primacy of good faith, equality, the dignity of the human person and respect for proportionality, under penalty of illegality of the procedure.

Third, and carried out all the planning under the collection of the personal *data* of the tax obliged, the tasks mentioned above should be carried out in order to obtain the necessary information and give it the treatment that is appropriate to the desired desiderates. Thus, at this stage, it will be necessary to collect the desired personal data in order for them to be stored in the databases that the administrations have in order to give it further processing.

Fourth, the data collected and stored will be processed by the competent bodies and may serve to create profiles of risk sectors or activities whose aptitude may be tended to be aimed at the practice of acts of evasion and tax fraud, as well as the creation of profiles aimed at a certain class of taxpayers whose aptitude is identical. However, they can also serve to detect possible artifice systems created by taxpayers or specialists that aim solely at deferring or dishonoring the tax liability due (Sanches, 2007).

Fifth and lastly, based on the processing of personal data collected and stored, subsequent acts will be carried out that will allow the mitigation of pathological situations of the tax legal relationship, correcting the tax situation as if there had never been any noncompliance on the part of the tax obliged. It will seek to adopt the measures considered necessary and appropriate to respond to the mechanisms of tax evasion and fraud, in order to act in accordance with the primacy of seeking material truth and taxation according to the demonstrated contributory capacity and that deserves attention from the legal and tax rules. In this way, action is achieved faster, appropriate, and proportionate to existing interests, the methods used by both parties, and the necessary corrective or safeguard measures.

6.5   THE POSITION OF TAXPAYERS FACING SOCIAL ANALYTICS BY THE TAX ADMINISTRATION

Conceived the ontology and systemtology of social analytics from the perspective of the tax system, it is up to us to analyze the repercussions that it assumes for taxpayers and their legal sphere, since we will be faced with a real action that is assumed to be possibly harmful to the rights and interests legally protected of these.

First, we must take into account that the collection of data and information allows the creation of highly detailed profiles about people and their quality, being especially problematic when it concerns an individualized person, or the data processed relate to an individualizable person in whom decisions will resonate especially. This legal figure is now enshrined as a figure belonging to the right of things and the protection of personal data, which is an important matter on the rise in the legal area, given its relevance in the economic, social, and legal world, and the need for protection of data subjects and the profile created by that data subject.

The notion of profiling is currently given by the new General Data Protection Regulation, adopted by Regulation (EU) 2016/679 of the European Parliament and the Council, April 27, 2016, which can be defined, in accordance with Article 4(4), as "any form of automated processing of personal data consisting in using such personal data to assess certain personal aspects of a natural person, in particular to analyze or predict aspects related to his or her professional performance, his economic situation, health, personal preferences, interests, reliability, behaviour, location or travel." However, as the Article 29 working group stated: "Automated decisions can be made with or without profiling; profiling can take place without making automated decisions. However, profiling and automated decision-making are not necessarily separate activities. Something that starts off as a simple automated decision-making process could become one based on profiling, depending upon how the data is used" (DATA, Guidelines on Automated individual decision-making and Profiling for the purposes of Regulation 2016/679 2017).

As discussed, from this legal definition can be removed three substantive requirements necessary for a given performance to have classified as profiling, namely: (i) must be a form of automated treatment, (ii) must be carried out on personal data, (iii) and its purpose should be to assess the personal aspects of a natural person. In other words, it can be said, in brief terms, that profiling turns out to be the possibility of making decisions based solely on the processing of personal data, which are intended to assess economic, personal or social aspects with a view to evaluating future acts that may be carried out by the data subject. This definition of profile can range from the analysis of the data to assume the income that a person will obtain in a given fiscal year, to assess his economic situation or even to assess the possibility of acting with a view to concealing income in countries or territories more fiscally favorable. For example, on the basis of information obtained through the automatic exchange of information and the information obtained through internal standards, the profile of a certain taxpayer who, often investing in the purchase and sale of real estate and yielding them by way of lease, removing the fruits obtained from it, will be easy to realize that he will obtain real estate income, and must be declared for tax purposes, even if the income is obtained by real estate located in any other state, provided that the holder of the same is resident here. If the taxpayer concerned does not declare any income in the category due, the Tax Administration may, based on the information obtained, automatically decide on the procedural and procedural acts due for the omission of this declarative obligation of the tax liability.

All these policies created by domestic legislation, but also by the European Union itself, thus make available through the processing of the information provided a very precise and assertive profile on the standard of certain tax obliged, and can, based on this profile created, be correlated certain activities that may be attributable to the data subject. Of course, such a profile of taxpayers appears to be of great value in combating the harmful practices of international tax evasion and fraud, because it allows, in a timely manner, to combat and prevent conduct that is in conformity with the desiderates sought by the states (Politou, 2019).

However, such a possibility cannot be left to the discretion of the entities responsible for the processing of personal data, because in the case of the definition of putative acts of taxpayers, without remaining the same and entering a purely subjective domain, these conducts may be harmful to taxpayers' fundamental rights and actions, and thus a balance point should be found that allows both legal positions to be satisfied (Politou, 2019).

For these reasons, it became necessary for the law to regulate these actions, which, tended to arise within the various entities engaged in the treatment of these metadata for the determination of conduct or practice of the data subjects, thus combating possible abusive practices of their privacy. It had therefore become necessary for data subjects to be able to know this profiling, allowing them to inspect, correct, or request the payment of any data that were mishandled, that is, in noncompliance with the guiding legal principles of this matter. To this end, the new General Data Protection Regulation, adopted by Regulation (EU) 2016/679 of the European Parliament and the Council of April 27, 2016, establishes a set of measures and instruments aimed mainly at the legal regulation of this legal institute, bringing it closer to the data and information subjects themselves that serve as the basis for profiling and subsequent automated decision-making.

First, the General Data Protection Regulation determines that profiling can only occur when appropriate measures are applied that make the protection of the rights, freedoms, and guarantees of data subjects, that is, only when the legal requirements are met, the processing of the data can be done with the design of profiling and decision-making based on them. In this sense, the profile of a particular taxpayer may only be carried out when the taxpayer is informed of the decision that may be taken as a result of the profile created and when that decision is directed at the production of legal effects that significantly affect his legal sphere. As anchored in Article 22(1) of that legal document, "the data subject has the right not to be subject to any decision taken solely on the basis of automated processing, including profiling, which has effects in his legal sphere *or affects him significantly in a similar way*" (we stress). In other words, the processing of data and automated decision-making based on profiles created by the Tax Administration can only be carried out when, cumulatively, three material requirements are met, namely:

1. The taxpayer is informed that the decision taken automatically may affect his legal sphere.
2. The tax obligor may exercise, in a timely manner, the right of the decision taken to be made with human intervention, in particular by the data controller.
3. The processing is authorized by the legislation in force.

This is because, axiologically, recital 60 of the General Data Protection Regulation states that the principles of fair and transparent processing require the data subject to be informed of the data processing operation and its purposes and must also be informed of the definition of profiles and the consequences that come from it. Furthermore, recital 63 goes in the same direction, stating that each data subject should have the right to know and be informed, inter alia, of the purposes for which personal data are processed, where possible from the period during which the data are processed, the identity of the recipients of the personal data, the logic underlying the possible automatic processing of personal data and, at least when it is based on profiling, its consequences.

However, recital 71 of the General Data Protection Regulation is one that effectively turns out to be more assertive and actionable in its statements, since it states that the data subject should have the right not to be subject to a decision, which may include a measure, which assesses personal aspects concerning him, which is based solely on automated processing and which produces legal effects concerning him or significantly affects him or affects him significantly in a similar manner, such as the automatic refusal of an electronic credit application or electronic recruitment practices without any human intervention. Such processing includes profiling by means of any form of automated processing of personal data to assess personal aspects relating to a natural person, in particular the analysis and forecasting of aspects related to professional performance, economic situation, health, preferences or personal interests, reliability or behaviour, location or travel of the data subject, when it produces legal effects that concern him or her significantly affect it in a similar way. However, decision-making on the basis of such processing, including profiling, should be permitted if expressly authorised by Union or Member State law applicable to the controller, including for the purposes of fraud control and prevention and tax evasion, conducted in accordance with the regulations, standards and recommendations of the Union institutions or national control bodies, and to ensure the safety and reliability of the service provided by the controller, or if it is necessary for the conclusion or performance of a contract between the data subject and the controller, or with the explicit consent of the controller. In any case, such processing should be accompanied by appropriate safeguards, which should include specific information to the data subject and the right to obtain human intervention, to express his point of view, to obtain an explanation of the decision taken following that assessment and to challenge the decision. This measure should not concern a child.

However, we must stress that such a legal institute is configured, in the field of combating tax evasion and fraud, as an instrument that should be used to the fullest of the possibilities allowed, but without neglecting the legally protected interests of tax data subjects. For these reasons, it is necessary to state that the data subject enjoys a set of rights that he may assert before the Tax Administration, taking into account the existence of such processing by the tax authorities, as well as that the processing of the data should be done in compliance with the *criteria* mentioned above.

Cousin, we must take into account that the taxpayer should be notified of the content of the automated decisions that may be taken based on the creation of profiles based on the analysis of the tax data processed by the Administration, which may require the updating, rectification, or payment of the information when they are in conformity with the reality that they aim to demonstrate (see Article 13(2) (f) of the General Data Protection Regulation); second, the tax authority should be given the possibility to consult all the information that the Tax Administration has on it, and it must be provided, without delay smashes or associated costs, the information requested, whenever and when it does not aim at the burden or dilation of the desiderates pursued by the Administration (see Article 15(h) of the General Data Protection Regulation).

So, the processing of tax data by the Tax Administration and the creation of profiles based on automated decision-making that prove necessary to combat tax evasion and fraud can only be carried out when the rules relating to the protection of privacy and personal data of tax-obliged people are provided and complied with, using a set of instruments that can assert against the misuse of this legal instrument. The preparation of the same will thus involve informing the taxpayer of the existence of the profiles developed and may necessitate that no decision be made simply on the basis of computerized services and taking into consideration the data processed and the profiles established. All treatment and decision-making made in violation of the preceding provisions shall be considered unlawful treatment and, as such, all subsequent prosecutions based on those choices and profiles generated in violation of the preceding principles shall be nullified. Second, it remains to be seen whether the legitimacy with which the competent tax administration is used to collect the necessary data and treat it for the purposes under consideration is ontologically attributed by the desiderates and for the publicist purpose that the tax obligation has underlying.

It should be observed that it continues to serve the public interest, particularly via the collection of unpaid taxes, the examination of compliance with tax duties, and even the assistance and cooperation provided to taxpayers. The GDPR addresses the legality of administrations along this axiological route, and data processing can be carried out without the agreement of the data subject, since the pursuit of a public interest authorizes the competent authority to collect and process the data for these reasons (see Article 6(1)(e) of the GDPR) (Da Silva and Rocha, 2019).

It should be noted, however, that the data are processed for purposes other than those originally intended, because if they were freely placed by the holder on pages whose opening it allows in a more or less conditioned manner, it must be considered whether the processing for purposes other than those originally intended will be legitimate.

To resolve this challenge, the GDPR eventually authorizes treatment for distinct purposes if the tax administration is entitled under the norms of union law or domestic legislation of the Member State, as provided for in Article 6(3)(b) of the GDPR, "the purpose of the processing shall be determined on that legal basis or, with regard to the treatment referred to in point (e), it shall be necessary to perform public-interest functions or to exercise the public authority in which the controller is vested." Furthermore, paragraph 4 of that legal precept which may be processed by personal data for purposes other than those for which personal data was collected without the consent of the data subject or on the basis of provisions of Union or Member State law, provided that they constitute a necessary and proportionate measure in a democratic society to safeguard the objectives referred to in Article 23(1) of the same European legislation.

Thus, the processing of taxpayers' personal data collected in databases constituting social networks and which are partially accessible to any person may be collected and processed for purposes other than those initially shared in public by its holder, provided that such processing is necessary to safeguard public interests pursued by EU law or the legislation of the Member State. As the pursuit of the public interest and compliance with the tax system as one of the main desiderates of the State in order to answer tax and extra-tax issues, the processing for purposes other than those originally provided for at the time of the transfer of the data will be shown to be legitimate.

Third, we must raise genuine questions of proportionality inherent in the collection and processing of personal data, because it should be seen that, while the legitimacy for collection is legal in the face of desires to combat pathological phenomena such as tax evasion or fraud, this legitimacy does not prove discretionary and limitless. It should be noted that the GDPR says that the processing of personal data must be necessary and reasonable to the objectives pursued by the data controller in this regard.

Without our objective on the objective and teleological content of the aforementioned principle of personal data, we must, however, take into account that the collection of personal data by the tax authorities should be guided by criteria of adequacy and proportionality. In other words, we are faced with a real guideline that orders it to collect data that is strictly necessary for the objectives to be achieved, preventing measures and actions that are not in conformity with those mentioned. To this end, article 5 (1) (c) provides that the processing of data is lawful when "appropriate, relevant and limited to what is necessary for the purposes for which they are processed." This seeks to minimize the data against the purposes pursued, only by legitimizing the collection and processing of data which are strictly necessary for the desiderates pursued.

Consequently, even if legitimized to that end, the GDPR ends up by deeming in point (b) of Article 6(3) that "the purpose of the processing is determined on that legal basis (...) it should be necessary for the exercise of public interest functions or the exercise of the public authority vested in the controller," adding that "Union or Member State law must respond to an objective of public interest and be proportionate to the legitimate objective pursued." It ends up continuing the aforementioned, because the legitimacy granted through the granting of a public interest does not grant an unlimited and discretionary power, because the collection and processing of the personal data of taxpayers end up being guided by criteria of adequacy and proportionality in relation to the aforementioned purposes of the entity responsible for the processing. For this reason, it should be concluded here that the legitimacy that is conferred on tax administrations to collect and process taxpayers' personal data must comply with criteria that respect the primacy of the dignity of the human person and the protection of trust, which stand as fundamental in a democratic rule of law.

6.6 CONCLUSION

We end by emphasizing something that has traveled absconded in each of the pointed reflections: one is not devoid of magical solutions that enable the author to offer the definitive solution for a quarrel that begins, but that arises to last in the future. It is intended solely to make a contributions problem which, although *sui generis*, is described as relevant in the legal system given the specificities and vicissitudes that each of the counterpoints presents. To arrogate us with certainties on a ground that is considered "swampy" and uneven is, at the very least, to assume pride and arrogance.

However, some premises that are important to conclude can affirm them: first, social analytics stands as one of the *instruments that* appears tended to be a tool of great relevance for the realization of tax interests by the state, since they constitute important sources of data and information that will allow, when well used, to measure important manifestations of wealth by taxpayers. However, there will be no need to find mathematical and exact sciences to find answers to this problem, and it should be investigated on a case-by-case basis to find a better solution to the problem posed, in view of the legal problems that arise in its implementation.

A second premise to be concluded arises in the opposition and difficult balance of legal texts, because the implementation of this instrument, although innovative, questions about axiological values that cast doubt on its legitimacy in the face of the current legal primacy. For this reason, we walk with some the positive notes and try to find solutions and formulate proposals according not only to the legal texts, but also to the coherence of the legal system as a whole and one, without contradictions and hierarchically well organized and equitably distributed.

We cannot, therefore, live chained to platonic ideals, dogmatizing an ideal world and ignoring the throbbing of reality and associated problems, thus trying to provide a support of some solutions *that very humbly seem* to suit the interests of all the actors.

KEYWORDS

- **big data**
- **tax law**
- **personal data**
- **tax personal data**
- **intelligence artificial**
- **tax evasion**
- **tax fraud**
- **profiling**
- **predictive models**

REFERENCES

Abraham, M.; Catarino, J. O Uso da Inteligência Artificial na Aplicação do Direito Público: O Caso Especial da Cobrança Dos Créditos Tributários—Um Estudo Objetivado nos Casos Brasileiro e Português. *e-Pública: Revista Eletrónica de Direito Público 193*, 2019.

Bathaee, Y. The Artificial Intelligence Black Box and the Failure of Intent and Causation. *Harv. J. Law Technol.* **2008,** *31* (2, Spring), 890–938.

Cockfield, A. Protecting Taxpayer Privacy Rights Under Enhanced Cross-Border Tax Information Exchange: Toward a Multilateral Taxpayer Bill of Rights. *Univ. Br. Columbia Law Rev.* **2010,** *42.*

Cockfield, A. Big Data and Secrecy. *18 Fla. Tax Rev. 483*; University of Florida, 2016.

Da Silva, H. F. *Privatização do Sistema de Gestão Fiscal*; Coimbra Editora: Coimbra, 2014.

Da Silva, H. F., Da Rocha, J. F. *Teorial Geral da Relação Jurídica Tributária*; Almedina: Coimbra, 2019.

Hildebrandt, M. Who Is Profiling Who? Invisible Visibility. In *Reinventing Data Protection?*; Gutwirth S., Poullet Y., De Hert P., de Terwangne C., Nouwt S., Eds.; Springer: Cham, 2009.

Holmes, D. *Big Data: A Very Short Introduction*; Oxford University Press: Oxford, 2017.

Katal, A., Wazid, M., Goudar, R. H. Big Data: Issues, Challenges, Tools and Good Practices. In *2013 Sixth International Conference on Contemporary Computing (IC3)*, 2013; pp 404–409.

Politou, E. Profiling Tax and Financial Behaviour with Big Data under the GDPR. *Comput. Law Secur. Rev.* **2019.** doi:10.1016/j.clsr.

Riahi, Y. Big Data and Big Data Analytics: Concepts, Types and Technologies. *Int. J. Res. Eng.* **2018,** *5* (9), 524–528.

Ribeiro, J. S.; Carrero, J. Limite ao Uso da Inteligência Artificial no Controlo Fiscal: A Experiência Francesa (Décision no. 2019-796 DC). *Cadernos de Justiça Tributária n. 26, Out-Dez*, 2019.

Salvatore, S. Diritto e Intelligenza artificiale. Alcune riflessioni nell'ambito del paradigma argomentativo. *Inf. Dir, XXV Ann.* **1999,** *VIII* (1).

Sanches, J. L. S. *Os Limites ao Planeamento Fiscal*; Coimbra Editora: Coimbra, 2007.

Warren, S.; Brandeis, L. The Right of Privacy. *Harv. Law Rev.* **1890,** *IV* (December, 5).

CHAPTER 7

IS THE INTELLIGENT PARTICIPATORY BUDGET (i-PB) THE NEXT GENERATION OF DEMOCRACY AND GOVERNANCE?

JOHNNY CAMELLO[1] and MARIA JOSÉ SOUSA[2]

[1]*School of Sociology and Public Policy (ESPP), ISCTE—University Institute of Lisbon, Lisbon, Portugal*

[2]*Instituto Universitário de Lisboa, Lisbon, Portugal*

ABSTRACT

In the same way that artificial intelligence is revolutionizing the market/consumers relationship, it will also revolutionize the relationship between public organizations/citizens. Its ability to process large amounts of data and machine learning will enable the emergence of intelligence that will be able to unite the biological, the physical, and the digital. More than 30 years of participatory budgeting experience have already been available worldwide. During this journey, it survived political sabotage, and every year the number of communities that adopt it as a mechanism for managing and administering democratic collective demands and public budgets is growing. This chapter analyzes the evolution of the incorporation of new technologies in participatory budgeting processes over time and how artificial intelligence will impact it. The literature on the two themes will be reviewed, seeking to project the application of technology in the structural phases of participatory budgeting. The result of this merger is the emergence of the

Incorporating AI Technology in the Service Sector: Innovations in Creating Knowledge, Improving Efficiency, and Elevating Quality of Life. Maria José Sousa, Subhendu Kumar Pani, Francesca Dal Mas, & Sérgio Sousa (Eds.)

© 2024 Apple Academic Press, Inc. Co-published with CRC Press (Taylor & Francis)

intelligent Participatory Budget (i-PB) that will have the ability to integrate multilevel (local, regional, national, and international) and multidimensional (social, economic, political, technological, and environmental) participatory budgeting processes. Smart participatory budgeting will transform the world into a global village.

7.1   INTRODUCTION

The Participatory Budget (PB) was born in the city of Porto Alegre, Brazil, in 1989, 1 year after the promulgation of the new Federal Constitution that reestablished democracy in the country after 21 years of military dictatorship. The new constitutional text allowed states and municipalities to create mechanisms of popular participation in public management, especially the PB, which allowed citizens/taxpayers to act in the phases of preparation and execution of the public budget in a complementary way to traditional political representation (Fedozzi, 2002). The PB model from Porto Alegre, for its pioneering, longevity, and innovation, has become a national and international reference, recognized by international organizations such as the UN and the World Bank as a practice of good governance and popular participation (Camello, 2019; Fedozzi, 2002).

Currently, the PB is used as a budget management tool in thousands of cities around the world, as well as in schools and other institutions (Participatory Budgeting Project, 2016). The experiences of PBs developed for more than three decades—in heterogeneous social, economic, cultural, and political contexts—have shown that their practice, in a way, has provided the strengthening of communities and promotion of citizenship in the sociopolitical dimension, changing the relationship of the population with the traditional model of governance. For, while communities were empowered in decision-making, it was also evidenced the dimensioning of the coresponsibilities of citizens concerning the application of public resources (Fedozzi, 2002; Matheus and Ribeiro, 2010) and the maturing of the democratic debate between community and government in the definitions of budget investment priorities.

In the public organizational dimension, various years of implementation of the PB reinforced the perception that it promoted the decentralization and plurality of decision-making actors, significantly reducing the risk of patrimonialism practices and corruption in governments and making decisions concerning the priorities of public budgets more equitable, impersonal, and democratic. In addition, the PB has demonstrated strong resilience to the various crises and attempts to boycott and sabotage promoted by politicians and policies during all these years, with a view to the continued growth of its adoption as a mechanism of democratic citizen participation held account-able in public budgets around the world. Perhaps it is because, at the end of the day, the PB concerns the old human dichotomy that is the management of their collective demands in a territory with the resources available.

With the advent of the emergence of information and communication technologies (ICTs) in the late 1990s, the PB became also digital, incorporating these technologies into its operating processes, either only as support or as an electronic participation channel. The use in the process of technologies such as applications for high-speed mobile telephony, Internet of Things, Internet of Everything, big data, and artificial intelligence (AI), design transformative and impactful scenarios of how citizens and governments will manage and administrate collective demands and public investments.

The continuous incorporation of technologies into people's routines since the late 1990s has provoked a real revolution at the social, economic, and political levels. The migration from "analog life" to digital has given people access to products, services, information, and media in an almost unrestricted, unlimited, and freeway. This condition has radically changed the market/consumer relationship for goods and services, as well as govern-ment/citizen for the definition and execution of public policies (Camello, 2019; Neves, 2001; Novelli, 2006; Sæbøa et al., 2008).

The capacity for information, communication, interaction, reach, speed, and mainly mobilization of individuals through ICTs forced the market to constantly adapt its commercial, financial, logistics, and ethical productive strategies for commercialization of goods and services. Similarly, even with delay and with a lower speed than the market, public management and politics had to adapt and reshape themselves to deal over this period with much better informed, plural, demanding, participatory, and supervisory citizens, and in particular, with a fast and disseminated individual and collective power of manifestation through digital tools, provoking in both the market and government, new questions, ignorance, and confusion about which way to follow the speed of technological evolution and its economic and sociopolitical impact (Harari, 2016; Sæbøa et al., 2008; Sampaio and Peixoto, 2014).

There is evidence that the first time that ICTs were used as a tool in PB processes occurred in the Brazilian cities of Porto Alegre, RS, and Ipatinga, MG, in 2001. In the case of Porto Alegre, the city council used the internet as an information resource and consultation of its electronic Participatory Budget (e-PB) by creating a page on the city's website. Through this place, the population and the participants of the PB could inform themselves about the agenda of the phases of the process, as well as follow the stage of execution of the projects chosen in the previous PBs. The Ipatingian experience took a step forward in the use of ICTs in its PB, because, in addition to the informative and consultative functions of the website, the city made available to the participants of the process and citizens the possibility of sending through the internet—either on the city's website or in computer terminals placed in public places—project proposals for the municipal PB.

In 2006, the city of Belo Horizonte presented an innovation that in a way became a historical milestone for the evolution of e-PB, the use of the Internet in the voting phase of the city's PB projects. Proposals for regional projects that could only be voted on the internet were defined with the support of the Committee for the accompaniment and oversight of the e-PB.

Another important Brazilian experience for the evolution of the e-PB was that of the city of Recife, PE, in the northeast region of the country. In the city's e-PB in 2008, the population can vote on the Internet and electronic ballot boxes, in the list of priorities chosen in the regional and thematic plenary sessions (Ferreira, 2012; Matheus and Ribeiro, 2010; Sampaio, 2016; Sampaio and Peixoto, 2014).

In general, ICTs have been used since the 2000s in different stages of the PBs to facilitate the participation of citizens, as well as for the management of the phases of the PB itself (Sampaio, 2016). In this sense, there are already several international experiences of fully digital PBs with their advantages and disadvantages in relation to only face-to-face OPs (Sampaio and Peixoto, 2014). This issue has been the subject of a wide and intense debate on the e-OP.

Many people argue that e-PB should not be a total replacement option for face-to-face PBs. From their point of view, the e-PB should be used only in a mixed way or complementary to the traditional face-to-face PB (Ritchie, 2016). The arguments used to defend this point of view are the most varied. However, the most common is that the e-PB does not promote physical interaction, and in this sense, does not strengthen the affective bonds and the feeling of community or belonging of the participants of the process. Others, on the other hand, argue otherwise. They believe that the e-PB is inclusive because it affects a population that wants to participate in the process, however, using the internet and mobile telephony technologies as an option (Sampaio, 2016).

The fact is that with the dissemination of the use of new technologies by citizens and governments, the growth of e-PB has been confirmed over the last two decades. Countries, such as Germany, Portugal, and Brazil, lead the initiatives to promote e-PB as a form of e-participation and e-deliberation. Whether mixed, complimentary, or digital, the e-PB is increasingly gaining strength in the preference of citizens as a powerful tool of participation and democratic deliberation (Sampaio, 2016).

A good example to illustrate this growth was the PB 2021 of the city of Tallinn, capital of Estonia, considered the most digital society in the world. The city's e-PB was structured to receive the proposals of projects from citizens online and by e-mail. The projects selected to compete for the preference of the communities received 19,570 votes, and 94.90% of them were electronic votes (ERR, 2021).

In this sense, the performance of three motivating forces for the use of new technologies in PB processes can be seen: the first of a modernizing character of the managerial and administrative processes of public organizations, the second of a contextual nature about technological development and innovation and its incorporation into people's daily routines and the third of the need for public organizations to adapt their services and democratic processes to an increasingly hypertechnological society (Sampaio, 2016).

Therefore, it is understood that the incorporation of new technologies into the processes of the PB, whether or not they are wanted, will occur naturally and its intensity and speed related to the technological, sociopolitical, and economic reality of each country (Pogrebinschi, 2017). In general, today the technologies used in e-PB—web tools, mobile applications, electronic devices—are basic, limiting the digitization of the bureaucratic management and administrative routines of traditional PB processes, as well as in the stages of proposition and voting of projects and programs. However, the integrated use of AI in the PB can revolutionize not only PB processes but also the relationship between citizens and public organizations.

7.2   ARTIFICIAL INTELLIGENCE

According to Luger's definition (2013, p. 1), AI is "the branch of computer science that deals with the automation of intelligent behavior" (Luger, 2013, p. 1) being classified into four categories of systems by Stuart J. Russell and Peter Norvig (2020, pp. 2–4): those who think as human; those who act like humans; those who think rationally and those who act rationally. However, to analyze the impact of the use of AI on PB, we will focus on the development of AI systems that act rationally, that is, those that act in a way that achieves the best results, or when there is doubt, the best-expected result (Russell and Norvig, 2020).

AI's ability to process an enormous amount of data is the central part of this technology because it far exceeds that of the human brain (Aldama, 2019). The evolution of the power of computers and the creation of the World Wide Web favored the creation of an abundance of data, known as Big Data. This "mass" of data consists of trillions of text words, billions of images and hours of speech and video, large amounts of genomic and vehicle tracking data, *clickstream*, and social networks. AI, through the use of specially designed learning algorithms, can produce information, which at first would be impossible to compile by conventional forms of research and data analysis (Russell and Norvig, 2020). According to Lee (2019, p. 22) "the data 'trains' the program to recognize patterns, providing many examples, and computational power allows the program to analyze these examples at high speed."

Currently, the public sector is the sector that holds the most data, and at the same time, the one that uses AI less to take advantage of it. This demonstrates the enormous potential of its use in the sector (*Foster Government Innovation*, s.d.). In this sense, several countries and international organizations such as the UN, OECD, and the European Union (EU) have started to treat AI as a strategic and unpredictable technology for global economic development, and because of this, in recent years they have defined principles and regulations for its use (European Commission, Joint Research Centre, 2020; OECD Working Papers, 2019; Ochigame, 2019).

There are already several cases around the world of the use of AI in the public sector. In the EU, for example, numerous experiences of its application have been identified in image recognition solutions, natural language processing, pattern recognition, robotic process automation, and unclassified robotics. The expectation of those involved in these projects is to achieve in general several benefits such as significant gain in quality, effectiveness, and consistency of services provided to citizens, improvement of formatting and implementation of public policies, transparency in the use of taxpayer money, and interaction and active participation of the population in decision-making (Misuraca et al., 2020).

However, the literature and empirical cases of the use of AI in the PB process are rare, and, why not say, nonexistent. What we have is a vast literature and case studies on the use of new technologies in the phases of the PB such as e-petition, e-participation, and e-vote. Therefore, to analyze the impact of the use of AI in the PB it is necessary to project existing experiences of its use in other areas—both in the public and private sectors—in the context and dynamics of the PB and to verify the probable trends and future scenarios arising from this use. However, to take advantage of the data processing power of AI, it is important to work on multidimensional (social, economic, political, technological, and environmental) and multilevel (local, regional, national and international) perspectives and data.

As we have mentioned above, in the end, the PB concerns territory, population, common needs, resources, and the management of these variables by group organizations, a millenary and constant need in the evolution of the human race. Understanding this logic is very important to analyze the impact of the use of AI on the PB, and indeed, on the very structure of the state as a collective organization to administer and manage collective demands. Because only in this way can you understand that even in the 21st century, we continue to do the same thing that our ancestors did 12,000 years ago. However, in an unprecedented social, economic, political, environmental, and technological context that with the use of AI in the PB can completely change the way we manage our collective demands in the next 30 years.

7.3   INTELLIGENT PARTICIPATORY BUDGETING

It is in the territories and their respective populations that the PBs are executed. That is, they are the platforms for processes. In many PB experiences around the world, the division of territory and population is delimited at the local, regional level, and in some countries such as Portugal, South Korea, and Taiwan national (Dias and Júlio, 2019). In this sense, the PB process fosters the debate of ideas and projects at all territorial and population levels, producing an abundance of valuable data concerning the demands, projects, and multilevel budgets, ranging from asphalt paving of a street in a neighborhood to the construction of a large interstate highway.

These data bring in their "DNA" intrinsic characteristics of the collective needs of the populations, from the small village in a remote region to the entire national territory. Data represent the social, cultural, economic, and environmental diversities of each group of individuals and the group of these groups. The power of algorithms to search for patterns in the data and associate them with series and results enables the intelligent Participatory Budget (i-PB) to produce unprecedented and impossible evaluations so far by conventional methods of data analysis. And we can do a lot more. Just as ICTs have eliminated geographical distances and barriers to information and communication of individuals, the i-PB can eliminate geographical, linguistic, technical, and financial limitations of public and private organizations in managing the collective demands of populations at local, regional, national, and international levels.

However, to see the size and possibilities of the i-PB, it is necessary to rethink the concept, methodology, and platform, in general, of traditional PBs processes. It is necessary a total change of mentality, attitude, and the notion of amplitude about its dynamics and objective. Because the i-PB is a process within the process, in an unprecedented historical context. The i-PB is directly related to the process of change that we are experiencing now as the structural, behavioral, and environmental transformation of society, a new global order, more fragmented, the expansion of individual power, and the radical change of the way we will produce and consume in the future imposed by the fourth industrial revolution (Camello, 2019; Schwab, 2018).

Strategic planning is essential for any organization, whether public or private. It is through it that they can formulate short-, medium-, and long-term strategies to operationalize the present and design the future. They seek through him the continuous learning of what they are, do, and why they do it (Bryson, 2004; Poister, 2010; Vieg, 1942). Based on this, it is possible, at first, to see the i-PB as a tool for planning, managing, and administering collective demands that coordinate an economic, political, social, cultural, technological, and environmental digital biosphere. For this, it uses structured dynamics and logic of operation, both in the production of data and in its use by algorithms. This i-PB mechanism should be led by techniques and methods of planning, execution, and management of projects that optimize both the generation of information by project variables, as well as the way to cross and integrate them for the production of possible scenarios and simulations of results by AI.

In this sense, it proposes a platform for the implementation of the decentralized and integrated i-PB at the same time, with continuous and discontinuous territories. Another important issue to be highlighted is the question of the dimensions of action of the i-PB. Based on the processing capacity of large amounts of AI data, i-PB can act much more widely and in multiple dimensions simultaneously, shared and integrated (social, cultural, economic, technological, and environmental).

7.4 TERRITORY, POPULATION, AND COLLECTIVE DEMANDS

As so, the territory and the population are the basis of the i-PB processes, because they are the ones that produce the data that will be processed by AI and transformed into information. In this sense, it is important to establish updated prerogatives concerning the dynamics of territory, population, and collective demands management. According to Camello (2019) "there is a Buddhist proverb that says: instead of wanting to cover the world with carpets, wear sandals and that in medicine there is a maxim that states that healthy cells form a healthy body." In this sense, the i-PB assumes that the more decentralized the platforms at the level of management, administration, and representation, the richer the intrinsic information will be the data generated by the process.

Thus, in a broader view, the mechanism of operation of the i-PB performs better in modern public organizations (states), in which the creation and implementation of public policies are *bottom-up,* horizontal, decentralized, and supported by freedom of opinion and pluralism of ideas (Amaral, 2010; Camello, 2019). This model of public organization brings the bond between government and citizens closer together, favoring local initiatives (Caupers, 1994) and systematically recognizes, according to Reigado (2000, p. 177), the "sociocultural peculiarities of each human leaf, by which there is no single or exportable formula that guarantees the referral to sustainable development."

After the platforms (territory and population), the next step in the i-PB's strategic planning is the definition of collective demands that will be executed. But what are collective demands?

According to Camello (2019):

> It is the sum of the individual demands of citizens for public services and apparatus, financed through the apportionment of their costs (taxes), among the individuals who make up this social nucleus. Demands can be current, strategic, or emergency. Short, medium, or long term. Local, regional, national, or international. Integrated or isolated at the geopolitical level. In the structural aspect, they are always multidimensional and processed by organizations (State, NGOs, and private companies), responsible for producing and delivering to their financiers, citizens, the services, and public equipment requested. (pp 40–41)

In an i-PB process, collective demands are identified through the use of sequential realization of debates, suggestions, and definition of ideas and projects of each level, which, when finalized, will become data to be analyzed by algorithms (Table 7.1). First, we work on the local i-PBs, then the regional, national, and international ones consecutively. Always remembering that i-PB works with data production and processing by AI, so it is important that this sequence is respected. Because only in this way, it is possible for algorithms to identify patterns and connections in multilevel and multidimensional demands, to be shared and integrated at the technical, financial, execution, inspection, and analysis levels. This dynamic can be operationalized by multiple actors and organizations as long as data processing is done first at each level and then shared and integrated. Thus, the result of the identification of the collective demands of the process by the algorithms will express the needs from the population of a street to that of the entire international community.

TABLE 7.1   Multilevel and Multidimensional Collective Demands Dynamic.

Multidimensional collective demands			
Location	Local	Regional	National	International
Priority	1	2	3	4
Term	Short	Short	Short	Short
	Medium	Medium	Medium	Medium
	Long	Long	Long	Long
Integration	Global multilevel integration			

Author: Johnny Camello.

Although this analysis may seem complex, considering the multiple levels and multiple dimensions involved in the process, in fact, it is not. AI can eliminate any geographic, linguistic, economic, logistical, technological, and information barriers to data processing. At the same time, they can instantly and accurately identify the possibilities for optimizing material, technical, technological, human, and financial resources, from the local to the global level. And then, propose technical, operational, logistical, and budgetary solutions that make each demand viable, whether isolated or integrated. The result is the possible multilevel and multidimensional scenarios of viable and executable projects and programs to be evaluated by the participants in the process and later voted on by the population. This is possible through the process of machine learning which is the ability of AI to improve its performance with experience (Tegmark, 2020).

Regarding the management of the execution, inspection, and account-ability of projects and programs chosen by the population in the i-PB, the AI greatly facilitates these tasks. The algorithms manage, through the control variables of the schedules, expenses, resources, risks, and budgets of the processes, to monitor these actions with surgical precision in a much more effective and transparent way. Another benefit is the feasibility of active participation and involvement of the population in these stages of the process. Through the use of multiple analog and digital information and communication channels, i-PB can interact individually and collectively with all community members and at all levels. In this way, it is possible to monitor and inspect the execution of the i-PB by the entire population, who can closely monitor the performance of the participants in the process, as well as the commitment to deliver the services and public equipment required.

7.5 CONCLUSION

The i-PB will provide public, private, and nonprofit organizations, in an unprecedented way, the capacity to manage in an integrated, shared, solidary and sustainable way, their territories, resources, and global demands. It is very likely that over time, the i-PB will help to correct social, economic, technological, and environmental imbalances, promoting the development of poor territories and populations and the true distribution of income at a global level. Through the i-PB, it is possible to manage the collective demands of any size of groups of individuals, transforming the world into a large global village. However, the challenges to its implementation are proportionate to its benefits. In addition to the resistance and political sabotage recorded in the PBs last 30 years of history, i-PB needs to address digital security issues and the privacy and protection of citizens' personal data. There are two fundamental issues to be considered for the future development of the i-PB. The first is the awareness of the international community that the environmental, technological, economic, and social threats existing today will only be overcome with global actions, but at the same time, through the strong role of governments in solving basic multidimensional bottlenecks at local levels. The second and most important, identified by James E. Lovelock in 1974 with his Gaia Hypothesis, is the urgent need for human beings' deep understanding that they are part of a living, interconnected, and interdependent biosphere and the pandemic of COVID-19 demonstrated that even being the dominant race on the planet, a simple virus can stop it. The relevance and sociological, economic, political, technological, and environmental impact of this topic needs to be studied in detail in the future to verify the feasibility of its implementation at all geopolitical levels. Finally, this possibility represents the rescue of the genuine ancestral reason for the existence of collective organizations, which has always been to manage the collective demands of populations.

KEYWORDS

- artificial intelligence
- participatory budgeting
- public organizations
- collective demands
- public budget
- income distribution
- administrative decentralization

REFERENCES

Aldama, Z. Surgirá Uma Inteligência Maior Do Que a Humana? *El País*, 2019, julho 29. https://brasil.elpais.com/brasil/2019/07/29/tecnologia/1564354846_969018.html

Bryson, J. M. What to Do When Stakeholders Matter—A Guide to Stakeholder Identification and Analysis Techniques. *Publ. Manage. Rev.* **2004**, *6* (1), 21–53.

Camello, J. *CAPAS: Célula Administrativa Pública Autossustentável: Contributo Para a Gestão da Administração Pública: Uma Visão*, 2019. https://repositorio.iscte-iul.pt/bitstream/10071/19338/1/master_johnny_camello.pdf

Caupers, J. *A Administração Periférica do Estado. Estudo de Ciência da Administração*; Aequitas—Editorial Nacional, 1994.

Dias, N.; Júlio, S. *Trinta anos de Orçamentos Participativos no Mundo. Entre o passado, as Tendências Mais Recentes e os Desafios Futuros*; Epopeia/Oficina, 2019. https://www.oficina.org.pt/30anosopmundo.html

ERR, E. N. *Tallinn Participatory Budget Winning Projects Announced*; ERR, 2021, Fevereiro 4. https://news.err.ee/1608097354/tallinn-participatory-budget-winning-projects-announced

European Commission, Joint Research Centre. *AI Watch, Artificial Intelligence in Public Services: Overview of the Use and Impact of AI in Public Services in the EU*; Publications Office, 2020. https://data.europa.eu/doi/10.2760/039619

Fedozzi, L. J. *O eu e os Outros: A Construção da Consciência Social No Orçamento Participativo de Porto Alegre*, 2002. https://lume.ufrgs.br/handle/10183/85057

Ferreira, D. E. S. *Participação e Deliberação: Análise Do Impacto Dos Usos Das Novas Tecnologias Digitais Na Dinâmica Dos Orçamentos Participativos De Belo Horizonte e Recife*, 2012; p 300.

Foster Government Innovation. The Alan Turing Institute. Recuperado 2 de julho de 2021, s.d.. https://www.turing.ac.uk/research/challenges/foster-government-innovation

Harari, Y. N. *Homo Deus—Uma Breve História do Amanhã*; Companhia das Letras, 2016.

Lee, K.-F. *Inteligência Artificial [Recurso Eletrônico]: Como os Robôs Estão Mudando o Mundo, a Forma Como Amamos, Nos Relacionamos, Trabalhamos e Vivemos*, 1ª; Globo Livros, 2019.

Luger, G. *Inteligência artificial*, 6ª ed.; Pearson Universidades: London, 2013.

Matheus, R.; Ribeiro, M. M. *Case Studies of Digital Participatory Budgeting in Latin America: Models for Citizen Engagement*, 2010, 6.

Misuraca, G.; van Noordt, C.; Boukli, A. The Use of AI in Public Services: Results from a Preliminary Mapping across the EU. In *Proceedings of the 13th International Conference on Theory and Practice of Electronic Governance*, 2020; pp 90–99. https://doi.org/10.1145/3428502.3428513

Neves, A. *Para Uma Cultura de Gestão na Administração Pública*, 2001, 228.

Novelli, A. L. C. R. O Papel Institucional da Comunicação Pública para o Sucesso da Governança. *Organicom* **2006**, *3* (4), 77–89.

OECD Working Papers. Hello, World: Artificial Intelligence and Its Use in the Public Sector; *OECD Working Papers on Public Governance No. 36*; OECD Working Papers on Public Governance, Vol 36, 2019. https://doi.org/10.1787/726fd39d-en

Ochigame, R. *How Big Tech Manipulates Academia to Avoid Regulation*, 2019; p 19.

Participatory Budgeting Project. Next Generation Democracy. *The Participatory Budgeting Project*, 2016. https://www.participatorybudgeting.org/white-paper/

Pogrebinschi, T. *Digital Participatory Budgeting*; LATINNO Dataset, 2017. https://www.latinno.net/en/case/3173/

Poister, T. H. The Future of Strategic Planning in the Public Sector: Linking Strategic Management and Performance. *Publ. Admin. Rev.* **2010**, *9*. https://doi.org/10.1111/j.1540-6210.2010.02284.x

Reigado, F. M. *Desenvolvimento e Planeamento Regional. Uma Abordagem Sistémica*; Editorial Estampa, 2000.

Ritchie, S. *Digital Participatory Budgeting: Opportunities and Challenges*; PB Network, 2016. https://pbnetwork.org.uk/digital-participatory-budgeting-opportunties-and-challenges/

Russell, S. J.; Norvig, P. *Artificial Intelligence: A Modern Approach*, 4th ed.; Pearson: London, 2020.

Sæbøa, Ø.; Roseb, J.; Flak, L. *The Shape of eParticipation: Characterizing an Emerging Research Area*; Elsevier: Amsterdam, 2008; pp 400–428.

Sampaio, R. C. e-Orçamentos Participativos Como Iniciativas de e-Solicitação: Uma Prospecção dos Principais Casos e Reflexões Sobre a e-Participação. *Rev. Admin. Públ.* **2016**, *50* (6), 937–958. https://doi.org/10.1590/0034-7612152210

Sampaio, R. C.; Peixoto, T. Electronic Participatory Budgeting: False Dilemmas and True Complexities. *Hope for Democracy—25 Years of Participatory Budgeting Worldwide, in Loco Association*, 2014.

Schwab, K. Globalization 4.0—What Does It Mean? In *World Economic Forum Annual Meeting*, 2018.

Tegmark, M. *Vida 3.0—Os Seres Humanos na Era da Inteligência Artificial*; Benvirá, 2020.

Vieg, J. A. In *Developments in Government Planning. In the Future of Government in the United States*; White, L. D.; University of Chicago Press: Chicago, IL, 1942.

CHAPTER 8

ARTIFICIAL INTELLIGENCE AND HEALTHCARE CONNECTION: A STATE-OF-THE-ART DISCUSSION AMONG ACADEMICS AND PRACTITIONERS

SILVANA SECINARO[1], DAVIDE CALANDRA[1], ROBERTO MARSEGLIA[2], and FEDERICO LANZALONGA[1]

[1]*Department of Management, University of Turin, Turin, Italy*

[2]*Department of Management, University of Venice Ca' Foscari, Venice, Italy*

ABSTRACT

The challenge of artificial intelligence (AI) in healthcare seems to have been launched. Numerous applications and connections are now possible thanks to the use of data and collaboration between information systems. Despite the multiple studies published so far in the scientific literature by academics or in the professional literature by managers and healthcare professionals, there are no comparisons and exploratory investigations between the two sources of thought. The book chapter aims to investigate the link between AI and healthcare by understanding how technology and deep learning can change preexisting scenarios. The chapter proposes an experimental research perspective. Indeed, on the one hand, we select 102 peer-reviewed articles from Scopus in business, management, and accounting; on the other hand, 64 articles from blogs, newspapers, and journals from the Europresse database. The results suggest to us that the discussion covers topics such as

Incorporating AI Technology in the Service Sector: Innovations in Creating Knowledge, Improving Efficiency, and Elevating Quality of Life. Maria José Sousa, Subhendu Kumar Pani, Francesca Dal Mas, & Sérgio Sousa (Eds.)
© 2024 Apple Academic Press, Inc. Co-published with CRC Press (Taylor & Francis)

applications, integration, and challenges. However, differences in thinking between the two groups exist. In particular, we find that practitioners require academics to design technology and develop a theory to apply AI. Finally, we conclude by providing practical and managerial implications through the McKinsey 7S Framework.

8.1 INTRODUCTION

Digital technology and medical integration are opening possibilities to reshape the entire healthcare system (Rippa and Secundo, 2019), and unlocking significant innovation and digitization (Cohen et al., 2017). However, the digital transformation challenge's relevance should aim to develop new medical practices and affect internal procedures (Sousa et al., 2019; Vaska et al., 2021), seeking for improvement in patient access to information and pursuing increasing accountability (Wang et al., 2020). Enabling the process of transformation involves implementing innovative technologies able to change the complete organizational structures in which operations take place (Sousa and Rocha, 2019; Yoo et al., 2010). The rise of artificial intelligence (AI) applications in both medicine and management and the growing applications of blockchain, identify the field as a flourishing one for investigation (Bardhan et al., 2020; Ting et al., 2020). Indeed, COVID-19, as a pandemic outbreak, demonstrated the importance for health systems to rethink their overall strategies from resilience to antifragility (Cobianchi et al., 2020a). Therefore, the importance of identifying AI fields is recognized as one of the purposes for the near future, and this field has not yet been fully explored in the healthcare environment (Wang et al., 2020).

Nowadays, AI is applied in different medical fields such as cancer, neurology, cardiology, and stroke detection (Jiang et al., 2017; Secinaro et al., 2021b). Significantly, the branch of computer science can analyze complex medical data and use relationships in databases to treat and predict clinical scenarios (Ramesh et al., 2004). Several types of AI have been applied in the medical field. Either as employed by payers and care providers (Davenport and Kalakota, 2019) or through algorithms, software, and hardware implementation for biomedical information processing and biomedical research (Rong et al., 2020). The recent literature shows how AI is gradually changing medical practice in digitized data acquisition, machine learning, and IT infrastructure, which was thought to be only the preserve of human experts (Yu et al., 2018). AI has involved developing deep neural networks, natural language processing, computer vision, and robotics to integrate into the healthcare system (Reddy et al., 2019). According to Esteva et al. (2019), AI developments, including deep learning in computer vision, natural language processing, and reinforcement learning can impact modern medicine. Deep learning can enable effective learning models to translate big biomedical data into better human health (Miceli et al., 2021; Miotto et al., 2018). The healthcare system appears to be ideal for applying this technique because it offers a large and varied data set (Faust et al., 2018). Moreover, conventional rule-based models cannot capture the underlying knowledge; therefore, deep learning can simulate human thought processes and learn in a unified model (Liang et al., 2014; Sousa et al., 2021).

This chapter aims to comprehend the conceptual elements to verify the differences between academia and practitioners regarding the state of the art in integrating AI in healthcare. The sudden digitization has created numerous applications of AI. However, solutions appear to be disaggregated, and there seems to be a need for a model that can connect the different tools and techniques available. Therefore, the study aims to answer the following questions:

RQ: What is the impact of AI in healthcare from an academic and practitioner perspective?

To answer this question, our research offers a perspective including thematic and content analysis (Krippendorff, 2018) on both academic articles and professional documents based on business cases, newspaper articles, press releases, and specialized blogs. The research draws its sources from two different databases. Our study used the Scopus database to identify 102 peer-reviewed papers written in English to collect the scholar's discussions. On the other hand, to define the practitioner's point of view, we extract 64 articles focused on the topic by blog, newspaper's report, and magazines provided by Europresse (Aykut et al., 2012). Subsequently, we adopted Leximancer software to implement the analysis and search and extract thesaurus-based concepts from the text data (Dal Mas, 2019; Massaro et al., 2020). Application of the rigorous methodology allows for insight into knowledge between academics and practitioners. Furthermore, to interconnect the elements available to healthcare in a dimension of integrating tools and understanding future challenges by offering future research fields for academics.

The chapter is organized as follows. The following section will detail the rigorous methodology followed by the authors. Next, we will present the results highlighting what emerges for academics' papers and practitioners' blogs. Finally, a section will be dedicated to discussing the results and conclusions, showing the implications, limitations, and future research.

8.2 METHODOLOGY

8.2.1 *THEMATIC AND CONTENT ANALYSIS*

According to Krippendorff (2018), written texts and multimedia content can be explored through qualitative methodologies as thematic and content analysis. A detailed examination of individual research streams can be achieved through content analysis (Hsieh and Shannon, 2005). It is utilized in different research streams to highlight specific literature trends and themes (Landrum and Ohsowski, 2018; Nobre and Tavares, 2020). According to Massaro et al. (2020), content analysis can be used to compare the state-of-the-art knowledge of academics with findings from the practitioners' sphere. However, content analysis has had other purposes as well. It can be implemented to understand intellectual capital knowledge within specific literature (Dal Mas, 2019; Dumay, 2014) or investigate how companies report information as a case study (Sihvonen and Partanen, 2017). For example, in healthcare, it has been used to explore service quality (Ponsignon et al., 2015) or migrants' access to healthcare (Ledoux et al., 2018).

Therefore, the content analysis appears to be a methodology allowing for conventional, direct, and summative scientific research (Hsieh and Shannon, 2005). Consequently, following the literature review on AI (Rong et al., 2020), this study investigates thematic and content analysis related to technologies likely to benefit the healthcare industry.

8.2.2 *DATA COLLECTION AND ANALYSIS*

The study aims to achieve the research objective using the Scopus database to collect 102 scientific papers. According to several authors, the database is one of the most widely used databases in keyword research (Biancone et al., 2020; Dal Mas, 2019; Secinaro et al., 2021a). The analysis was conducted in August 2021 through the following search key, connected by Boolean operators (Uluyol et al., 2021):

TITLE-ABS-KEY "Artificial Intelligence" AND "Healthcare."

The search key did not benefit from further specification to provide a holistic view of what is present on the topic (Secinaro et al., 2020). The first stage revealed 5189 papers. Subsequently, the authors restricted the field to management articles only, considering many sources (Massaro et al., 2016). A further restriction was done by considering peer-reviewed articles in English (Secinaro and Calandra, 2020), obtaining 102 papers for the academics' sphere.

From the practitioners' perspective, the Europresse database was used. According to Aykut et al. (2012), the data set allows information acquisition through blogs, newspaper reports, and magazines. Therefore, it qualifies as a good source regarding practitioners (Massaro et al., 2020) and allows searching through the same keywords used for academics. There were 64 sources consistent with our study.

The analysis took advantage of Leximancer software to implement the analysis as a final step. Leximancer searches and extracts thesaurus-based concepts from text data using automated content analysis (Smith and Humphreys, 2006). As confirmed by several studies, the software uses two different algorithms for extracting cooccurrence, semantic, and relational information (Dal Mas et al., 2019; Massaro et al., 2020; Smith and Humphreys, 2006). Therefore, the use of Leximancer allows the mapping of relationships between AI and healthcare concepts. Using its technical features, the analysis was performed to open and read each extracted document by coding the content and using an in-vivo approach (Miles et al., 2014). Through this two-step process, comparisons were made between results from academic and practical sources.

8.3 RESULTS

8.3.1 AI FOR HEALTHCARE IN ACADEMICS' VIEW

The following section explains academics' themes investigating the link between AI and healthcare, focusing on theories, applications, and case studies. As shown in Figure 8.1, the main subject of AI is linked to many other concepts as "challenges," "systems," "learning," "data," and "patients." The first research topic considers the challenges that healthcare is facing in understanding the use of intelligent algorithms. Other research topics address the analysis of intelligent systems, and thus, applications, predictive, and training uses that algorithms have. Finally, the role of data in clinical decision-making is emphasized. More elements can be found in Table 8.1.

The first general theme that we discover when looking at the research area concerns the countless applications that AI can have in healthcare. We find that algorithms can be used both in the patient-care process and in back-office document management. For example, Srivastava et al. (2020) discuss the Microsoft case study. As defined by the authors, the software company is seeing value in healthcare management. For this reason, it is investing in and testing its "Hospital Management System" application in several Indian hospitals by integrating deep-learning algorithms for the fast analysis of X-rays. This choice corresponds to the need to ensure healthcare services in countries with a larger population than doctors. Therefore, as confirmed by the authors and other studies, the role of future technology also seems to be to bridge the gaps in healthcare due to inadequate healthcare staffing and medical governance (Brescia et al., 2019; Meskó et al., 2018; Srivastava et al., 2020). Related to the previous example, Coccia (2020) focuses primarily on hospital radiology departments that are typically expensive and have problems with film storage. Digital conversion in these departments can take place thanks to two technologies. First, blockchain for the immutability of medical records, and second, AI, which with the development of analytical algorithms makes it possible to read, understand, and learn from radiological findings and support the physician in clinical decision-making. In addition, AI's ability to train on big data is the opportunity to identify subtypes of cancer or ongoing genetic mutations from analyses (Coccia, 2020).

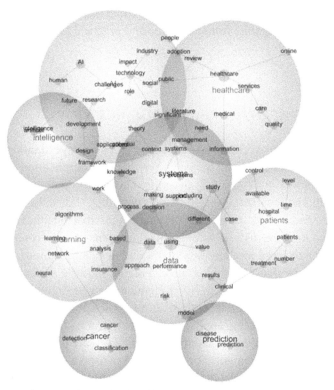

FIGURE 8.1   Themes under academics' discussion.

As discussed by Au-Yong-Oliveira et al. (2021) and Cobianchi et al. (2020b) at the heart of these opportunities is a digitization and the potential of big data in a transformative logic. This allows the valorization of paper reports and the development of solid algorithms for automatic analysis (Calandra and Favareto, 2020). Therefore, even in this specific field, the literature sees an opportunity for the scalability and sharing of programming languages for reading and detecting pathogens (Fruehwirt and Duckworth, 2021). Another interesting application of the algorithms is in the field of the heart. As discovered by Dwivedi et al. (2021), deep learning also makes it possible to detect patients with reduced left ventricular ejection fraction through electrocardiogram applications. This indirectly makes it possible to prevent and limits more costly specialist examinations. Therefore, according to numerous researchers, the combination of AI and examination analysis can play a role in terms of limiting economic costs due to both preventive medicines (with a better reading of medical outcomes) and limiting further specialist examinations (Bennett and Hauser, 2013; Jung and Pfister, 2020).

The second theme we discover concerns the debate on integrating AI applications and healthcare. According to Haleem and Javaid (2020), the new healthcare solutions respond to the "Medical 4.0" model. Several players (developers) constructively create applications linked to the Internet for healthcare treatment and medical surveillance. However, if left ungoverned, this theoretical assumption brings with it innumerable problems. First, the creation of a gap between the will of decision-makers and technology providers. Second, the effective implementation of changes in healthcare departments. Third, the lack of organization in the management of AI with different applications in each department. Therefore, these issues confront healthcare decision-makers with the need to integrate systems and ensure that they can always communicate with each other (Alami et al., 2020). This is also confirmed by Lam et al. (2021, p. 19) which discusses connectivity both inside and outside hospitals. According to the authors, the increase in AI applications creates diversification. Nevertheless, data reading and exploitation should take place in standardized environments. Therefore, systems such as AIoT-based Domestic Care Service Matching System allow wearable devices, thermometers, blood glucose meters, and other devices to communicate to collect and monitor all information effectively, aggregate it, and transmit it in a unified way.

Finally, the third research topic concerns the challenges that AI creates. In particular, we discover how the debate among academics aims to analyze security engineering approaches to AI design and procedural safeguards

TABLE 8.1 Academic's Debate on Artificial Intelligence and Healthcare.

Macrotopics	Themes/Case study	Original quotes
Applications	Microsoft and Indian hospitals	Thus, Telangana has become the pioneer in India for using AI techniques in public health delivery. Narayana Health at Bengaluru, in collaboration with Microsoft cloud solution, has developed Hospital Management System. Besides this, the hospital has also tied up with Microsoft Research, focusing on using the Deep Learning Project for predictive analysis using medical imaging (Srivastava et al., 2020)
	Radiology	With the conversion to digital images, Radiology has reduced costs eliminating film, chemicals, developers, and the storage of films. Moreover, radiology departments and labs with digital images have also solved the loss of films and transporting films to operating rooms, emergency departments, and intensive care units (Coccia, 2020)
	Cancer detection	Hence, deep learning technology can assist pathologists in the detection of cancer subtypes or gene mutations with a save of time and costs; moreover, poor regions with these new technologies can have benefited by sending the digital images to labs of other developed regions, generating a reduction, whenever possible, of the current gap in healthcare among different regions worldwide (Coccia, 2020)
	Electrocardiogram	Anderson (2019) analysed the potential of combining Deep Learning technology with electrocardiogram (ECG) applications to detect patients with reduced left ventricular ejection fraction (rLVEF). Detecting patients with rLVEF would be helpful in patients for whom echocardiography or other imaging modalities are not available or too expensive (Dwivedi et al., 2021).
	Paper analysis	Complete digital documentation of provenance and consent up to the deployment of AI solutions would be desirable (Jung and Pfister, 2020)
Health integration	Constructivist theory	Medical 4.0 seems a better technological solution for evidence-based care with a clear healthcare strategy. This medical revolution will provide practical solutions in fulfilling the various healthcare challenges in this ongoing pandemic. It opens new possibilities in healthcare by collecting all information of the patient through internet-connected devices. [...] Technologies used in this medical revolution predicted the progress after performing the treatment. It helps to improve surveillance systems (Haleem and Javaid, 2020)

TABLE 8.1 *(Continued)*

Macrotopics	Themes/Case study	Original quotes
		However, the current context is marked by a perplexing gap between the willingness of decision-makers and technology promoters to capitalize on AI applications and the reality on the ground, where it is challenging to initiate the changes needed to realize their full benefits while avoiding their negative impacts. Conceptualizing AI as an object of transformation in healthcare organizations may help to reduce this gap. Thus, it is necessary to pay more attention to organizational readiness for AI. This is crucial for successful integration and avoiding unnecessary investments and costly failures (Alami et al., 2020)
	Connectivism	Three types of IoT devices, wearable devices, thermometers, and blood glucose meters, are provided to effectively collect and monitor the health of the elderly at home. Figure 8.2 shows the architecture of the IoT networking in the AIoT-based Domestic Care Service Matching System (AIDCS), which comprises three layers: perception layer, network layer, and application layer. Through the connection with the wireless communication technology of Wi-Fi or 4G network in the network layer, the collected biometric data in the perception layer can be transmitted to the external cloud and then stored in the web-based server of the application layer (Lam et al., 2021, p. 19)
Challenges	Secure and stable algorithms	Approaches to Achieving Safety in AI Accuracy of prediction, the causality of predictive models, the human effort for labeling out-of-sample cases, and reinforcement and learning of systems contribute to making applications safe for use in healthcare. Four critical strategies of safety engineering are applied to the safety of AI in healthcare: (1) safe design, (2) safety reserves, (3) safe fail, and (4) procedural safeguards (Ellahham et al., 2020)
	Privacy	Ever-increasing digital stores of personal health information (PHI) hold the promise of improving efficiencies, efficacy, and precision of clinical medicine (Murdoch and Detsky, 2013) via big data analytics and artificial intelligence (AI)/machine learning. On the other hand, there are growing concerns about protecting individual privacy and the security of the data while also facilitating their use to enhance clinical research and societal welfare (Winter and Davidson, 2019)

Source: Author's elaboration.

(Ellahham et al., 2020). This dialog is vital, primarily as algorithms work in significant health and personal data environments (Winter and Davidson, 2019). Therefore, an AI management model in the health field will not do without future intellectual capital capable of maximizing cybersecurity practices (Alfiero et al., 2021).

8.3.2   AI FOR HEALTHCARE IN PRACTITIONERS' VIEW

The following section explains practitioners' themes investigating the link considering blog and magazine interviews. As shown in Figure 8.2, in this case, the main subject of AI is linked to many other concepts as "solutions," "devices," "home," "time," and "rights." More precisely, here too, it is possible to classify the results by considering the application of AI and the aspects of health integration. More elements can be found in Table 8.2.

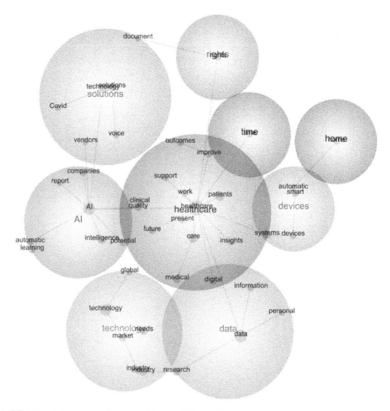

FIGURE 8.2   Themes under practitioners' discussion.

Also, in the case of practitioners, we discover how the relevant topic concerns AI applications and operational solutions. In this respect, the applications we find out confirm what the academics have analyzed. However, we focus primarily on the extra insights practitioners can provide us with to trigger future research insights. For example, very popular in the COVID-19 pandemic is applying deep learning to global data sets on vaccinations, the number of infected people and traces of infected patients. Similarly, AI is now being used to optimize and allocate the medical workforce to perform vaccinations (The Nation, 2020). Therefore, the role of AI in healthcare will increasingly become—as confirmed by ASEAN vice-president for IT company Infor Fabio Tiviti—"mission critical." This is confirmed by both the worldwide development of AI projects and future growth estimates. The "mission critical" is also established by the opportunity to use AI to predict and prevent hospital readmissions and optimize treatment practices thanks to large-scale analysis of medical reports (Krotz, 2019). Or, by predicting and calculating that a patient may suffer from a chronic disease, adopt mitigation strategies as early as possible (Choudhury, 2019).

In addition, there is much more discussion among professionals about smart home assistants such as Alexa, Google Assistant, and Siri and their role in healthcare. According to Davis (2020a), such systems provide complementary healthcare. This is relevant for those who have no problems with technology and can therefore better benefit from voice contact with a virtual assistant. In a subsequent contribution, Davis (2020b) illustrates how, in the pandemic management phase, the US Centers for Disease Control provided a voice questionnaire to patients confirming or eliminating the diagnosis of COVID-19. This reduced misinformation and, at the same time, limited temporary access to emergency rooms. Thus, here again, we discover how AI and voice recognition can be supplementary tools to healthcare, especially in prevention and managing large-scale emergencies such as pandemics.

The last two areas of discussion concern the role of countries and the scalability of algorithms. The case study of the United Arab Emirates (UAE) through the Ministry of Health and Prevention provides whole light on the opportunity to develop strategies to offer healthcare and remote monitoring benefiting from AI. In particular, this is part of a broader strategy to invest in technology and digitization by creating a solid innovation hub in the country (Ministry of Health and Prevention, 2020). Finally, the accessibility of algorithms and their applications should ensure access and scalability to other clinicians and research teams, especially where patients' health and economic benefit is clear (Kharpal, 2018a).

The second and final area of discussion concerns healthcare integration. As defined by Jai Verma, CEO and Board Member of Cigna DIFC, an insurance company: "AI, the internet of things, will change the way we deliver healthcare in the future" (Chandran, 2019). This is primarily due to the pre-AI data not being valued holistically. Finally, we discover how the concept of compatibility and interoperability between digital technologies, connected systems, and created algorithms emerges. According to Spronk (2019), digital environments should be more and more integrated. This makes it possible to maintain the healthcare services offered to patients without having to change technology providers. Therefore, initiatives such as Microsoft's "Healthcare NExT" and investments by Ministries of Health can be promoted if AI can then be applied to common virtual spaces (Kharpal, 2018b).

8.4   DISCUSSION AND CONCLUSION

This chapter aimed to compare academic and professional sources regarding the open discussion on the role of AI in healthcare. The research team adopted a mixed qualitative research approach based on thematic and content analysis to do so.

The qualitative analysis allowed us to find three relevant themes of debate for academics. We find how there is strong interest in AI applications (Cobianchi et al., 2020b; Coccia, 2020; Ellahham et al., 2020). At the same time, we discover an undercurrent of discussion for valuing health integration and the multiple sources of data available today (Haleem and Javaid, 2020). Specifically, as Alami et al. (2020) discussed, there is a need for investments in AI to be targeted and integrated into healthcare processes. The risk is to do projects for their own sake and without opportunities for development and enhancement on patients. These concepts are reflected in design theory applied to technology. Indeed, according to Feng and Feenberg (2008), for the design, we refer to the process of conscious modeling capable of creating results suitable for specific goals and environments. Therefore, it is possible to find approaches to produce concrete devices available to stakeholders even within technology.

Alongside this, academics also recognize some relevant challenges. These include the security and stability of AI, especially in a healthcare field with vast amounts of personal data at its disposal (Ellahham et al., 2020; Winter and Davidson, 2019). The discussion coincides with a specific and interdisciplinary area of research such as cybersecurity within digital environments

TABLE 8.2 Practitioners' Debate on Artificial Intelligence and Healthcare.

Macrotopics	Themes	Original quotes
AI applications	Critical mission	Fabio Tiviti, Asean vice president for global software company Infor. added that AI in healthcare would become "mission critical." Over the next year, we will see the accelerated adoption of AI across many areas of healthcare. By applying machine learning to real-time global data sets, healthcare professionals can more accurately track contact between staff and infected patients, enable accurate diagnoses, utilise predictive analytics to track personal protective equipment [PPE], optimise workforce allocations, and develop more effective and lasting vaccinations (The Nation, 2020)
		Available AI tools range from readmission predication and prevention (a top priority for all healthcare organizations using AI or not) to avoidable ED visits and the prediction and prevention of hospital-acquired diseases. We also found tools that help discover treatment best practices, chronic disease management, clinical research, clinical trial matching, patient engagement, and education (Krotz, 2019)
	Time savings	It has developed AI systems that it says can predict the likelihood of a patient suffering from a specific chronic illness even before physical symptoms are present or identify infectious diseases in advance with high accuracy. Its programs claim to spot abnormalities in medical image scans that would typically take doctors much longer to do manually.
		"We can take it down to like five minutes, so it's a lot more efficient, a lot more accurate, also," Chan said. "Afterwards, we can even have AI technologies do follow up with the patients." (Choudhury, 2019)
	Voice as a health-care management solution	Voice biomarkers as an AI solution have a tremendous potential to supplement virtual healthcare services. The ability to apply these solutions with smartphones, telemedicine audio, and call centers will create another level of healthcare management that will improve care quality and outcomes. The ability to identify potential chronic illnesses or patient conditions that can prove fatal from a patient's conversation with a care provider is likely to reduce deaths and expensive emergency or acute care (Davis, 2020a)
		Smart home assistants such as Amazon Alexa, Google Assistant, and Apple HomePod are being developed to support healthcare services for their customers. All these solutions provide voice recognition services supported by AI algorithms. Alexa can present consumers with the US Centers for Disease Control COVID-19 questionnaire to assess potential COVID-19 infection and provide recommendations on what to do next to confirm or eliminate the diagnosis. The new feature arrives about a week after Apple added a

TABLE 8.2 (Continued)

Macrotopics	Themes	Original quotes
		version of the same quality for Siri and is one of a handful of updates made to Alexa as part of Amazon's response to the current pandemic. Amazon, Google, and Apple have established a content-evaluation process of their catalogues to eliminate misinformation related to COVID-19 (Davis, 2020b)
	Innovation strategy	Al-Ajmi pointed out that MoHAP has taken the lead globally in implementing AI technologies in health-care as part of the United Arab Emirates Artificial Intelligence Strategy and predictive data analysis. This would lead to supporting future medical decisions, remote monitoring of patients conditions, providing preventive healthcare, and reducing healthcare costs (Ministry of Health and Prevention, 2020)
	Scalability	Tonight's results clearly illustrate how AI-augmented health services can reduce the burden on healthcare systems around the world. Our mission is to put accessible and affordable health services into the hands of every person on Earth Ali Parsa, CEO of Bablyon, said in a statement (Kharpal, 2018a)
Health integration	Connections	"We are building telemedicine in our apps today where you can consult a doctor from the convenience of your homes, not for an emergency," said Jai Verma, CEO and board member of insurance company Cigna DIFC, and global head of government solutions at Cigna International. "I think AI, internet of things, is going to change the way we deliver healthcare in the future (Chandran, 2019).
	Interoperability	[...] But many companies are neglecting a critical issue that is becoming increasingly essential—digital technologies and connected devices must be compatible with existing systems. For too long, interoperability was a secondary consideration. Sometimes it was not a consideration at all (Spronk, 2019)
	Investments	Last year, Microsoft started an initiative called Healthcare NExT which aims to apply its cloud and artificial intelligence (AI) products to the industry. One example is how Microsoft uses AI and cloud computing to help doctors scan medical imagery to diagnose conditions (Kharpal, 2018b)

Source: Author's elaboration.

(Ehrenfeld, 2017). We advocate greater disciplinary exchange, especially between academics in the computer-management area and practitioners/users in this context.

Entering the specifics of professionals, we discover how the macrothemes of discussion are only the first two: AI applications and healthcare integration. We find vital the definition of "Critical Mission" as a theoretical junction of reference. Moreover, we show that practitioners juxtapose AI with the concept of strategic innovation and scalability. This is demonstrated by the UAE case study that saw AI and its developments as an opportunity for economic growth spread over several strategic sectors (Ministry of Health and Prevention, 2020).

In addition, we also find interest among practitioners in the integration, connection, and interoperability of technology systems and AI applications in healthcare. This is part of the scope of design theory (Feng and Feenberg, 2008) and can further be read theoretically from designing technology and developing theory (Schubert and Kolb, 2021). Indeed, technological systems require collaborative activities and cooperative work supported by human-computer interaction that can be managed with multidisciplinary approaches. Thus, the results demonstrate common discussion points and expertise exchanges between academics (theoretical approaches) and practitioners (Massaro et al., 2020; Romme et al., 2018).

Considering the divergence between the two study groups, practitioners have more control over AI solutions, opportunities, and response timelines. Furthermore, we show how innovation enabled voice assistants to support patients during the COVID-19 pandemic. Interestingly, practitioners give a lot of weight to the topic, and in academics, there is only one dedicated strand of research.

Our study has interesting practical implications for managers and healthcare personnel. The thematic research of the results allowed us to discover many applications and concepts that are functional for creating AI applications. At the level of practical implications, we think it is helpful to share Figure 8.3 with the McKinsey 7S Framework. According to Baishya (2015), the framework is a management model developed by business consultants such as Robert H. Waterman, Jr. and Tom Peters in the 1980s and allows for shared structures, strategies, and competencies in a project. The model can be used to assess and monitor changes in an organization's internal situation. As shown, at the core is the concept of scalability derived from outcomes. Alongside, insist six additional concepts that look at sharing, integration, communication, training, compatibility and interoperability of AI applications and, more generally, digital systems. Each concept is then reflected in explanatory questions for adopting the model in healthcare settings.

Therefore, we address managers and practitioners with three outcomes. First, we point out some possible applications for AI in healthcare settings. Second, we give them concepts through a practical model that can be used before developing AI applications. Third, we provide them with a vision for raising awareness of more significant investment at the government level as done in the UAE.

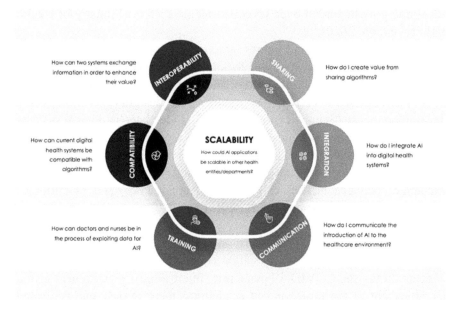

FIGURE 8.3   McKinsey 7S Framework on artificial intelligence and healthcare application.

8.4.1   *LIMITATIONS AND FUTURE RESEARCH PERSPECTIVES*

Our study, like every research, has some limitations and related research opportunities. The first one is related to the keywords used and the research limitations adopted to study business, management, and accounting. This may allow new exploratory studies to understand the evolution of AI in healthcare and other scientific fields. The second limitation concerns the sample of sources of the studied professionals. Again, future research may shed light and investigate larger samples of sources. Finally, the survey was conducted using a qualitative methodology that aimed to validate the entire literature. This may prompt future research to diversify by adopting quantitative and qualitative methods to investigate exploratory and interventionist case studies.

KEYWORDS

- **artificial intelligence**
- **digital transformation**
- **health applications**
- **deep learning**
- **radiology**
- **voice management**
- **management**

REFERENCES

Alami, H.; Lehoux, P.; Denis, J.-L.; Motulsky, A.; Petitgand, C.; Savoldelli, M.; Rouquet, R.; Gagnon, M.-P.; Roy, D.; Fortin, J.-P. Organizational Readiness for Artificial Intelligence in Health Care: Insights for Decision-Making and Practice. *J. Health Organ. Manage.* **2020**, *ahead-of-print* (ahead-of-print). https://doi.org/10.1108/JHOM-03-2020-0074

Alfiero, S.; Brescia, V.; Bert, F. Intellectual Capital-Based Performance Improvement: A Study in Healthcare Sector. *BMC Health Serv. Res.* **2021**, *21* (1), 73. https://doi.org/10.1186/s12913-021-06087-y

Au-Yong-Oliveira, M.; Pesqueira, A.; Sousa, M. J.; Dal Mas, F.; Soliman, M. The Potential of Big Data Research in Healthcare for Medical Doctors' Learning. *J. Med. Syst.* **2021**, *45* (1), 13. https://doi.org/10.1007/s10916-020-01691-7

Aykut, S. C.; Comby, J.-B.; Guillemot, H. Climate Change Controversies in French Mass Media 1990–2010. *Journal. Stud.* **2012**, *13* (2), 157–174. https://doi.org/10.1080/1461670X.2011.646395

Baishya, B. *McKinsey 7s Framework in Corporate Planning and Policy* 2015, Whatfix; p 4.

Bardhan, I.; Chen, H.; Karahanna, E. Connecting Systems, Data, and People: A Multidisciplinary Research Roadmap for Chronic Disease Management. *Manage. Inf. Syst. Q.* **2020**, *44* (1), 185–200.

Bennett, C. C.; Hauser, K. Artificial Intelligence Framework for Simulating Clinical Decision-Making: A Markov Decision Process Approach. *Artif. Intell. Med.* **2013**, *57* (1), 9–19. https://doi.org/10.1016/j.artmed.2012.12.003

Biancone, P. P.; Saiti, B.; Petricean, D.; Chmet, F. The Bibliometric Analysis of Islamic Banking and Finance. *J. Islam. Acc. Bus. Res.* **2020**. https://doi.org/10.1108/JIABR-08-2020-0235

Brescia, V.; Indelicato, A.; Chmet, F.; Maglio, P.; Muraca, L.; Mazzei, A.; Guzzo, M. L.; Cardona, R.; Bisogni, K.; Notarangelo, M.; De Fina, M. Multidisciplinarity in the Treatment Process: An Essential Element in Clinical Governance. *Int. J. Manage. Sci. Bus. Res.* **2019,** *10* (7), 47–62. http://dx.doi.org/10.5281/zenodo.3491482

Calandra, D.; Favareto, M. Artificial Intelligence to Fight COVID-19 Outbreak Impact: An Overview. *Eur. J. Soc. Impact Circ. Econ.* **2020,** *1* (3), 84–104. https://doi.org/10.13135/2704-9906/5067

Chandran, K. *Can AI Ever Replace Human Doctors? Health Tech Experts Weigh in*; CNBC; 2019, November 20. https://www.cnbc.com/2019/11/20/can-ai-ever-replace-human-doctors-health-tech-experts-weigh-in.html

Choudhury, S. R. *AI Can Improve Health Care in China, Says Ping an Technology CEO*; CNBC, 2019, July 9. https://www.cnbc.com/2019/07/09/ping-an-tech-ceo-says-ai-can-improve-health-care-in-china.html

Cobianchi, L.; Dal Mas, F.; Peloso, A.; Pugliese, L.; Massaro, M.; Bagnoli, C.; Angelos, P. Planning the Full Recovery Phase: An Antifragile Perspective on Surgery after COVID-19. *Ann. Surg.* **2020a,** *272* (6), e296.

Cobianchi, L.; Dal Mas, F.; Piccolo, D.; Peloso, A.; Secundo, G.; Massaro, M.; Takeda, A.; Garcia Vazquez, A.; Verde, J.; Swanstrom, L.; Marescaux, J.; Perretta, S.; Gallix, B.; Dimarcq, J.-L.; Giménez, M. *Digital Transformation in Healthcare. The Challenges of Translating Knowledge in a Primary Research, Educational and Clinical Centre*, 2020b, May 1.

Coccia, M. Deep Learning Technology for Improving Cancer Care in Society: New Directions in Cancer Imaging Driven by Artificial Intelligence. *Technol. Soc.* **2020,** *60*, 101198. https://doi.org/10.1016/j.techsoc.2019.101198

Cohen, B.; Amorós, J. E.; Lundy, L. The Generative Potential of Emerging Technology to Support Startups and New Ecosystems. *Bus. Horizons* **2017,** *60* (6). doi:10.1016/j.bushor.2017.06.004.

Dal Mas, F. The Relationship between Intellectual Capital and Sustainability: An Analysis of Practitioner's Thought. In *Intellectual Capital Management as a Driver of Sustainability*; Springer: Cham, 2019; pp 11–24.

Dal Mas, F.; Piccolo, D.; Cobianchi, L.; Edvinsson, L.; Presch, G.; Massaro, M.; Skrap, M.; Ferrario di Tor Vajana, A.; Stanislao d'auria, S.; Bagnoli, C. *The Effects of Artificial Intelligence, Robotics, and Industry 4.0 Technologies. Insights from the Healthcare Sector*, 2019, October. https://doi.org/10.34190/ECIAIR.19.015

Davenport, T.; Kalakota, R. The Potential for Artificial Intelligence in Healthcare. *Fut. Healthc. J.* **2019,** *6* (2), 94. https://doi.org/10.7861/futurehosp.6-2-94

Davis, M. *eTech Insight—Voice Biomarkers Become a Key Disease Detection Solution—Klas Blog*. Klas Research, 2020a. https://klasresearch.com/blog/etech-insight-voice-biomarkers-become-a-key-disease-detection-solution/815

Davis, M. *eTech Insights—Smart Home Assistant Products Emerge as Consumer Healthcare Managers—Klas Blog*. Klas Research, 2020b. https://klasresearch.com/blog/etech-insights-smart-home-assistant-products-emerge-as-consumer-healthcare-managers/687

Dumay, J. 15 Years of the *Journal of Intellectual Capital* and Counting. *J. Intellect. Cap.* **2014**. https://doi.org/10.1108/JIC-09-2013-0098

Dwivedi, Y. K.; Hughes, L.; Ismagilova, E.; Aarts, G.; Coombs, C.; Crick, T.; Duan, Y.; Dwivedi, R.; Edwards, J.; Eirug, A.; Galanos, V.; Ilavarasan, P. V.; Janssen, M.; Jones, P.; Kar, A. K.; Kizgin, H.; Kronemann, B.; Lal, B.; Lucini, B.; et al. Artificial Intelligence (AI): Multidisciplinary Perspectives on Emerging Challenges, Opportunities, and Agenda for Research, Practice and Policy. *Int. J. Inf. Manage.* **2021,** *57,* 101994. https://doi.org/10.1016/j.ijinfomgt.2019.08.002

Ehrenfeld, J. M. WannaCry, Cybersecurity and Health Information Technology: A Time to Act. *J. Med. Syst.* **2017,** *41* (7), 104. https://doi.org/10.1007/s10916-017-0752-1

Ellahham, S.; Ellahham, N.; Simsekler, M. C. E. Application of Artificial Intelligence in the Health Care Safety Context: Opportunities and Challenges. *Am. J. Med. Qual.* **2020,** *35* (4), 341–348. https://doi.org/10.1177/1062860619878515

Esteva, A.; Robicquet, A.; Ramsundar, B.; Kuleshov, V.; DePristo, M.; Chou, K.; Cui, C.; Corrado, G.; Thrun, S.; Dean, J. A Guide to Deep Learning in Healthcare. *Nat. Med.* **2019,** *25* (1), 24–29. https://doi.org/10.1038/s41591-018-0316-z

Faust, O.; Hagiwara, Y.; Hong, T. J.; Lih, O. S.; Acharya, U. R. Deep Learning for Healthcare Applications based on Physiological Signals: A Review. *Comput. Methods Programs Biomed.* **2018,** *161,* 1–13. https://doi.org/10.1016/j.cmpb.2018.04.005

Feng, P.; Feenberg, A. Thinking about Design: Critical Theory of Technology and the Design Process. In *Philosophy and Design: From Engineering to Architecture*; Kroes, P., Vermaas, P. E., Light, A., Moore, S. A., Eds.; Springer Netherlands, 2008; pp 105–118. https://doi.org/10.1007/978-1-4020-6591-0_8

Fruehwirt, W.; Duckworth, P. Towards Better Healthcare: What Could and Should Be Automated? *Technol. Forecast. Soc. Change* **2021,** *172,* 120967. https://doi.org/10.1016/j.techfore.2021.120967

Haleem, A.; Javaid, M. Medical 4.0 and Its Role in Healthcare During COVID-19 Pandemic: A Review. *J. Ind. Integr. Manage.* **2020,** *05* (04), 531–545. https://doi.org/10.1142/S2424862220300045

Hsieh, H.-F.; Shannon, S. E. Three Approaches to Qualitative Content Analysis. *Qual. Health Res.* **2005,** *15* (9), 1277–1288. https://doi.org/10.1177/1049732305276687

Jiang, F.; Jiang, Y.; Zhi, H.; Dong, Y.; Li, H.; Ma, S.; Wang, Y.; Dong, Q.; Shen, H.; Wang, Y. Artificial Intelligence in Healthcare: Past, Present and Future. *Stroke Vasc. Neurol.* **2017,** *2* (4). https://doi.org/10.1136/svn-2017-000101

Jung, H.; Pfister, F. Blockchain-enabled Clinical Study Consent Management. *Technol. Innov. Manage. Rev.* **2020,** *10* (2), 14–24. https://doi.org/10.22215/timreview/1325

Kharpal, A. *Health Care Start-Up Says A.I. Can Diagnose Patients Better Than Humans Can, Doctors Call That "Dubious."* CNBC, 2018a, June 28. https://www.cnbc.com/2018/06/28/babylon-claims-its-ai-can-diagnose-patients-better-than-doctors.html

Kharpal, A. *Microsoft Health Unit Is a "Multi-Billion Dollar Business," Medical Chief Says.* CNBC, 2018b, July 26. https://www.cnbc.com/2018/07/26/microsofts-health-unit-is-a-multi-billion-dollar-business.html

Krippendorff, K. *Content Analysis: An Introduction to Its Methodology*; Sage Publications: Thousand Oaks, CA, 2018.

Krotz, L. *Leveraging AI in Healthcare—Top Use Cases and Outcomes—Klas Blog*; Klas Research, 2019. https://klasresearch.com/blog/leveraging-ai-in-healthcare-top-use-cases-and-outcomes/631

Lam, H. Y.; Ho, G. T. S.; Mo, D. Y.; Tang, V. Enhancing Data-Driven Elderly Appointment Services in Domestic Care Communities under COVID-19. *Ind. Manage. Data Syst.* **2021,** *121* (7), 1552–1576. https://doi.org/10.1108/IMDS-07-2020-0392

Landrum, N. E.; Ohsowski, B. Identifying Worldviews on Corporate Sustainability: A Content Analysis of Corporate Sustainability Reports. *Bus. Strat. Environ.* **2018,** *27* (1), 128–151. https://doi.org/10.1002/bse.1989

Ledoux, C.; Pilot, E.; Diaz, E.; Krafft, T. Migrants' Access to Healthcare Services within the European Union: A Content Analysis of Policy Documents in Ireland, Portugal and Spain. *Glob. Health* **2018**, *14* (1), 1–11. https://doi.org/10.1186/s12992-018-0373-6

Liang, Z.; Zhang, G.; Huang, J. X.; Hu, Q. V. Deep Learning for Healthcare Decision Making with EMRs. In *2014 IEEE International Conference on Bioinformatics and Biomedicine (BIBM)*, 2014; pp 556–559. https://doi.org/10.1109/BIBM.2014.6999219

Massaro, M.; Dumay, J.; Guthrie, J. On the Shoulders of Giants: Undertaking a Structured Literature Review in Accounting. *Account., Audit. Account. J.* **2016,** *29* (5), 767–801. https://doi.org/10.1108/AAAJ-01-2015-1939

Massaro, M.; Secinaro, S.; Mas, F. D.; Brescia, V.; Calandra, D. Industry 4.0 and Circular Economy: An Exploratory Analysis of Academic and Practitioners' Perspectives. *Bus. Strat. Environ.* **2020**. https://doi.org/10.1002/bse.2680

Meskó, B.; Hetényi, G.; Győrffy, Z. Will Artificial Intelligence Solve the Human Resource Crisis in Healthcare? *BMC Health Serv. Res.* **2018,** *18* (1), 545. https://doi.org/10.1186/s12913-018-3359-4

Miceli, L.; Dal Mas, F.; Biancuzzi, H.; Bednarova, R.; Rizzardo, A.; Cobianchi, L.; Holmboe, E. S. Doctor@Home: Through a Telemedicine Co-production and Co-learning Journey. *J. Cancer Educ.* **2021**. https://doi.org/10.1007/s13187-020-01945-5

Miles, M. B.; Huberman, A. M.; Saldana, J. *Qualitative Data Analysis: A Methods Sourcebook*; Sage Publications: Thousand Oaks, 2014.

Ministry of Health and Prevention. In *MoHAP Organizes the 1st Conference on Artificial Intelligence in Healthcare—Ministry of Health and Prevention—UAE*, 2020. https://www.mohap.gov.ae/en/MediaCenter/News/Pages/2322.aspx

Miotto, R.; Wang, F.; Wang, S.; Jiang, X.; Dudley, J. T. Deep Learning for Healthcare: Review, Opportunities and Challenges. *Brief. Bioinform.* **2018,** *19* (6), 1236–1246. https://doi.org/10.1093/bib/bbx044

Nobre, G. C.; Tavares, E. Assessing the Role of Big Data and the Internet of Things on the Transition to Circular Economy: Part II: An Extension of the ReSOLVE Framework Proposal through a Literature Review. *Johnson Matthey Technol. Rev.* **2020,** *64* (1), 32–41.

Ponsignon, F.; Smart, A.; Williams, M.; Hall, J. Healthcare Experience Quality: An Empirical Exploration Using Content Analysis Techniques. *J. Serv. Manage.* **2015**. https://doi.org/10.1108/JOSM-10-2014-0265

Ramesh, A. N.; Kambhampati, C.; Monson, J. R.; Drew, P. J. Artificial Intelligence in Medicine. *Ann. R. Coll. Surg. Engl.* **2004,** *86* (5), 334. https://doi.org/10.1308/147870804290

Reddy, S.; Fox, J.; Purohit, M. P. Artificial Intelligence-Enabled Healthcare Delivery. *J. R. Soc. Med.* **2019,** *112* (1), 22–28. https://doi.org/10.1177/0141076818815510

Rippa, P.; Secundo, G. Digital Academic Entrepreneurship: The Potential of Digital Technologies on Academic Entrepreneurship. *Technol. Forecast. Soc. Change* **2019,** *146*, 900–911. https://doi.org/10.1016/j.techfore.2018.07.013

Romme, A. G. L.; Broekgaarden, J.; Huijzer, C.; Reijmer, A.; van der Eyden, R. A. I. From Competition and Collusion to Consent-Based Collaboration: A Case Study of Local Democracy. *Int. J. Publ. Admin.* **2018,** *41* (3), 246–255. https://doi.org/10.1080/01900692.2016.1263206

Rong, G.; Mendez, A.; Assi, E. B.; Zhao, B.; Sawan, M. Artificial Intelligence in Healthcare: Review and Prediction Case Studies. *Engineering* **2020,** *6* (3), 291–301. https://doi.org/10.1016/j.eng.2019.08.015

Schubert, C.; Kolb, A. Designing Technology, Developing Theory: Toward a Symmetrical Approach. *Sci., Technol., Human Values* **2021,** *46* (3), 528–554. https://doi.org/10.1177/0162243920941581

Secinaro, S.; Calandra, D. Halal Food: Structured Literature Review and Research Agenda. *Br. Food J.* **2020,** *123* (1), 225–243. https://doi.org/10.1108/BFJ-03-2020-0234

Secinaro, S.; Brescia, V.; Calandra, D.; Biancone, P. Employing Bibliometric Analysis to Identify Suitable Business Models for Electric Cars. *J. Clean. Prod.* **2020,** *264,* 121503.

Secinaro, S.; Calandra, D.; Petricean, D.; Chmet, F. Social Finance and Banking Research as a Driver for Sustainable Development: A Bibliometric Analysis. *Sustainability* **2021a,** *13* (1), 330. https://doi.org/10.3390/su13010330

Secinaro, S.; Calandra, D.; Secinaro, A.; Muthurangu, V.; Biancone, P. The Role of Artificial Intelligence in Healthcare: A Structured Literature Review. *BMC Med. Inform. Decis. Mak.* **2021b,** *21* (1), 125. https://doi.org/10.1186/s12911-021-01488-9

Sihvonen, S.; Partanen, J. Eco-Design Practices with a Focus on Quantitative Environmental Targets: An Exploratory Content Analysis within ICT Sector. *J. Clean. Prod.* **2017,** *143,* 769–783. https://doi.org/10.1016/j.jclepro.2016.12.047

Smith, A. E.; Humphreys, M. S. Evaluation of Unsupervised Semantic Mapping of Natural Language with Leximancer Concept Mapping. *Behav. Res. Methods* **2006,** *38* (2), 262–279. https://doi.org/10.3758/BF03192778

Sousa, M. J.; Rocha, Á. Strategic Knowledge Management in the Digital Age: JBR Special Issue Editorial. *Journal of Business Research* **2019,** *94,* 223–226. https://doi.org/10.1016/j.jbusres.2018.10.016

Sousa, M. J.; Pesqueira, A. M.; Lemos, C.; Sousa, M.; Rocha, Á. Decision-Making Based on Big Data Analytics for People Management in Healthcare Organizations. *J. Med. Syst.* **2019,** *43* (9), 290.

Sousa, M. J.; Dal Mas, F.; Pesqueira, A.; Verde, J. M.; Cobianchi, L. The Potential of AI in Health Higher Education to Increase the Students' Learning Outcomes. *TEM J.* **2021,** *10* (2), 488–497.

Spronk, R. *Why Medtech Needs to Be Interoperable by Design*; Medtech Views, 2019. http://www.medtechviews.eu/article/why-medtech-needs-be-interoperable-design

Srivastava, S.; Pant, M.; Agarwal, R. Role of AI Techniques and Deep Learning in Analyzing the Critical Health Conditions. *Int. J. Syst. Assur. Eng. Manage.* **2020,** *11* (2), 350–365. https://doi.org/10.1007/s13198-019-00863-0

The Nation. *Infor's Top Three Technology Predictions for 2021*; Nationthailand, 2020. https://www.nationthailand.com/tech/30400040

Ting, D. S. W.; Carin, L.; Dzau, V.; Wong, T. Y. Digital Technology and COVID-19. *Nat. Med.* **2020,** *26* (4), 459–461.

Uluyol, B.; Secinaro, S.; Calandra, D.; Lanzalonga, F. Mapping WAQF Research: A Thirty-Year Bibliometric Analysis. *J. Islam. Acc. Bus. Res.* **2021.** https://doi.org/10.1108/JIABR-01-2021-0031

Vaska, S.; Massaro, M.; Bagarotto, E. M.; Dal Mas, F. The Digital Transformation of Business Model Innovation: A Structured Literature Review. *Front. Psychol.* **2021,** *11,* 3557. https://doi.org/10.3389/fpsyg.2020.539363

Wang, C. J.; Ng, C. Y.; Brook, R. H. Response to COVID-19 in Taiwan: Big Data Analytics, New Technology, and Proactive Testing. *JAMA* **2020,** *323* (14), 1341–1342.

Winter, J. S.; Davidson, E. Big Data Governance of Personal Health Information and Challenges to Contextual Integrity. *Inf. Soc.* **2019,** *35* (1), 36–51. https://doi.org/10.1080/01972243.2018.1542648

Yoo, Y.; Henfridsson, O.; Lyytinen, K. Research Commentary—The New Organizing Logic of Digital Innovation: An Agenda for Information Systems Research. *Inf. Syst. Res.* **2010,** *21* (4), 724–735.

Yu, K.-H.; Beam, A. L.; Kohane, I. S. Artificial Intelligence in Healthcare. *Nat. Biomed. Eng.* **2018,** *2* (10), 719–731. https://doi.org/10.1038/s41551-018-0305-z

CHAPTER 9

PEOPLE ANALYTICS AND THE COVID-19 PANDEMIC: HOW EMPATHY AND PRIVACY TURNED OUT THE HOT TOPICS

ANTÓNIO PIMENTA DE BRITO

BRU-ISCTE/ESCAD—IP Luso, ISCTE-Instituto Universitário de Lisboa/IP Luso—Universidade Lusófona, Lisbon, Portugal

ABSTRACT

People analytics (PA) is a field of HR that uses the techniques of artificial intelligence, social sciences, and innovation to extract insights from employee data for business decision-making. This is an area that has shown growing interest from organizations, industry, and academia in the last decade. PA trends before the COVID-19 pandemic were mostly around the need to extract business value from the amalgamation of user data provided and data privacy. The latter is the most pressing. After the outbreak of the COVID-19 pandemic, PA managers' concerns focused on empathy and data privacy were intensified. Through a literature review and content analysis of interviews and case studies on the internet, this evolution in PA trends is proven and a review on this topic to date is done.

9.1 INTRODUCTION

According to Tursunbayeva et al. (2018, p. 231) "People Analytics is an area of HRM practice, research and innovation concerned with the use of information

Incorporating AI Technology in the Service Sector: Innovations in Creating Knowledge,
Improving Efficiency, and Elevating Quality of Life. Maria José Sousa, Subhendu Kumar Pani,
Francesca Dal Mas, & Sérgio Sousa (Eds.)
© 2024 Apple Academic Press, Inc. Co-published with CRC Press (Taylor & Francis)

technologies, descriptive and predictive data analytics and visualization tools for generating actionable insights about workforce dynamics, human capital, and individual and team performance that can be used strategically to optimize organizational effectiveness, efficiency and outcomes, and improve employee experience."

According to a survey by Deloitte Insights (2018), the participants considered PA as the second biggest human capital trend in 2018 (Tursunbayeva et al., 2021).

The big data revolution also has echoes in people management. In a modern approach to HRM in which people are the competitive advantage of the organization (Sullivan, 2013), similarly to marketing, which aims to put the customer first, in the HR area, the internal customer is the one the company wants to serve. To serve, the company needs to know who it serves.

Kitchin (2014, p. 68) defines big data this way: "huge in volume, high in velocity, diverse in variety, exhaustive in scope, fine-grained in resolution, relational in nature, and flexible in trait."

In the field of business and society, for example, in the consumer goods distribution sector, a supermarket receives thousands of customers a day. At one point, it was necessary to store and process the amount of data generated by millions of transactions, whether the amounts spent, the items purchased, the time the purchase was made, the buyer profile, and so on. All data with value for the CRM (customer relationship management) systems allowed one-to-one marketing, up to the latest big data concept, integrating artificial intelligence, and predictive models. Through patterns and associations, how will managers be able to anticipate the new consumption trend, this is one of the questions that can be raised from a big data strategy. Through these data, managers can predict based on the type of items purchased which item the customer will buy next, what psychographic profile can be drawn, and so on.

With the rise of the internet came the data revolution. If in the first phase, the so-called Web 1.0, was read only and with a passive participation of the user. In the second phase, came the revolution of social networks with high interactivity and user participation in the production of contents (Almeida, 2017)—the Web 2.0. With the Web 2.0, came the revolution of content, but the majority of all that data tend to be unstructured. With Web 3.0 and specially Web 4.0 began to develop tools and methodologies that would make these data, from unstructured to structured, from raw data, into valuable knowledge to generate useful insights for industry and for scientific research, be it in the natural sciences or in the social sciences.

People management cannot ignore this need to make decisions based on evidence and not just relying on the quality of relationships established in the company or in simple common sense.

Web 4.0 has several definitions and encompasses several dimensions and each of them offers a different, but complementary view of the 4.0 paradigm. Social networks and technologies such as the Internet of things, big data, artificial intelligence, and machine-to-machine communication offer a comprehensive image of the Web 4.0 application (Almeida, 2017; de Brito, 2022).

The National Bank of Australia (Green, 2020a) has demonstrated that a highly motivated and involved employee contaminates the client and makes him more satisfied. The next question was, what causes this? And it turned out to be the leaders, so it was decided to select better leaders, provide them with better training and support. The National Bank of Australia therefore believes it will achieve these results. This value chain is created for everyone, employees, and customers. This example shows that the organization can only apply measures and make decisions based on verified evidence from the data.

First in this chapter, a review of the literature on the topic of people analytics (PA) to date will be made. It will be focused on the most mentioned subjects in academic and industry literature, such as the strategic component of PA and the issue of privacy. The paradigmatic and pioneering case of Google will also be highlighted. Then, based on the consultation and content analysis of case studies and interviews on the internet, conclusions will be drawn on what are the PA trends before and after the COVID-19 pandemic. Once these conclusions are generated, recommendations will be made and future suggestions for deepening the theme will be pointed out.

9.2 THEORETICAL FRAMEWORK

The area of PA "it's hotter than hot" (Jones, 2014, p. 43) because nowadays we live in the modern world of digital transformation and the "data gold rush" (Kennedy et al., 2015, p. 172). The term has increasingly appeared in HR circles (Deloitte Insights, 2017). The most majority of studies about PA come from the industry, not the academy, and specifically from the area of organizational psychology and psychometrics, but recently the trend is the area of computing and data sciences (Tursunbayeva et al., 2018). In scientific articles, the area most represented is business, management, and accounting.

Since 2004, according to a Google Trends query, the term PA has been increasingly sought after by internet users (Figure 9.1).

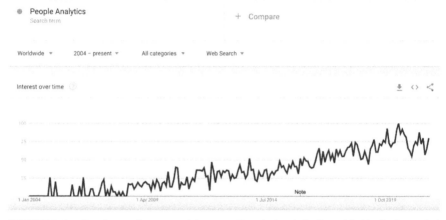

FIGURE 9.1   Google trends output of the term "People Analytics" worldwide, in the period between 2004 and 2021.

PA is a relatively recent term. "Human Resource Analytics," first appeared in the literature in 2003–2004 (Marler and Boudreau, 2016). Lawler et al. (2004) make the difference between "Analytics" and "metrics." HR metrics are measures of important HR results, for example, indicators like efficiency, effectiveness, or impact. On the contrary, Lawler et al. (2004) affirm that HR analytics are not measures but rather social sciences techniques, based on statistical tools and tests to assess HR policies and practices (Marler and Boudreau, 2016). Therefore, PA is an area that crosses statistics with business strategy. It is not about metrics, as it can be confused, but about generating valuable business insights from the data. It is about predicting the future, it is not also just about randomly analyzing data, but asking the right questions and with the help of data generating value for employees and ultimately for the organization. It is essential to start from the problems that the organization is going through, or the most pressing issues related to people (Green, 2020a).

Changes in PA terminology suggest new and evolving needs in human resources management, such as administrative functions, the introduction of technology to generate insights, HR strategy (Tursunbayeva et al., 2018), the issue of privacy, and, finally, empathy as discussed in this study (Green, 2020a, 2020b, 2020c).

Many PA strategies focus on performance assessment and employee lifetime values, gender issues in compensation, onboarding, culture fit, and engagement. Another dominant category found in the literature is workforce planning, including studies on new scheduling models or identifying and estimating employee expertise. Other studies are focused on the use of PA for churn and retention, wellness, sourcing, and acquisition/hiring (Tursunbayeva et al., 2018).

A data analyst will be better prepared for his job with the following skills: analytical or technical skills, knowledge of the sector, soft skills like storytelling, team-working, analytics mindset, creativity, and curiosity. He will also need to be equipped with the methods and tools of a social science researcher, such as quantitative data collection, analysis and presentation, performance of basic and intermediate data analyses, multivariate models, and research and survey design (Bakhshi, 2014; Levenson, 2011).

9.2.1 PA VENDORS

In a recent, academic, and complete review of PA (Tursunbayeva et al., 2018), a search was made by the most common vendors of PA consulting. An internet search for PA vendors showed that most results were links of IBM's HR analytics homepage. Also, other search terms retrieved: to news (Forbes), research (Harvard Business Review), PA-related communities (Kaggle), organizations/platforms providing access to educational materials on PA (HCA Group webpage—Copenhagen Business School PA research group, Coursera) or specific training programs in which PA is a component (Human Resources MBA), and conferences (Wharton PA conference) (Tursunbayeva et al., 2018).

Commonly vendors offer a consulting service of implementing and managing a strategy of PA in companies. Generally, they offer different value propositions. Accenture, IBM, Kronos, and Cornerstone were found to have the most complete value propositions offered, including (a) improved strategic management through access to information and analytical tools; (b) better data management processes using innovative approaches to data collection, combination, analysis, and interpretation; (c) improved people management resulting from greater efficiencies and HR decision-making; (d) new technological solutions for collecting, storing, or analyzing HR data, including automating these processes; (e) direct impacts on HR or strategic business outcomes, such as optimizing human resource assets to increase income relevant to payroll; and (f) employee-oriented benefits such as improved work experience or job satisfaction (Tursunbayeva et al., 2018).

9.2.2 GOOGLE CASE

This was what Google wanted when it created the Oxygen research project—which later turned into strategy (Sullivan, 2013): it started to create a team dedicated to PA. Thus, by extracting data about employees, wanted not only to know them but also to serve them better, as soon realized that they are their most valuable asset. It has been proven that the use of these techniques has improved performance, increased retention, and worker satisfaction. This view is not strange, knowing that Google is looking for the best of the best talent with the desire of not leaving the company. Through the tools of research and data, it seeks this goal of retention of talents.

There are two reasons for Google to invest in this area of HR. First, to serve the employee, which is the company's most precious asset; second, to save costs, as the investment in people accounts for 60/70% of the total company costs (Isson and Harriott, 2016, p. 69). PA models allow predicting behavior and, thus, possible undesirable unforeseen events. For example, if it can be predicted the level of retention of a worker, a lot of money can be saved. Namely, in hiring, training, and retaining that, it would have to be spent on a new worker if the one hired left the company.

Through this project, Google created the "Oxygen 10 behaviours for great managers" to train and select its leaders. Sullivan (2013) found 10 practices that shape Google's PA policy and still place it at the forefront of this area:

1. Improvement of leadership: by analyzing large amounts of internal company data, Google figured out that additionally to technical skills, a major characteristic of great leaders is the periodic one-to-one coaching of workers and frequent feedback;
2. The PiLab—is a unique subgroup within Google, which develops experiences within the company in order to understand what drives performance, productivity, happiness at work, health, and well-being;
3. Google has developed an algorithm that predicts which workers will be a retention issue. This approach allows managers to act preventively;
4. People management at Google has a predictive perspective: models and "what if" analysis;
5. Google also uses algorithms to improve diversity across the company. Through these models, what causes poor diversity in recruitment and

promotions can be calculated. The results it produced in recruitment and retention were dramatic and measurable;

6. An effective algorithm—when recruiting Google calculates the probability of a person failing to recruit. This feature allowed for drastic reduction of time to recruit. In their investigation, it was found that little value was added after four interviews. Strategic recruitment is also independent and thus safer as decisions are made by a group, avoiding personal preferences when choosing employees, such as the tendency to recruit people for short-term goals;

7. Google has developed a way to differentiate top performers from average performers in the company. In this way, it values talent and invests in hiring, retaining, and developing exceptional talent;

8. Workplace design at Google increases collaboration among employees in different roles, being innovation the result of discovery (learning), collaboration, and fun;

9. On-job learning is done in a practical way and not through classes. Two skills promoted at Google are self-directed continuous learning and adaptability through project rotations, mistakes, and events promotion with celebrities (e.g., Al Gore or Lady Gaga);

10. The final key to the success of the Google Team PA happens, not when researching, but when recommendations are made to managers and executives. Before imposing, it uses data and facts to convince. This is easy to do because executives all have an analytic view that understands this data-driven mindset and performance.

Google's "Oxygen" experience came out with three lessons to guide a good PA management: (1) to invest in data infrastructure (2) to answer the questions that really matter. At the beginning, PA Google team tried to answer each question by turning out to be time consuming and ineffective. At the end, they focused on the important questions; (3) At Google, there is not only one Social Science research team. There are various departments and a network: business intelligence group, people operations, voice and people innovation lab teams, business partnership insights team, the "Google People Analytics Ecosystem" (Nicol, 2019).

9.2.3 THE SEVEN PILLARS OF A SUCCESSFUL PA

In a large survey done to companies and published in a seminal work about PA (Isson and Harriott, 2016), the seven most important talent management stages that the leaders consider critical when it comes to creating business value from their talent data are (1) workforce planning; (2) sourcing; (3) acquisition/hiring; (4) onboarding, culture fit, and engagement; (5) employee churn and retention; (6) performance assessment and development and employee lifetime value; and (7) employee wellness, health, and safety.

Focusing on Isson and Harriot's (2016), seven pillars for a successful PA strategy are as follows:

9.2.4   WORKFORCE PLANNING

Workforce planning is an essential pillar of PA. This planning "helps organizations to identify the target segment of employees needed in order to achieve business goals" (Isson and Harriott, 2016, p. 129). Instead of acting in a reactive way to what the market offers in terms of workforce, the company establishes a plan and clearly identifies the profile of employees it wants and also where it will seek them. This profile has to do with technical and nontechnical skills and then the company establishes a strategy for attracting, recruiting, and retaining these same employees. This workforce planning is at the service of corporate strategy and includes all business and top managers, at all stages of the process. Workforce planning helps organizations reduce personnel costs in talent acquisition and development. When carrying out a workforce planning, the company foresees recruitment needs and optimizes the balance of shortages and excesses of human resources.

9.2.5   TALENT SOURCING

The demand for talent has existed for a long time in companies and organizations. This search can be for hundreds of hires, as for dozens. However, a new world has come: the internet, big data, social media, mobile, and the cloud, the latter have made the amount of data explode and have enabled connectivity unprecedented in the previous world. This amount of data allowed the use of analytics in order to optimize sourcing activities and strategies. Today's workforce is made up of different generations and it was estimated that by 2020, more than 50% of this would be Millennials. Companies have to adapt to this reality and plan how they will attract, select, develop, and retain job seekers and those who are already employed.

The STEM (science, technology, engineering, and mathematics) area is the one that meets the greatest needs in terms of recruitment and companies have to adapt and use alternative and sophisticated means to combat the shortage of talent in these areas. Social networks, talent communities, and other big data solutions and service providers to reach candidates are actively and passively looking for work. There has to be a dialog in order to understand which channels they prefer to interact with.

It has been proven that referral (word of mouth) is the most effective method of recruiting, so it is necessary to leverage this channel. However, it is necessary to segment the market and understand which channels are best for each one.

Predictive analytics and big data will help a company to optimize their sourcing results. There are job board solutions that rely on big data, such as semantic search, which executes a search through hundreds of millions of resumes and candidate profiles. These solutions minimize and optimize the recruitment process. Through these solutions, the search for candidates can be done, check their work, their participation in social networks or niche sites, even interaction with the prospective candidates directly and exchange views about opportunities with them.

In this battle for talent, recruitment strategies have to be increasingly analytical and sophisticated in order to capture the best talent. Through big data analytics, it is possible to integrate a set of data from different sources, such as talent CRM systems, applicant-tracking systems, job boards, social media, and employee referrals, to have an overall view, in order to increase talent community and the scope of demand. This is where the company needs to be, where the candidates are. In these places, the recruiter can attract, promote, interact, create content, and retain candidates, just like in a marketing process, but here the product/service is the employee.

9.2.6 TALENT ACQUISITION ANALYTICS

As it has already been highlighted, the techniques of attracting customers used in marketing, namely, those programmed on the internet, for example, search engine optimization is the same used in PA for talent acquisition. Here, too, the companies' online relevance plays a key role. A content strategy here is key as is online engagement. How does the prospective candidate interact online, how it is rated on professional networks and communities such as professional sites as Glassdoor, GitHub, Stack Overflow, and Twitter? Through predictive models of the PA, the "finding" effect is reduced and decisions are better based on evidence. It can be used as a first filter for recruitment, for example, automatic curriculum screening. As Google's Eric

Schmidt said, "hiring is the most important thing you do" (Schmidt and Rosenberg, 2014, p. 510).

There is also a cost-cutting effect in the recruitment process, as the number of interested candidates narrows down through the data, based on a set of criteria. Otherwise, whether it was through manual search or through a simple guess, HR efforts were dispersed and at the same time, the reliability of the choice was jeopardized. There is also a reduction in costs downstream, as if the recruitment process is also "tailor made" as in marketing, there is less likelihood that the candidate will not be loyal and competent. The loyalty part is essential because through PA the turnover costs are reduced.

Recruiting talent today should involve companies' brains and wit, managers with a PA mindset understand that a good hire is a mix of experience, hunch and facts, and data (Isson and Harriott, 2016).

9.2.7   ONBOARDING AND CULTURE FIT

The time when the candidate enters the company is very sensitive. A first impression counts a lot, and the organization has to make efforts not only to make a good impression but to imprint its culture and organizational vision from the very first moment. This vision and culture is what makes the company unique and that is why it has to be cultivated from the first moment. It is the organization's desire to look for talent that is in line with the company's values and behaviors, otherwise the employee can be very competent but not acclimatized to "the way things are done around here." As soon as the company is authentic with its way of being and acting, the candidate will adhere more easily, as it creates trust and retention.

The onboarding process has several phases and takes several months. It is necessary to look for early wins (Watkins, 2013) in the way in which the vision and values are communicated to the new candidate, so that he is involved from the very beginning and facilitates his work.

A model was created to monitor the onboarding process, called OPEN (orient, provide, engage, and next) (Isson and Harriott, 2016).

9.2.8   TALENT ENGAGEMENT ANALYTICS

After the attraction and recruitment of the employee comes the necessary engagement with the company. This engagement is performance related. As pointed out, this involvement must be authentic and based on what makes the company unique. Questionnaires are often used, but it is not enough, in order to try to understand what motivates an employee involved. These worker engagement questionnaires should influence the success of the business objectives and predict them. Through data collection, one company should seek to find patterns and metrics related to engagement. Here there has to be an alignment of the company's leaders regarding the desired business objectives, in order to be efficient. Direct contact with the employee is a more effective practice as it allows to measure the signs of risk of the employee leaving.

9.2.9 ANALYTICAL PERFORMANCE MANAGEMENT

Along the path taken by the employee in the company, analyses on his performance are carried out, and these are essential for the company to remain competitive. These performance analyses are based on the impact generated for the company and consequent rewards. This analysis has to be proactive and done globally. Performance indicators have to be in line with the company's strategy but also the needs and preferences of the workforce. The analytics tools should help predict and assist in promoting employees.

9.2.10 EMPLOYEE LIFETIME VALUE AND COST MODELING

There are three important indicators for measuring the impact of a role in a company. Performance, cost, and attrition provide information for decision-making. These metrics contribute to indicators such as employee lifetime value (ELTV). Measures like this assess the duration and performance of a worker. It is mostly used in high-volume, high-turnover jobs. Based on the analysis of these indicators, the company is permanently learning and acting in areas such as recruitment, engagement, and performance (Isson and Harriott, 2016).

9.2.11 RETENTION ANALYTICS

Retention is an objective no less important than recruiting the right person. The biggest cost in a company is the cost of people. If a company hired someone highly valuable and was able to attract and recruit but after a while this person leaves the company, the company is wasting important resources.

It is a combination of things like compensation, performance, feedback, learning and development, and confidence in leadership that, at the end, can be measured by the simple result of, the person stayed or left? Measures such as ROI are also used here.

Big data and analytics tools help predict attrition risks in terms of knowing who can leave the company, when, and why. It is important here to prioritize who to measure, that is, those resources that give a greater return to the company should be more measured and taken care of. This logic is the same as in the marketing and manufacturing sectors, for example. In a one-to-one marketing, CRM, or big data, the measurement and prediction effort is greater in that slice of customers that bring more revenue to the company. Through the predictive models of the PA, we can anticipate trends, situations, problems, incidents, which can give the company a lot of resource savings. ELTV, combined with retention metrics, provides the company with valuable data in order to inform which employees have the highest ELTV and then understand potential reasons to leave the company and concrete strategies to retain people.

9.2.12   EMPLOYEE WELLNESS, HEALTH, AND SAFETY

There is now evidence that a company that places employee wellness at the heart of its strategy will create a more productive workforce. The 2008 financial crisis made companies want to get back to the numbers quickly and invested heavily in leveraging productivity, but without a healthy and motivated workforce, it is very difficult to achieve its results. A company that offers the candidate a good work–family balance, employer branding, and a value proposition that promotes a good place to work will also be an extra attraction for the employee. The best companies to work for proved that there is a causal link between organizational well-being, health, and safety, with profitability, and the analytics systems in the wellness area of these companies prove this link between well-being and productivity. This is essential, as there may be a vague or intuitive idea that the better employees feel, the more they produce, but using analytics tools, we can measure these indicators accurately, because as Peter Drucker said, "if you can't measure it, you can't manage it."

What is employee wellness? Workplace wellness encourages workers to take preventive care in relation to their health and lifestyle changes, such as increasing physical activity, improving nutrition habits, reducing stress, reducing or decreasing tobacco use, lifestyle coaching, and so on.

These preventive measures lead to a decrease in absenteeism, an increase in workers' morale, and a consequent increase in engagement. Workplace wellness programs consist of a variety of training and behavior change initiatives.

9.2.13 IS PEOPLE ANALYTICS A FAD?

Despite the buzz created around the topic, a broader literature review leads to the conclusion that even so PA is not as implemented in companies as expected (Marler and Boudreau, 2016). There was an idea that PA would be linked to increased organizational performance, but some evidence questions this. Falleta (2014) conducted a survey to determine the use of HR analytics across Fortune 1000 firms. With a sample of 220 firms, Falleta (2014) reported that only 15% of respondents claimed HR analytics as a central role in determining or implementing HR strategy. Furthermore, HR analytics primarily consisted only of analyzing employee survey data. Lawler et al. (2004) and Lawler and Boudreau (2015) report the results of a survey over 100 Fortune 500 companies suggesting less than a third of these companies have HR analytics that measures the relationship between HRM processes and people and business impact. Marler and Boudreau (2016) explain that the main causes for this to happen can be little decision-making capacity of the superiors, lack of analytical skills of the teams, and, finally, lack of IT capacity in the HR area.

There is a difference between conducting surveys or extracting data, even using certain criteria for decision-making. HR analytics is a social science activity, pulling large amounts of data and performing correlations, extracting insights, operations that, without the use and mastery of social science research tools, is difficult to succeed. HR teams are not known to be analytics-driven, conclude Marler and Boudreau (2016).

Google's case clearly underlines that PA is an area of "research," and the literature distinguishes between metrics and analytics. That is why, if companies do not hire specialized personnel, data analysts, they will hardly be able to put into practice such tremendous power that they have in their hands—data. Ownership of the infrastructure and software is also not a *sine qua non* to be able to say that you have a PA system. It matters more what you do with the data than ownership of the data itself.

Another hypothesis pointed out is that businesses are still in a phase of early adoption of PA, and those that advance are the most innovative and take more risks. According to the marketing product lifecycle model, if there are consistent results of the feedback of a product in the market, more customers with less risk tolerance, will follow the pioneers (innovators and risk takers) and thus reinforce the growth in the adoption of the product, until it is skyrocketed to the next stage: maturity.

In a seminal paper about PA, Rasmussen and Ulrich (2015) pointed out four suggestions to avoid PA being a management fad: focusing the work of PA on business problems, taking analytics out of HR, remembering the human in human resources, and training HR professionals to have an analytical mindset (Green, 2020a).

In that article, the coauthor argued that there was a real danger that people from HR analytics could become a little alienated from the functional areas of the company and could be analyzing data that were not relevant to the real problems of the company. So, the proposal of removal of HR analytics from HR and penetrate the functional areas of the company. Operations, finance, marketing, customer service, and so on thus seeking to understand the issues of each department, starting from the problems and not the data. Nowadays (2020), Rasmussen maintains that it is necessary to start with the real problems of the business, but he backs away from the need for the department to leave HR, as he concludes that, in fact, certain specific techniques are needed such as applied social sciences, automation, machine learning, and metrics of specialized nature. Finally, he concludes that it is necessary to be close to decision makers and business problems, but he does not do it without the specialized factor of his work. In conclusion, defends a "hub & spoke" system, in which there are data resources centralized in the PA, but these can be accessed by other areas in a "data lake," centralized, but in contact with the functional areas of the company (Green, 2020a). Again, the manager addresses a critical issue mentioned by PA literature, the need of more specialized knowledge and preparation from HR analytics professionals (Marler and Boudreau, 2016).

9.2.14 ETHICS AND PRIVACY IN PEOPLE ANALYTICS

PA is sought to improve the results of a company and through data manage efficiently the workforce. Additionally, it can be a tool in service of employee performance and well-being, but also a threat.

When extracting data about users whether their personal details, performance, or actions, a sensitivity can be reached—employee's privacy. This is a topic that, despite everything, has not been addressed by literature and industry. In fact, the latter almost only extols the qualities of PA, barely addressing its dark side (Tursunbayeva et al., 2018, 2021). It is possible with analytics to monitor employee e-mails, their social networks and interactions with digital devices, wearables, and apps. It is possible, for example, through the e-mail system to understand when the worker is or is not at the desk, not to mention wearables, sometimes used to measure health indicators, but that can be used for other purposes like surveillance and manipulation. These methodologies can be an argument for improving the employee experience, but also a way of 24/7 monitoring of their location, activity, state of mind, health, and social life. In particular, in productivity and wellness apps (Ajunwa et al., 2017), through work gamification (Cardador et al., 2017), tools which seek, through the execution of games and interactive tasks, greater motivation, and productivity in the job, and nudging (Green, 2020a). "Nudging" is a behavioral economics strategy that seeks to make the user perform certain actions/tasks that, even if in their interest, meet the service provider's needs. Nudging is used every day, for example, in marketing and the customer experience, but also in the employee experience. It can be seen as customer/employee service but also manipulation.

Despite the privacy risks posed by PA for individuals and companies, there is a great lack of applicable legislation. The European General Data Protection Regulation (GDPR) has wide application in Europe and seeks to alert to some risks and vulnerabilities of some innovations but leaves some room for interpretation (Politou and Nicol, 2019). The United States is something of a case of "wild west" when it comes to this issue. It is reported how in many cases companies monitor their workers without a clear and restrictive legal framework (Ajunwa et al., 2017; Tursunbayeva et al., 2018, 2021).

The potential risks of lack of privacy in the use of PA are six (Tursunbayeva et al., 2021): operationalizing bias and discrimination, psychological or social profiling, behavior shaping, reducing performance/people to numbers, creating inconvenience or income security, and threatening privacy or autonomy through tracking and surveillance.

When it comes to operationalizing bias and discrimination, PA tools are made with the good intention of using objective data and not simple human common sense, in order to make the best decisions about people in an organization. Although as human beings are biased by nature and the algorithms are made by them, the results can also be biased.

There is the classic Amazon case, where a recruiting algorithm for software engineers exhaustively screened many résumés and learned that men were more competent in the field than women. Amazon decided to abandon this strategy as it was not meeting its intended diversity policy.

When it comes to behavior shaping, the so-called nudging mentioned previously can be seen as manipulative and intrusive. Teams and people can be reduced to simple machines, and the diversity and complementarity of each one's skills can be ignored. Many PA projects are criticized for only considering groups and organizations, not teams and individuals.

There is also a risk of creating inconvenience or income insecurity. There are cases in which due to data analysis, workers' hours are changed instantly and unpredictably. For example, the case of Starbucks, which used diverse types of data as weather and pedestrian patterns in its scheduling software, resulting in uncertainty about available shift work (Tursunbayeva et al., 2021). However, there is evidence that most workers accept being watched (Mann et al., 2018). One recommendation might be to communicate and educate workers well about monitoring, as this will be the best way to receive their consent (Kim, 2017).

PA projects can also be a risk for organizations. At the dawn of an era of "consent," whether in data or relationships, if companies do not adopt ethical, prudent, and user-focused behavior, they risk jeopardizing their work and the damage may be greater than the expected return on these tools. For this reason, PA projects are also starting to consider, in addition to the return to the business, the risk to the business as well. One observation is that this topic should begin to be worked by specialists in human behavior and ethics instead of technicians, computer scientists, or PA vendors (Calvard and Jeske, 2018).

Furthermore, in the event of the COVID-19 pandemic in which a large part of the workforce was forced to go home to work, these concerns became more demanding as the risk of surveillance and monitoring in remote work is more severe. It becomes more urgent in the future, as the pandemic has changed the work landscape and accelerated the digital transformation in society and companies.

It is also necessary a legal framework and transparency practices on the companies' side, seeking to make workers feel that the data belongs to them. Otherwise, the investment made in these technologies can be undermined, the social contract between employers and employees jeopardized and, ultimately, the sustainability of the organization compromised.

9.2.15   EMPIRICAL RESEARCH APPROACH

The methodology applied to this study was first to do a literature review of the most recent academic review studies on PA, on one hand, industry-related material, on the other hand, and finally the content analysis of information, business cases, and interviews on the Internet. The business case more developed is Google's as is seen as one of the first companies implementing PA in a broader, structured, and innovative way. The interviews analyzed in more depth were done to human capital analytics practitioners from two companies, Merck and the National Bank of Australia. Rabobank was used as a case study. All of business cases and interviews were used with three objectives: (1) understand PA practices, (2) assess PA strategies and practices during the COVID-19 pandemic (Chamorro-Premuzik and Bailie, 2020), and (3) compare the practices and trends before and after the outbreak of the COVID-19 pandemic. The reason for choosing these companies is because they are companies of considerable size, some multinationals, and with prestige in the market. Some of its directors are opinion makers in international circles about PA, which makes their opinion more credible and generalizable. For this reason, this is not only interviews with professionals in the field but also experts in the field (Flick, 2005). Second, in all of them—Rabobank, Merck, and the National Bank of Australia—the subject of PA and the COVID-19 pandemic is addressed.

The analyzed results can be generalizable and reproducible for other realities, namely, for the advancement in the knowledge and practice of PA, for the knowledge of the new challenges generated by the pandemic crisis, and for the HRM area in general.

The interviews analyzed the trends and biggest challenges of PA before and after the COVID-19 pandemic. A content analysis work was done, interpreting the text by classification, categorization, and subjective interpretation (Lai and To, 2015). Then, the major themes that are the concern of HR managers were isolated and patterns searched in them. Finally, conclusions and recommendations will be issued based on reading the literature and collecting and treating the data from the interviews.

9.3 RESULTS AND DISCUSSION

By analyzing the interviews with HR managers from the two companies mentioned, Merck and National Bank of Australia and the case study by Rabobank (Green, 2020a, 2020b, 2020c), there are recurrent subjects that we can establish as the current trends—and in a postpandemic world—in PA and data-driven HRM:

1. Driving business value from data (strategic HR)
2. Empathy/Listening employees/Connection/Wellness

3. Privacy
4. More COVID-19-related challenges and trends:
    • Acceleration of trends/Knowledge/PA
    • Reformulation of the function analysis
    • Remote work

9.3.1 DRIVING BUSINESS VALUE FROM DATA

Starting with the first, it can be considered as what constitutes any PA strategy. Through data, create value for the organization. Instead of using common sense or a hunch, rely on facts, gather information, find patterns, establish relationships, and step into the unknown, ask the right questions, and ultimately create valuable insights for decision-making. PA shows where the value is and where can the company cut costs and improve customer satisfaction. Then the next step is to act upon these findings in changed behavior (Green, 2020a).

This quest to create value is not just about mastering statistics but also asking the right questions and focusing on business results rather than procedural issues. PA is also about predicting trends and needs and not looking back on what has already happened in terms of employee experience and other areas of HR. In a quote by Wayne Gretsky, already repeated by Steve Jobs and Warren Buffett about anticipating market trends:

> "it is not about knowing where the puck is, but it is about knowing where it is going to be if you want to win." (Green, 2020a)

Jeremy Shapiro, from Merck, also mentions the increasingly predominant role that strategic human resources management plays in the company, no longer just another actor in the functional hierarchy, but a key role in creating business value (Green, 2020c).

9.3.2 EMPATHY

With regard to empathy, due to the outbreak of the COVID-19 pandemic, it is constantly mentioned by the two interviewees and the case study about PA in COVID times analyzed, as a growing need in organizations. This objective of permanent listening, in order to obtain coherent results for decision-making, is analogous to a customer-centered strategy; here the customer is the employee. The pandemic brought to society and companies a vulnerability that had to be monitored by those who take care of people, adopting a close posture, focused on the needs of employees, and constantly auditing the health and safety of the workforce.

Jeremy Shapiro, from Merck, mentions the theme of the need to show empathy for employees, as HR and PA posture, seven times. In his comments, the related terms are "wellbeing," "connection," "empathy." With the COVID-19 event, the priority became to check how the worker is doing and then, yes, to ensure that the company's operations are carried out (Green, 2020c).

In a Google Trends search, we can see how the search for the term "empathy" has increased in recent times, reaching the maximum score in the given period (100) in September 19th, 2020 (Figure 9.2).

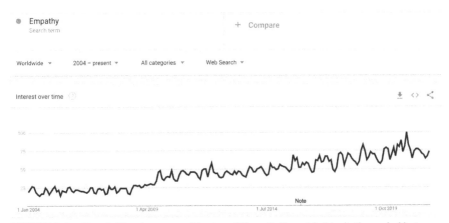

FIGURE 9.2   Google Trends output of the term "Empathy" worldwide, in the period between 2004 and 2021.

This thoughtful leadership marked HR management during the pandemic and brought back the term empathy as never before. Once again, it is clear, through catastrophic events, how people are not a simple resource, but that without them, nothing happens in the company. Furthermore, this type of leadership, the one based on consideration and proximity, the one that wants to build trust, is the most correlated with remote work performance, which was massively present as a way to protect against the virus. The telecommuter has unique needs that may dictate the leader's best style (Dahlstrom, 2013). Hackman and Johnson (1991) make the point that leadership is best understood from a communication standpoint. Moreover, Timmerman and Scott (2006) show that responsiveness and thoroughness (of the leader), and communication channel selection to maintain connectedness, have solid correlation with virtual team outcomes, such as identification, trust, and communication satisfaction. Baker et al. (2006) also make the point that a manager's trust (a nontechnical support and type of relationship-oriented behavior) had broad impact on employees' reactions to home-based telecommuting.

The experience of Rabobank's managers is similar, the theme of empathy, support, and wellness is mentioned seven times in their compilation of ideas learned about PA in COVID-19 times (Green, 2020b).

Thomas Rasmussen, responsible for employee experience, digital, HR strategy, and PA at the National Bank of Australia, also highlights the importance of empathy in PA's strategy in a postpandemic context or not, but specially in that situation:

> "And the starting point always becomes, have empathy, respect data privacy and understand that you are dealing with people (…) that you get some feedback as well." (Green, 2020a)

9.3.3   DATA PRIVACY

The issue of privacy is something that is present before and after the pandemic. As the interviews were carried out before and after, it is possible to verify this recurrence. In fact, as pointed out by the literature earlier in this study, it is one of the challenges, if not the biggest one that PA faces. Here, the interviewees are unanimous that privacy is a topic that is no longer questioned, but that it should be accompanied by more legislation (Green, 2020c). For Rasmussen, it should be the main concern and even if something can be done, it does not mean that it should be done (Green, 2020a). And, it is known that the possibilities of PA are endless but so are its data security and privacy vulnerabilities.

9.3.4   MORE COVID-19'S PEOPLE ANALYTICS TRENDS

Regarding the COVID-19 pandemic, the themes on which everyone agrees is, as already highlighted, the need for connection and empathy, as a form of internal listening. Then, workforce wellness gains a notable preponderance here, as the pandemic situation has brought to the focus of organizations, health needs (physical and mental), well-being, work–life balance, fighting stress and anxiety, remote management, and privacy, which gained more relevance as people worked from home. Data security, on the one hand, surveillance, on the other, were areas of risk and vulnerability. There was also, according to respondents in a Merck's inquiry, an acceleration of trends (Green, 2020c), including digitization and remote work, which includes PA. As the configuration of functions in the company was questioned and changed, due to circumstances, the design was also. According to the two interviewees Rasmussen and Shapiro, agree that the configuration of roles in their companies were questioned, whether because of the physicality of the function or assigning the right people to the right jobs with the right skills very quickly (Green, 2020a, 2020c).

9.4 CONCLUSION, LIMITATIONS, AND FUTURE DIRECTIONS

Based on the content analysis of the internet material and the literature review, the PA priorities before the pandemic were essentially centered on two areas: strategic business value and data privacy. First, the area of PA is at the service of business strategy, in which people play a central role; second, the issue of data privacy as a priority in PA. In a world post-Enron, post-Cambridge Analytica, and post-MeToo, transparency and authenticity are values increasingly considered by societies. If PA is a strategy to achieve results, it will have to be done with people and not at the expense of people, because in the end no employee will feel on the same boat if he perceives he is being used as a mere means to an end and not as an own end.

With the pandemic event, the areas of PA and human resources management in general, changed priorities and focus. With the outbreak of the pandemic, topics, such as need for connection, well-being, empathy, digital and overall acceleration of trends, and human resource strategic management, are unanimously addressed by the analyzed PA directors' interviews. Therefore, if the main topics before the pandemic were business value, privacy, now they continue to be, but the employee's well-being gains preponderance in relation to the company's operations. Before the operation, one tries to find out if the worker is doing well. The pandemic questioned many conceptions, namely, which functions can be performed online and offline, as well as the human value and empathy toward the worker. In this prioritization, the management of human resources gains new breath in the set of areas of the company, highlighted in relation to the business area. With this pandemic, it was realized that if companies do not value more and take care of their employees, the businesses will not advance much. Here, the strategic management of human resources also gains a special role in the set of functional areas of the company. Physically and emotionally unhealthy people will hardly produce and return results.

Finally, the academic and industry literature analyzed to date also seems to reflect these concerns, business value and privacy, as well as empathy, but in particular the academic literature is more cautious about the real effectiveness of PA techniques. On the one hand, despite the hype created around PA mainly leveraged by the industry, the academic literature seems suspicious about it (Marler and Boudreau, 2016), claiming more case studies on the area are needed. On the other hand, many case studies are accessible in some sources (Isson and Harriott, 2016) and through the analysis of the interviews, it is palpable the structured and strategized work that is being done, and also in the case of Google. Nevertheless, the expectable high number of companies implementing these technologies was not fulfilled. Three of the possible reasons for the PA not to grow more is the need to prepare human resources, that is, the so-called data analysts, the poor IT infrastructure in companies, and finally, the lack of legislation and regulations regarding data privacy. These three factors may be the main curtailers of PA.

As recommendations, in addition to the ostensible disclosure of the benefits of PA for the business, a broader debate on ethical issues is needed. Second, clear legislation is needed on the limits of the use of employee data, otherwise the expected growth of this area can be halted, and PA can become a nuisance for the workforce and not a unifying factor of care and growth.

The limitations of this study may be the small number of companies analyzed but given their size and the influence of their leaders as experts in the field, it can be compensated. Areas of study to deepen in the future include PA ethics, privacy, ways to create empathy with workers through PA, and finally, more in-depth studies on lessons from COVID-19 and its application to PA.

KEYWORDS

- people analytics
- workforce analytics
- HR analytics
- big data
- artificial intelligence
- social sciences
- human resources
- business value
- human resources strategic management
- employer branding
- data privacy
- empathy
- COVID-19

REFERENCES

Ajunwa, I.; Crawford, K.; Schultz, J. Limitless Worker Surveillance. *Calif. Law Rev.* **2017,** *105* (3), 735–776.

Alepis, E.; Patsakis, C. Forgetting Personal Data and Revoking Consent under the GDPR: Challenges and Proposed Solutions. *J. Cybersecur.* **2018,** *4* (1), tyy001.

Almeida, F. Concept and Dimensions of Web 4.0. *Int. J. Comput. Technol.* **2017,** *16* (7), 7040–7046.

Baker, E.; Avery, G.; Crawford, J. Home Alone: The Role of Technology in Telecommuting. *Inf. Resour. Manage. J.* **2006,** *19,* 1–22.

Bakhshi, H. Model Workers. How Leading Companies Are Recruiting and Managing Their Data Talent. *Nesta,* 2014. Retrieved from: http://www.rss.org.uk/Images/PDF/influencing-change/rss-nesta-model-workers-data-talent-recruitment-2014.pdf

Bersin, J. Predictions for 2017: Everything Is Becoming Digital. *Bersin by Deloitte,* 2016.

Calvard, T.S.; Jeske, D. Developing Human Resource Data Risk Management in the Age of Big Data. *Int. J. Inf. Manage.* **2018,** *43,* 159–164.

Cardador, M. T.; Northcraft, G. B.; Whicker, J. A Theory of Work Gamification: Something Old, Something New, Something Borrowed, Something Cool? *Human Resour. Manage. Rev.* **2016,** *27* (2), 353–365.

Chamorro-Premuzic, T.; Bailie, I. Tech Is Transforming People Analytics. Is That a Good Thing? *Harv. Bus. Rev.* **2020.** Retrieved from: https://hbr.org/2020/10/tech-is-transforming-people-analytics-is-that-a-good-thing

Dahlbom, P.; Siikanen, N.; Sajasalo, P.; Jarvenpää, M. Big Data and HR Analytics in the Digital Era. *Balt. J. Manage.* **2019,** *15* (1), 120–138.

Dahlstrom, T. R. Telecommuting and Leadership Style. *Publ. Person. Manage.* **2013,** *42* (3), 438–451.

Deloitte Insights. *2017 Deloitte Global Human Capital Trends Report: Rewriting the Rules for the Digital Age,* 2017. Retrieved from: https://www2.deloitte.com/cn/en/pages/human-capital/articles/global-human-capital-trends-2017.html

Deloitte Insights. The Rise of the Social Enterprise. *2018 Deloitte Global Human Capital Trends,* 2018. Retrieved from: https://www2.deloitte.com/content/dam/insights/us/articles/HCTrends2018/2018-HCtrends_Rise-of-the-social-enterprise.pdf

de Brito, A. P. Using Google Trends and Twitter to Analyse the Phenomenon of Telework during the COVID-19 Pandemic—A Social Media Analytics Review and Study. In *Innovations and Social Media Analytics in a Digital Society*; Sousa, M. J., Marques, C., Eds.; Taylor and Francis Book: London, 2022; pp 90–111.

Falletta, S. In Search of HR Intelligence: Evidence-Based HR Analytics Practices in High Performing Companies. *People Strat.* **2014,** *36,* 28–37.

Flick, U. *Métodos Qualitativos na Investigação Científica*; Monitor: Lisboa, 2005.

Green, D. Episode 37: How National Australia Bank Has Scaled People Analytics (Interview with Thomas Rasmussen). *My HR Future*; Insight 222, May 2020a. Retrieved from: https://www.myhrfuture.com/digital-hr-leaders-podcast/2020/5/19/how-national-australia-bank-has-scaled-people-analytics

Green, D. How Rabobank Uses Continuous Listening to Understand Employee Sentiment During COVID-19. *My HR Future*; Insight 222, May 2020b. Retrieved from: https://www.myhrfuture.com/blog/2020/5/12/how-rabobank-uses-continuous-listening-to-understand-employee-sentiment-during-covid-19

Green, D. Episode 39: How People Analytics Has Progressed in the Last 10 Years (Interview with Jeremy Shapiro). *My HR Future*; Insight 222, June 2020c. Retrieved from: https://www.myhrfuture.com/digital-hr-leaders-podcast/2020/6/2/how-people-analytics-has-progressed-in-the-last-10-years

Hackman, M.; Johnson, C. *Leadership: A Communication Perspective*; Waveland Press: Prospect Heights, IL, 1991.

Isson, J. P.; Harriott, J. S. *People Analytics in the Era of Big Data: Changing the Way You Attract, Acquire, Develop, and Retain Talent*; John Wiley & Sons: New Jersey, 2016.

Jones, K. Conquering HR Analytics: Do You Need a Rocket Scientist or a Crystal Ball? *Workforce Solut. Rev.* **2014**, *5*, 43–44.

Kennedy, H.; Moss, G.; Birchall, C.; et al. Balancing the Potential and Problems of Digital Methods through Action Research: Methodological Reflections. *Inf., Commun. Soc.* **2015**, *18* (2), 172–186.

Kim, P. Data-Driven Discrimination at Work. *William Mary Law Rev.* **2017**, 48, 857–936.

Kitchin, R. *The Data Revolution: Big Data, Open Data, Data Infrastructures & Their Consequences*; Sage: Thousand Oaks, CA, 2014.

Lai, L. S.; To, W. M. Content Analysis of Social Media: A Grounded Theory Approach. *J. Electr. Commerce Res.* **2015**, *16* (2), 138.

Lawler, E. E.; Boudreau, J. W. *Global Trends in Human Resource Management: A Twenty-Year Analysis*; Stanford University Press: Stanford, CA, 2015.

Lawler, E. E.; Levenson, A.; Boudreau, J. W. HR Metrics and Analytics: Use and Impact. *Human Resour. Plann.* **2004**, *27*, 27–35.

Lazer, D.; et al. Computational Social Science. *Science* **2009**, *323*, 721–723.

Levenson, A. Using Targeted Analytics to Improve Talent Decisions. *People Strat.* **2011**, *34*, 34–43.

Mann, H.; Neale, C.; Kumar, T. People Analytics: Ethical Considerations. *Analytics in HR*, 2018. Available at: https://www.analyticsinhr.com/blog/people-analytics-ethical-considerations/

Marler, J. H.; Boudreau, J. W. An Evidence-Based Review of HR Analytics. *Int. J. Human Resour. Manage.* **2016**, *28* (1), 3–26.

Meister, J. The Future of Work: The Intersection of Artificial Intelligence and Human Resources. *Forbes*, 2017. Retrieved from: https://www.forbes.com/sites/jeannemeister/2017/03/01/the-future-of-work-the-intersection-of-artificial-intelligence-and-human-resources/2/#517bbd5c67ee

Newman, D. T.; Fast, N. J.; Harmon, D. J. When Eliminating Bias Isn't Fair: Algorithmic Reductionism and Procedural Justice in Human Resource Decisions. *Organ. Behav. Human Dec. Process.* **2020**, 160, 149–167.

Politou, E.; Nicol, C. *Case Study: How Google Uses People Analytics*; Sage: Thousand Oaks, CA, 2019. Retrieved from: https://www.sage.com/en-au/blog/case-study-how-google-uses-people-analytics/

Rasmussen, T.; Ulrich, D. Learning from Practice: How HR Analytics Avoids Being a Management Fad. *Organ. Dyn.* **2015**, *44* (3), 236–242.

Rego, A.; Cunha, M. P.; Gomes, J. F.; Cunha, R. C.; Cardoso, C. C.; Marques, C. A. *Manual de Gestão de Pessoas e do Capital Humano*; Sílabo: Lisboa, 2015.

Sullivan, J. How Google Became the #3 Most Valuable Firm by Using People Analytics to Reinvent HR. *ERE Recruiting Intelligence*, 2013. Retrieved from: https://www.ere.net/how-google-became-the-3-most-valuable-firm-by-using-people-analytics-to-reinvent-hr/

Timmerman, E.; Scott, C. Virtually Working: Communicative and Structural Predictors of Media Use and Key Outcomes in Virtual Work Teams. *Commun. Monogr.* **2006,** *73,* 108–136.

Schmidt, E.; Rosenberg, J. *How Google Works*; Grand Central Publishing: New York, NY, 2014.

Tursunbayeva, A.; Di Lauro, S.; Pagliari, C. People Analytics—A Scoping Review of Conceptual Boundaries and Value Propositions. *Int. J. Inf. Manage.* **2018,** *43,* 224–247.

Tursunbayeva, A.; Pagliari, C.; Di Lauro, S.; Antonelli, G. The Ethics of People Analytics: Risks, Opportunities and Recommendations. *Personn. Rev.* **2021,** *51* (3), 900–921.

Watkins, M. D. *The First 90 Days Updated and Expanded: Proven Strategies for Getting Up to Speed Faster and Smarter*; Harvard Business Review Press: Boston, MA, 2013.

CHAPTER 10

PARADIGM SHIFT IN HIGHER EDUCATION MODEL BY USING ARTIFICIAL INTELLIGENCE: CHALLENGES AND FUTURE PERSPECTIVES IN INDIA AND OMAN

SANGEETA TRIPATHI

Mass Communication Department, University of Technology and Applied Sciences Salalah, Dhofar, Sultanate of Oman

ABSTRACT

Advance technology and the internet revolution have accentuated the use of digital learning. The COVID-19 pandemic has made it more evident. In such a scenario, artificial intelligence (AI) has become a buzzword in our daily life, business, and education. The current scenario brings a new paradigm shift where people can use the maximum machine to connect the virtual world as real. Awareness is the key to the success of AI as it can apply to gauge up efficient utilization of community teaching assistance productivity and enhance interaction with MOOC learners. Today, communicologists are working hard on developing a new model of education based on AI in different parts of the world. As per Lewis, 1898, the AIDA model for personal selling emphasizes "awareness" as the initial stage leading to action.

This chapter explores the status of awareness regarding AI among students and teachers and examines emerging technologies in education that evolve new ways of teaching and learning. The chapter tries to discover

Incorporating AI Technology in the Service Sector: Innovations in Creating Knowledge, Improving Efficiency, and Elevating Quality of Life. Maria José Sousa, Subhendu Kumar Pani, Francesca Dal Mas, & Sérgio Sousa (Eds.)
© 2024 Apple Academic Press, Inc. Co-published with CRC Press (Taylor & Francis)

the challenges and intricacies of AI in the education system in two different demographics India and Oman and its future perspectives in higher education. The conclusion helps as a reference document in policy-making for future use of higher education.

10.1   INTRODUCTION

Artificial intelligence (AI) has become a buzzword in our daily life, business, and education. Machine learning and deep learning have made AI a reality. The advent of the smartphone facilitates its reach to the masses. AI origin can be traced since 1956 when a group of experts assembled to conduct a research project for the Dartmouth Summer Research project on AI (Mccarthy, 2006). It was not a solemn start. However, research work in this area got accelerated steadily. Later machine learning thrived from 1980 onward. Practically, AI got highlighted in 2010 (Reynoso, 2021). After machine learning, deep learning brought a great potential to make AI a reality in this world. It became more noticeable and popular when connected with the voice assistant tool to electronic gadgets. Alexa smart speaker is a voice-controlled Amazon-assistant device that converts word commands into actions. Google Assistant, Apple Siri, and Microsoft Cortana virtual assistant are some popular voice assistant tools of AI. Initially, voice assistant tools got implanted in smartphones and personal speakers. Later, a voice identification program has introduced to communicate with the electronic device. In this way, these devices receive audiodirectives to turn them into actions. Looking at the unabridged research papers on AI in recent years, the mass appeal of AI cognitive approaches is apparent. These research papers help not only upgrade this field but also help to create awareness for its further usage. The worldwide increasing market value displays the emerging demand for AI. According to the grand research report, the estimated revenue for AI global market for the year 2021 is 93.53 billion US dollars (The Report, 2021). The AI revenue forecast has been estimated at 997.77 billion US dollars during the year 2021–2028. Since 2017, the AI education market has also experienced growth. It shared 20% machine learning revenue, 55% learning platform, virtual facilitator applications, and 60% learner model market. North America from the Global North has dominated AI in the education market in the year 2020. AI market predictors forecast its market value to grow at a CAGR of 47.77% by 2022 (Anders, 2020). The United Kingdom, Germany, Australia, and South Africa are emphasizing AI in education. Global south counties such as Brazil, Africa, China, India, and the Middle East countries are trying to compete in the international learning environment by adopting AI in education. AI has all to replace the traditional analytic tools that have been used in education, healthcare, and business. This effort will help in generating a large amount of data to promote AI that can be owned privately (Preeti Wadhwani, 2021).

The beginning of AI research had been sporadic in India. The first time Master's program in Computer Science started at IIT, Kanpur, was in 1963. Professor Dr. H.N. Mahabala was the person behind this drive. Only nine students got registered for this course. Nobody was aware of computers in India. Jobs opportunities for such computer graduates were zero in the country because nobody uses computers in those days (Sadagopan, 2019). The year 1980 is considered as took off for AI in India. The Indian government launched a knowledge-based computing program in association with the United Nation Development Programme. From 1986 to 1995, some nodal agencies such as IIT Madras, Tata Institute of Fundamental Research, and Indian Statistical Institute Kolkata had been set up to work on critical aspects of AI. "Eklaya" a knowledge-based program had been designed by IIT Madras as an effort to support community healthcare workers (Digital, 2018). Indian government's interest in AI can be traced to its feasibility for socio-economic benefits. NITI Aayog, the think tank of India, has supported AI applications for growth and accuracy in agriculture, diabetic retinopathy diagnosis, and developing a language processing platform for various Indian languages. Indian research and development capabilities have been growing up steadily from 2010 to 2017. IIT Hyderabad has become the first institution to offer a full B-Tech course in AI, in India (Verma, 2019).

India ranked globally at 10th position for Ph.D. research in AI. A lot of efforts are being made to implement AI techniques more accurately, multilaterally, and dextrous as it has greater potential to transform teaching and learning than traditional classrooms. AI and the latest innovations allow teachers and students to have better prospects to advance the learning processes (Iftikhar, 2018).

The outbreak of the COVID-19 pandemic emerged as a high risk to human existence and confined the whole world. It causes a massive impact on world businesses and the education system. To flatten the curve of infection, each country's government has taken many decisions. It changed the sociocultural behavior dramatically. It emerged as an opportunity for AI in the business, service sector, and education system. Several IT giants and start-ups started working to facilitate remote working and learning through a different digital platform to alleviate the impact of virus infection. Digital media platforms turned into a primary medium for work, communication, and other engagement for the people during their stay in quarantine. In the medical sector, different diagnostic algorithms had developed to detect COVID-19 cases. Computed tomography scan Alibaba's Research Institute Damo Academy's and Lunit's AI solution for X-ray analysis were some techniques of AI-empowered computer systems that help in inferring and nursing COVID patients (Cloud, 2020).

In the education sector, with the shutdown of universities since the spring 2020, millions of teachers and students were forced into an unexpected online learning trial. Many countries were not prepared for this as it requires robust internet infrastructure. The disruption continued in the new academic year 2020–2021. It forced schools, colleges, and universities' administration and teachers to work on effective plans. In the absence of classroom learning, online live sessions with the help of Google Meet, Google Classroom, and Microsoft Team have become gigantic support to teachers and students. AI systems have played a lot as it has become the need of the hour to optimize online learning. Increasing dependency on digital platforms in the education system indicates different prospects, dissimilar from paradigms of a traditional classroom. This chapter mainly underlines three points to understand the components for the success of AI in higher education, awareness about AI among the masses, identify intricacies to ensure AI bright prospects, and understand the potential of AI for the future learner. This chapter focuses on two beamy regions of the world—India as an Asian country and the Sultanate of Oman represent a Middle East country.

10.2 EMERGING TREND IN INDIA AND OMAN EDUCATION SYSTEM

AI works to produce and study the machine intended processes to simulate human intelligence. It helps in optimizing routine work methods to improve work speed and efficiency. Due to the increasing demand for AI, several establishments worldwide are adopting AI to grow continuously. India and Oman have also understood the significance of AI. Digital, AI-enabled technology-based education is the way forward for next-generation learning that helps in facilitating a global learning environment. It allows accessing course content without geographical boundaries, anywhere, anytime. Research-related deliberation and discussion on AI have been discussed since the inception of its idea. But the COVID-19 pandemic gave a kick start as it changed the global market, education system, and other service sectors. The abrupt closure of universities and other academic institutions has forced physical learning to shift to online remote learning. It helps to safeguard academics and learners' well-being.

SWAYAM MOOC learning initiative was started July 9, 2017 by the Ministry of Human Resource Development. However, it has received abundant success during the pandemic lockdown in India. It has been considered a big step toward AI-powered personalized learning. SWAYAM, with nine national coordinators, offers massive online open courses, aiming at a large-scale population with no learning cost. SWAYAM has changed the landscape of higher education in India. More AI-learning apps like BYJU's learning, Merit nation, TED, SOLO learning, and Grammarly apps have proven profuse support in enhancing knowledge. It is beneficial for the students as they can adjust their learning timing according to their available time. Due to remote learning, SWAYAM has different pedagogies. The success of MOOC learning in India can be estimated by the enrollment of online students, which rose 61% since January 2020 (SWAYAM, 2017). SWAYAM learning targets 48% Indian population with the 15–40 age group. These students are highly aspired to achieve adroit education. Due to low income, they cannot access direct learning in higher education centers. With the pretty good penetration of smartphones and cheap internet availability in India, SWAYAM has become popular among the younger demographic. Here, 50% of Internet penetration in India plays a significant role in making way for SWAYAM. Different states and nonstate agencies use various tools and techniques to promote and deliver e-learning modules to online learners. Some other initiatives like E-Pathshala, SWAYAM Prabha free DTH education channel have begun in 2015 to strengthen AI efforts in India (SWAYAM, 2017).

India has adopted a unique tactic to its national AI strategy AIforALL. This strategy aims to empower national youth with the required skills for better opportunities (CBSC, 2021). The Indian government has launched an AI program, "Responsible AI for Youth." It aims to facilitate a new tech mindset that makes youngsters ready for future opportunities. To promote AI in India, many academic departments, institutions are working. Department of AI-IIT Hyderabad, Academic-Industry Collaboration on AI, Centre for AI IIT Kharagpur, and Centre for AI and Robotics, DRDO are some of them.

The National Institute of Transforming India (NITI Ayog) has taken several initiatives to promote AI in India. A task force had formed on August 24, 2017, under Commerce and Industry Department, India. It aims to transform the Indian economy. Niti Aayog and Asea Brown Boveri have signed a statement of intent in 2018 to integrate modern progress in robotic work and AI (Delhi Press, 2018). Niti Aayog has introduced an AI module for children with the help of Microsoft and Wipro company in 2020 and suggested investing 7500 crores to stimulate AI in India. This outlay focuses on healthcare, education, agriculture, developing smart cities infrastructure, and transportation. AI market size in education is increasing steadily. As of 2016, India's e-learning market size was 247 million US dollars which comprised 1.6 million users. By 2021, it has expected to reach 1.96 billion US dollars. This growth is eight times multiplied. The current user growth has been estimated by 44% CAGR to 9.6 million. With all these efforts, India's e-learning market has become the second-largest market after the USA (Foundation, 2021a).

The potential impact of AI in the Middle East can be seen as an AI market expected of the Middle East is expected 320 billion US dollars by 2030. In this whole scenario, Saudi Arabia seems leading among GCC countries. Due to AI contribution, their economy has expected to see the biggest gain of 135.2 billion US dollars by 2030. UAE has measured to be in the second position with 96.0 billion US dollars. AI contribution impact to GCC4 countries has speculated at around 45.9 billion US dollars which is 8.2% of their GDP (PWC, 2020). Qatar, Kuwait, Bahrain, and Oman have been included (PWC, 2020).

Oman Vision 2040 is distinctive in many ways as it fosters diversified economic development and employment creation under the Omanization process for Omani nationals in the existing digital economy. Getting ready for the fourth industrial revolution, Oman aims to advance the current education system by adopting AI. Oman's government has identified AI as a component to achieving Oman's vision for 2040. However, AI-enabled technology is at its nascent stages in Oman, but the Oman government seems enthusiastic to build IT infrastructure and maximum governance through e-services and AI, which has proven encouraging to AI drive. Oman's population is 5.16 million by January 2021, while 4.92 million people use the internet facility. Oman's Internet penetration is 95.2% which is pretty good. 5G network is also getting ready to meet the transition of the next generation (KEMP, 2021).

In the healthcare sector during 2019, the Ministry of Health informed the country that AI would be used to detect breast cancer. This project displayed the Ministry of Health's incessant efforts to enhance the quality of healthcare facilities in Oman (MOH, 2019).

The government is emphasizing the use of AI innovative technology in education. It aims to monitor the delivery of course material and tracking the performance growth of the students individually. MENA Innovation 2019 is considered very significant in this journey. Regional, international brands, Oman Academic Institution SMEs, Ministry of Education and Higher Education, Ministry of Communication, and multiple government stakeholders from the Middle East and North Africa have participated in this event. They devise ways to enhance Oman's education system with AI-based technology (Innovation, 2019). Ewathiq, an online Omani digital platform, is already getting used to help and support Omani students. Oman has also implemented an active learning policy that has shifted traditional teaching and learning (WATHIQ, 2021).

In 2020, a consortium had organized to promote AI solution facts, information, and skills with the collaboration of the Ministry of Technology and Communication, Gulf Business Machines, and The Research Council. They signed to implement AI projects in smart city platforms. In October 2020, a National AI and Education forum has been organized virtually by the Ministry of Education and Oman National Commission for Education, Science, and Culture. Experts from various fields such as education, AI professionals from regional and international, culture and science, Arab Bureau of Education for the Gulf States have participated in this forum. They discussed the prospects of Oman's education system to meet the requirement of the fourth industrial revolution. The main focus of the discussion was to introduce the purpose of AI, its different fields, the instrument to apply its various applications in education processes, and enable its immediate use during the COVID-19 pandemic. The discussion also included capacity building and the use of technology in education by Omani teachers (Communications, 2020). In another effort in the same year, Oman education services signed an exclusive agreement with Finland company Eduten. This agreement aimed to bring a high-quality AI-supported mathematics platform for Omani schools. Eduten platform offers several opportunities in math to set specific learning pathways to improve the performance of Omani students. AI-learning platforms help to transmute the traditional form of teaching and facilitate a way forward in learning and critical thinking among the students.

10.2.1 RELEVANCE OF THE AIDA MODEL IN IMPLEMENTATION OF AI IN EDUCATION

The AIDA model is a marketing model developed by an American businessman St. Elmo Lewis in 1898. In this model, he tried to explain personal selling (Model, 2011).

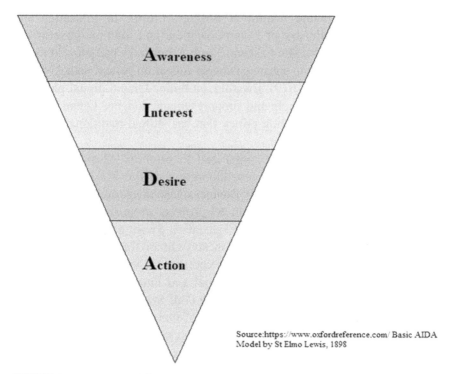

Source:https://www.oxfordreference.com/ Basic AIDA
Model by St Elmo Lewis, 1898

FIGURE 10.1   AIDA model.

Source: Oxford Reference.com.

10.2.2   HOW AIDA MODEL WORKS

The AIDA model looks like a funnel that consists of four stages. The first stage of the AIDA model is a cognitive phase that requires awareness and attention of the community to get success for any event. Through advertising and promotion, AI awareness can be achieved across societies. It generates interest, desire, and acceptance for the product, services, and technology for general use. At the cognitive stage of awareness, several participants participate, while moving toward the second, third, and fourth stages, some fraction of expectancy vanishes. It is not compulsory that everyone who gets aware of information will be interested and desire in action. There are many things such as need, utility, and a budget that works in the second stage to affect the target group to go to the next level.

AIDA is a marketing-based model. However, it is relevant for the success of AI in education too. At present, the education sector is treated as the service industry. Parents and youngsters are selecting school or higher education institutes after checking their academic performance, available rating, world-class learning with a rigorous competitive curriculum, technical support, qualified teaching staff, vibrant teachers' and students' relation, and personal needs with future career opportunities. Due to the increase of digital demand and the cause of pandemics, the whole world has shifted to online platforms. Several courses were running online by several institutions before the pandemic. At the beginning of online learning courses, they ensure the content quality with an additional feature to attract the target learners. It builds strong connections among the students and teachers and helps to hold their interest and desire for enrollment in online courses. Research of target learners' needs and mindset are the prerequisite for producing high-quality course content. It helps in sustaining their engagement in the current program and calls for other participants. For creating AI awareness, highlights and features of online content need to display to the target groups. It fascinates and creates curiosity among them. The use of urgency forces them to explore the course content immediately. Strategic communication about AI features holds interest and desire among learners to the next level. It facilitates understanding how AI addresses the distinct needs of prospects learning for the fourth industrial revolution, repercussions of not adopting AI in education and impact of AI in students' performance to meet future job requirements, and so on. It will easily persuade them for the value-added learning to attain better career opportunities. Through research papers and their results in story-telling form, we can create an aspiration among next-generation learners. Research papers on AI have become the cause of research environment to different fields and accelerated a mechanism to apply AI technologies in healthcare, education, industries and corporates, and so on. Discussion and debate over AI's particular features, utilities, and benefits create a desire to implement AI. The cognitive phase of awareness builds up a reaction in favor or against something. Favorable interest leads them to a suitable disposition toward the product, services, or technological use. The second and third components of the AIDA funnel can be considered an emphatic stage. AIDA model is not relevant only in marketing but in all spheres of life. If the interest succeeds in creating strong desire, it means the promotion event has successfully connected the mass to the product, services, or technology. In marketing, this action calls purchase. In terms of AI, it is called the trial and experiment of AI to accomplish definite tasks. AI implementation accelerated after 2015. Global North country North America is dominating in the use of AI in different sectors. Countries like the United

Kingdom, Germany, South Africa, and Australia have already started AI use in education and several industries. Global South countries like India, China, Africa, and the Middle East countries are also emphasizing on AI. India and Oman's efforts to embrace AI are still in the nascent stage. So here, the AIDA model becomes more relevant. If people get aware of AI and its benefits, it will create a pathway for interest and desire to adopt AI-enabled technology. In this way, a country will be able to build the capacity to empower its economy.

FIGURE 10.2   Description of AIDA model, self-designed by the author on AIDA-based component.

10.2.3   AWARENESS STATUS REGARDING AI IN INDIA AND OMAN

As the AIDA model discussed, awareness is a primordial component for the success of any event. The current chapter explores the status of awareness regarding AI among students and teachers in India and Oman. A pilot study has been conducted. The 243 samples have obtained from the University of Technology and Applied Sciences, Salalah, Oman, and Galgotia University, Greater Noida, Uttar Pradesh, India. Two separate self-administered questionnaires have been developed in English and Arabic language for Indian and Omani communities. Two set questionnaire links have been created and distributed through e-mail and WhatsApp to the target respondents. The questionnaire mainly focuses on 12 points under the AIDA element, shown in Figure 10.3.

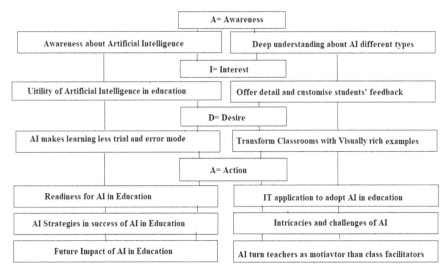

FIGURE 10.3   Relevance AIDA elements to research questions.

The first part examines the awareness status of AI dispersion, deep knowledge about its different types, and various emerging applications in education in India and Oman. The second part of the figure shows two elements—interest and desire. Awareness creates interest and desire to possess or use the technology. Here, AI utilities, efficiency to offer details, and customized feedbacks arise interests among the masses. It encouraged them to go to the next level. The desire to adopt AI has been linked with making the learning experience great with less trial and error. AI features and visually rich content have all potential to transform the traditional class-room into advanced learning platforms. The final part focuses on readiness, AI strategies in education, intricacies, and challenges encountered by both countries.

Frequency Chart 10.1 shows awareness and readiness status about AI among teachers and students in India and Oman. Increasing digital demand and accessibility of the internet facility have encouraged AI proliferation in both countries. India's readiness for AI in education is 44.6%. Its awareness rate is 81.9% which is pretty good. About 59% of Indian respondents say they are fully aware of all four types of AI—reactive machines, limited memory, theory of mind, and self-awareness. During the pandemic, many emerging technologies like virtual reality, live streaming, social learning, augmented reality, asynchronous, microlearning, stimulation, and game learning have been used for distance learning.

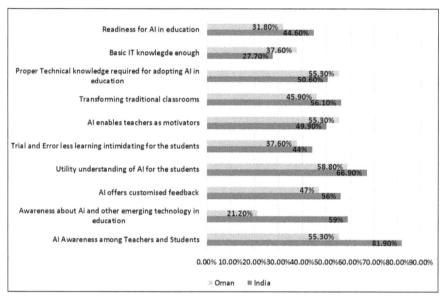

CHART 10.1   AI awareness in education India and Oman, based on data.

In Oman, the awareness rate about AI is lesser than in India. About 55.3% of respondents are aware of the AI concept, while 21.2% know it's all types. These are not sufficient. The students use live sessions, synchronous, asynchronous learning, and gaming applications to accomplish their routine learning. However, the concept of AI is new, its dispersion is growing steadily. Since 2019, awareness regarding the benefits of AI in different sectors created interest and desire to adopt new technology. Different dimensions of AI research, discussions, and debates promote AI in education and make a way forward for India and Oman's education system. The significant factor of rising interest toward adopting AI in education is its utilities and facilities for teachers and students. About 66.9% of Indian respondents agree that AI helps in increasing efficiency through a digital neural network and machine learning. It facilitates customized learning for the learners and helps teachers to identify knowledge gaps among the students. About 56% of Indian respondents say that AI offers detailed and customized feedback to the students, which helps in improving course material and its delivery system.

In Oman, 58.8% of respondents say that AI utilities help improve student's performance. AI can fill the knowledge gap by personalized machine learning. About 47% of Omani respondents believe that AI provides detailed feedback to improve content and teaching methods. Due to machine learning algorithms, computational storage capacity has increased. It has reduced the cost of data managing. Practical applications of AI have promoted the desire to adopt machine learning. AI applications have become affordable because of the smartphone, large storage capacity, and cloud share without adding upfront costs. Now students are less intimidating and more encouraged toward learning as AI offers less trial-and-error learning mode. About 44% of Indian respondents and 37.6% of Omani respondents agreed to this fact. Machine-powered learning proves diagnostics solutions for the students' problems. Deep-learning-based superpowered videos and educational platforms have the potential to provide personalized learning methods to students. It helps in enhancing learning outcomes through a different way of students' assessment. Figure 10.4 shows clearly how three components of AI-enabled learning help to facilitate learning. Communication and feedbacks play a significant role to provide support outside of the classroom.

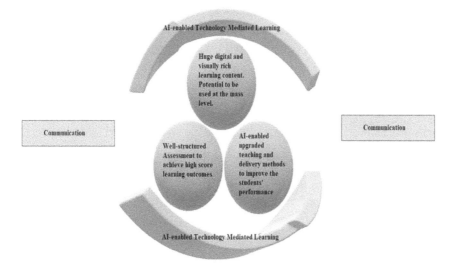

FIGURE 10.4   Three-layer work process of AI in education, based on data.

56.1% Indian and 45.9% Omani respondents believe that AI can change traditional learning. About 50.6% of Indian respondents say that proper IT training and robust infrastructure are the basic requirements for adopting

AI in education. About 27.7% believe that basic knowledge of IT is enough for AI in education. In Oman, 55.3% of respondents agreed that proper IT training is necessary for adopting AI, while 37.6% say that basic IT training is enough for adopting AI in education. About 49.4% Indian respondents and 55.3% Omani respondents say that AI has a long way to outbid. However, it can transform our traditional classrooms to modern and our teachers as a motivator than class facilitators.

Though India has made plausible strides in escalating its educational system since independence, the present education system is a well-organized and transformed system through collective efforts and progressive policies. Since Renaissance, Oman has also made remarkable progress in the education sector. Now both countries are giving pace to advance technology and have well-acknowledged AI potential. Many collaborative efforts from the government, researchers, educators, and the innovation industry have been taken to promote quality education in the country. In this direction, they adopt AI solutions to overcome shortcomings in education. However, some steep barriers persist along the way to peddling a wide-scale implementation of AI in India and Oman. The sudden closure of academic activities and then shifting to online teaching due to the COVID-19 pandemic has posed many questions and impediments. Respondents from India and Oman have many concerns regarding challenges that have originated according to the existing social conditions of each country. That is reflecting from Chart 10.2.

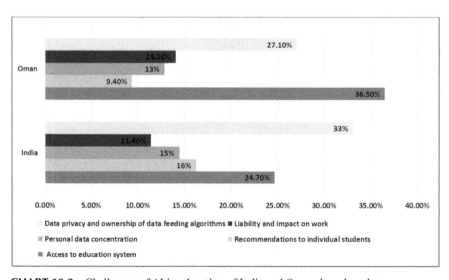

CHART 10.2   Challenges of AI in education of India and Oman, based on data.

About 36.5% of Omani students and teachers understand that data access to the education system is a big challenge for AI in Oman education, whereas 24.7% of Indian respondents consider it as an impediment to AI in India's education. Data privacy and ownership of data-feeding algorithms are the biggest challenges for India. It holds the second position on the challenge list for Oman. About 33% of Indian and 24.10% of Omani respondents consider it the second primus challenge to AI in Oman, and 14.10% of Omani and 11.40% of Indian respondents agree that apprehension and lack of awareness regarding AI liability and impact on work are creating hindrances to the adoption process of AI in education. The frequency percentage of the responses from both countries is close to each other. Thirteen percent of Omani respondents say that personal data concentration is also a challenge to AI. It may cause personal data misuse. It may allow a specific firm or digital platform to achieve substantial competency, but at the same time, it raises distrust too. Fifteen percent of Indian respondents agree to this. About 9.40% of Omani respondents say that recommendation to individual students is difficult to manage as it needs a mechanism or system to track the particular student's performance and generate a report to recommend for further improvement, whereas 16% of Indian respondents consider it as a challenge to AI in education.

10.2.4   CHALLENGES AND INTRICACIES OF AI IN TWO DIFFERENT COUNTRY CONTEXTS

There are some more intricacies and challenges that can slow down AI implementation in India and Oman.

10.2.5   LACK OF AWARENESS ABOUT AI AMONG PEOPLE

Lack of awareness creates a vast impediment to adopt new technologies. It has been noticed that AI awareness is limited to technology experts, academics, and research scholars. The above survey data from both countries have disclosed awareness about AI in India and Oman. Less comprehension of AI leads to slow proliferation in the country. In the present scenario, some SMEs and private sector industries want to use innovative techniques to increase their production by understanding consumer behavior, online sell-out, and purchase, resource management effectively. Due to a lack of awareness and knowledge, they are bound to use the traditional or normal way of working. They do not know the technoservice provider companies like Amazon internet services, Microsoft and Google cloud, and so on. The same situation implies to the education sector too. AI augmentation in the classroom and syllabus is missing. Teachers and students know about AI, but they are not deeply aware of the benefits of AI in advanced learning. They are not aware, how do AI works and what applications to use under AI.

10.2.6 LACK OF COMPREHENSIVE AI STRATEGY FOR ACADEMIC SECTOR

On the economic front, businesses and industries seem enthusiastic to adopt AI-based solutions that help in generating job requirements related to AI skills shortly. It forms a solid imperative background for the education sector to include a curriculum related to AI. This requires the formulation of national policies and strategies. However, neither India nor Oman is having such nationwide comprehensive AI strategy-related intelligence automation for their education sector. The slow policy response to intelligent automation keeps these two countries at a nascent stage.

10.2.7 LACK OF DIGITAL DATA AND ITS PRIVACY ISSUES OF AI IN EDUCATION

AI-enabled learning begins with the data. It requires an advanced pedagogical framework, huge digital and visually rich content, effective curriculum, well-structured assessment, and innovative educational tools along with good communication networks. Due to the initial stage of AI implementation in India and Oman, these kinds of data availability are missing in the country. It is a time-taking process that can foster the collaboration of technology and the academic industries. It reinforces the link between academic circles and the education industry by facilitating technology transfer and exposing knowledge gaps among students to compete in future challenges.

10.2.8 DATA ACCURACY, SUBSTANDARD DATASET, AND RELIABILITY ISSUE

The accurate data are AI's backbone as it vigorously works on the massive dataset. AI applications work perfectly and build up correct inference for action if the dataset is put accurately. At present, India and Oman are at the beginning stage of adopting AI in education. Due to this, a massive data environment is not available in the country. A vast IT infrastructure is needed to create a gigantic data environment with accuracy. In the digital data-driven age, the threat of substandard data has increased too. One lousy data can destroy business, competitiveness, set back to research work, and hinder the process of innovation. Due to substandard data, the loss is expected 3 trillion US dollars per year all over the world. Commonly, data users are not bothered about the data source, explain their needs, and help in eliminating the root cause of poor data. For education, substandard data are a big threat as it is being used to build up the future of students. This problem is not only faced by India and Oman but other countries of the world too. Data reliability is also a big concern for both the country. The Indian government has taken many initiative steps to collect data from higher education institutions. Still, there is a huge gap that can be noticed between actual data and pulled data by the information system. The Indian government has launched a national academic depository to keep a duly digitized record of all academic certificates, mark sheets, and diplomas but still a long road to go. The reason is India's giant population, regional, national, and state boundaries' complications. Oman's country condition is different than India but AI in education is still not started fully. So, these challenges can slow down the process of AI adoption in education and awareness about AI use.

10.2.9   LACK OF CLOUD COMPUTING AND IT INFRASTRUCTURE

Cloud computing is very significant for AI-enabled learning as it includes many features like server, database storage, networking, software, data analytics, and intelligence over the internet. Due to cloud computing, resources become flexible. We became able to get fast innovation at an economic rate. It helps in reducing hardware costs and enhances computing power along with strong storage capacity. The cloud computing market is underdeveloped in India and Oman, which creates a big challenge for adopting AI in education in both countries. Oman government has emphasized upscale inlying cloud computing market and infrastructure. Two local companies—Datamount (Green Mountain Data Centre) and ETCO (International Emerging Technology Company)—signed up to work with a big Chinese company Alibaba Group Cloud (Times of Oman, 2021). The aim behind this effort is to bring advance and secure cloud services to Oman. One step ahead, the Ministry of Commerce, Industry, and Investment

Promotion of Oman has announced that all commercial activities will go cashless with effect from January 1, 2022. This decision has been taken to reduce cash circulation in the market and to enhance digital transformation. These moves are stepping stones in alignment with the roadmap of Oman's vision for 2040 (NFCW, 2021).

In India, the cloud computing market is better. However, due to huge demand, it requires more improvement, security, and reliability. To enhance IT infrastructure, the Indian government has allocated 7.31 billion US dollars in the union budget for 2021. Though India's IT industry is growing and contributed 8% of the total GDP in 2020, a lot more needs to be done in remote and rural areas to strengthen the IT infrastructure. Lack of IT infrastructure creates a digital divide in the country and can be a jerk to a fully AI society (Foundation, 2021b).

10.2.10   THE CHALLENGES OF DIGITAL DIVIDE

The digital divide is still a challenge for many countries. It has been a vital topic of discussion for decades among the technology circle, researcher scholars, and policymakers. Due to COVID-19, the digital divide has gained a prominent place of discussion among all impediments to AI. About 59% of rural American parents from the low-income group showed their apprehension that their children might face digital barriers to their schoolings such as a lack of strong internet connection at home, unavailability of computer devices, or software to complete assigned projects (Pew Research, 2020).

In India, the digital divide is a big challenge for the adoption of AI and machine learning. Metropolitan cities and private academic institutions are adopting and accessing information technologies and handling ICT tools as well, whereas other remote areas and villages have less access to ICT infrastructure. Government schools and higher educations are not well equipped with such facilities. In Oman, the digital divide can be seen in the mountains and remote areas where ICT facilities are limited to access. When the academic activity has been transferred to digital platforms during the pandemic, some students have dropped their semester, and some have chosen such courses that do not require many electronic gadgets. Smartphones have become great saviors for them. In such a situation, an AI-like new concept needs to take more time for its proliferation among the masses. Less reach of AI creates limited awareness status of AI in Oman.

10.2.11   NETWORK SPEED AND TRANSMISSION ISSUE

AI-based learning is based on visually rich data content, which requires a high-speed network. Network speed issues are not only in India and Oman but experienced by other countries of the world. In rural America, academic institutions were scrambling to engage all their students after several months of the COVID-19 outbreak (Khazan, 2020). Due to slow internet speed and undersized IT infrastructure, educators and students did not get what they required for routine learning. According to a Pew Research survey, rural America's major problem is income. That affects the services (Pew Research, 2020). The United Kingdom's situation is also not different than the USA. An estimated 1 million students and their families are still not able to access connectivity at home (Wakefield, 2021). Due to this, they are not able to complete their assignments. When world-leading countries' position in the accessibility of good network speed is suffering, the condition of developing countries can be understood. Due to the pandemic, all activities are getting done online. Several complaints regarding slow internet connection despite unlimited high-speed internet data and bloated bills despite less consumption have been reported in India and Oman. Such an issue can cause trouble for AI in education.

10.2.12   LACK OF COMMUNICATION NETWORKS

Communication networks are required to enhance learning outcomes and course delivery efficiency. It helps teachers to improve teaching methods to understand the knowledge gap among students. Through classwork, assignments, exams, and student's behavior in the discussion, teachers can collect personalized data from the students for further counseling. Lack of communication networks can affect AI-based learning.

10.2.13   LACK OF AI EXPERTS AND SKILL-BASED TRAINING

AI entails highly qualified and expert professionals. AI-skilled human resources are limited in both countries. It creates several challenges to AI drive in India and Oman. There will be no innovation in lack of talent. To prepare AI-skilled professionals, academic institutions need to come forward and embrace AI courses and operate high-equipped AI labs for future hands-on practices. Still, such kinds of efforts are missing at a high level. Sufficient AI resources need to deploy to meet future AI demand.

10.3   CONCLUSION AND RECOMMENDATIONS

The detailed analysis in this chapter establishes an explicit status of AI, its intricacies, and challenges in India and Oman. It displays that AI use is increasing steadily in businesses and industries to improve competency in both countries at its initial stage. However, its diffusion is still limited in the education sector. Due to the COVID-19 pandemic, online shifting of teaching and learning has accelerated the AI implementation process and prepared a solid background to the paradigm shift in high education. However, to promote the acquisition of AI-based learning in both countries, some basic points require development.

10.3.1   ENHANCE AI AWARENESS AND TECHNICAL KNOWLEDGE-SHARING COLLABORATION

Awareness about AI is the foundation stone as it debunks several systematic myths about AI and eases the pathway for the successful adoption of AI in education and other sectors. Strategic communication and its different platforms play a very significant role in this regard. After creating awareness about AI, the second step is to introduce AI-related courses and degrees in public and private colleges and universities. A systematic orientation of AI courses and their prospects can help in creating interest and desire among the students. Sharing of research results among people to create understanding about its utilities and further collaboration to national and international solutions can speed up AI adoption in public and private sector institutions. Such platforms need to be opened under the flagship of Oman and the Indian government. Both countries' governments' research centers can promote awareness about emerging technology, its utilities, and engagement to the masses.

10.3.2   CREATING COMPLETE DATASET AND SHARING STRATEGY

AI in education requires a huge dataset. As India and Oman are at their initial stage of adopting AI, both countries' local data banks are yet to be developed. Both the countries' governments can explore other alternative data sources and data-sharing platforms from AI-leading countries. As India and Oman's governments are truly encouraged to adopt AI to meet their upcoming economic goals, self-data creation will be very significant for their drive to make an AI-enabled digital society. In such a situation, the Indian and Oman governments can take the help of current statistical agencies that can develop their dataset repository. A proper mechanism needs to be defined by both governments to work forward.

10.3.3   BUILDING BRIDGE FOR ACADEMIC, INDUSTRY, AND GOVERNMENT PARTNERSHIP

A collaborative bridge needs to build up among government, industry, and academic institutions to speed up AI in education. To create a young AI-skilled talent pool, academic institutions always need to work in collaboration with industries. Course revision is also getting done according to the requirement of the industries. Due to emerging technology and digital need, a huge job opportunity for AI-skilled talent has been generated. This cycle promotes the AI ecosystem and helps in boosting up the country's economy. This also supports different types of start-ups in the country. Oman and the Indian government can invite public and private industries along with colleges and universities to promote innovative drives and address local problems of the country. This partnership need not to be limited to the national boundaries only. International collaboration can facilitate new knowledge that can help in the adoption of AI in India and Oman. This effect can boost up the hardware industry which is still lagging behind in both countries.

10.3.4   NEW EDUCATION FRAMEWORK

To promote AI adoption in education, we require a digital pedagogical framework that needs to emphasize understanding the value and practices of ICT in education. The new framework should focus on three layers of education—enhancing IT literacy among students, deepening their knowledge with hands-on practices, and accelerate innovations. The framework should include extracurricular activities for better learning, quick-witted assignments with logical assessment criteria, professional training of the teachers, and additional support to administrative and institutional work. The teachers' training is required not only to manage AI-based applications and technologies in learning but also helps them to bring out possible solutions for ICT use.

10.3.5   ASSIGNED AN UNDERLYING AGENCY TO PROMOTE AI DIFFUSION IN EDUCATION

In India, a task force had been founded in 2017. It aimed to create policies and legal frameworks for deploying AI and provide recommendations to the concerned government, industries, and research. Later, it had turned into an underlying agency that needs to work under the government (Elonnai Hickok, 2018). However, its responsibilities and working nature are still not clear. It should be more cleared and defined. In Oman, such nodal agencies are yet to be identified with defined responsibilities. It should aim to promote AI drive not only in education but also in other sectors. Different sectors have different requirements. So, these nodal agencies need to assign experts of a particular area who can understand the specific needs of that sector. Academic experts need to include in assigned nodal agencies to provide suggestions to upgrade the country's education system.

10.3.6   PROMOTING AI EXPERTS TO BRIDGE AI SKILLS GAPS

In India and Oman, AI experts are lagging behind that creates a huge AI skill talent gap in both countries. Outsourcing of AI experts can be done to increase AI skills in both countries. These experts can train our young generation to fulfill the need for a completely digital society in the future. A handsome salary package and other incentives can attract AI experts to migrate from their native countries to Oman and India. Along with colleges and universities, easily accessible training and workshop programs can be arranged to facilitate knowledge and hands-on practice in the country.

KEYWORDS

- higher education
- machine learning
- artificial intelligence
- education system
- pandemic
- AI-powered personalized learning
- innovation
- online platform
- digital platforms
- awareness
- interest
- desire
- AI-based learning
- MOOC learners
- AI in the Middle East

REFERENCES

Anders, B. A. *Sovorel Learning for Life*, 2020, January 1. Retrieved from Sovorel publishing: https://sovorelpublishing.com/index.php/2020/01/01/top-7-higher-education-trends-for-2020/

CBSC. *Central Board of Secondary*, 2021, July 29. Retrieved from https://www.cbse.gov.in/: https://www.cbse.gov.in/cbsenew/documents//Prime%20Minister%20launches%20%E2%80%98AI%20For%20All%E2%80%99-converted.pdf

Cloud, A. *CT Image Analytics for COVID-19*, 2020. Retrieved from https://www.alibabacloud.com/solutions/ct-image-analytics

Communications, M. O. *ITA News*, 2020, February 24. Retrieved from www.ita.gov.om: https://www.ita.gov.om/itaportal/mediacenter/NewsDetail.aspx?NID=80926

Delhi Press. *Press Information Bureau*, 2018, May 23. Retrieved from https://pib.gov.in/: https://pib.gov.in/Pressreleaseshare.aspx?PRID=1533208

Digital, I. R. *LandScape of AI, ML in India*, 2018. https://itihaasa.com/. Retrieved from https://itihaasa.com/public/pdf/LandscapeofAI-MLResearch.pdf

Elonnai Hickok, S. M. *The Center for Internet Society*, 2018, June, 27. Retrieved from cis-india.org/: https://cis-india.org/internet-governance/blog/the-ai-task-force-report-the-first-steps-towards-indias-ai-framework

Foundation, I. B. *Education & Training Industry in India*, 2021a, July 28. Retrieved from ibef.org: https://www.ibef.org/industry/education-sector-india.aspx

Foundation, I. B. *IBEF*, 2021b, August 11. Retrieved from IBEF: https://www.ibef.org/industry/information-technology-india.aspx

Iftikhar, F. *IIT Delhi to Push Research in Artificial Intelligence*; Hindustan Times, 2018. Retrieved from https://www.hindustantimes.com/education/iit-delhi-to-push-research-in-artificial-intelligence/story-rWqdOjTpvs1BiL6BJ34TOI.html

Innovation, 2. M. *Mena-Innovation*; 2019, September 15–17. Retrieved from mena-innovation.com: https://mena-innovation.com/2019/event-summary/

KEMP, S. *Digital 2021: Oman*, 2021, February 12. Retrieved from datareportal.com: https://datareportal.com/reports/digital-2021-oman

Khazan, O. *The Atlantic*, 2020, August 17. Retrieved from theatlantic.com: https://www.theatlantic.com/technology/archive/2020/08/virtual-learning-when-you-dont-have-internet/615322/

Mccarthy, J. M. A Proposal for the Dartmouth Summer Research Project on Artificial Intelligence. *AI Magazine* 2006, December 1, 27. Retrieved from https://www.researchgate.net/publication/245009465_A_Proposal_for_the_Dartmouth_Summer_Research_Project_on_Arti_cial_Intelligence

Model, A. *Oxford Reference*, 2011. Retrieved from oxfordreference.com: https://www.oxfordreference.com/view/10.1093/oi/authority.20110803095432783

MOH. *Ministry of Health, Oman*, 2019, November 21. Retrieved from moh.gov.om: https://www.moh.gov.om/en/-/--1149

NFCW. *NFCW*, 2021, July 27. Retrieved from www.nfcw.com: https://www.nfcw.com/whats-new-in-payments/oman-to-make-it-mandatory-for-all-merchants-to-accept-cashless-payments/

Pew Research. *Pew Research*, 2020, September 10. Retrieved from www.pewresearch.org: https://www.pewresearch.org/fact-tank/2020/09/10/59-of-u-s-parents-with-lower-incomes-say-their-child-may-face-digital-obstacles-in-schoolwork/

Preeti Wadhwani, S. L. *Artificial Intelligence (AI) in Education.* Global Market Insights, June 2021. Retrieved from https://www.gminsights.com/industry-analysis/artificial-intelligence-ai-in-education-market

PWC, M. E. *PWC Middle East*, 2020. Retrieved from https://www.pwc.com/: https://www.pwc.com/m1/en/publications/potential-impact-artificial-intelligence-middle-east.html

The Report, M. A. *Artificial Intelligence Market Size Analysis Report. Market Analysis Report*, 2021 June. Retrieved from grandviewresearch.com: https://www.grandviewresearch.com/industry-analysis/artificial-intelligence-ai-market

Times of Oman. *Times of Oman*, 2021, June 7. Retrieved from TimesofOman.com: https://timesofoman.com/article/102310-agreement-signed-for-cloud-services-in-oman

Reynoso, R. A Complete History of Artificial Intelligence. *G2 AI & Machine Learning Operationalization Category* (2021, June 25). Retrieved from https://www.g2.com/articles/history-of-artificial-intelligence

Sadagopan, A. P. Icons of Indian IT. *IEEE India Info.,* 2019 Jul–Sep.; p 3. Retrieved from http://site.ieee.org/indiacouncil/files/2019/10/p53-p56.pdf

Swayam, M. L. *Massive Open Online Course Learning,* 2017. Retrieved from https://swayam.gov.in/about

Verma, P. IIT Hyderabad to Offer a Full-Fledged B.Tech. Program in Artificial Intelligence. *Economic Times*, 2019. Retrieved from https://economictimes.indiatimes.com/industry/services/education/iit-hyderabad-to-offer-full-fledged-b-tech-program-in-artificial-intelligence/articleshow/67570229.cms?from=mdr

Wakefield, J. *BBC*, 2021, January 11. Retrieved from BBC.com: https://www.bbc.com/news/technology-55573803

WATHIQ. *Centre, Sas for Entrepreneurship*, 2021. Retrieved from www.sas.om: https://www.sas.om/SASEN/Pages/about.aspx

CHAPTER 11

MACHINE LEARNING FOR MENTAL HEALTH: FOCUS ON AFFECTIVE AND NONAFFECTIVE PSYCHOSIS

MARIA FERRARA[1,2], GIORGIA FRANCHINI[3], MELISSA FUNARO[4], MARTINO BELVEDERI MURRI[1], TOMMASO TOFFANIN[1], LUIGI ZERBINATI[1], BEATRICE VALIER[1], DARIO AMBROSIO[1], FEDERICO MARCONI[1], MARCELLO CUTRONI[1], MARTA BASALDELLA[1], SEBASTIANO SENO[1], and LUIGI GRASSI[1]

[1]*Department Neuroscience and Rehabilitation, Institute of Psychiatry, University of Ferrara, Ferrara, Italy*

[2]*Department of Psychiatry, Yale School of Medicine, New Haven, CT, USA*

[3]*Department of Mathematics and Computer Science, University of Ferrara, Ferrara, Italy*

[4]*Harvey Cushing/John Hay Whitney Medical Library, Yale University, New Haven, CT, USA*

ABSTRACT

Machine learning is developing at a fast pace, providing the ability to analyze large volumes of data quickly and delivering insight without a-priori assumptions. Thus, this technique represents a promising tool in the field of mental healthcare, given the challenges faced by this field including the lack of biological markers of disease and prognosis, the large heterogeneity in

Incorporating AI Technology in the Service Sector: Innovations in Creating Knowledge, Improving Efficiency, and Elevating Quality of Life. Maria José Sousa, Subhendu Kumar Pani, Francesca Dal Mas, & Sérgio Sousa (Eds.)
© 2024 Apple Academic Press, Inc. Co-published with CRC Press (Taylor & Francis)

clinical presentation, and the lack of reliable predictors of treatment response. Machine learning has been widely applied, especially in neuroimaging studies, but still largely confined in an early phase of deployment and with a varying degree of efficacy. This chapter discusses the most recent applications of this technology in severe psychotic illnesses (schizophrenia spectrum and bipolar disorders), focusing on application of machine learning in early detection, differential diagnosis, treatment management, and response prediction. Pilot attempts to use machine learning for mental health service design and implementation are also discussed. For each key point, a review of updated literature is provided.

11.1   INTRODUCTION

Psychosis affects 3% of the global population over their lifetime (Bhugra, 2005). Psychosis that includes both bipolar disorder (BD) and schizophrenia-spectrum disorders (SCZ) is a psychiatric condition characterized by auditory hallucinations, thoughts disorders, and disorganized/dangerous behaviors. Twenty million people are currently living with schizophrenia, while BD affects around 45 million worldwide (World Health Organization, 2019a, 2019b); both are considered chronic conditions associated with considerable disability (World Health Organization, 2019a). The economic burden of these mental disorders is also substantial, both in terms of lost work productivity and direct costs (medications and hospitalizations) (Simon, 2003). Individuals affected by psychosis have a high likelihood of relapse, with reported rates up to 81.9% 5 years after an initial recovery (Robinson et al., 2019); patients also have a higher risk for suicide, especially during the first episodes of psychosis (FEP) (Melle et al., 2006) and a rate of suicide attempt during the first year of treatment as high as 10% (Simon et al., 2018b). The personal toll suffered by patients diagnosed with psychosis and their caregivers in addition to the economic burden for the community make psychosis prevention a public health priority (Malla and McGorry, 2019).

More than 20 years of research conducted in different countries and health systems have proven that early detection and intervention in psychosis improves outcomes up to 10 years later (Lieberman et al., 2019; Ten Velden Hegelstad et al., 2013).

The growing interest in artificial intelligence (AI) has involved investments by public and private companies in the last few decades and has contributed to a considerable development of machine learning (ML) methodologies. ML and AI are also pervasive in the domain of health care. Within AI, ML tools offer promise for early detection (i.e., to detect first signs of psychosis and to discern those who are affected by psychosis and those who are not) and prognosis (to identify those who will convert to full-blown psychosis from a clinical high-risk condition). Moreover, ML techniques can help clinicians with differential diagnosis, as many symptoms of psychiatric disorder(s) are transdiagnostic and can fluctuate over time. Finally, once the diagnosis is made, treatment can be tailored around users' clinical characteristics and their needs: ML can provide valuable information about treatment response and efficacy.

Lastly, AI can help decision-makers and program leaders draw insights from research based on electronic health records (EHRs): this represents a complex but invaluable source of information that is passively collected in routine clinical care but infrequently analyzed.

This chapter will summarize the most relevant and up-to-date findings on the use of ML techniques in the mental health scenario, with a focus on the most resource-consuming and potentially invalidating mental disorder, psychosis.

11.2   ML FOR EARLY DETECTION

An overwhelming amount of evidence supports the benefits of implementing early detection and intervention in psychotic disorders (Correll et al., 2018). Consistently with the critical period hypothesis (Birchwood and Fiorillo, 2000) or the assumption that care can have the strongest impact on long-term outcome, if provided over a limited time interval after psychosis onset (Birchwood et al., 1998). Early detected patients show less severe symptoms at care presentation, better global functioning and an overall better quality of life at 2 years (Lieberman et al., 2019), lower rates of suicidal behaviors (Melle et al., 2006) and risk of hospitalizations (Robinson et al., 2019), reduced encounters with the criminal justice system (Pollard et al., 2020), and overall better outcomes up to 10 years after their first episode (Ten Velden Hegelstad et al., 2013).

Psychotic disorders are usually preceded by a period of time of variable duration characterized by subthreshold symptoms of psychosis, known as prodromes (Powers et al., 2020). However, not all the subjects who will experience prodromal symptoms, or defined of being high risk for psychosis (CHR-P), will progress to frank psychosis: it has been estimated that up to 30% will convert to psychosis in 3 years (Fusar-Poli et al., 2012), and 35% in up to 10 years (Cannon et al., 2008; Fusar-Poli et al., 2012; Salazar de Pablo et al., 2020, 2021; Yoviene Sykes et al., 2019). Thus, most UHR individuals will not develop a psychotic disorder; therefore, some authors have suggested that preventative treatment should be offered to those who will benefit from it the most (van Os and Guloksuz, 2017). Identifying biomarkers that could be used to determine who will progress to psychosis within a CHR-P condition would allow the delivery of preventative measures to the subgroup that would most benefit from them (Gifford et al., 2017). Research studies have struggled so far to identify valid biomarkers of progression to psychosis: functional and structural imaging features, genetic data, EEG patterns, speech features, blood markers, and more have been investigated for this purpose, with no definitive success. In fact, while several models able to predict progression to psychosis in a UHR individual have been developed within research settings, their value is determined by their ability to translate this risk calculation in tangible benefits to patients, their families, and the network of care (Hunter and Lawrie, 2018). Thus, ML can be employed to uncover patterns of risk of conversion to psychosis that could enable clinicians and stakeholders to implement timely intervention to delay or prevent psychosis.

The vast majority of the studies focusing on prediction of psychosis conversion applied ML to resting state MRI. Koutsouleris et al. (2009, 2011) found that it was possible to increase by 40% the diagnostic certainty of subjects who will convert to frank psychosis by applying the MRI-based biomarker, specifically the prefrontal perisylvian and subcortical brain structures. Transition outcomes were correctly predicted in 80% of test cases using MRI-based predictors, which increased prognostic certainty by 36% (sensitivity: 76%, specificity: 85%) (Koutsouleris et al., 2014).

Kambeitz et al. (2017) tried to test an ML tool to predict global functioning outcomes at the individual level, by focusing on cortical area reductions in superior temporal, inferior frontal, and inferior parietal areas, with an accuracy of 82%, underlining the utility of ML in stratifying the risk to progression toward psychosis in UHR individuals.

One more parameter that has been studied as potential biomarker of psychosis is the disrupted functional asymmetry: this value in the left thalamus discriminated control versus FEP/UHR individuals with high sensitivity (68.42% and 81.08%, respectively) (Zhu et al., 2019).

Given that psychotic disorders are often characterized by disorganized speech (loosening of associations) and content disorders (delusions, echolalia), investigators have applied supervised linear discriminant analysis (LDA) and supervised leave-one-subject-out cross-validation + convex hull classifier to perform speech analysis to identify SCZ and BD early in the course of the disease. For example, an LDA-based algorithm had a classification accuracy of 79.4% (specificity = 83.6%, sensitivity = 75.2%) based on temporal, energy, and vocal pitch features automatically isolated from the recordings of individuals with SCZ and healthy controls (Rapcan et al., 2010). In prodromal individuals, later psychosis development was predicted by a latent semantic analysis measure of semantic coherence, maximum phrase length, and use of determiners with 100% accuracy, outperforming classification based on clinical interviews (Bedi et al., 2015).

A further study conducted in prodromal individuals found that language alterations including reduced usage of possessive pronouns and semantic coherence had an 83% accuracy in predicting psychosis onset in the training dataset (and 79% in a further independent prodromal sample) and an accuracy of 72% in discriminating patients who recently converted from psychosis from controls (Corcoran et al., 2018).

It is important to note that the same tool can be accurate and sensitive in the classification of a specific phase of illness: for example, it has been found that random forest algorithms applied to voice features taken from everyday life phone calls were more accurate in identifying manic or mixed states (AUC = 0.89) compared to depressive states (AUC = 0.78) (Faurholt-Jepsen et al., 2016) in BD. Given the availability of passive data from electronic devices such as smartphones or smartwatches, it is easy to postulate that such data will become extremely helpful for the early identification of the transition between the different phases of illness (Hays et al., 2020; Rodriguez-Villa et al., 2021).

Blood biomarkers have also been studied as a potential candidate that could identify individuals at risk of developing psychosis early in the course of illness (van Os and Guloksuz, 2017). Peripheral plasma proteomic data (mostly indicating a dysregulated complement and coagulation cascade) paired with baseline clinical data were successfully used to identify those individuals who will convert from clinical high risk to frank psychosis: ([AUC], 0.95; [PPV], 75.0%; [NPV], 98.6%) (Mongan et al., 2021). Moreover, the model was able to predict who, 6 years later, will have psychotic experience (PPV, 67.8%; and NPV, 75.8%) providing a tool that can help clinicians with early detection and stratification strategies (Mongan et al., 2021). Supervised ML has been also used to analyze biomarkers including neurotrophins, inflammatory (IL-10), and oxidative stress markers (e.g., glutathione peroxidase), associated with psychosis: the supervised algorithm failed to distinguish BD from SCZ (accuracy = 49%) but was able to reach a prediction accuracy of 77.5% and 72.5% to identify, respectively, patients with SCZ and BD from controls (Pinto et al., 2017). It is possible that affective and nonaffective psychosis share the same pathophysiological mechanisms so that it is hard to distinguish them by using these biological markers (Goldsmith et al., 2016; Goodkind et al., 2015).

Genetic analysis is also becoming popular in the field, given the initial evidence of a potential role of both inherited as well as de-novo mutation variants (Li et al., 2016) in neuronally expressed genes (Goetzl et al., 2020, 2021), contributing to synaptic dysfunction in the pathogenesis of SCZ.

Trakadis et al. (2019) applied the supervised eXtreme Gradient Boosting (XGBoost) with regularization in a case-control study (2545 SCZ and 2545 controls) to identify genetic markers of a risk for developing SCZ (accuracy = 0.85, sensitivity = 0.85, specificity = 0.86) including genes that regulate neurogenesis and neuronal development, synaptic plasticity, memory, and axonal development. A larger schizophrenia case-control study (Trakadis et al., 2019) of 11,853 subjects applied supervised support vector machines (SVMs) with linear and radial basis function kernel methods to identify possible genes contributing to the risk of developing SCZ: the sensitivity and specificity were lower compared to the Trakadis study (AUC 0.60–0.66); moreover, its prediction accuracy was lower than that obtained by the use of polygenic risk score (Escott-Price et al., 2015; International Schizophrenia et al., 2009; Vivian-Griffiths et al., 2019). A further study (Zheutlin et al., 2018) tried to test the effect of 77 risk loci known to be strongly associated with SCZ to predict six different cognitive phenotype in subjects with schizophrenia, finding that polygenic risk scores and random forest had similar predictive strength and error.

Finally, as Yang et al. (2010) underlined in their research on individuals with schizophrenia, ML tools can become even more precise predictive tools when combining genetic and brain morphology data.

11.3   ML FOR DIFFERENTIAL DIAGNOSIS

ML might represent a useful tool that could guide differential diagnosis (Kambeitz et al., 2017). The high clinical heterogeneity of psychiatric disorders, the kaleidoscopic presentation at onset, and the dynamic evolution often lead the same individual to receive different diagnoses over the course of their lives.

ML applied to imaging research has been widely used in psychosis studies. Anticevic et al. (2014), for example, investigated thalamocortical dysconnectivity in SCZ and BD patients versus healthy controls, while Schnack et al. (2014) trained three SVM to recognize patients with schizophrenia from healthy subjects with an accuracy of 0.76, patients with SCZ from those with BD with an accuracy of 0.66, and bipolar patients from healthy subjects with an accuracy of 0.61 focusing their attention on gray matter density images.

Structural MRI seems important to help differential between SCZ and healthy controls, as underlined by Iwabuchi et al. (2013), but also to distinguish patients with SCZ by those with autism-spectrum disorder patients as verified by Pinaya et al. (2019): with an accuracy of 0.62, SVM was utilized to develop a deep auto-encoder for detecting neuroanatomical abnormalities in individual patients. Koutsouleris et al. (2011) investigated whether patients with SCZ, at high risk for psychosis (ARMS) and other diagnosis diverted from the development of normal brain by applying SVM. The brain age gap estimation, BrainAGE, calculated as the difference between the neuroanatomical and the chronological age was highest in SCZ (+5.5 years) group, followed by MDD (+4.0), BPD (+3.1) and the ARMS (+1.7) groups. A larger gap of BrainAGE was related to earlier disease onset in MDD and BPD groups.

Many studies focused on functional aspect of the brain with the help of fMRI and SVM: resting state cerebral networks (in different regions such as frontal, supplementary motor, precuneus, parietal, cingulate, cerebellar, supramarginal cortices, and insula) were used by Du et al. (2015) to discriminate healthy control from SCZ, BP, and schizoaffective (SAD) patients; in contrast to prior assertions that SAD is an unusual form of SCZ/BP, their data support the idea that SAD is a single entity with many subtypes. They also demonstrated that the SCZ and SAD groups are relatively near to one another, similar to the BP and HC groups, with a 68.75% accuracy.

Individual structural and functional connectivity networks can help to distinguish subjects with SCZ from healthy controls, as shown by Arbabshirani et al. (2014) and Han et al. (2019). These networks were analyzed by Wei Han et al. using SVM in SCZ and MDD patients. Supervised convex nonnegative matrix factorization was successfully employed to draw the distinct characteristics of the two diagnoses, with a 82.6% of accuracy. In areas of the prefrontal cortex, particularly the superior frontal gyri, patients with SCZ differed from those with major depression. The inferior parietal lobule, middle cingulate, and cingulate cortex were the most discriminative areas in terms of functional properties: as Zeng et al. (2018) pointed out, those regions are the ones involved in the salience, control, and default network. Qureshi et al. (2017) focused on functional connectivity as a potential biomarker of SCZ, with an accuracy of 0.99, sensitivity 1, and specificity of 0.99. Moreover, aberrant connectivity in temporal and occipital regions resulted in a good prediction marker, according to Li et al. (2019).

Anticorrelated networks between subcortical and cortical areas were found to be a strong marker of schizophrenia (accuracy = 0.69, sensitivity = 0.68, specificity = 0.72 (Ramkiran et al., 2019). Zhuang et al. (2019) conducted a study in drug-naïve FEP discovering that the cerebellar connections and the default mode network are functional markers of psychosis, while the limbic system and the prefrontal-thalamo-hippocampal circuit are structural markers. These findings confirmed an earlier study that showed a high predictive value of using ML to analyze data on identified regions in the brain to separate SCZ patients from healthy controls (Bae et al., 2018).

Sensorimotor circuits also might play a relevant role in the pathogenesis or clinical presentation of SCZ, as demonstrated by the high specificity (0.96), sensitivity (0.93), and accuracy (0.95) of the ML approach (SVM) applied by Guo et al. (2017).

Costafreda et al. (2011) instead used a verbal fluency task to investigate executive function in SCZ and BD, finding both abnormal shared circuitry (such as increased activation in the left dorsolateral prefrontal cortex) and distinct functional differences, for example, patients with SCZ engaged selected regions on the right side of the brain in a more pronounced way than both healthy participants and BD patients (accuracy was 0.92 for the SCZ and 0.79 for BD).

Expectation maximization was used to analyze EEG data (measured after 10 days of medication withdrawal) to differentiate major depression from BD, SCZ or controls, MFA outperformed LDA, NN, and SVM classifiers; according to this study (Khodayari-Rostamabad et al., 2010b) the proposed EEG-based methodology, which combined Peng's feature selection method and the MFA classification procedure, has been demonstrated to be very effective for diagnosing psychiatric diseases, with an accuracy of 0.871. As already tested by Erguzel et al. (2015), quantitative EEG cordance, specifically selected featured from alpha- and theta-frequency bands, showed that an ANN–PSO approach was able to distinguish unipolar from BD with a 89.89% overall classification accuracy (BD Sens 0.8387; MDD Sens 0.931, AUC 0.905). Similar tests were run by Li and Fan (2005): they applied BP ANN and self-organizing competitive ANN for the discrimination of three different groups of subjects (10 healthy controls, 10 with SCZ, and 10 with depression). ANN resulted as an effective approach to differentiate these three groups, but BP ANN performed better than self-organizing competitive ANN technique.

Struyf et al. (2008) focused their attention on 20 genes possibly associated with SCZ or BD. They included clinical and demographic data (alcohol and drug use, smoking, age, sex, brain pH) to distinguish among controls, SCZ, and bipolar patients applying six classification algorithms: SVM, nearest neighbor, nearest shrunken centroids, naïve Bayes, ensemble of voters, and decision trees. It appears that gene expression within the brain is massively changed in both SCZ and BD, and SVM has a substantial advantage over other frequently used statistical classification and ML methods for this task (SCZ vs. HC, AUC: 0.94. BD vs. HC AUC: 0.97).

Inflammatory markers, neurotrophins, and oxidative stress markers usually correlated to BD and SCZ were also tested (Pinto et al., 2017). The SVM algorithm performed well in BD versus HC test and SCZ versus HC test but failed to differentiate BD versus SCZ. Most relevant biomarkers for BD were eotaxin-1 (CCL11) and glutathione S-transferase and for SCZ were IL-6 and eotaxin-1 (CCL11).

11.4 ML FOR TREATMENT OUTCOME AND OPTIMIZATION

There are many known predictors of psychosis outcomes: for example, it has been shown across many clinical and research samples, health services, and countries that delaying access to antipsychotic, resulting in a prolonged duration of untreated psychosis, that is, associated to poorer outcomes (Penttila et al., 2014). Other predictors of poor prognosis are male sex, insidious onset of symptoms (Díaz-Caneja et al., 2015), younger age at the first episode, being born in winter (Suvisaari et al., 2001), traumatic events (Varese et al., 2012), parental age (Frans et al., 2015), hormones, urbanicity (Castillejos et al., 2018; Vassos et al., 2012), immigrant status (Bourque et al., 2011; Castillejos et al., 2018), being part of a minority (Oduola et al., 2021; Schofield et al., 1954), and asocial premorbid personality. They all predict poorer outcomes at a group level (Schofield et al., 1954), stressing the difficulty of predicting the development of illness in individual patients (Mechelli, 2019).

Multiple attempts have been made to predict the course of psychosis in research using ML (Mourao-Miranda et al., 2012; Santesteban-Echarri et al., 2017), with inconsistent accuracy (up to 70%). However, we lack a reliable model for predicting long-term outcomes of SCZ at a patient level that can guide the clinician in routine practice. One of the first studies that used ML to predict outcomes in an FEP sample was conducted by Koutsouleris et al.: lower education, functional deficits, unemployment, and unmet psychosocial needs were identified as the most accurate predictors of 4 and 52-week outcomes (with accuracy of 73.8–75%). A similar study was conducted a few years later on a sample of 523 subjects diagnosed with schizophrenic disorders, by applying a linear SVM and recursive feature elimination within a nested cross-validation design to recognize patterns in a wide range of genetic, clinical, and environmental variables. The accuracy in predicting symptomatic outcome was 62.2–64.7%, while global outcome was 63.5–67.6%. The most important predictors were global assessment of functioning areas, psychotic and depressive symptoms, broad quality-of-life indicators and overall functioning, antipsychotics use, and psychosocial needs were confirmed as strong predictor also in this study (de Nijs et al., 2021). Interestingly, in all models, it was found that poor long-term consequences are strongly predicted by lack of insight, hypothesizing a mediating role of poor adherence and service disengagement.

Another study examined whether clinical information (including the presence of disorganized and negative symptoms, thoughts disorders, poor functioning, and severity of attenuated positive symptoms) could be utilized to develop individual outcome predictions in patients at UHR: attention disturbances, anhedonia-asociality, and disorder of thought content were the best predictors of global functioning, with an accuracy of 62.5% (Mechelli et al., 2017).

Antipsychotics represent the core component of any comprehensive psychosocial treatment for psychosis (Correll et al., 2017). However, two features have characterized psychosis treatment so far: no biomarker or clinical characteristic has been identified as indicator of antipsychotic response, leaving the prescribers complete freedom and at the same time a significant degree of uncertainty about the response for the individual patient (Martinuzzi et al., 2019); second, treatment-resistant psychosis emerges in up to a third of patients (Kapur et al., 2012; Meltzer, 1997) and there are no reliable tools to predict the lack of response to a certain antipsychotic. Thus, ML holds the promise to help clinicians in moving toward a more personalized pharmacotherapy to increase accuracy and relevance of predictions for pharmacological treatment outcomes (Korda et al., 2021). There are only few available studies on antipsychotic response in FEP, reporting only moderate accuracies: for example, Sarpal et al. (2016), using resting-state functional MRI, found that 91 regions that have functional connections with the striatum were an accurate prognostic tool for treatment response to antipsychotic in acutely psychotic patients; however, the accuracy was 78%.

In 2010, a pilot study (Khodayari-Rostamabad et al., 2010a) was conducted in 23 adults with schizophrenia then validated in an independent sample of 14. It showed that pretreatment EEG features were used as potential indicators of responders to clozapine treatment, with a specificity of 85% of performance by applying KPLSR. This study was somehow replicated by using a measure of effective connectivity (the symbolic transfer entropy) and ML techniques; first, a brain source localization procedure using the linearly constrained minimum variance beam-forming approach: they found that response to clozapine treatment can be predicted by the symbolic transfer entropy features with an accuracy of 95.83% (Ciprian et al., 2020). Also, a supervised feature selection algorithm followed by a fuzzy c-mean algorithm was used to provide an insight on the mechanisms of clozapine in the brain by using odd-ball auditory evoked potentials in adults with schizophrenia and healthy volunteers (Ravan et al., 2012).

Given the high incidence of treatment-resistant schizophrenia, a growing number of studies are delving into the pharmacogenomics of antipsychotics, but despite the efforts that have been made so far, no reliable predictive markers have been identified that might be employed in clinical management and that could enhance the quality of life of these patients. However, recent studies implemented ML methods to investigate the genetics of treatment-resistant schizophrenia, reporting promising findings that could pave the way for application of pharmacogenomics in the clinical practice (Pisanu and Squassina, 2019).

11.5 ML FOR SERVICE IMPLEMENTATION/BIG DATA/ELECTRONIC HEALTH RECORD

Outcomes of affective and nonaffective psychotic disorders can vary substantially among individuals, hence the necessity of tailoring a more personalized treatment for each patient affected by the disorder. In fact, some patients are likely to recover spontaneously, including patients with substance-induced psychotic symptoms, but other patients might require a more stringent follow-up. In order to offer a precision medicine approach, it might be necessary to create more population-based data reflecting the real incidence of mental disorders and to use EHRs. In that regard, EHRs have a lot of potential for speeding up clinical research and for helping clinicians to predict the outcome for each patient (Simon et al., 2017).

For instance, Simon et al. (2018a) used EHR data to estimate overall incidence of symptoms of psychosis at first presentation to care for psychosis in five large healthcare systems. The incidence rates they estimate were markedly higher than those previously reported providing a more precise estimate that must be considered when planning service provision.

If applied to this study, ML would have hastened the process, replacing the training of medical record abstractors, and the manual revision of the EHRs.

However, topic extraction from clinical narratives derived by psychiatric EHRs represents a real challenge: for instance, the terminology employed is quite diverse and context-dependent; moreover, the same symptom can be described with different words, both remaining valid (e.g., the patient reports he hears voices vs. he complaints about having auditory hallucinations).

Within outcomes in the mental health field, suicide risk and hospital readmission after discharge are particularly relevant for care planning and resource utilization. Reducing the likelihood of readmission is a significant unmet need in psychiatric care, as readmissions are not only disruptive for patients and their families, but they also represent a major contributor to healthcare expenditure. Holderness et al. (2019) used two types of artificial neural networks (ANN), multiple multilayer perceptron (MMP), and RBF, to predict whether sentences in a patient's EHR are linked to one or more of the identified risk factor domains for readmission. Overall agreement was good when compared to annotators, with a mean accuracy of 80.5%. Senior et al. (2020) developed a natural language processing in order to extract variables from clinical notes to predict risk factor for suicide in 57 patients with SCZ and BD. In comparison to the manual evaluation the overall accuracy was good (the overall microprecision was 0.77, recall was 0.90 and F1 was 0.83).

Miotto et al. (2016) used random forest classifiers to predict 78 diagnosis, including SCZ, within 1-year range, with an overall accuracy of 92.9% in EHR of 700,000 patients accessing a general hospital facilities (inpatient, outpatient, and emergency room). Therefore, deep learning (DL) techniques applied to EHRs can represent useful tools to generate patient representations that could improve clinical predictions by adding ML to the clinical decision tree (Miotto et al., 2016).

11.6 SUMMARY

Almost all the studies considered in this chapter have applied supervised ML techniques, which is quite common in the context of both classifications (binary and multiple) and regression. On the other hand, studies combining unsupervised ML techniques, for the preprocessing part, with supervised ML techniques, for the classification part, obtained better performance measures. For example, in Koutsouleris et al. (2009), the authors initially use principal component analysis (PCA) to decrease the number of input features (data source: imaging) and then pass the preprocessed data to an SVM, resulting in a higher score in a similar setting without the use of PCA (Koutsouleris et al., 2011, 2014). None of the studies reviewed in this chapter analyzed used exclusively nonsupervised ML techniques.

It has been documented a growing interest in DL over the last years; however, the amount of data needed to apply ANNs must be very big, at least of the order of thousands. For this reason, it is reasonable to see methodologies of a standard type, such as the SVM and the RF, being more often employed. In fact, of all the studies included in this chapter, only two (Trakadis et al., 2019; Vivian-Griffiths et al., 2019) had sufficient data for applying DL methodologies.

On the other hand, it is also interesting to assess the longitudinal dimension of the data. In medical studies, the single data are often composed of a high number of features, especially when the data source is imaging. For this reason, DL methodologies are often successfully employed, even with a limited number of patients, improving the accuracy of the results. For example, Zeng et al. (2018) reported that the accuracy increased by 4% using DL techniques.

Most of the studies used SVMs, either linear or with Gaussian kernels. The successful use of SVM by so many authors is surely driven by the great knowledge of this technique as well as the wide availability of fully automatic computer tools for its use. However, it is interesting to note that performance (in the case of binary classification) varies from 0.49, which is to be considered total noise, to over 0.90. These results are fully justified by different factors, some of which may be attributable to the preprocessing of the data, the variety of the data, and the setting of hyperparameters (parameters not learned during the training phase of the methodology but set by the architect of the software).

11.7 CONCLUSIONS

As a discipline, psychiatry suffers from some main challenges: first, there is a lack of biological markers of disease and prognosis; second, there is a large heterogeneity in clinical presentation, treatment response, and progression; third, most of the research studies, with a very selected and neat population, do not always translate into real-world practice. Thus, even ML might help guide routine clinical work but with limited accuracy.

While DL techniques would not be able to provide any insights into the psychopathology of psychosis, they might unveil a pattern, by using large and various sources of data (biological, clinical, passive data from wearable electronic devices on patients, EHRs) not based on epistemological assumptions. This will allow a better understanding of the disease and provide useful tools to personalize the treatment, and tailor services around users' needs.

KEYWORDS

- machine learning
- psychosis
- mental health
- schizophrenia
- bipolar disorder
- early detection
- differential diagnosis

REFERENCES

Anticevic, A.; Cole, M. W.; Repovs, G.; Murray, J. D.; Brumbaugh, M. S.; Winkler, A. M.; et al. Characterizing Thalamo-Cortical Disturbances in Schizophrenia and Bipolar Illness. *Cereb. Cortex* **2014,** *24* (12), 3116–3130. doi:10.1093/cercor/bht165.

Arbabshirani, M. R.; Castro, E.; Calhoun, V. D. Accurate Classification of Schizophrenia Patients Based on Novel Resting-State fMRI Features. *Annu. Int. Conf. IEEE Eng. Med. Biol. Soc.* **2014,** *2014,* 6691–6694. doi:10.1109/EMBC.2014.6945163.

Bae, Y.; Kumarasamy, K.; Ali, I. M.; Korfiatis, P.; Akkus, Z.; Erickson, B. J. Differences between Schizophrenic and Normal Subjects Using Network Properties from fMRI. *J. Digit Imaging* **2018,** *31* (2), 252–261. doi:10.1007/s10278-017-0020-4.

Bedi, G.; Carrillo, F.; Cecchi, G. A.; Slezak, D. F.; Sigman, M.; Mota, N. B.; et al. Automated Analysis of Free Speech Predicts Psychosis Onset in High-Risk Youths. *NPJ Schizophr.* **2015,** *1* (1), 15030. doi:10.1038/npjschz.2015.30.

Bhugra, D. The Global Prevalence of Schizophrenia. *PLoS Med.* **2005,** *2* (5), e151; quiz e175. doi:10.1371/journal.pmed.0020151.

Birchwood, M.; Fiorillo, A. The Critical Period for Early Intervention. *Psychiatr. Rehab. Skills* **2000,** *4* (2), 182–198. doi:10.1080/10973430008408405.

Birchwood, M.; Todd, P.; Jackson, C. Early Intervention in Psychosis. The Critical Period Hypothesis. *Br. J. Psychiatry Suppl.* **1998,** *172* (33), 53–59. Retrieved from https://www.ncbi.nlm.nih.gov/pubmed/9764127

Bourque, F.; van der Ven, E.; Malla, A. A Meta-Analysis of the Risk for Psychotic Disorders among First- and Second-Generation Immigrants. *Psychol. Med.* **2011,** *41* (5), 897–910. doi:10.1017/s0033291710001406.

Cannon, T. D.; Cadenhead, K.; Cornblatt, B.; Woods, S. W.; Addington, J.; Walker, E.; et al. Prediction of Psychosis in Youth at High Clinical Risk: A Multisite Longitudinal Study in North America. *Arch. Gen. Psychiatry* **2008,** *65* (1), 28–37. doi:10.1001/archgenpsychiatry.2007.3.

Castillejos, M. C.; Martin-Perez, C.; Moreno-Kustner, B. A Systematic Review and Meta-Analysis of the Incidence of Psychotic Disorders: The Distribution of Rates and the Influence of Gender, Urbanicity, Immigration and Socio-Economic Level. *Psychol. Med.* **2018,** 1–15. doi:10.1017/S0033291718000235.

Ciprian, C.; Masychev, K.; Ravan, M.; Reilly, J. P.; Maccrimmon, D. A Machine Learning Approach Using Effective Connectivity to Predict Response to Clozapine Treatment. *IEEE Trans. Neural Syst. Rehabil. Eng.* **2020,** *28* (12), 2598–2607. doi:10.1109/tnsre.2020.3019685.

Corcoran, C. M.; Carrillo, F.; Fernandez-Slezak, D.; Bedi, G.; Klim, C.; Javitt, D. C.; et al. Prediction of Psychosis across Protocols and Risk Cohorts Using Automated Language Analysis. *World Psychiatry* **2018,** *17* (1), 67–75. doi:10.1002/wps.20491.

Correll, C. U.; Rubio, J. M.; Inczedy-Farkas, G.; Birnbaum, M. L.; Kane, J. M.; Leucht, S. Efficacy of 42 Pharmacologic Cotreatment Strategies Added to Antipsychotic Monotherapy in Schizophrenia: Systematic Overview and Quality Appraisal of the Meta-Analytic Evidence. *JAMA Psychiatry* **2017,** *74* (7), 675–684. doi:10.1001/jamapsychiatry.2017.0624.

Correll, C. U.; Galling, B.; Pawar, A.; Krivko, A.; Bonetto, C.; Ruggeri, M.; et al. Comparison of Early Intervention Services Vs. Treatment as Usual for Early-Phase Psychosis: A Systematic Review, Meta-analysis, and Meta-Regression. *JAMA Psychiatry* **2018,** *75* (6), 555–565. doi:10.1001/jamapsychiatry.2018.0623.

Costafreda, S. G.; Fu, C. H.; Picchioni, M.; Toulopoulou, T.; McDonald, C.; Kravariti, E.; et al. Pattern of Neural Responses to Verbal Fluency Shows Diagnostic Specificity for Schizophrenia and Bipolar Disorder. *BMC Psychiatry* **2011,** *11*, 18. doi:10.1186/1471-244X-11-18.

de Nijs, J.; Burger, T. J.; Janssen, R. J.; Kia, S. M.; van Opstal, D. P. J.; de Koning, M. B.; et al. Individualized Prediction of Three- and Six-Year Outcomes of Psychosis in a Longitudinal Multicenter Study: A Machine Learning Approach. *NPJ Schizophr.* **2021,** *7* (1), 34. doi:10.1038/s41537-021-00162-3.

Díaz-Caneja, C. M.; Pina-Camacho, L.; Rodríguez-Quiroga, A.; Fraguas, D.; Parellada, M.; Arango, C. Predictors of Outcome in Early-Onset Psychosis: A Systematic Review. *NPJ Schizophr.* **2015,** *1*, 14005–14005. doi:10.1038/npjschz.2014.5.

Du, Y.; Pearlson, G. D.; Liu, J.; Sui, J.; Yu, Q.; He, H.; et al. A Group ICA Based Framework for Evaluating Resting fMRI Markers When Disease Categories Are Unclear: Application to Schizophrenia, Bipolar, and Schizoaffective Disorders. *NeuroImage* **2015,** *122*, 272–280. doi:10.1016/j.neuroimage.2015.07.054.

Erguzel, T.; Sayar, G.; Tarhan, N. Artificial Intelligence Approach to Classify Unipolar and Bipolar Depressive Disorders. *Neural Comput. Appl.* **2015,** *27*, 1607–1616.

Escott-Price, V.; Kirov, G.; Rees, E.; Isles, A. R.; Owen, M. J.; O'Donovan, M. C. No Evidence for Enrichment in Schizophrenia for Common Allelic Associations at Imprinted Loci. *PLoS One* **2015,** *10* (12), e0144172. doi:10.1371/journal.pone.0144172.

Faurholt-Jepsen, M.; Busk, J.; Frost, M.; Vinberg, M.; Christensen, E. M.; Winther, O.; et al. Voice Analysis as an Objective State Marker in Bipolar Disorder. *Transl. Psychiatry* **2016,** *6*, e856. doi:10.1038/tp.2016.123.

Frans, E.; MacCabe, J. H.; Reichenberg, A. Advancing Paternal Age and Psychiatric Disorders. *World Psychiatry* **2015,** *14* (1), 91–93. doi:10.1002/wps.20190.

Fusar-Poli, P.; Bonoldi, I.; Yung, A. R.; Borgwardt, S.; Kempton, M. J.; Valmaggia, L.; et al. Predicting Psychosis: Meta-Analysis of Transition Outcomes in Individuals at High Clinical Risk. *Arch. Gen. Psychiatry* **2012,** *69* (3), 220–229. doi:10.1001/archgenpsychiatry.2011.1472.

Gifford, G.; Crossley, N.; Fusar-Poli, P.; Schnack, H. G.; Kahn, R. S.; Koutsouleris, N.; et al. Using Neuroimaging to Help Predict the Onset of Psychosis. *NeuroImage* **2017**, *145*, 209–217. doi:10.1016/j.neuroimage.2016.03.075.

Goetzl, E. J.; Srihari, V. H.; Guloksuz, S.; Ferrara, M.; Tek, C.; Heninger, G. R. Decreased Mitochondrial Electron Transport Proteins and Increased Complement Mediators in Plasma Neural-Derived Exosomes of Early Psychosis. *Transl. Psychiatry* **2020**, *10* (1), 361. doi: 10.1038/s41398-020-01046-3.

Goetzl, E. J.; Srihari, V. H.; Guloksuz, S.; Ferrara, M.; Tek, C.; Heninger, G. R. Neural Cell-Derived Plasma Exosome Protein Abnormalities Implicate Mitochondrial Impairment in First Episodes of Psychosis. *FASEB J.* **2021**, *35* (2), e21339. doi:10.1096/fj.202002519R.

Goldsmith, D. R.; Rapaport, M. H.; Miller, B. J. A Meta-Analysis of Blood Cytokine Network Alterations in Psychiatric Patients: Comparisons between Schizophrenia, Bipolar Disorder and Depression. *Mol. Psychiatry* **2016**, *21* (12), 1696–1709. doi:10.1038/mp.2016.3.

Goodkind, M.; Eickhoff, S. B.; Oathes, D. J.; Jiang, Y.; Chang, A.; Jones-Hagata, L. B.; et al. Identification of a Common Neurobiological Substrate for Mental Illness. *JAMA Psychiatry* **2015**, *72* (4), 305–315. doi:10.1001/jamapsychiatry.2014.2206.

Guo, W.; Liu, F.; Chen, J.; Wu, R.; Li, L.; Zhang, Z.; et al. Using Short-Range and Long-Range Functional Connectivity to Identify Schizophrenia with a Family-Based Case-Control Design. *Psychiatry Res.: Neuroimag.* **2017**, *264*, 60–67. doi:10.1016/j.pscychresns.2017.04.010.

Han, W.; Sorg, C.; Zheng, C.; Yang, Q.; Zhang, X.; Ternblom, A.; et al. Low-Rank Network Signatures in the Triple Network Separate Schizophrenia and Major Depressive Disorder. *Neuroimage Clin.* **2019**, *22*, 101725. doi:10.1016/j.nicl.2019.101725.

Hays, R.; Keshavan, M.; Wisniewski, H.; Torous, J. Deriving Symptom Networks from Digital Phenotyping Data in Serious Mental Illness. *BJPsych Open* **2020**, *6* (6), e135. doi:10.1192/bjo.2020.94.

Holderness, E.; Miller, N.; Cawkwell, P.; Bolton, K.; Meteer, M.; Pustejovsky, J.; Hall, M.-H. Analysis of Risk Factor Domains in Psychosis Patient Health Records. *J. Biomed. Semant.* **2019**, *10* (1), 19. doi:10.1186/s13326-019-0210-8.

Hunter, S. A.; Lawrie, S. M. Imaging and Genetic Biomarkers Predicting Transition to Psychosis. *Curr. Top Behav. Neurosci.* **2018**, *40*, 353–388. doi:10.1007/7854_2018_46.

International Schizophrenia, C.; Purcell, S. M.; Wray, N. R.; Stone, J. L.; Visscher, P. M.; O'Donovan, M. C.; et al. Common Polygenic Variation Contributes to Risk of Schizophrenia and Bipolar Disorder. *Nature* **2009**, *460* (7256), 748–752. doi:10.1038/nature08185.

Iwabuchi, S.; Liddle, P.; Palaniyappan, L. Clinical Utility of Machine-Learning Approaches in Schizophrenia: Improving Diagnostic Confidence for Translational Neuroimaging. *Front. Psychiatry* **2013**, *4* (95). doi:10.3389/fpsyt.2013.00095.

Kambeitz, J.; Cabral, C.; Sacchet, M. D.; Gotlib, I. H.; Zahn, R.; Serpa, M. H.; et al. Detecting Neuroimaging Biomarkers for Depression: A Meta-Analysis of Multivariate Pattern Recognition Studies. *Biol. Psychiatry* **2017**, *82* (5), 330–338. doi:10.1016/j.biopsych.2016.10.028.

Kapur, S.; Phillips, A. G.; Insel, T. R. Why Has It Taken So Long for Biological Psychiatry to Develop Clinical Tests and What to Do about It? *Mol. Psychiatry* **2012**, *17* (12), 1174–1179. doi:10.1038/mp.2012.105.

Khodayari-Rostamabad, A.; Hasey, G. M.; MacCrimmon, D. J.; Reilly, J. P.; Bruin, H. D. A Pilot Study to Determine Whether Machine Learning Methodologies Using Pre-treatment Electroencephalography Can Predict the Symptomatic Response to Clozapine Therapy. *Clin. Neurophysiol.* **2010a**, *121* (12), 1998–2006. doi:10.1016/j.clinph.2010.05.009.

Khodayari-Rostamabad, A.; Reilly, J. P.; Hasey, G.; Debruin, H.; Maccrimmon, D. Diagnosis of Psychiatric Disorders Using EEG Data and Employing a Statistical Decision Model. *Annu. Int. Conf. IEEE Eng. Med. Biol. Soc.* **2010b,** *2010,* 4006–4009. doi:10.1109/IEMBS. 2010.5627998.

Korda, A. I.; Andreou, C.; Borgwardt, S. Pattern Classification as Decision Support Tool in Antipsychotic Treatment Algorithms. *Exp. Neurol.* **2021,** *339,* 113635. doi:10.1016/j. expneurol.2021.113635.

Koutsouleris, N.; Meisenzahl, E. M.; Davatzikos, C.; Bottlender, R.; Frodl, T.; Scheuerecker, J.; et al. Use of Neuroanatomical Pattern Classification to Identify Subjects in At-Risk Mental States of Psychosis and Predict Disease Transition. *Arch. Gen. Psychiatry* **2009,** *66* (7), 700–712. doi:10.1001/archgenpsychiatry.2009.62.

Koutsouleris, N.; Borgwardt, S.; Meisenzahl, E. M.; Bottlender, R.; Möller, H.-J.; Riecher-Rössler, A. Disease Prediction in the At-Risk Mental State for Psychosis Using Neuroanatomical Biomarkers: Results from the FePsy Study. *Schizophr. Bull.* **2011,** *38* (6), 1234–1246. doi:10.1093/schbul/sbr145.

Koutsouleris, N.; Riecher-Rössler, A.; Meisenzahl, E. M.; Smieskova, R.; Studerus, E.; Kambeitz-Ilankovic, L.; et al. Detecting the Psychosis Prodrome across High-Risk Populations Using Neuroanatomical Biomarkers. *Schizophr. Bull.* **2014,** *41* (2), 471–482. doi:10.1093/schbul/sbu078.

Li, Y. J.; Fan, F. Y. Classification of Schizophrenia and Depression by EEG with ANNs. *Conf. Proc. IEEE Eng. Med. Biol. Soc.* **2005,** *2005,* 2679–2682. doi:10.1109/IEMBS.2005. 1617022.

Li, J.; Cai, T.; Jiang, Y.; Chen, H.; He, X.; Chen, C.; et al. Genes with De Novo Mutations Are Shared by Four Neuropsychiatric Disorders Discovered from NP De Novo Database. *Mol. Psychiatry* **2016,** *21* (2), 290–297. doi:10.1038/mp.2015.40.

Li, J.; Sun, Y.; Huang, Y.; Bezerianos, A.; Yu, R. Machine Learning Technique Reveals Intrinsic Characteristics of Schizophrenia: An Alternative Method. *Brain Imag. Behav.* **2019,** *13* (5), 1386–1396. doi:10.1007/s11682-018-9947-4.

Lieberman, J. A.; Small, S. A.; Girgis, R. R. Early Detection and Preventive Intervention in Schizophrenia: From Fantasy to Reality. *Am. J. Psychiatry* **2019,** *176* (10), 794–810. doi:10.1176/appi.ajp.2019.19080865.

Malla, A.; McGorry, P. Early Intervention in Psychosis in Young People: A Population and Public Health Perspective. *Am. J. Publ. Health* **2019,** *109* (S3), S181-S184. doi:10.2105/ AJPH.2019.305018.

Martinuzzi, E.; Barbosa, S.; Daoudlarian, D.; Bel Haj Ali, W.; Gilet, C.; Fillatre, L.; et al. Stratification and Prediction of Remission in First-Episode Psychosis Patients: The OPTiMiSE Cohort Study. *Transl. Psychiatry* **2019,** *9* (1), 20. doi:10.1038/s41398-018-0366-5.

Mechelli, A. *Machine Learning: Methods and Applications to Brain Disorders,* 1st ed.; Elsevier: San Diego, 2019.

Mechelli, A.; Lin, A.; Wood, S.; McGorry, P.; Amminger, P.; Tognin, S.; et al. Using Clinical Information to Make Individualized Prognostic Predictions in People at Ultra High Risk for Psychosis. *Schizophr. Res.* **2017,** *184,* 32–38. doi:10.1016/j.schres.2016.11.047.

Melle, I.; Johannesen, J. O.; Friis, S.; Haahr, U.; Joa, I.; Larsen, T. K.; et al. Early Detection of the First Episode of Schizophrenia and Suicidal Behavior. *Am. J. Psychiatry* **2006,** *163* (5), 800–804. doi:10.1176/ajp.2006.163.5.800.

Meltzer, H. Y. Treatment-Resistant Schizophrenia—The Role of Clozapine. *Curr. Med. Res. Opin.* **1997,** *14* (1), 1–20. doi:10.1185/03007999709113338.

Miotto, R.; Li, L.; Kidd, B. A.; Dudley, J. T. Deep Patient: An Unsupervised Representation to Predict the Future of Patients from the Electronic Health Records. *Sci. Rep.* **2016,** *6* (1), 26094. doi:10.1038/srep26094.

Mongan, D.; Focking, M.; Healy, C.; Susai, S. R.; Heurich, M.; Wynne, K.; et al. Development of Proteomic Prediction Models for Transition to Psychotic Disorder in the Clinical High-Risk State and Psychotic Experiences in Adolescence. *JAMA Psychiatry* **2021,** *78* (1), 77–90. doi:10.1001/jamapsychiatry.2020.2459.

Mourao-Miranda, J.; Reinders, A. A. T. S.; Rocha-Rego, V.; Lappin, J.; Rondina, J.; Morgan, C.; et al. Individualized Prediction of Illness Course at the First Psychotic Episode: A Support Vector Machine MRI Study. *Psychol. Med.* **2012,** *42* (5), 1037–1047. doi:10.1017/S0033291711002005.

Oduola, S.; Das-Munshi, J.; Bourque, F.; Gayer-Anderson, C.; Tsang, J.; Murray, R. M.; et al. Change in Incidence Rates for Psychosis in Different Ethnic Groups in South London: Findings from the Clinical Record Interactive Search-First Episode Psychosis (CRIS-FEP) Study. *Psychol. Med.* **2021,** *51* (2), 300–309. doi:10.1017/S0033291719003234.

Penttila, M.; Jaaskelainen, E.; Hirvonen, N.; Isohanni, M.; Miettunen, J. Duration of Untreated Psychosis as Predictor of Long-Term Outcome in Schizophrenia: Systematic Review and Meta-Analysis. *Br. J. Psychiatry* **2014,** *205* (2), 88–94. doi:10.1192/bjp.bp.113.127753.

Pinaya, W. H. L.; Mechelli, A.; Sato, J. R. Using Deep Autoencoders to Identify Abnormal Brain Structural Patterns in Neuropsychiatric Disorders: A Large-Scale Multi-Sample Study. *Human Brain Mapp.* **2019,** *40* (3), 944–954. doi:10.1002/hbm.24423.

Pinto, J. V.; Passos, I. C.; Gomes, F.; Reckziegel, R.; Kapczinski, F.; Mwangi, B.; Kauer-Sant'Anna, M. Peripheral Biomarker Signatures of Bipolar Disorder and Schizophrenia: A Machine Learning Approach. *Schizophr. Res.* **2017,** *188*, 182–184. doi:10.1016/j.schres.2017.01.018.

Pisanu, C.; Squassina, A. Treatment-Resistant Schizophrenia: Insights from Genetic Studies and Machine Learning Approaches. *Front. Pharmacol.* **2019,** *10*, 617. doi:10.3389/fphar.2019.00617.

Pollard, J. M.; Ferrara, M.; Lin, I. H.; Kucukgoncu, S.; Wasser, T.; Li, F.; Srihari, V. H. Analysis of Early Intervention Services on Adult Judicial Outcomes. *JAMA Psychiatry* **2020**. doi:10.1001/jamapsychiatry.2020.0448.

Powers, A. R.; Addington, J.; Perkins, D. O.; Bearden, C. E.; Cadenhead, K. S.; Cannon, T. D.; et al. Duration of the Psychosis Prodrome. *Schizophr. Res.* **2020,** *216*, 443–449. doi:10.1016/j.schres.2019.10.051.

Qureshi, M. N. I.; Oh, J.; Cho, D.; Jo, H. J.; Lee, B. Multimodal Discrimination of Schizophrenia Using Hybrid Weighted Feature Concatenation of Brain Functional Connectivity and Anatomical Features with an Extreme Learning Machine. *Front. Neuroinf.* **2017,** *11*, 59. doi:10.3389/fninf.2017.00059.

Ramkiran, S.; Sharma, A.; Rao, N. P. Resting-State Anticorrelated Networks in Schizophrenia. *Psychiatry Res. Neuroimag.* **2019,** *284*, 1–8. doi:10.1016/j.pscychresns.2018.12.013.

Rapcan, V.; D'Arcy, S.; Yeap, S.; Afzal, N.; Thakore, J.; Reilly, R. B. Acoustic and Temporal Analysis of Speech: A Potential Biomarker for Schizophrenia. *Med. Eng. Phys.* **2010,** *32* (9), 1074–1079. doi:10.1016/j.medengphy.2010.07.013.

Ravan, M.; MacCrimmon, D.; Hasey, G.; Reilly, J. P.; Khodayari-Rostamabad, A. A Machine Learning Approach Using P300 Responses to Investigate Effect of Clozapine Therapy. *Annu. Int. Conf. IEEE Eng. Med. Biol. Soc.* **2012,** *2012*, 5911–5914. doi:10.1109/EMBC.2012.6347339.

Robinson, D. G.; Schooler, N. R.; Rosenheck, R. A.; Lin, H.; Sint, K. J.; Marcy, P.; Kane, J. M. Predictors of Hospitalization of Individuals With First-Episode Psychosis: Data From a 2-Year Follow-Up of the RAISE-ETP. *Psychiatr. Serv.* **2019,** *70* (7), 569–577. doi:10.1176/appi.ps.201800511.

Rodriguez-Villa, E.; Mehta, U. M.; Naslund, J.; Tugnawat, D.; Gupta, S.; Thirtalli, J.; et al. Smartphone Health Assessment for Relapse Prevention (SHARP): A Digital Solution toward Global Mental Health. *BJPsych Open* **2021,** *7* (1), e29. doi:10.1192/bjo.2020.142.

Salazar de Pablo, G.; Catalan, A.; Fusar-Poli, P. Clinical Validity of DSM-5 Attenuated Psychosis Syndrome: Advances in Diagnosis, Prognosis, and Treatment. *JAMA Psychiatry* **2020,** *77* (3), 311–320. doi:10.1001/jamapsychiatry.2019.3561.

Salazar de Pablo, G.; Radua, J.; Pereira, J.; Bonoldi, I.; Arienti, V.; Besana, F.; et al. Probability of Transition to Psychosis in Individuals at Clinical High Risk: An Updated Meta-Analysis. *JAMA Psychiatry* **2021.** doi:10.1001/jamapsychiatry.2021.0830.

Santesteban-Echarri, O.; Paino, M.; Rice, S.; González-Blanch, C.; McGorry, P.; Gleeson, J.; Alvarez-Jimenez, M. Predictors of Functional Recovery in First-Episode Psychosis: A Systematic Review and Meta-Analysis of Longitudinal Studies. *Clin. Psychol. Rev.* **2017,** *58*, 59–75. doi:10.1016/j.cpr.2017.09.007.

Sarpal, D. K.; Argyelan, M.; Robinson, D. G.; Szeszko, P. R.; Karlsgodt, K. H.; John, M.; et al. Baseline Striatal Functional Connectivity as a Predictor of Response to Antipsychotic Drug Treatment. *Am. J. Psychiatry* **2016,** *173* (1), 69–77. doi:10.1176/appi.ajp.2015.14121571.

Schnack, H. G.; Nieuwenhuis, M.; van Haren, N. E.; Abramovic, L.; Scheewe, T. W.; Brouwer, R. M.; et al. Can Structural MRI Aid in Clinical Classification? A Machine Learning Study in Two Independent Samples of Patients with Schizophrenia, Bipolar Disorder and Healthy Subjects. *NeuroImage* **2014,** *84*, 299–306. doi:10.1016/j.neuroimage.2013.08.053.

Schofield, W.; Hathaway, S. R.; Hastings, D. W.; Bell, D. M. Prognostic Factors in Schizophrenia. *J. Consult. Psychol.* **1954,** *18* (3), 155–166. doi:10.1037/h0056083.

Senior, M.; Burghart, M.; Yu, R.; Kormilitzin, A.; Liu, Q.; Vaci, N.; et al. Identifying Predictors of Suicide in Severe Mental Illness: A Feasibility Study of a Clinical Prediction Rule (Oxford Mental Illness and Suicide Tool or OxMIS). *Front. Psychiatry* **2020,** *11* (268). doi:10.3389/fpsyt.2020.00268.

Simon, G. E. Social and Economic Burden of Mood Disorders. *Biol. Psychiatry* **2003,** *54* (3), 208–215. doi:10.1016/S0006-3223(03)00420-7.

Simon, G. E.; Coleman, K. J.; Yarborough, B. J. H.; Operskalski, B.; Stewart, C.; Hunkeler, E. M.; et al. First Presentation with Psychotic Symptoms in a Population-Based Sample. *Psychiatr. Serv.* **2017,** *68* (5), 456–461. doi:10.1176/appi.ps.201600257.

Simon, G. E.; Stewart, C.; Hunkeler, E. M.; Yarborough, B. J.; Lynch, F.; Coleman, K. J.; et al. Care Pathways before First Diagnosis of a Psychotic Disorder in Adolescents and Young Adults. *Am. J. Psychiatry* **2018a,** *175* (5), 434–442. doi:10.1176/appi.ajp.2017.17080844.

Simon, G. E.; Stewart, C.; Yarborough, B. J.; Lynch, F.; Coleman, K. J.; Beck, A.; et al. Mortality Rates after the First Diagnosis of Psychotic Disorder in Adolescents and Young Adults. *JAMA Psychiatry* **2018b,** *75* (3), 254–260. doi:10.1001/jamapsychiatry.2017.4437.

Struyf, J.; Dobrin, S.; Page, D. Combining Gene Expression, Demographic and Clinical Data in Modeling Disease: A Case Study of Bipolar Disorder and Schizophrenia. *BMC Genom.* **2008,** *9*, 531. doi:10.1186/1471-2164-9-531.

Suvisaari, J. M.; Haukka, J. K.; Lönnqvist, J. K. Season of Birth among Patients with Schizophrenia and Their Siblings: Evidence for the Procreational Habits Hypothesis. *Am. J. Psychiatry* **2001,** *158* (5), 754–757. doi:10.1176/appi.ajp.158.5.754.

Ten Velden Hegelstad, W.; Haahr, U.; Larsen, T. K.; Auestad, B.; Barder, H.; Evensen, J.; et al. Early Detection, Early Symptom Progression and Symptomatic Remission after Ten Years in a First Episode of Psychosis Study. *Schizophr. Res.* **2013,** *143* (2–3), 337–343. doi: 10.1016/j.schres.2012.10.027.

Trakadis, Y. J.; Sardaar, S.; Chen, A.; Fulginiti, V.; Krishnan, A. Machine Learning in Schizophrenia Genomics, a Case-Control Study Using 5,090 Exomes. *Am. J. Med. Genet., B: Neuropsychiatr. Genet.* **2019,** *180* (2), 103–112. doi:10.1002/ajmg.b.32638.

van Os, J.; Guloksuz, S. A Critique of the "Ultra-High Risk" and "Transition" Paradigm. *World Psychiatry* **2017,** *16* (2), 200–206. doi:10.1002/wps.20423.

Varese, F.; Smeets, F.; Drukker, M.; Lieverse, R.; Lataster, T.; Viechtbauer, W.; et al. Childhood Adversities Increase the Risk of Psychosis: A Meta-Analysis of Patient-Control, Prospective- and Cross-Sectional Cohort Studies. *Schizophr. Bull.* **2012,** *38* (4), 661–671. doi:10.1093/schbul/sbs050.

Vassos, E.; Pedersen, C. B.; Murray, R. M.; Collier, D. A.; Lewis, C. M. Meta-Analysis of the Association of Urbanicity with Schizophrenia. *Schizophr. Bull.* **2012,** *38* (6), 1118–1123. doi:10.1093/schbul/sbs096.

Vivian-Griffiths, T.; Baker, E.; Schmidt, K. M.; Bracher-Smith, M.; Walters, J.; Artemiou, A.; et al. Predictive Modeling of Schizophrenia from Genomic Data: Comparison of Polygenic Risk Score with Kernel Support Vector Machines Approach. *Am. J. Med. Genet., B: Neuropsychiatr. Genet.* **2019,** *180* (1), 80–85. doi:10.1002/ajmg.b.32705.

World Health Organization. *Mental Disorders*; 2019a. Retrieved from https://www.who.int/news-room/fact-sheets/detail/mental-disorders

World Health Organization. *Schizophrenia*; 2019b. Retrieved from https://www.who.int/news-room/fact-sheets/detail/schizophrenia

Yang, H.; Liu, J.; Sui, J.; Pearlson, G.; Calhoun, V. A Hybrid Machine Learning Method for Fusing fMRI and Genetic Data: Combining both Improves Classification of Schizophrenia. *Front. Human Neurosci.* **2010,** *4* (192). doi:10.3389/fnhum.2010.00192.

Yoviene Sykes, L. A.; Ferrara, M.; Addington, J.; Bearden, C. E.; Cadenhead, K. S.; Cannon, T. D.; et al. Predictive Validity of Conversion from the Clinical High Risk Syndrome to Frank Psychosis. *Schizophr. Res.* **2019.** doi:10.1016/j.schres.2019.12.002.

Zeng, L. L.; Wang, H.; Hu, P.; Yang, B.; Pu, W.; Shen, H.; et al. Multi-Site Diagnostic Classification of Schizophrenia Using Discriminant Deep Learning with Functional Connectivity MRI. *EBioMedicine* **2018,** *30*, 74–85. doi:10.1016/j.ebiom.2018.03.017.

Zheutlin, A. B.; Chekroud, A. M.; Polimanti, R.; Gelernter, J.; Sabb, F. W.; Bilder, R. M.; et al. Multivariate Pattern Analysis of Genotype–Phenotype Relationships in Schizophrenia. *Schizophr. Bull.* **2018,** *44* (5), 1045–1052. doi:10.1093/schbul/sby005.

Zhu, F.; Liu, Y.; Liu, F.; Yang, R.; Li, H.; Chen, J.; et al. Functional Asymmetry of Thalamocortical Networks in Subjects at Ultra-High Risk for Psychosis and First-Episode Schizophrenia. *Eur. Neuropsychopharmacol.* **2019,** *29* (4), 519–528. doi:10.1016/j.euroneuro.2019.02.006.

Zhuang, H.; Liu, R.; Wu, C.; Meng, Z.; Wang, D.; Liu, D.; et al. Multimodal Classification of Drug-Naïve First-Episode Schizophrenia Combining Anatomical, Diffusion and Resting State Functional Resonance Imaging. *Neurosci. Lett.* **2019,** *705*, 87–93. doi:10.1016/j.neulet.2019.04.039.

CHAPTER 12

ARTIFICIAL INTELLIGENCE, EDUCATION, AND DIGITAL ECONOMY IN INDIA

MOHD NAYYER RAHMAN[1], BADAR ALAM IQBAL[2], NIDA RAHMAN[3], and MUNIR HASSAN[4]

[1]Department of Commerce, Aligarh Muslim University, Aligarh, Uttar Pradesh, India

[2]Monarch Business School, Zug, Switzerland

[3]Research and Information System for Developing Countries, New Delhi, India

[4]Department of Economics, Kuwait University, Kuwait City, Kuwait

ABSTRACT

The chapter aims to conceptualize and study policies pertaining to artificial intelligence (AI), digital economy (DE), and education in India. AI is growing technological advancement and is applicable to all the domains of economic, political, and social life. AI is an innovative technology capable of integrating and transforming the DE. Already, developed countries have progressed in the area by the application of AI. As an emerging economy in Asia, India has a promising future and it aspires to become the largest economy of the world. However, the challenges of the future will emerge out of the association between AI and DE. Education policies can create a workforce suited for the DE. With Industrialization 4.0 at the door, it is high time for India to gear up.

Incorporating AI Technology in the Service Sector: Innovations in Creating Knowledge, Improving Efficiency, and Elevating Quality of Life. Maria José Sousa, Subhendu Kumar Pani, Francesca Dal Mas, & Sérgio Sousa (Eds.)
© 2024 Apple Academic Press, Inc. Co-published with CRC Press (Taylor & Francis)

The chapter explores the tripartite relationship between AI, education, and DE in India and evaluates the policy initiatives undertaken. Brainstorming and converging the past studies, conceptual quadrant models are generated for AI, DE, and education. The findings indicate 11 macropolicy initiatives taken by India along with New Education Policy with the expectation of incremental progress in ADE trident.

12.1   INTRODUCTION

Technological advancement and progress are continued endeavor of economies with the objective of achieving scale benefits, political power, and technological edge. In the postmodern world, technology creates digital economy (DE) and with it an economy can rise to an empire. The political economy of technology is powerful and plays a dominant role in the international economic order. Technologically advanced countries are the most developed countries of the world. The economic history of the world suggests that great empires were built due to technological advancement. Technological advancement and universal education have an age-old connection, in the sense that, universal education became a reality due to the industrial revolution (Allen, 2011). Currently in the Industrialization 4.0 age, the outcome of education as a factor in promoting this new form of industrialization is required. Thus, education and technological advancement go hand in hand. If a country wants to master in any field, it has to train its workforce, particularly the young ones. This can be accomplished with incentives and reforms in the education sector. India holds an interesting place in the global political order. India is an emerging economy and has become an attraction for the global MNCs. Due to the global domination of China, the United States and allies consider India to be the power-balancing player in the region. India's economic and military might has grown over the last few decades, and it has to its advantage a rich diaspora all around the world. India aspires to become an economic and political leader in the future. However, the future of the global economy cannot be just determined by power, it requires countries to be technologically advanced. The future trends suggest that Industrialization 4.0 will transform a real economy into DE, and several steps have already been taken in this regard such as digital currencies, gig economy of consumption, e-commerce, and so on. India has also introduced several key policies that will push to the DE. The skill set requirement for the workforce is gradually shifting to more subtle forms of knowledge and technical know-how.

12.1.1   INDIAN SCENARIO

As per the latest UNCTAD report, India is a developing and emerging economy. When India liberalized its economy in 1991, the GDP of the country was US$ 291,200 million and today as per the latest statistics it is US$ 2679,578, indicating accelerating growth rate (UNCTAD Statistics, 2021). Over the last three decades, India has shown considerable influence, regionally and globally. The political, social, and economic indicators of India have improved in the last three decades (Iqbal et al., 2019). It is interesting to study education and DE in order to understand the political economy of artificial intelligence (AI) in India and how it can be improved to the advantage of India. India is one of the countries that will face huge technology disruption due to automation. Already this has been witnessed in the pandemic period when educational institutions were working in online mode. A large percentage of students in India do not have any access to the technologies/gadgets supporting online education program. India needs to gear up its digital infrastructure and learning. The study is to explore the policies in India for a tripartite relationship between AI, DE, and education.

12.2   LITERATURE ON AI, EDUCATION, AND DE IN INDIA

It is only recently that research on AI in India has been in focus. There is lack of policy studies focusing on India but technical aspects have been touched. A review of Indian-specific AI studies is the focus of this section. A review of "National Strategy for AI in India" with the help of focused group discussions reveals that the current strategy needs improvement. More focus is required on security and privacy issues (Chatterjee, 2020). In 2016, it was predicted that internet connectivity in India will boost AI proliferation and this has come true due to 4G networking in India. However, barriers still persist in rural and suburban areas. India requires to fund AI research and should learn from global lessons (Vempati, 2016). Application of AI in education sector has been subject of study in India. AI-based chatbots can enhance the student learning experience, and it will add to the positive change in Indian education sector. Applying a quantitative approach to collect survey data on chatbots in India, it has been found that chatbot developers have a job to play in improving the student learning experience in India (Sandu and Gide, 2019). India's future depends on application of AI technologies and an analysis of opportunities and challenges is required. Cross-cutting opportunities for India include bridging India's linguistic divisions and mining public data.

India will have to counter social issues that hinder the progress of AI such as ethical concerns and privacy issues (Kalyanakrishnan et al., 2018). AI is the backbone of the fourth industrial revolution. India's strength being workforce, it is important to perceive the future and train them accordingly. Due to implementation of AI technologies, a new wave of automation will sweep all the sectors. Thus, necessary infrastructure along with policy is required for India to excel (Srivastava, 2018). The three stages of AI policy the data, model, and application need to be considered skeptically for data-driven decision-making. For India to use AI for policy decisions, the limitations of the AI systems must be reckoned with. The ethical and social concerns of AI technology implementation should not be ignored (Marda, 2018). With respect to application of AI, Indian start-ups in healthcare have already used AI technologies to bridge the gap between decisions and data. In the times of COVID crisis, application of AI in healthcare has increased and this is a good signal for a developing country like India. AI has helped monitoring and screening of the clinical studies for patients in India (Vijai and Wisetsri, 2021). Indian higher education sector is a complex system of public and private universities, the increasing load on the instructors can be reduced smartly with the application of AI technologies. With the application of "Unified Theory of Acceptance and Use of Technology" (UTAUT) model on 329 survey responses, adoption of AI in higher education and attitude toward AI technologies was explored. Higher education institutions in India will achieve greater efficiency with the application of AI (Chatterjee and Bhattacharjee, 2020). The Indian education scenario is becoming smart with the use of technologies; this includes universities, institutions as well as schools. It has been found that personalized learning, recommendation systems, and adaptive assessments are helping students and supporting teachers (Jaiswal and Arun, 2021). Indian higher education has opened a new chapter with the adoption of AI in learning environments. The potential of AI cannot be undermined in a digital age. The future of the Indian education sector will be determined on how best the AI technologies are applied to education sector (Bhatnagar, 2020).

Industrialization 4.0 is the term coined to indicate the use of digitization and digitalization in the economic system. India is progressing to transform its economy toward complete digitization and digitalization. While digitization is the use of numeric indicators across social and industrial sectors, digitalization is the process and application of technologies. India has already implemented a good number of digitalization mechanisms for monetary economy, one of the indicators is the use of cashless economy with the promotion of digital payment systems and digital wallets (Shankar, 2017). DE initiatives started in India with the liberalization policy of 1991 but the masses were directly affected after demonetization in India in 2016. Demonetization motivated and forced people to try digital payment systems. This created a familiarity with the digital payment's usage. Research conducted on the perception of Indians on recent digital revolution reveals a negative perception toward digital payment system in rural areas. The most important reason for this is the barriers of accessibility. In India, more people are using digital systems as a status symbol and women are lagging behind in using them (Sen, 2020). These microdigital efforts generate public opinion in favor of DE. The foundations for a DE are digital literacy, infrastructure, and internet penetration. In 2016, Government of India launched national program toward digitalization named Digital India wherein innovators, practitioners, and learners were targeted to focus on development of DE in India. The present government has emphasized on the importance and relevance of DE in India. Developing DE infrastructure has also been the objective of India and National Information Network is another feather in the hat for India. India's NIN focuses on cloud services, network sharing, bandwidth allocation, and internet penetration (Gokilavani and Durgarani, 2017). Countries have started focusing on DE, and several initiatives have been introduced in this direction. Although India did not perform well on the Network Readiness Index (World Economic Forum, 2016) with a rank of 91, still the recent efforts are hope toward DE in India (Jarwal, 2017). DE and financial markets interaction are paving way for a hybrid economic and political system and digital financialization. Financial inclusion is important for the developing countries, and the future digital structure needs a grinding of digital mechanism and financial technologies. In India, coercive measures have been adopted for digitalization such as demonetization and for digitization such as Aadhar project of national identity. India's narrative of digital financialization appears to be based on technocultural nationalism (Jain and Gabor, 2020).

As a developing country (UNCTAD, 2021) and a lower income country (World Bank), India has to build policies and infrastructure for supporting a DE. However, digital divide in India is a major issue, needed to be sorted out at the earliest. Digital divide and social inequalities are an area of concern for the researchers. In Indian perspective, research conducted on the linkages between social inequalities and digital divide using national data of 40,000 households indicates less educated with lower-income group along with low strata are negatively affected as they lack ICT assets and necessary skills. Households who own organized business in India own and use ICT assets more in comparison to those dependent on wage income (agricultural or nonagricultural). ICT ownership and usage as an indicator of DE differ in India along different socio-economic groups. There is a need to focus on the social paradigm of DE, otherwise social inequalities will be amplified (Tewathia et al., 2020).

A density map using VOS viewer for 266 published papers is developed as per the Web of Science database with terms AI and DE. The green networks connect the constructs of DE, while the blue networks connect with social and economic dimensions. The red network area is linkages of different AI technologies with terms such as data and methods that are central to AI mechanism. The red density is more than green and blue indicating the domination of published literature on specific AI technologies and jargons. Figure 12.1 highlights that published research in AI and DE is interconnected and myriad layers of knowledge are involved in it.

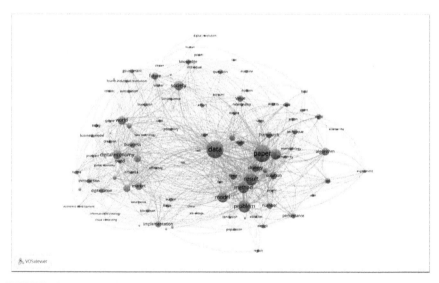

FIGURE 12.1   VOS Literature Network Map: artificial intelligence and digital economy.

Figure 12.2 is the density and network graph for 5000 published papers as per Web of Science database on AI and education from 2011 to 2021. Red networks represent education, while green and blue represent AI technologies and usage area, respectively. The yellow density dots (which are few) shows the hardware side of AI technologies like device, sensors, and so on. It is clear from the figure that the density of education is lowest while its networking with AI technologies (green) is high. This gives an indication that future link-ages between AI and education with mediation of hardware systems (yellow) is a natural outcome. The specific domains where AI application has been used (blue) have linkages with education (red). These linkages add to the knowledge base of a particular discipline. For example, application of AI in cancer will enhance the present human knowledge and understanding of cancer. In turn, the new knowledge will be transmitted to students currently in medical science, opening up new avenues for innovation and progress in cancer research.

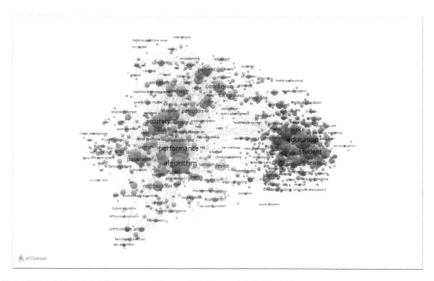

FIGURE 12.2   VOS Literature Network Map: artificial intelligence and education.

12.3   CONCEPTUALIZING AI, EDUCATION, AND DE IN INDIA

The concepts of AI, education, and DE have been duly explored in the literature. However, conceptualizing relationship is missing in the existing literature. In this section, focus is to develop a conceptual quadrant model encompassing the expected outcomes. A quadrant model with two variables at a time (two-dimensional) with permutation can maintain the principle of parsimony. The three key terms are not a portmanteau and thus there will be no objection of that sort. First, conceptualization deals with AI and education. The changing paradigm of education due to application of AI is greatly observed. Development in AI technologies presents new challenges for the education sector, like remote teaching, virtual labs, that needs to be inculcated with the teaching syllabus. The development in AI is also making the current syllabus archaic, in the sense, that issues need to be discussed in the light of technological development and disruption.

The quadrant model of conceptualization reflects the outcomes due to the collision of AI with education without focus on directionality. The first quadrant indicates the positive outcomes with the positive interaction of AI and education. Application of AI in education has several advantages, but the most common is time-saving and the efficiency achieved in imparting education. With the use of AI technologies, time consumed in delivering the content is minimized and it makes the learning process interesting and attractive applying AI visualizations and simulations. AI technologies, when applied in education, give opportunity for personalized learning experience, by creating chatbots necessary feedback from the students can be taken. The technology loop can then provide a personalized learning curve with the best knowledge provided in a best manner (Holmes et al., 2019). The second partition denotes positive education (+) and negative AI (−), referring to the outcomes. Not everything is good with the interaction of AI and education, there are issues of concern as well. In a social setup, human interaction is a psychological need and not just a luxury. With the application of AI, the human interaction in education may be hampered. The teacher–student relationship becomes more of a mechanical process, rather than having humane approach. Privacy issues that emerge with the interaction of AI and education needs due consideration, particularly the age constraint and the type of content to which students are exposed. With no global ratified agreement on AI for education from an ethical and legal perspective, the move is always prone to errors and may open up gates of hazards for the children (Chen et al., 2020). The third section of the quadrant represents the negative outcomes due to the interaction of AI and education, human resource displacement, and initial higher cost. With advancement in AI and application in the education sector, human resource is at the risk of displacement. Transition role of trainers is at risk, the less brainstorming knowledge can be easily acquired without a human teacher. AI-assisted programs, chatbots, early recognition systems, and voice recognition systems are sufficient, thus displacing the human resources in the education sector. Displacing is an appropriate term as it denotes that an upgradation in skills can bring them back to the job market, such as teaching of AI mechanisms will be the most relevant job in future market. Currently, AI technologies are being explored and the institutional cost of acquiring them is high, gradually it will go on decreasing and will be easily accessible to all. Initial high cost is a challenging task for the lower and middle-income countries (Ciolacu et al., 2018). Fourth and the final section of the quadrant presents the positive AI (+) and negative education (−), indicating the outcomes after interaction and reduced attention span and flexibility. Education philosophers and psychologists have strong evidence to believe that with technological advancement and social media platforms, attention span of the students is declining (Kies, 2018; Heflin et al., 2017). With AI in education, retaining attention span in human interaction will be a challenging task. This may lead to psychological problems particularly among children. Students need concentrated efforts and attention span is complementary to concentration. Though the applications such as virtual reality may specifically target to counter this challenge, it may not be accessible to all (Anusha, 2017). The high cost of the installation of AI technologies at educational institutions is a matter of concern. Once an AI system is procured for an institution, the students have to habitat with it, leaving little room for flexibility. The evaluation system allows, particularly in the low and middle-income countries, for uniformity among students, thus, allowing less room for flexibility (Pedro et al., 2019).

The second quadrant model (Figure 12.3) conceptualizes the relationship between DE and education. The outcomes of the interaction between DE and education are depicted as positive (+) or negative (−). The first area of the quadrant outlines the positive outcomes of DE and education interaction in the form of DE and Education 3.0 and 4.0. With progress in DE, as measured by spending on ICT (UNCTAD), education sector has an opportunity for developing a digital learning environment (Bogoslovskiy et al., 2019). The environment is facilitated by use of computers, application of software, simulations platforms, writing, and visualization software as well. Digital learning environments provide a great opportunity for learning real problem-solving skills. The technological convergence and transformation of education sector is paving way for Education 3.0 and 4.0, connoting the use of technology to transform education practices. Education has been significantly linked to industrial revolutions (Allen, 2011), and with the advent of Industrialization 4.0, the education sector is going to be affected by it. Gaming, simulations, predictive modeling, data visualizations, and so on are going to be part of the student curriculum to fulfill the future needs of the industry (Gueye and Exposito, 2020).

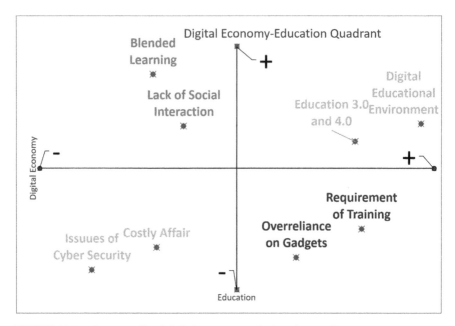

FIGURE 12.3   Conceptualized digital economy and education quadrant.

The second space of the quadrant highlights positive education (+) and negative DE (−), meaning thereby the outcomes with the interaction of DE and education. One of the advantages derived is the concept of blended learning; physical interaction plus technological application wherever and whenever feasible is required. Blended learning in the COVID-19 crisis became challenging due to restricted human movement, but once the pandemic ends, the option would be explored all around the world. The other aspect is lack of social interaction due to the application of DE. Social interaction here does not include social media interaction (it is virtual interaction/remote communication) and thus DE is promoting a culture of less social interaction among students due to gadgets usage (Sreehari et al., 1989). With reduced social interaction as the outcome of DE, consequences such as psychological problems, attention span syndrome, and cognitive shocks can become widespread among students (Klimuk and Lazdins, 2019). The third section of the quadrant captures the negative outcomes of DE and education, referring to the outcomes. Issues of cybersecurity are a matter of concern, particularly for students as they are open to several kinds of threats and crimes. In this new era of DE, cybersecurity issues are becoming complex day by day. Therefore, the education setup will not be free from the suspicious attack of cybersecurity in the educational institutions and training centers. The way education is developing in the DE, cybersecurity, and privacy issues of students are a matter of concern (Maymina et al., 2018). The costs associated with implementing DE technologies in education sector are currently high, as is the case with AI technologies, already discussed in Figure 12.4. Especially, this is true for underdeveloped and developing countries, where per capita income is low. With the interaction of positive DE and negative education, the outcomes such as training requirement and overreliance on gadgets are identified. As economies move toward digitalization, the workforce with a constant set of knowledge and skills becomes redundant, it is where training is key to upgrade and be part of Industrialization 4.0. The transformations in the education sector require that the faculty, instructors, and teachers are imparted training to cope up with changing requirement of technology. However, as more and more gadgets are used in the education sector, overreliance on them may become a problem in terms of cognitive abilities (Gupta, 2019; Mariam et al., 2018).

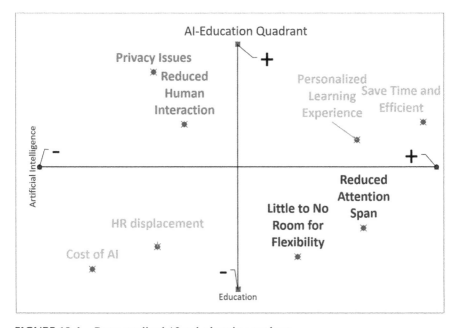

FIGURE 12.4   Conceptualized AI and education quadrant.

12.4   AI POLICY IN INDIA

With India's liberalization policy of 1991, a new era of economic growth and technological development opened up. India's economic policy initially focused on foreign direct investment but underlying objective was technology transfer. Due to the policy in the late 1990s, India witnessed a boom in ITES and IT sector. Bangalore became a popular city with the title "India's Silicon Valley." Technology start-ups emerged and India became a BPO service hub. However, education sector remained isolated to train people in ITES with schools not having a prescribed subject for it. Basic computer literacy was at the target of the education policy. With the advent of AI/ML technologies in the late 2000s, India still was not having a focus on AI/ML learning and knowledge transfer. The first policy document came in 2018 titled National Strategy on AI presented in the Fiscal Budget 2018–2019. The policy document enshrined NITI Ayog (newly found in 2014) to formulate and continuously work on a national AI policy. NITI Ayog has adopted a three-point approach to implement a comprehensive AI policy in India. Figure 12.5 illustrates the three focus points of AI policy by NITI Ayog.

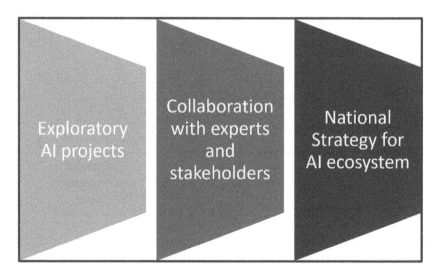

FIGURE 12.5   NITI Ayog national policy objective.

First objective is to explore proof-backed AI projects in different areas. As per the policy paper (NITI, 2018), focus areas for AI intervention in India are healthcare, agriculture, education, smart cities and infrastructure, and smart mobility and transportation. However, other areas are underway by respective ministries. For example, Information and Broadcasting Ministry has already identified key areas to apply AI technologies. Second objective is the collaboration with experts and stakeholders for research in AI at the national level. India produced around 2.6 million STEM graduates in the year 2016, and it is expected to go up considering the expansion in educational and training institutions. India ranks second in terms of its output in STEM education. For the second objective, it is important to bring AI technologies into the education sector particularly training the young ones who are the future of the country. Third objective is a comprehensive national strategy for AI ecosystem in the country. NITI Ayog proposes the establishment of Centres of Research Excellence in Artificial Intelligence (CORE) and International Centre for Transformational Artificial Intelligence (ICTAI). It is proposed that CORE with a focus on the fundamental research on AI must guide India to develop a knowledge hub for India's requirement of the future technologies. ICTAI will foster application-based technology development and deployment. Ministerial objectives for AI technologies will also be explored. It appears that a strong theoretical policy has already been developed in India.

12.5 AI, DE, AND EDUCATION INITIATIVES IN INDIA

It would be a good idea to discuss the current policy initiatives taken for Indian economy that directly or indirectly affects AI, DE, and education trident (now on, ADE trident) in India. The ADE trident requires a comprehensive policy for a developing country like India. Having discussed the national AI Policy, the ADE trident requires a different set of policy instruments. The government of India has introduced New Education Policy in 2020 (MHRD, 2020) with constraints that will benefit the ADE trident. The government policy document on NEP exclusively mentions the importance of AI and the need to train school children in this mechanism. NEP document mentions AI seven times under the headings of technology, training, multilinguist, to name a few (FND, 2020). The schools have started implementing subjects such as programming language (python), introduction to machine learning (through games and analytical cases), robotics (technological upgradation), and so on. This will pave way for the future generation to be trained in ADE trident activities. The ADE trident is so diverse that basic skills are sufficient enough to push the student. With the changing scenario and demand, students can decide what is to be learned for the future. Keeping this in view, the universities in India have started providing an option of picking online courses on ADE trident. Upon completion of the courses, it will be reflected as credits in their degree program, a decision that will surely motivate the university students to use their creativity in learning ADE trident activities. The New Education Policy will open a new chapter of ADE trident activities in the education sector in India.

With respect to DE under ADE trident, implementation of the direct-benefit transfer schemes in India has provided the foundation for ADE trident. The social security system of India, Aadhaar, which was the first digitized mechanism for the masses has now become digitalized, with its linkage with schemes including vaccination drive in India. The ICT expenditure in India is also going incrementally up which indicates the progress of the DE. Digital payment systems and wallets have grown to a maximum in the last decade and their usage has become common in India, both urban and rural. The national initiatives of India for the ADE trident have also been recognized by international agencies such as Organization for Economic Cooperation and Development (OECD). The OECD AI database has identified 11 key policy initiatives having a significant impact on not only AI but also on the ADE trident due to the multidisciplinary approach of the initiatives. Table 12.1 highlights key AI policy initiative in India.

The first policy initiative targeting the ADE trident is the Artificial Intelligence Task Force for India's Economic Transformation setup by Ministry of Commerce and Industry, GOI. The theme of the policy initiative was the formulation of national AI policies. The policy has three clear objectives of leveraging AI for economic benefits, creating a policy and legal framework to accelerate the deployment of AI technologies, and to issue concrete 5-year horizon recommendations for specific government, industry, and research programs. The policy is bringing brainstorming policy documents and strategies for the ADE trident in India. However, for the current program, private funding is not allowed which restricts the reach of the policy to the masses. Also, any structural changes are not expected as the task force is focusing more on recommendations and awareness, rather than on implementing changes. The policy instrument is targeting inclusive growth, sustainable development, and well-being of the country. The second policy initiative benefitting the ADE trident is The DNA Technology (Use and Application) Regulation Bill which is legal in nature, implemented in the year 2019. The objectives of the policy legal framework are recognizing the need for regulation of the use and application of deoxyribonucleic acid (DNA) technology in the country, establishing identity of missing persons, victims,

TABLE 12.1 AI Policy Initiatives in India.

Title	Start date	Theme area(s)	Target group(s)
Artificial Intelligence Task Force for India's Economic Transformation	2017	National AI policies	Civil society, established researchers, higher education institutes, national government, private research and development lab, public research institutes
The DNA Technology (Use and Application) Regulation Bill	2019	Value-based principles	Entrepreneurs, large firms (250 or more employees), micro-enterprises (10 or less employees), multinational enterprises, private investors, private research and development lab, public research institutes, SMEs (10–249 employees)
National Strategy on Artificial Intelligence	2018	National AI policies	Entrepreneurs, established researchers, industry associations, large firms (250 or more employees), micro-enterprises (10 or less employees), multinational enterprises, national government, private investors, public research institutes, SMEs (10–249 employees)
National Guidelines for Gene Therapy Product Development and Clinical Trials	2019	Value-based principles	Entrepreneurs, established researchers, firms of any age, firms of any size, private research and development lab, public research institutes, technology transfer offices
Biological Data Storage, Access and Sharing Policy of India	2019	Value-based principles	Entrepreneurs, firms of any age, firms of any size, national government, private investors, private research and development lab, public research institutes, technology transfer offices
National Ethical Guidelines for Biomedical and Health Research Involving Human Participants	2017	Value-based principles	Academic societies/academies, entrepreneurs, established researchers, firms of any age, firms of any size, private research and development lab, public research institutes
AI Standardisation Committee	2018	Value-based principles	Civil society, labor force in general, large firms (250 or more employees), Multinational enterprises, national government
Centre of Excellence for Internet of Things (IOT) and AI	2015	National AI policies	Civil society, established researchers, firms of any age, firms of any size, incubators, accelerators, hubs, Large firms (250 or more employees), multinational enterprises, postdocs, and other early-career researchers, private investors, private research and development lab, public research institutes, SMEs (10–249 employees)

TABLE 12.1 *(Continued)*

Title	Start date	Theme area(s)	Target group(s)
National Artificial Intelligence Resource Portal	2019	National AI policies	Civil society, established researchers, firms of any age, firms of any size, national government, postdocs and other early-career researchers, private research and development lab, public research institutes
National Programme for Government Schools: Responsible AI for Youth	2020	National AI policies	Civil society, higher education institutes, labor force in general, National government, Ph.D. students, postdocs, and other early-career researchers, public research institutes, secondary education students, teachers, undergraduate and master students
AI COVID-19 Response	2020	National AI policies	Civil society, national government, private research and development lab, public research institutes

Source: OECD AI database: https://oecd.ai/dashboards/countries/India

offenders, under trials, and unknown deceased persons. The unique feature of the bill is that it is using value-based principles as opposed to utilitarian principles used in general AI technologies. With value-based principles, a human-centric AI system approach is targeted that will immensely benefit human–machine interaction. The bill envisages that every data bank will maintain indices like the crime scene index, suspects' or undertrials' index, offenders' index, missing persons' index, and unknown deceased person index. The legislation also seeks to establish a DNA Regulatory Board. Every laboratory that analyzes DNA samples to establish the identity of an individual has to be accredited by the board. Under the bill, a written consent by individuals is required to collect DNA samples from them. Consent is not required for offences with punishment of more than 7 years of imprisonment or death. It also provides for the removal of DNA profiles of suspects on filing of a police report or court order and of undertrials on the basis of a court order. Profiles in the crime scene and missing persons' index will be removed on a written request. The estimated budget for the implementation of the bill is between 5 million USD and 20 million USD. Unlike AI taskforce, the bill is looking forward for structural reforms in the industry. It is providing both guidance and regulation in the ADE trident and will substantially help the usage of AI technologies. With its regulatory and ethical advice nature, the future of ADE trident will be a positive boom for the economy. The third policy initiative as per OECD is the national strategy on AI initiated in the year 2018. The policy recognizes AI as a potential to transform economies and the need for India to strategize its approach, Finance Minister of India, in her budget speech in 2018 mandated NITI Aayog to establish the national program on AI, with a view to guiding the research and development in new and emerging technologies. The motive of the policy strategy is "AI for all" which indicates that AI technologies can benefit everyone depending on how they are used and implemented. Under the policy initiative, several policy documents have been released and several other policies have been influenced, including the New Education Policy, 2020. One of the foci in this policy initiative is to highlight and discuss critical AI issues such as bias, ethics, and privacy.

Out of the 11 policy initiatives, next 4 are all focused on value-based principles for ADE trident. They are "National Guidelines for Gene Therapy Product Development and Clinical Trials" initiated in 2019, "Biological Data Storage, Access and Sharing Policy of India" initiated in 2019, "National Ethical Guidelines for Biomedical and Health Research Involving Human Participants" in 2017, and "AI Standardisation Committee" initiated in 2018.

All these initiatives involve humans as either subjects or a moderator for a human–machine interaction with mediating effect of AI technologies. Thus, they can only be guided by an ethical framework and value-based principles. Globally, very few gene therapy products are present and there is a huge market for gene therapy products. India with an early policy can benefit and significantly contribute in the gene therapy market. The government has earmarked an annual budget of 20–50 million USD for the gene therapy infrastructure. India with a huge population generates huge biological data and this can be significantly used for scientific advancement. The biological data storage by the government can be easily shared among the scientists for advancement of biotechnology and even to check the present efficacy of pharmaceutical products. However, misuse is a concern, and thus under this policy, rules and regulations are formulated to be followed strictly. Under the AI policy jargon, the initiative will come under regulatory oversight and ethical advice body. The national ethical guidelines is another policy initiative deliberating on ethical issues concerning human participants for biological technological testing. The social and religious aspects of India differ from the developed countries, generating a need for a socially acceptable policy on human trials. It is to devise a human-centric AI in the context of Indian social order. These guidelines are applicable to all biomedical, social, and behavioral science research for health conducted in India involving human participants, their biological material, and data. Five to 20 million USD is the earmarked amount for implementation of the policies across the nation. Though private sector funding is not yet opened, the structural changes it will bring surely push for private sector involvement in the future. The AI Standardisation Committee set up by the Government of India in 2018 applies value-based principles for ADE trident policies. The committee works under the Department of Telecommunications with stakeholders from ABB, BOSCH, NASSCOM, TCS, IIT Delhi, DSF, IIT Kanpur, NITI Aayog, Mahindra, IIT Patna, and Intel. It is a good example of public–private part-nership in the ADE trident.

Big data, Internet of Things, and AI have emerged as an integral area for businesses and other organizations. Eighth policy initiative is the establishment of "Centre of Excellence for Internet of Things (IOT) and AI" in 2015. The objective is to frame national AI policies, and it has been observed that the current New Education Policy (2020) has relied on the center for including ADE trident skills. The center has also looked into the digitalization of government sector for efficient mechanism. The center is targeting start-ups, innovators, government sector, and enterprises. The

Digital India initiative by the Government of India is a sister initiative and both go hand-in-hand. The National AI Resource Portal setup in 2019 is a web-based platform with all the AI resources for learning. The platform is cloud computational with free access to the public. The two main objectives are promoting research and development in the field of AI and providing a cloud-based computation platform so users have access to computational resources required for learning and practicing with the techniques of AI and machine learning. In 2020, there were two policy initiatives to push the ADE trident, "Schools: Responsible AI for Youth" and "AI COVID-19 Response." The former targets students, faculty members, researchers and postdoctoral fellows to identify challenges and opportunities for ADE quadrant. This is a parallel policy with New Education Policy that targets potential contributors to the existing body of knowledge with respect to AI trident. The latter is the AI-based response to the COVID-19 scenario in India. The havoc caused due to COVID-19 deaths in India forced nationwide lockdown and remote working was promoted. The policy has successfully used the resources to share COVID-19 data with concerned stakeholders. It would be justified to state that these policy initiatives (Table 12.1) will provide foundation for the future strength of India in terms of AI, DE, and education.

12.6 CONCLUSION

With the advent of Industrialization 4.0 and advancement of AI technologies, significant disruption in the economy is going to happen. Amid this disruption, India as a developing country has started devising policies to become competitive for the future. The study conceptualizes AI, DE, and education to develop a concept of ADE trident. The multidisciplinary nature of AI policies will impact ADE trident. India has introduced the New Education Policy (2020) where ADE trident constraints are present. The study identifies 11 policy initiatives by India as reported by OECD and have found them relevant and efficient steps to furthering the objective of achieving a competitive ADE trident. Future research to develop an ADE trident model for India can help to measure the comprehensive impact on AI, DE, and education in India. India has to go a long way to increase the per capita access to digital infrastructure. The current policies, if efficiently implemented, will provide necessary and sufficient infrastructure to at least lead in the Asian region in terms of ADE trident.

KEYWORDS

- artificial intelligence
- digital economy
- education
- India
- ADE trident
- AI policy
- Industrialization 4.0
- Education 4.0

- new education policy
- Internet of Things
- big data
- human-centric AI
- privacy
- data visualization
- cognitive attention span

REFERENCES

Allen, R. C. *Global Economic History: A Very Short Introduction*; Oxford University Press, 2011; Vol 282.

Anusha, S. Effectiveness of Virtual Reality Therapy upon Attention Span and Concentration among Secondary School Students; *Doctoral Dissertation*, Apollo College of Nursing: Chennai, 2017. Retrieved from http://repository-tnmgrmu.ac.in/5871/

Bhatnagar, H. Artificial Intelligence—A New Horizon in Indian Higher Education. *J. Learn. Teach. Digit. Age* **2020,** *5* (2), 30–34. Retrieved from https://dergipark.org.tr/en/pub/joltida/issue/55766/763068

Bogoslovskiy, V. I.; Busygina, A. L.; Aniskin, V. N. Conceptual Foundations of Higher Education in the Digital Economy. *Samara J. Sci.* **2019,** *8* (1), 223–230. https://doi.org/10.17816/snv201981301

Chatterjee, S. AI Strategy of India: Policy Framework, Adoption Challenges and Actions for Government. *Transform. Govern.: People, Process Policy* **2020.** https://doi.org/10.1108/TG-05-2019-0031

Chatterjee, S.; Bhattacharjee, K. K. Adoption of Artificial Intelligence in Higher Education: A Quantitative Analysis Using Structural Equation Modelling. *Educ. Inf. Technol.* **2020,** *25* (5), 3443–3463. https://doi.org/10.1007/s10639-020-10159-7

Chen, L.; Chen, P.; Lin, Z. Artificial Intelligence in Education: A Review. *IEEE Access* **2020,** *8,* 75264–75278. doi:10.1109/ACCESS.2020.2988510.

Ciolacu, M.; Tehrani, A. F.; Binder, L.; Svasta, P. M. Education 4.0—Artificial Intelligence Assisted Higher Education: Early Recognition System with Machine Learning to Support Students' Success. In *2018 IEEE 24th International Symposium for Design and Technology in Electronic Packaging (SIITME)*; IEEE, October 2018; pp 23–30. https://doi.org/10.1109/SIITME.2018.8599203

FND. *Artificial Intelligence (AI) Policies in India—A Status Paper*; Future Networks (FN) Division, Telecommunication Engineering Centre, 2020. Retrieved from https://www.

tec.gov.in/public/pdf/Studypaper/AI%20Policies%20in%20India%20A%20status%20 Paper%20final.pdf

Gokilavani, D. R.; Durgarani, D. R. Evolution of Digital Economy in India. *Int. J. Mark. Human Resour. Manage.* **2017,** *9* (1), 31–39. Retrieved from ijmhrm.9.1.2018-with-cover-page-v2.pdf (d1wqtxts1xzle7.cloudfront.net)

Gueye, M.; Exposito, E. University 4.0: The Industry 4.0 Paradigm Applied to Education. In *IX Congreso Nacional de Tecnologías en la Educación*, October 2020. Retrieved from https://hal-univ-pau.archives-ouvertes.fr/hal-02957371/document

Gupta, G. Education and Digital Economy: Trends, Opportunities and Challenges. In *Proceedings of the 2019 4th International Conference on Machine Learning Technologies*, June 2019; pp 88–92. https://doi.org/10.1145/3340997.3341013

Heflin, H.; Shewmaker, J.; Nguyen, J. Impact of Mobile Technology on Student Attitudes, Engagement, and Learning. *Comput. Educ.* **2017,** *107*, 91–99. https://doi.org/10.1016/j.compedu.2017.01.006

Holmes, W.; Bialik, M.; Fadel, C. *Artificial Intelligence in Education*; Center for Curriculum Redesign: Boston, 2019. Retrieved from https://curriculumredesign.org/wp-content/uploads/AIED-Book-Excerpt-CCR.pdf

Iqbal, B. A.; Rahman, M. N.; Hasan, M. Social Indicators: A Comparison among Selected Countries. *J. Dev. Policy Pract.* **2019,** *4* (2), 123–144. https://doi.org/10.1177%2F2455 133319862405

Jain, S.; Gabor, D. The Rise of Digital Financialisation: The Case of India. *New Polit. Econ.* **2020,** *25* (5), 813–828. https://doi.org/10.1080/13563467.2019.1708879

Jaiswal, A.; Arun, C. J. Potential of Artificial Intelligence for Transformation of the Education System in India. *Int. J. Educ. Dev. Using Inf. Commun. Technol.* **2021,** *17* (1), 142–158. Retrieved from https://files.eric.ed.gov/fulltext/EJ1285526.pdf

Jarwal, D. Digital Economy and India. *Chart. Secretary* **2017,** *47* (06), 55–57. Retrieved from https://ssrn.com/abstract=3405961

Kalyanakrishnan, S.; Panicker, R. A.; Natarajan, S.; Rao, S. Opportunities and Challenges for Artificial Intelligence in India. In *Proceedings of the 2018 AAAI/ACM conference on AI, Ethics, and Society*; December 2018; pp 164–170. https://doi.org/10.1145/3278721.3278738

Kies, S. C. Social Media Impact on Attention Span. *J. Manage. Eng. Integr.* **2018,** *11* (1), 20–27. Retrieved from https://www.proquest.com/docview/2316725647?pq-origsite=gsch olar&fromopenview=true

Klimuk, V. V.; Lazdins, A. Interaction of Education, Science and Business in Terms of Digital Economy Development. In *Economic Science for Rural Development Conference Proceedings*, No. 52, September 2019.

Marda, V. Artificial Intelligence Policy in India: A Framework for Engaging the Limits of Data-Driven Decision-Making. *Philos. Trans. R. Soc. A: Math., Phys. Eng. Sci.* **2018,** *376* (2133), 20180087. https://doi.org/10.1098/rsta.2018.0087

Mariam, F.; Kamal, M. Y.; Lukman, Z. M.; Azlini, C.; Normala, R. The Effect in Cognitive, Affective, and Behavior of Using Electronic Gadget among University Students. *Tablet* **2018,** *37*, 10–15.

Maymina, E.; Puzynya, T.; Egozaryan, V. Development Trends of the Education in Russia under Digital Economy. *Rev. ESPACIOS* **2018,** *39* (30). Retrieved from http://www.revistaespacios.com/a18v39n30/18393023.html

MHRD. *New Education Policy 2020*; Government of India, 2020. Retrieved from https://niepid.nic.in/nep_2020.pdf

NITI. *National Strategy for Artificial Intelligence*, 2018. Retrieved from https://www.niti.gov. in/sites/default/files/2019-01/NationalStrategy-for-AI-Discussion-Paper.pdf

Pedro, F.; Subosa, M.; Rivas, A.; Valverde, P. *Artificial Intelligence in Education: Challenges and Opportunities for Sustainable Development*, 2019. http://repositorio.minedu.gob.pe/handle/MINEDU/6533

Sandu, N.; Gide, E. Adoption of AI-Chatbots to Enhance Student Learning Experience in Higher Education in India. In *2019 18th International Conference on Information Technology Based Higher Education and Training (ITHET)*; IEEE, September 2019; pp 1–5. https://doi.org/10.1109/ITHET46829.2019.8937382

Sen, D. A Narrative Research Approach: Rural–Urban Divide in Terms of Participation in Digital Economy in India. *J. Manage.* **2020,** *7* (1). Retrieved from https://ssrn.com/abstract=3574674

Shankar, K. U. Digital Economy in India: Challenges and Prospects. *Int. J. Res. Manage. Stud.* **2017,** *2* (11), 6–11. Retrieved from http://www.ijrms.com/olvolume2issue11/Uma Shankar-2.pdf

Sreehari, E.; Mohan, A. K.; Indu Nair, V. Impact and Prevalence of Electronic Gadgets on Life Style among University Students. A Formative Research Study on the Health Seeking Behaviour of Individuals with Post-Polio Syndrome in Telangana, India. *Protect. Fact. Person.* **1989,** *6* (1), 38.

Srivastava, S. K. Artificial Intelligence: Way Forward for India. *J. Inf. Syst. Technol. Manage.* **2018,** *15.* https://doi.org/10.4301/S1807-1775201815004

Tewathia, N.; Kamath, A.; Ilavarasan, P. V. Social Inequalities, Fundamental Inequities, and Recurring of the Digital Divide: Insights from India. *Technol. Soc.* **2020,** *61*, 101251. https://doi.org/10.1016/j.techsoc.2020.101251

UNCTAD Statistics. *Gross Domestic Product at Current Prices in USD Million for India*; UNCTAD Statistics Data Centre, 2021. Retrieved from https://unctadstat.unctad.org/wds/TableViewer/tableView.aspx

Vempati, S. S. *India and the Artificial Intelligence Revolution*; Carnegie Endowment for International Peace, 2016. https://www.jstor.org/stable/pdf/resrep12855.pdf

Vijai, C.; Wisetsri, W. Rise of Artificial Intelligence in Healthcare Startups in India. *Adv. Manage.* **2021,** *14* (1), 48–52. Retrieved from https://www.researchgate.net/publication/349604103_Rise_of_Artificial_Intelligence_in_Healthcare_Startups_in_India

World Economic Forum. *Networked Readiness Index*, 2016. Retrieved from https://reports.weforum.org/global-information-technology-report-2016/networked-readiness-index/

CHAPTER 13

ARTIFICIAL INTELLIGENCE AND CLINICAL DECISION-MAKING IN EMERGENCY SURGERY: A RESEARCH PROTOCOL

LORENZO COBIANCHI[1], FRANCESCA DAL MAS[2], FAUSTO CATENA[3], and LUCA ANSALONI[1]

[1]*Department of Clinical, Diagnostic and Pediatric Sciences, University of Pavia, Pavia, Italy*

[2]*Department of Management, Lincoln International Business School, University of Lincoln, Lincoln, United Kingdom*

[3]*General and Emergency Surgery Department, Cesena Bufalini Hospital, Cesena, Italy*

ABSTRACT

Artificial intelligence and machine learning represent two of the most disruptive technologies, which are going to affect a variety of different industrial fields, including several medical specialities. The chapter aims to investigate the importance of artificial intelligence and machine learning applications in supporting clinical decision-making and the ethical concerns that may arise in their development and deployment. Starting from the recent literature, a detailed research protocol is designed to explore the acceptance of such new technologies and the barriers and ethical concerns in their adoption by their users. The context is a challenging one, that of emergency surgery, in collaboration with the World Society of Emergency Surgery.

Incorporating AI Technology in the Service Sector: Innovations in Creating Knowledge, Improving Efficiency, and Elevating Quality of Life. Maria José Sousa, Subhendu Kumar Pani, Francesca Dal Mas, & Sérgio Sousa (Eds.)
© 2024 Apple Academic Press, Inc. Co-published with CRC Press (Taylor & Francis)

13.1   INTRODUCTION

13.1.1   ARTIFICIAL INTELLIGENCE AS A DISRUPTIVE TECHNOLOGY

Artificial intelligence (AI) stands today as one of the most disruptive technologies, gaining traction in most industry and service sectors. AI refers to machines' ability to think like humans and learn, reason, perceive, and make judgments rationally and intelligently. A current definition of AI describes it as a machine's or operative system's ability to understand its environment and take actions, increasing its chances of attaining its objectives. A subset of AI is machine learning (ML), which entails machines that learn to gain results independently, based on the data they are fed, and with a minimum of programming (Bukht and Heeks, 2018; Heeks, 2016). ML allows data to be used to create a mathematical model that includes a large number of unknown variables (Mjolsness and DeCoste, 2001). The settings are defined as the algorithm progresses through the learning phase, which involves finding and classifying associations using training data sets. The designers select the various ML algorithms (Heeks, 2018) based on the complexity of the jobs to be completed (grouping, decision tree). These methods are usually divided into three groups: human-supervised learning, unsupervised learning, and reinforced unsupervised learning (Arel et al., 2010). These three categories integrate many techniques such as neural networks, deep learning, and others.

AI-based applications lead to increased operating efficiencies, faster production, higher equipment performance, decreased waste, and lower maintenance costs (de Sousa et al., 2019). AI advancements may potentially pave the way for a hybrid civilization in which humans and computers coexist. As a result, AI is transforming businesses in every sector, making them more efficient (Ransbotham et al., 2017; Toniolo et al., 2019). Furthermore, new business opportunities and new business processes emerge as the result of the human–machine interaction in dealing with vast amounts of data (Hoffman, 2016), allowing managers and professionals to boost their decision-making abilities (Davenport and Ronanki, 2018; Duchessi et al., 1993; Pomerol, 1997).

While several authors warn about the loss of several types of jobs because of the new technologies (Daugherty et al., 2019), others highlight how AI will create new positions, involving more conceptual tasks and including creativity and emotions that humans can only express. Humans and AI-empowered robots and machines will need to find ways to collaborate

(Vallverdú et al., 2018; Vanzo et al., 2020), and education should change accordingly (Roll and Wylie, 2016; Sousa et al., 2021).

Therefore, AI-related technologies are expected to affect society and organizations profoundly (Makridakis, 2017), including new jobs, work and educational practices, and types of relationships, as well as new business models (Bagnoli et al., 2018; Toniolo et al., 2019) and leadership strategies (Glikson and Woolley, 2020).

13.1.2   *ARTIFICIAL INTELLIGENCE IN HEALTHCARE AND SURGERY*

The number of AI-related biomedical studies is on the rise, and so is the interest of both practitioners and academics in several medical specialities toward the development and deployment of AI-based applications. A search was performed in the scientific database Scopus in September 2021, using the search key "TITLE-ABS-KEY (artificial AND intelligence) AND (LIMIT-TO (SUBJAREA, "MEDI"))." The result led to more than 27,000 research products, of which more than 22,000 in the period from 2008 to 2021, as reported in Table 13.1.

TABLE 13.1   Artificial Intelligence Publications.

Year	Number of publications
2021	4631
2020	4915
2019	3033
2018	1869
2017	1424
2016	836
2015	769
2014	815
2013	724
2012	592
2011	521
2010	535
2009	528
2008	859

Source: Author's elaboration from Scopus.

AI is gradually disrupting medical practice. AI-related applications in medicine can be employed in clinical, diagnostic, rehabilitative, surgical, and prognostic treatments (Secinaro et al., 2021). Several studies have underlined how the most relevant AI-based applications are in disease diagnosis and supporting clinical decision-making (CDM) (Byerly et al., 2021; El Hechi et al., 2021). Therefore, AI systems can ingest, analyze, and report vast amounts of data from several sources, employing different calculations (Loftus et al., 2020a). AI applications can deal with the massive amounts of data generated and uncover fresh information that would otherwise be lost in clinical big data.

The surgical literature has underlined the potential of AI in supporting surgical decision-making (Arambula and Bur, 2020; Byerly et al., 2021; Loftus et al., 2020b). Still, at the current time, it cannot totally replace the surgeon's judgment (Loftus et al., 2020b). The use of AI and AI-empowered robots depends on the specific situation and needs that may arise (O'Sullivan et al., 2019). AI-based robots controlled remotely have been employed to perform surgical operations in isolated or dangerous situations, like in war to assist injured soldiers or long space missions (Yang et al., 2017). In such cases, even the surgeon's skill set may change, from clinical guesswork ability to dexterity in handling, understanding, and make effective use of numbers (Dal Mas et al., 2020c). The more the AI system can work independently, the more ethical concerns arise in developing, deploying, and availing such surgical applications (Arambula and Bur, 2020).

13.1.3 ETHICAL CONCERNS ABOUT THE USE OF ARTIFICIAL INTELLIGENCE IN SURGERY

The applications of AI technologies in surgery brings some ethical dilemmas. Ethical issues arise when assessing the application's training model. Indeed, the algorithm is expected to become more and more reliable and accurate over time as it digests and absorbs more data gathered from its use on the job. Therefore, those surgeons and patients who employ the algorithm's early and less educated versions are to receive less accurate decision support. Still, data-hungry algorithms will not become as precise and comprehensive as they should be without proper training and past experiences (Vokinger et al., 2021). Thus, before relying on AI to support their clinical decisions, surgeons must be aware of the state-of-the-art of their training model. Surgeons should therefore assess the model's fitness compared to their set of patients. Moreover, they should be mindful of the motivations and state of data of the development and training of their algorithm at the time of the evaluation. Open data reporting would detect eventual domain shifts between the patients' population used during AI training and testing and the patients' population of interest.

If surgeons rely on AI predictions for their patients, the algorithm and computations should be fully revealed. The so-called explainable AI is critical for improving transparency and fostering trust between patients and physicians (O'Sullivan et al., 2020; Thomas and Haertling, 2020). However, the outputs of a model frequently cannot be explained. Even algorithms with significant prediction accuracy cannot explain some features' influence a priori (Lauritsen et al., 2020).

High-quality and adequately trained AI-based surgical applications will be able to support the clinical staff by suggesting the best surgical option, taking into account a variety of data, elements, pros, and cons. However, in a modern patient-centric health-care system (Cheng et al., 2009), the patient's preferences, wishes, and concerns should always be taken into account. Shared decision-making (Shay and Lafata, 2015; Woltz et al., 2018), coproduction (Dal Mas et al., 2020a; Elwyn et al., 2020; Petersson et al., 2019), and a multistakeholder engagement (Cobianchi et al., 2021a) do represent the crucial paradigms of the new health-care scenario. Therefore, the (theoretically) ideal clinical option selected by the AI-based application, among many more, may not represent the best choice according to the patient's wishes and lifestyle (Arambula and Bur, 2020).

Last but not least, the costs for the development, training and testing of surgical AI applications are often expensive, and so are the machines and equipment which use AI technologies for surgical use. High investments are, therefore, required by health-care institutions, hospitals, or clinics. Private organizations in wealthier countries are the ones that most likely will be able to afford such costs, leading to discrimination in the access to care for developing or low-income countries (El-Deiry and Giaccone, 2021; Torain et al., 2016).

13.1.4 THE CONTEXT OF EMERGENCY SURGERY

Emergency surgery refers to those surgical activities "required to deal with an acute threat to life, organ, limb or tissue caused by external trauma, acute disease process, acute exacerbation of a chronic disease process, or complication of a surgical or other interventional procedure" (European Union of Medical Specialists, 2021). Emergency surgery is complex. Members of an emergency or trauma surgical team must work under tremendous pressure in a stressful and complicated environment characterized by time constraints. Saving the life of an injured patient is often a matter of minutes, and decision-making processes are particularly critical. Emergency teams often have no awareness of the trauma causes, the patients' identity, their current circumstances or conditions, and their desires or wishes about the treatment options, with the risk of unforeseen incidents (Cobianchi et al., 2021b). In such a scenario, soft (or nontechnical) skills appear just as relevant as mastering technical aspects. Indeed, nearly half of all errors in the operating room have been attributed to surgeons' behavior and decision-making (Dal Mas et al., 2021; Maschuw et al., 2011).

Emergency teams are multidisciplinary by definition, as they include clinical professionals (from the medical and nursing staff) of different specialities, including emergency medicine, general surgery, orthopedic, and anesthesiology. Emergency teams are coordinated by a team leader, who has the final responsibility to coordinate the team and make decisions. Such a leader should feature nontechnical skills like leadership, communication, teamwork, ethics, and professionalism (Cobianchi et al., 2021c; Rehim et al., 2017; Roberts et al., 2015). Fostering emergency surgery teams' performance is not easy because of the circumstances above. Indeed, traditional and technical organizational practices like surgical techniques or clinical guidelines may sometimes be less effective in boosting performance and optimizing clinical outcomes if not accompanied by the development and training of adequate soft skills. Still, decision-making appears the most critical process for emergency teams.

13.1.5   ARTIFICIAL INTELLIGENCE IN EMERGENCY SURGERY

AI-based applications in surgery can support CDM (Loftus et al., 2020b). Such an aim appears particularly suitable for emergency surgeons, especially when managing severely injured patients or in the resuscitation phase.

AI- or ML-related applications have been used, for example, for the diagnosis and classification of acute appendicitis in children (Reismann et al., 2019), to spot and monitor variations in colorectal surgery (Maheshwari et al., 2019), to forecast surgical shunts in male patients with ischemic priapism (Masterson et al., 2020), in the surgical treatment of pediatric intestinal obstruction (Qiu et al., 2021), in the detection, localization, and segmentation of ischemic infarct in noncontrast computerized tomography human brain scans (Nowinski et al., 2020). The POTTER Calculator experience, developed by the Massachusetts General Hospital and Harvard Medical School together with the Massachusetts Institute of Technology (Bertsimas et al., 2018; El Hechi et al., 2021; Maurer et al., 2021), starts from the assumption that the influence of risk factors is linear and cumulative in most risk assessment techniques. The team aimed to develop an interactive, nonlinear risk calculator for emergency surgery using an ML approach. The starting database comprised all 382,960 emergency surgery patients listed in the American College of Surgeons National Surgical Quality Improvement Program from 2007 to 2013. ML algorithms were trained using optimal classification trees to predict postoperative mortality, morbidity, and 18 particular complications (like surgical-site infection or sepsis). The algorithms' interactive and user-friendly interface was then translated into an application for both IOS and Android smartphones, later named as POTTER—Predictive OpTimal Trees in Emergency Surgery Risk. In the POTTER app, the user's response to one question interactively influences the next enquiry. Therefore, the number of queries required to forecast mortality for any given patient ranges from 4 to 11. The POTTER app stands, for surgeons, as an effective instrument for preoperative counseling of emergency surgery patients, facilitating their engagement, whenever possible, and that of their families.

Although applications like the POTTER Calculator can represent valid decision aids for Emergency surgeons operating in challenging settings, physicians may still have concerns or experience barriers in adopting such new technologies, being such issues of ethical or different nature.

Starting from this premise, we designed a research protocol to investigate the understanding of CDM, involving new technologies like AI and ML and the barriers and ethical concerns in their adoption. The present chapter aims to outline the research protocol, the way the survey was designed, and what outcomes can be expected from its data collection and analysis.

13.2 METHODOLOGY

13.2.1 SURVEY DEVELOPMENT AND DESIGN

An online survey has been designed following the CHERRIES checklists for e-surveys (Eysenbach, 2004) and delivered through Google Forms. The investigation has gained the endorsement of the World Society of Emergency Surgery (WSES), one of the major scientific societies in the field of Emergency Surgery, with more than 900 members on all the continents. The survey was developed within the WSES Team Dynamics initiative (Cobianchi et al., 2021b, 2021c).

The questions have been designed following the recent literature in the field of AI and ML applied to surgery (Bertsimas et al., 2018; Byerly et al., 2021; El Hechi et al., 2021; Loftus et al., 2020a, 2020b; Maurer et al., 2021), knowledge translation in healthcare and surgery (Dal Mas et al., 2020b), Technology Acceptance Model (TAM) (Bashshur et al., 2011), and Unified Theory of Acceptance and Use of Technology (UTAUT) (Venkatesh et al., 2003). The survey was developed by a multidisciplinary committee of investigators coming from different countries (Italy, the United Kingdom, and the USA) comprising experts in academic emergency surgery, general surgery, strategic management, organization science, AI and ML, and biomedical informatics.

Given the type of study, no institutional review board approval was required.

The survey has eight questions. Some of them are open; some employ a 5-point Likert scale or a simple Yes/No answer. All the questions are mandatory to conclude the survey.

13.2.2   SURVEY CONTENT AND SUPPORTING LITERATURE

The first part of the questionnaire aims to collect some descriptive information about the sample. The questions' structure has been adapted by the WSES Team Dynamics I initiative, carried out during the months of January and February 2021 (Cobianchi et al., 2021b, 2021c). While the survey remains anonymous, data collected refer to the role of the emergency surgeon (senior or head of department vs. young certified surgeon or early-career resident), the years of experience in emergency surgery, the courses or research fellowships attended, the gender, the type of institution (academic versus nonacademic), the eventual membership to an official emergency/trauma team, and the perceived membership to a work team characterized by diversity among its members.

The first question aims to understand the practical tools that can facilitate CDM in general terms. Surgeons should rate a list of 11 items using a 5-point Likert scale, where 1 means "not suitable" and 5 "very suitable." The list of items is borrowed from the literature review of Dal Mas et al. (2020), investigating the tangible and nontechnical tools employed in the health-care sector to translate knowledge with different stakeholders (being them clinicians, patients, or other parties like industry partners, public entities, or citizens). Three more items, namely, risk stratification by additive scores using static variable thresholds, regression modeling and calculations, and AI/ML have been added following the study of Loftus and colleagues (2020). Items are summarized in Figure 13.1.

1. On a scale from 1 to 5, where 1 = not suitable and 5 = very suitable, which are the tools that, in your opinion, may facilitate clinical decision making?
Likert scale 1 to 5

1. Mobile electronic medical records and online tools, including telemedicine
2. Training
3. Networking and international experiences
4. Multidisciplinary committees and meetings
5. Publications
6. Clinical guidelines and cases
7. Time spent to engage patients
8. Non-technical skills
9. Risk stratification by additive scores using static variable thresholds.
10. Regression modelling and calculations
11. Machine learning and Artificial intelligence

FIGURE 13.1 Question 1.

Source: Adapted from Dal Mas et al. (2020b) and Loftus et al. (2020b)

The second question aims to map the challenges to CDM, using a series of 13 items to measure some latent variables grabbed from Loftus et al. (2020b). More in detail, the variables to be rated are complexity, values and emotions, time constraints and uncertainty, and bias. Surgeons will need to assess their agreement with the 13 items using a 5-point Likert scale, where 1 means "strongly disagree" and 5 means "strongly agree." Items are reported in Figure 13.2.

2. Think of how you take clinical decisions. On a scale from 1 to 5, where 1 = strongly disagree and 5 = strongly agree, how would you rate the following statements?
Likert scale 1 to 5

1. It is often too complicated to form a complete list of all likely diagnoses, all life-threatening diagnoses, and all unlikely diagnoses that may be considered if the initial workup excludes other causes.
2. It is often too complicated to recognize the strengths and limitations of available tests.
3. Errors and mistakes are likely all along the way.
4. Data are often incomplete.
5. Decisions must often be made before all relevant data can be retrieved
6. In-house calls happen often
7. Sometimes the clinical scenario presented is different than the surgeon would have perceived during an independent assessment
8. The surgeon often falsely perceives those weaknesses and failures disproportionately affect their peers
9. A surgeon tends toward action when inaction may be preferable
10. Patients are often informed of expected outcomes using data from aggregate patient populations without adjusting for their personalized risk profile
11. Recent experiences with a certain patient population or operation often affect disproportionately surgical decision-making than remote ones.
12. Potential outcomes are often predicted using personal beliefs rather than evidence-based guidelines
13. Digital technologies (e.g., artificial intelligence) support how I take clinical decisions

FIGURE 13.2 Question 2.

Source: Adapted from Loftus et al. (2020b)

Question 3 aims to collect the surgeons' opinions about their personal knowledge and understanding of AI, using a simple yes/no enquiry. While question 3 works as a self-assessment, in question 4, the participants are required to argue their understanding about AI applied to surgery through an open question. Such questions are reported in Figure 13.3.

---

3. Are you familiar with the terms Artificial Intelligence/Machine Learning?
Yes/No
1.   Yes
2.   No

4 What is your understanding of Artificial Intelligence/Machine Learning applied to surgery?
open question

FIGURE 13.3   Questions 3 and 4.

Questions 5 and 6 aim to collect the surgeons' opinions about the importance that AI- and ML-based applications play today and will have in a five-year horizon in surgery when supporting CDM, on a scale from 1 to 5 where 1 means "not relevant" and 5 "very relevant." The questions are reported in Figure 13.4.

---

5. On a scale from 1 to 5, where 1 = not relevant and 5 = very relevant, how relevant do you think that Machine learning and Artificial intelligence-based tools are today for clinical decision making?
Likert scale 1 to 5

6. On a scale from 1 to 5, where 1 = not relevant and 5 = very relevant, how relevant do you think that Machine learning and Artificial intelligence-based tools will be for clinical decision making in a five-year horizon?
Likert scale 1 to 5

FIGURE 13.4   Questions 5 and 6.

Question 7 explores the goal and benefits of AI- and ML-based applications in supporting CDM by using a Likert scale from 1 to 5, where 1 means "strongly disagree" and 5 means "strongly agree." The items are summarized in Figure 13.5.

Last, question 8 aims to investigate the potential issues in the adoption of AI- and ML-based applications by asking surgeons to rate 20 items on a scale from 1 to 5, where 1 means "strongly disagree" and 5 means "strongly agree." The items can be grouped in different ways to measure and assess some latent variables. Such variables can be connected to the ethical concerns and dilemmas in the adoption of AI-based tools, including the EU principles of technical robustness and safety, human agency and oversight, privacy and data governance, diversity, nondiscrimination, and fairness, transparency, societal, and environmental well-being and account-ability (High-Level Expert Group on Artificial Intelligence, 2019). The same items can be grouped to assess the performance expectancy, effort expectancy, social influence, and facilitating conditions as reported by the UTAUT according to Venkatesh and colleagues (2003). Again, they can be used to evaluate the social influence, facilitating conditions, trust, privacy, perceived risk, technological anxiety, resistance toward technology as distinct elements of the TAM (Bashshur et al., 2011). The items are reported in Figure 13.6.

---

7. On a scale from 1 to 5, where 1 = strongly disagree and 5 = strongly agree, how would you rate the following statements concerning the goal and benefits of Machine learning and Artificial intelligence-based applications in supporting clinical decision making?

Likert scale 1 to 5

1.   - it helps in scouting and reviewing publications.
2.   - it reduces the span of options.
3.   - it supports taking decisions regarding simple problems, so I can focus on high-value activities.
4.   - it supports in taking complex clinical decisions.
5.   - it helps in evaluating/validating decisions I would take.

FIGURE 13.5   Question 7.

13.2.3   DATA COLLECTION AND ANALYSIS

The WSES will send out an e-mail request to all its members to fill in the survey. A couple of reminders will be sent out. We expect to gather at least 400 fully filled questionnaires, reaching a target of approximately 45% of the total members. The survey will remain open from 1 to 2 months.

Once the investigation is completed, the responses will be downloaded into an Excel spreadsheet file. Most of the analysis will be run through the software R (RStudio Team, 2015). The research will include structural equation modeling, content analysis, and topic modeling, as previously done during the team dynamics I initiative and survey (Cobianchi et al., 2021c). The relationship between different variables and differences in the responses given by various groups (e.g., between male or female surgeons or academics versus nonacademics) will be investigated.

8. On a scale from 1 to 5, where 1 = strongly disagree and 5 = strongly agree, how would you rate the following statements concerning the issues that Machine learning and Artificial intelligence-based tools may arise?

Likert scale 1 to 5

1. AI-based clinical decision-making can experience fewer issues than traditional clinical decision-making
2. An optimal human-machine interface in surgery can change according to the specific situation
3. Non-technical skills should be adapted and change if new technologies like AI are involved.
4. It is important to keep collecting surgical data
5. If the quantity of surgical data is high, AI will work better
6. Low-quality data can lead to low-quality decisions
7. Simulations and real-life situations are entirely different
8. Preserving patients' privacy is fundamental
9. When big data are used, patients' privacy is not a concern
10. Data should be managed carefully
11. Data should be transparent
12. Patients should know how the decision was made
13. Today's surgical education supports the use of new technologies and tools
14. Surgical consent should change if technologies are involved.
15. Responsibilities of surgeons should change when technologies affect the surgical practice
16. Surgical responsibilities should be shared with the manufacturer of the technologies
17. Surgical responsibilities should be shared with the data manager
18. Surgical responsibilities should be shared with those in charge of the maintenance.
19. AI and ML algorithms and logic need to be interpretable
20. AI and ML algorithms are in general free from bias, such as race- or gender-related bias

FIGURE 13.6   Question 8.

13.3   CONCLUSIONS

Our survey will allow us to shed light on physicians' adoption of modern technologies like AI- and ML-based applications, underlining the barriers and ethical concerns in their practical use. The study will be conducted in one specific context: emergency surgery, characterized by time constraints and pressure and where decision-making processes appear challenging and often affected by tough ethical dilemmas.

The survey has been designed following the recent literature to test different theories and relations among variables, limiting the biases by the participants in assessing the various items. The endorsement of the WSES, one of the most prominent scientific societies in the emergency surgery context, will support the investigators in getting answers from a decent multinational sample.

While the development and deployment of AI- and ML-related tools is seeing the birth of accurate and valuable applications, like the POTTER Calculation, the concerns and opinions of their users must be taken into account to facilitate their adoption and plan adequate translation and training activities.

Results will be helpful for the scientific societies in taking the lead in educating their members in a correct, still effective, and valuable utilization and consumption of such new applications, to facilitate CDM in challenging settings for both medical doctors and their patients like the one of emergency surgery.

KEYWORDS

- artificial intelligence
- machine learning
- decision-making
- healthcare
- emergency surgery
- research protocol
- ethics
- nontechnical skills

REFERENCES

Arambula, A. M.; Bur, A. M. Ethical Considerations in the Advent of Artificial Intelligence in Otolaryngology. *Otolaryngol.—Head Neck Surg. (U.S.)* **2020,** *162* (1), 38–39. https://doi.org/10.1177/0194599819889686

Arel, I.; Rose, D. C.; Karnowski, T. P. Deep Machine Learning—A New Frontier in Artificial Intelligence Research. *IEEE Comput. Intell. Mag.* **2010,** *5* (4), 13–18. https://doi.org/10.1109/MCI.2010.938364

Bagnoli, C.; Massaro, M.; Dal Mas, F.; Demartini, M. Defining the Concept of Business Model. Searching for a Business Model Framework. *Int. J. Knowl. Syst. Sci.* **2018,** *9,* 48–64.

Bashshur, R.; Shannon, G.; Krupinski, E.; Grigsby, J. The Taxonomy of Telemedicine. *Telemed. J. E-Health* **2011,** *17* (6), 484–494. https://doi.org/10.1089/tmj.2011.0103

Bertsimas, D.; Dunn, J.; Velmahos, G. C.; Kaafarani, H. M. A. Surgical Risk Is Not Linear: Derivation and Validation of a Novel, User-friendly, and Machine-Learning-Based Predictive Optimal Trees in Emergency Surgery Risk (POTTER) Calculator. *Ann. Surg.* **2018,** *268* (4). https://journals.lww.com/annalsofsurgery/Fulltext/2018/10000/Surgical_Risk_Is_Not_Linear__Derivation_and.4.aspx

Bukht, R.; Heeks, R. *Development Implications of Digital Economies* (No. 6; DIODE Network), 2018.

Byerly, S.; Maurer, L. R.; Mantero, A.; Naar, L.; An, G.; Kaafarani, H. M. A. Machine Learning and Artificial Intelligence for Surgical Decision Making. *Surg. Infect.* **2021,** *22* (6), 626–634. https://doi.org/10.1089/sur.2021.007

Cheng, B.-W.; Luo, C.-M.; Chiu, W.-H.; Chen, K.-H. Applying Cluster Analysis to Build a Patient-Centric Healthcare Service Strategy for Elderly Patients. *Int. J. Technol. Manage.* **2009,** *47* (1–3), 145–160.

Cobianchi, L.; Dal Mas, F.; Massaro, M.; Bednarova, R.; Biancuzzi, H.; Filisetti, C.; Barcellini, A.; Orlandi, E.; Miceli, L.; Angelos, P. Hand in Hand: A Multistakeholder Approach for Co-production of Surgical Care. *Am. J. Surg.* **2022,** *223* (1), 214–215. https://doi.org/https://doi.org/10.1016/j.amjsurg.2021.07.053

Cobianchi, L.; Dal Mas, F.; Massaro, M.; Fugazzola, P.; Catena, F.; Ansaloni, L. Knowledge Management and Dynamics as Perceived by Emergency Surgery Teams: a quantitative study. In *Proceedings of the 22nd European Conference on Knowledge Management—ECKM2021*; Garcia-Perez, A., Simkin, L., Eds.; Academic Conferences & Publishing International Ltd., 2021b; pp 217–224. https://doi.org/10.34190/EKM.21.083

Cobianchi, L.; Dal Mas, F.; Massaro, M.; Fugazzola, P.; Coccolini, F.; Kluger, Y.; Leppäniemi, A.; Moore, E. E.; Sartelli, M.; Angelos, P.; Catena, F.; Ansaloni, L.; Team Dynamics Study Group. Team Dynamics in Emergency Surgery Teams: Results from a First International Survey. *World J. Emerg. Surg.* **2021c,** *16*, 47. https://doi.org/10.1186/s13017-021-00389-6

Dal Mas, F.; Biancuzzi, H.; Massaro, M.; Miceli, L. Adopting a Knowledge Translation Approach in Healthcare Co-production. A Case Study. *Manage. Decis.* **2020a,** *58* (9), 1841–1862. https://doi.org/10.1108/MD-10-2019-1444

Dal Mas, F.; Garcia-Perez, A.; Sousa, M. J.; Lopes da Costa, R.; Cobianchi, L. Knowledge Translation in the Healthcare Sector. A Structured Literature Review. *Electr. J. Knowl. Manage.* **2020b,** *18* (3), 198–211. https://doi.org/10.34190/EJKM.18.03.001

Dal Mas, F.; Piccolo, D.; Edvinsson, L.; Skrap, M.; D'Auria, S. Strategy Innovation, Intellectual Capital Management and the Future of Healthcare. The Case of Kiron by Nucleode. In *Knowledge, People, and Digital Transformation: Approaches for a Sustainable Future*; Matos, F., Vairinhos, V., Salavisa, I., Edvinsson, L., Massaro, M., Eds.; Springer: Cham, 2020c; pp 119–131.

Dal Mas, F.; Bagarotto, E. M.; Cobianchi, L. Soft Skills Effects on Knowledge Translation in Healthcare. Evidence from the Field. In *Soft Skills for Human Centered Management and Global Sustainability*; Lepeley, M. T., Beutell, N., Abarca, N., Majluf, N., Eds.; Routledge, 2021; pp 95–109. https://doi.org/10.4324/9781003094463-7-11

Daugherty, P. R.; Wilson, H. J.; Chowdhury, R. Using Artificial Intelligence to Promote Diversity. *MIT Sloan Manage. Rev.* **2019,** *60* (2), 1.

Davenport, T. H.; Ronanki, R. Artificial Intelligence for the Real World: Don't Start with Moon Shots. *Harv. Bus. Rev.* **2018,** *96* (1), 108–116.

de Sousa, W. G.; de Melo, E. R. P.; Bermejo, P. H. D. S.; Farias, R. A. S.; Gomes, A. O. How and Where Is Artificial Intelligence in the Public Sector Going? A Literature Review and Research Agenda. *Govern. Inform. Q.* **2019,** *36* (4), 101–392.

Duchessi, P.; O'Keefe, R.; O'Leary, D. A Research Perspective: Artificial Intelligence, Management, and Organizations. *Intell. Syst. Account., Finan., Manage.* **1993,** *2* (3), 151–159.

El-Deiry, W. S.; Giaccone, G. Challenges in Diversity, Equity, and Inclusion in Research and Clinical Oncology. *Front. Oncol.* **2021,** *11* (March), 1–4. https://doi.org/10.3389/fonc.2021.642112

El Hechi, M.; Ward, T. M.; An, G. C.; Maurer, L. R.; El Moheb, M.; Tsoulfas, G.; Kaafarani, H. M. Artificial Intelligence, Machine Learning, and Surgical Science: Reality Versus Hype. *J. Surg. Res.* **2021,** *264*, A1–A9. https://doi.org/10.1016/j.jss.2021.01.046

Elwyn, G.; Nelson, E.; Hager, A.; Price, A. Coproduction: When Users Define Quality. *BMJ Qual. Saf.* **2020,** *29* (9), 711–716. https://doi.org/10.1136/bmjqs-2019-009830

European Union of Medical Specialists. *Emergency Surgery*; European Union of Medical Specialists, 2021. https://uemssurg.org/divisions/emergency-surgery/

Eysenbach, G. Improving the Quality of Web Surveys: The Checklist for Reporting Results of Internet E-Surveys (CHERRIES). *J. Med. Intern. Res.* **2004,** *6* (3), 1–6. https://doi.org/10.2196/jmir.6.3.e34

Glikson, E.; Woolley, A. W. Human Trust in Artificial Intelligence: Review of Empirical Research. *Acad. Manage. Ann.* **2020,** *14* (2), 627–660. https://doi.org/10.5465/annals.2018. 0057

Heeks, R. *"Digital Development": The Shape of Things to Come?* (No. 64; GDI Development Informatics), 2016.

Heeks, R. *Information and Communication Technology for Development (ICT4D)*; Routledge: London, 2018.

High-Level Expert Group on Artificial Intelligence. *Ethics Guidelines For Trustworthy AI*, 2019. https://ec.europa.eu/digital-single-market/en/news/ethics-guidelines-trustworthy-ai

Hoffman, R. Using Artificial Intelligence to Set Information Free. *MIT Sloan Manage. Rev.* **2016,** *58* (1), 20.

Lauritsen, S. M.; Kristensen, M.; Olsen, M. V.; Larsen, M. S.; Lauritsen, K. M.; Jørgensen, M. J.; Lange, J.; Thiesson, B. Explainable Artificial Intelligence Model to Predict Acute Critical Illness from Electronic Health Records. *Nat. Commun.* **2020,** *11* (1), 3852. https://doi.org/10.1038/s41467-020-17431-x

Loftus, T. J.; Filiberto, A. C.; Balch, J.; Ayzengart, A. L.; Tighe, P. J.; Rashidi, P.; Bihorac, A.; Upchurch, G. R. Intelligent, Autonomous Machines in Surgery. *J. Surg. Res.* **2020a,** *253*, 92–99. https://doi.org/10.1016/j.jss.2020.03.046

Loftus, T. J.; Tighe, P. J.; Filiberto, A. C.; Efron, P. A.; Brakenridge, S. C.; Mohr, A. M.; Rashidi, P.; Upchurch, G. R.; Bihorac, A. Artificial Intelligence and Surgical Decision-Making. *JAMA Surg.* **2020b,** *155* (2), 148–158. https://doi.org/10.1001/jamasurg.2019.4917

Maheshwari, K.; Cywinski, J.; Mathur, P.; Cummings, K. C.; Avitsian, R.; Crone, T.; Liska, D.; Campion, F. X.; Ruetzler, K.; Kurz, A. Identify and Monitor Clinical Variation Using Machine Intelligence: A Pilot in Colorectal Surgery. *J. Clin. Monit. Comput.* **2019,** *33* (4), 725–731. https://doi.org/10.1007/s10877-018-0200-x

Makridakis, S. The Forthcoming Artificial Intelligence (AI) Revolution: Its Impact on Society and Firms. *Futures* **2017,** *90*, 46–60. https://doi.org/https://doi.org/10.1016/j.futures.2017. 03.006

Maschuw, K.; Schlosser, K.; Kupietz, E.; Slater, E. P.; Weyers, P.; Hassan, I. Do Soft Skills Predict Surgical Performance? A Single-Center Randomized Controlled Trial Evaluating Predictors of Skill Acquisition in Virtual Reality Laparoscopy. *World J. Surg.* **2011,** *35* (3), 480–486.

Masterson, T. A.; Parmar, M.; Tradewell, M. B.; Nackeeran, S.; Rainer, Q.; Blachman-Braun, R.; Heller, N.; Greer, A.; Hauser, N.; Kava, B. K.; Ramasamy, R. Using Artificial Intelligence to Predict Surgical Shunts in Men with Ischemic Priapism. *J. Urol.* **2020,** *204* (5), 1033–1038. https://doi.org/10.1097/JU.0000000000001183

Maurer, L. R.; Bertsimas, D.; Bouardi, H. T.; El Hechi, M.; El Moheb, M.; Giannoutsou, K.; Zhuo, D.; Dunn, J.; Velmahos, G. C.; Kaafarani, H. M. A Trauma Outcome Predictor:

An Artificial Intelligence Interactive Smartphone Tool to Predict Outcomes in Trauma Patients. *J. Trauma Acute Care Surg.* **2021**, *91* (1). https://journals.lww.com/jtrauma/Fulltext/2021/07000/Trauma_outcome_predictor__An_artificial.15.aspx

Mjolsness, E.; DeCoste, D. Machine Learning for Science: State of the Art and Future Prospects. *Science* **2001**, *293* (5537), 2051–2055. https://doi.org/10.1126/science.293.5537.2051

Nowinski, W. L.; Walecki, J.; Półtorak-Szymczak, G.; Sklinda, K.; Mruk, B. Ischemic Infarct Detection, Localization, and Segmentation in Noncontrast CT Human Brain Scans: Review of Automated Methods. *Peer J.* **2020**, *8*, e10444. https://doi.org/10.7717/peerj.10444

O'Sullivan, S.; Nevejans, N.; Allen, C.; Blyth, A.; Leonard, S.; Pagallo, U.; Holzinger, K.; Holzinger, A.; Sajid, M. I.; Ashrafian, H. Legal, Regulatory, and Ethical Frameworks for Development of Standards in Artificial Intelligence (AI) and Autonomous Robotic Surgery. *Int. J. Med. Robot. Comput. Assist. Surg.* **2019**, *15* (1), 1–12. https://doi.org/10.1002/rcs.1968

O'Sullivan, S.; Leonard, S.; Holzinger, A.; Allen, C.; Battaglia, F.; Nevejans, N.; van Leeuwen, F. W. B.; Sajid, M. I.; Friebe, M.; Ashrafian, H.; Heinsen, H.; Wichmann, D.; Hartnett, M.; Gallagher, A. G. Operational Framework and Training Standard Requirements for AI-Empowered Robotic Surgery. *Int. J. Med. Robot. Comput. Assist. Surg.* **2020**, *16* (5), e2020. https://doi.org/https://doi.org/10.1002/rcs.2020

Petersson, C.; Batalden, P.; Fritzell, P.; Borst, S.; Hedberg, B. Exploring the Meaning of Coproduction as Described by Patients after Spinal Surgery Interventions. *Open Nurs. J.* **2019**, *13* (1), 85–91. https://doi.org/10.2174/1874434601913010085

Pomerol, J.-C. Artificial Intelligence and Human Decision Making. *Eur. J. Oper. Res.* **1997**, *99* (1), 3–25. https://doi.org/https://doi.org/10.1016/S0377-2217(96)00378-5

Qiu, W.-R.; Chen, G.; Wu, J.; Lei, J.; Xu, L.; Zhang, S.-H. Analyzing Surgical Treatment of Intestinal Obstruction in Children with Artificial Intelligence. *Comput. Math. Methods Med.* **2021**, *2021*, 6652288. https://doi.org/10.1155/2021/6652288

Ransbotham, S.; Kiron, D.; Gerbert, P.; Reeves, M. Reshaping Business with Artificial Intelligence: Closing the Gap between Ambition and Action. *MIT Sloan Manage. Rev.* **2017**, *59* (1).

Rehim, S. A.; DeMoor, S.; Olmsted, R.; Dent, D. L.; Parker-Raley, J. Tools for Assessment of Communication Skills of Hospital Action Teams: A Systematic Review. *J. Surg. Educ.* **2017**, *74* (2), 341–351. https://doi.org/10.1016/j.jsurg.2016.09.008

Reismann, J.; Romualdi, A.; Kiss, N.; Minderjahn, M. I.; Kallarackal, J.; Schad, M.; Reismann, M. Diagnosis and Classification of Pediatric Acute Appendicitis by Artificial Intelligence Methods: An Investigator-Independent Approach. *PLoS One* **2019**, *14* (9), 1–11. https://doi.org/10.1371/journal.pone.0222030

Roberts, D. J.; Bobrovitz, N.; Zygun, D. A.; Ball, C. G.; Kirkpatrick, A. W.; Faris, P. D.; Stelfox, H. T. Indications for Use of Damage Control Surgery and Damage Control Interventions in Civilian Trauma Patients: A Scoping Review. *J. Trauma Acute Care Surg.* **2015**, *78* (6), 1187–1196. https://doi.org/10.1097/TA.0000000000000647

Roll, I.; Wylie, R. Evolution and Revolution in Artificial Intelligence in Education. *Int. J. Artif. Intell. Educ.* **2016**, *26*, 582–599.

RStudio Team. *RStudio: Integrated Development for R. RStudio*; RStudio, Inc.: Boston, MA, 2015.

Secinaro, S.; Calandra, D.; Secinaro, A.; Muthurangu, V.; Biancone, P. The Role of Artificial Intelligence in Healthcare: A Structured Literature Review. *BMC Med. Inform. Decis. Mak.* **2021**, *21* (1), 1–23. https://doi.org/10.1186/s12911-021-01488-9

Shay, L. A.; Lafata, J. E. Where Is the Evidence? A Systematic Review of Shared Decision Making and Patient Outcomes. *Med. Decis. Mak.* **2015**, *35* (1), 114–131. https://doi.org/10.1177/0272989X14551638

Sousa, M. J.; Dal Mas, F.; Pesqueira, A.; Lemos, C.; Verde, J. M.; Cobianchi, L. The Potential of AI in Health Higher Education to Increase the Students' Learning Outcomes. *TEM J.* **2021,** *10* (2), 488–497. https://doi.org/10.18421/TEM102-02

Thomas, J.; Haertling, T. AIBx, Artificial Intelligence Model to Risk Stratify Thyroid Nodules. *Thyroid* **2020,** *30* (6), 878–884. https://doi.org/10.1089/thy.2019.0752

Toniolo, K.; Masiero, E.; Massaro, M.; Bagnoli, C. Sustainable Business Models and Artificial Intelligence. Opportunities and Challenges. In *Knowledge, People, and Digital Transformation: Approaches for a Sustainable Future*; Matos, F., Vairinhos, V., Salavisa, I., Edvinsson, L., Massaro, M., Eds.; Springer: Cham, 2019; pp 103–117.

Torain, M. J.; Maragh-Bass, A. C.; Dankwa-Mullen, I.; Hisam, B.; Kodadek, L. M.; Lilley, E. J.; Najjar, P.; Changoor, N. R.; Rose, J. A.; Zogg, C. K.; Maddox, Y. T.; Britt, L. D.; Haider, A. H. Surgical Disparities: A Comprehensive Review and New Conceptual Framework. *J. Am. Coll. Surg.* **2016,** *223* (2), 408–418. https://doi.org/10.1016/j.jamcollsurg.2016.04.047

Vallverdú, J.; Nishida, T.; Ohmoto, Y.; Moran, S.; Lázare, S. Fake Empathy and Human-Robot Interaction (HRI): A Preliminary Study. *Int. J. Technol. Hum. Interact.* **2018,** *14* (1), 44–59.

Vanzo, A.; Riccio, F.; Sharf, M.; Mirabella, V.; Catarci, T.; Nardi, D. Who Is Willing to Help Robots? A User Study on Collaboration Attitude. *Int. J. Soc. Robot.* **2020,** *12* (2), 589–598. https://doi.org/10.1007/s12369-019-00571-6

Venkatesh, V.; Morris, M.; Davis, G. B.; Davis, F. D. User Acceptance of Information Technology: Toward a Unified View. *Mis Q.* **2003,** *27* (3), 425–478.

Vokinger, K. N.; Feuerriegel, S.; Kesselheim, A. S. Continual Learning in Medical Devices: FDA's Action Plan and Beyond. *Lancet Digit. Health* **2021,** *3* (6), e337–e338. https://doi.org/10.1016/S2589-7500(21)00076-5

Woltz, S.; Krijnen, P.; Pieterse, A. H.; Schipper, I. B. Surgeons' Perspective on Shared Decision Making in Trauma Surgery. A National Survey. *Patient Educ. Couns.* **2018,** *101* (10), 1748–1752. https://doi.org/10.1016/j.pec.2018.06.002

Yang, G.-Z.; Cambias, J.; Cleary, K.; Daimler, E.; Drake, J.; Dupont, P. E.; Hata, N.; Kazanzides, P.; Martel, S.; Patel, R. V.; Santos, V. J.; Taylor, R. H. Medical Robotics. Regulatory, Ethical, and Legal Considerations for Increasing Levels of Autonomy. *Sci. Robot.* **2017,** *2* (4). https://doi.org/10.1126/scirobotics.aam8638

CHAPTER 14

OPEN INNOVATION IN HEALTHCARE DURING THE COVID-19 PANDEMIC: THE CASE OF 3D-PRINTED VENTURI VALVES

LUIGI FACCINCANI[1], DAVIDE CIRIMBELLI[1], ALESSANDRO COMINELLI[2], FRANCESCA DAL MAS[3], CRISTIAN FRACASSI[4], and ANDREA PELLEGRINI[5]

[1]ASST Franciacorta, Chiari, Italy

[2]ATS Valpadana, Mantova, Italy

[3]Department of Management, Ca' Foscari University, Venice, Italy

[4]Isinnova SRL, Brescia, Italy

[5]ASST Lariana, Como, Italy

ABSTRACT

The COVID-19 pandemic has caused a disruption in several healthcare services. Italy was severely hit by the first wave of the pandemic at the beginning of 2020. Lombardy stood as one of the most affected regions, needing to cope with a severe number of patients with respiratory difficulties and few resources to meet their medical needs. The lack of respiratory valves named "Venturi" led one of the hospitals to think about self-production using an innovative 3D-printing technology. The search for a partner through a local newspaper allowed the public managers to meet a young entrepreneur leading an innovative startup. The partnership not only led to the production

Incorporating AI Technology in the Service Sector: Innovations in Creating Knowledge, Improving Efficiency, and Elevating Quality of Life. Maria José Sousa, Subhendu Kumar Pani, Francesca Dal Mas, & Sérgio Sousa (Eds.)
© 2024 Apple Academic Press, Inc. Co-published with CRC Press (Taylor & Francis)

of the needed Venturi valves but also to the creation of a different type of valves (later called "Charlotte") to allow the conversion of a popular snorkeling mask from the French retailer Decathlon into an effective ventilation device. The 3D projects were freely shared online to produce and print such valves worldwide. The case of Venturi valves stood as an open-innovation best practice during the COVID-19 pandemic.

14.1   INTRODUCTION

The COVID-19 pandemic (WHO, 2020a) at the beginning of 2020 has disrupted the entire healthcare system worldwide. After China (WHO, 2020b), the first wave hit Europe, especially Italy and Lombardy (Pisano et al., 2020). In the initial absence of vaccines or effective medications, nonpharmaceutical interventions like social distancing and the closure of schools and nonessential businesses were put in place (Massaro et al., 2021), and hospitals and healthcare institutions had to reorganize their people, resources, and processes (Dal Mas et al., 2021; Romani et al., 2021). Elective and nonurgent surgical interventions (Cobianchi et al., 2020c; Tseng et al., 2020) and testing and screening activities (Barcellini et al., 2020) were canceled or postponed, with the main paradigm shifting from patient-centric to public health ethics (Angelos, 2020).

This condition highlighted the need for new ways of managing innovation in this sector, supporting the relevance of more open innovation practices also in healthcare (e.g., hospitals and medical centers), besides life-science industry (like pharma, biotech, etc.) (Cobianchi et al., 2020b; Davies et al., 2019; Secundo et al., 2019).

While the healthcare crisis had to be managed to ensure resilience and "business as usual" (Cobianchi et al., 2020c), antifragile strategies (Derbyshire and Wright, 2014; Taleb, 2012) had to be planned for the "new normal" (Cobianchi et al., 2020a) to make sure that the best practices and lessons learned developed during the pandemic could represent valuable pillars to rebuild a stronger and more performing healthcare system. According to a recent study (Cobianchi et al. 2020a), one of the most valuable best practices developed within the COVID-19 pandemic refers to multidisciplinary experiences like the Decathlon "Easy Breath" snorkeling mask converted into a ventilation device for COVID patients (Fracassi, 2020) and the COVID-19 Bundled Response for Access—COBRA experience of the Massachusetts General Hospital (Albutt et al., 2020). Moreover, the same study underlined the relevance of new technologies to support the development of innovative solutions, even in the case of scarcity of resources.

Given this background, the present work investigates the case of the Venturi and Charlotte valves as an open innovation project between one of the hospitals more hit by the first wave of the pandemic at the beginning of 2020, and a local startup as a solution to quickly respond to an unexpected crisis, leading to a scarcity of resources. Both theoretical and managerial implications are discussed in the conclusions.

14.2 THE CASE STUDY

14.2.1 3D PRINTING AS A DISRUPTIVE TECHNOLOGY

3D printing is one of the technologies related to Industry 4.0 (Bagnoli et al., 2019). 3D printing creates three-dimensional objects through additive manufacturing, starting from a digital 3D model.

Additive technologies are defined as those processes that aggregate materials to create objects starting from their three-dimensional mathematical models, usually by superimposing layers and proceeding in the opposite way to what happens in subtractive (or chip removal) processes. The term "3D printing" is the synonym used in the media and the world of makers and personal manufacture. 3D printing refers to those additive processes that make products by depositing material through a print head, nozzles, or other printing technologies. This technology has been proven to support rapid prototyping and quick innovation, from both technical and organizational viewpoints (Denicolai et al., 2021; Strange and Zucchella, 2017).

14.2.2 THE MOTIVATIONS OF THE PROJECT

The case study concerns the various attempts to print some medical devices absent on the market during the COVID-19 pandemic—namely, the valves for "Venturi" oxygen therapy for COVID patients. The successful printing of the valve "Charlotte" transformed simple snorkeling masks into authentic ventilation devices for oxygen therapy, using, in particular, affordable masks sold by the French sporting goods retailer Decathlon (Cobianchi et al., 2020a; Fracassi, 2020). The case of the Charlotte valve jumped to the headlines of national and international news, showing how much technology, even the simplest one, can be oriented towards innovation. Interestingly, the case highlights open-minded leadership and collaboration among diverse players (in terms of culture, organizational size, and goals) as critical factors of success.

14.2.3   THE LACK OF VENTURI VALVES DURING THE COVID-19 PANDEMIC

The project was conceived at the beginning of 2020 at the hospital of Chiari, Brescia, located in one of the Italian areas of Lombardy mostly hit by the first unexpected wave of the epidemic (Pisano et al., 2020). Following an increasing number of COVID patients with breathing difficulties and the cancellation of most elective surgical operations (Cobianchi et al., 2020c), the hospital management decided to convert the beds in the surgical wards into places for subintensive care, as was happening in several other locations worldwide (Peters et al., 2020). Still, patients needed continuous positive airway pressure (CPAP) breathing masks. Meanwhile, the market was experiencing a general lack of medical goods, including sanitizers and personal protective equipment for clinical staff like surgical masks and gloves. The hospital was in need of CPAP devices. Still, domestic and international suppliers could only provide a limited number of masks, many of which could not be utilized without a "Venturi" valve.

The clinical engineering service of the hospital had a small 3D printer capable of producing a single piece at a time. Such a machine was generally used to build small mechanical parts, to be customized or no longer available on the market. The small 3D printer triggered the idea of self-producing missing Venturi valves. Still, its capacity would have never been enough to meet the demand of the hospital. For this reason, the hospital management decided to launch a call in the local newspaper, with the aim of finding support in the production of Venturi valves. An engineer, Cristian Fracassi, replied to the call on behalf of his company Isinnova, operating in the technology field, which motto is "Ideas are the engine of innovation, they are the lever of change, even when they are small and seem trivial."

Institutional theories (Suchman, 1995) and path dependence view (Sydow et al., 2010) suggest this condition leads to strategic paralysis/myopia in the vast majority of organizations like public hospitals. Nevertheless, the experimentation of Industry 4.0 technologies within the center of Chiari and the interaction with a startup—Isinnova—supported to explore an alternative way of dealing with the problem (Denicolai and Previtali, 2020; Neyens et al., 2010; Spender et al., 2017).

14.2.4   SELF-PRODUCTION AND TECHNICAL ATTEMPTS

The Venturi valve is a passive medical device that allows mixing oxygen and air in a predetermined concentration to obtain a correct mixture for oxygen therapy. The principle underlying its operation is the so-called Venturi principle, from the inventor's name, the Italian physicist Giovanni Battista Venturi (1746–1822).

The Venturi effect relates the pressure and speed of a fluid flowing inside a generally cylindrical duct. Specifically, as the speed of the fluid increases, there is a reduction in pressure. The Venturi valve plays on variations of cylindrical section and side windows: maintaining a constant flow of oxygen at the valve inlet (15 or 30 L/min), the passage of fluid from the cylindrical nozzle with a diameter of 0.8 mm in the area of the valve with a larger diameter and side windows generates air intake from the side windows. In this way, the two fluids, namely, air and oxygen, mix with a ratio that depends on the sections of the tube and the side openings, obtaining the desired proportion.

The goal of the project was to self-produce safe and effective Venturi valves in a few hours: starting from the prototyping phase, moving on to the production of first examples, to get to the production of the first pieces useful for therapeutic purposes.

The Chiari hospital made available to the research team one Venturi valve, already used by a patient and sterilized before collection. The engineering team investigated in depth the operating principles of the Venturi valve, assessing the clinical risks related to the geometric tolerances introduced by the chosen construction technique. Isinnova's engineers then elaborated a three-dimensional mathematical model in CAD format, built through the geometric measurements of the sample Venturi valve, obtained from precision instrumental measurements, varying them—where possible—according to the construction requirements.

The engineering staff tested three different 3D-printing options.

With the so-called fused deposition modeling (FDM) technique, printing times were approximately 2.5 h/piece. Two prototypes were made with this technology, one in white color and for use on the first patient and one in yellow used for immersion tests in ammonia solution. This technique uses less expensive machines and raw materials than laser technology but offers less definition. The cost of the material is about 20 €/kg. The piece weighs on average 25 g. Once printed, the product was processed by removal with a jewelry micromill to create a hole at the entrance with a diameter of less than a millimeter (0.8 mm). Following this process, the pieces were immersed in alcohol and bagged.

With resin printing (laser stereoligraphy), three white prototypes were created in about 20 h of printing. The pieces were then washed abundantly with water and alcohol, exposed to ultraviolet rays for 5 min and placed in an envelope. The cost of the material is around 100 €/kg, therefore five times more expensive than the FDM technique.

Samples were also made with powder technology (Powder Print). The polymer used is PA12 (nylon) with an aluminum additive to ensure high mechanical and thermal resistance. It underwent a thermal cycle up to 140° and was then washed abundantly with alcohol. Also, in this case, the 0.8 mm hole was corrected by hand with a microdrill to ensure the necessary geometric precision, and then it was rewashed with hot water and neutral soap and finally bagged.

14.2.5   CHOOSING THE BEST OPTION

The analysis of the results of the three types of 3D printing made it possible to identify the strengths and weaknesses of all three technologies and then select the best one for the objective.

FDM printing is undoubtedly the cheapest and most widespread in the world. This also supported a quick decision-making process and facilitated the openness to work with external players. The cost of an entry-level printer is just over €200 and, therefore, affordable for everyone. The filament is also, among the 3D-printing materials, the cheapest of all and allows colors of any type. However, such cheapness clashes with the accuracy of the product. The best possible quality has a definition of 0.1 mm. Therefore, the various layers can be seen with the naked eye. Moreover, it was not possible to produce the entire Venturi valve in a single shot, given the particular shape of the cap. One more positive aspect of FDM printing is the material used. Such material, named PLA, stands as a biodegradable substance, suitable for contact with the skin and food, derived from corn and completely odorless. Printing times are relatively fast but largely depend on the volume of the single piece. If it takes 2.5 h to print a Venturi valve, it takes exactly twice as long to print two. Finally, the surface of the piece is rough and not perfectly smooth. From some tests on the Venturi, good behavior has been shown, probably due to micro turbulences that mix better the two gases (oxygen and air).

Resin resulted in the absolute best definition printer. It is much slower than the FDM. Indeed, it takes about 12 h to make a Venturi valve. However, the timing, as is also the case for powder printers, does not depend on the volume but the piece's height. Since a maximum of three Venturi can fit on the plate of a resin printer, the printing time of one valve or three valves is exactly the same. The accuracy is 0.01 mm, and to the eye, it is impossible to distinguish the layers that make up the product. The resins are much harder than PLA, but at the same time, more brittle. A piece that falls to the ground behaves like a glass object, splinters, or shatters. A defect of resin printing is that of postprocessing. While with the FDM, a finished product is obtained immediately, with the resin, it is necessary to make a second step, the so-called cure. In fact, the piece, as soon as it comes out of the printer, is completely slimy and sticky. It must first be washed thoroughly to remove the excess resin and then pass it to a UV treatment to allow complete catalysis and relative hardening of the surface. Furthermore, the resins have a very unpleasant odor that tends to remain on the piece for days. In the case of a Venturi, through which oxygen and air pass, which then ends up in the lungs of a patient, it is absolutely not recommended. The surface of a resin-molded object is perfectly smooth.

Powder printing allows the creation of objects of any shape with extreme precision, definition, and replicability of the product. It is the slowest and most expensive technology. The most performing machines cost about €300,000, and the construction time of a Venturi valve is about 24 h. The positive aspect is the timing for making multiple valves which is identical since everything is based on the height of the piece and not on the overall volume. Having, therefore, a large print bed, Isinnova was able to produce 96 items in 24 h. Like for the resin method, a second step is also required to remove all excess unsintered powder. It was then essential to wash every single valve with soap and water to eliminate any residual dust left, given its use in the medical and respiratory fields. The surface is very precise, but at the same time, slightly wrinkled. This technology has been identified as the best for the purpose.

14.2.6 *TRANSFORMING THE EASYBREATH SNORKELING MASK INTO A VENTILATION DEVICE*

While the production of Venturi valves to be used with CPAP helmets was successful, the lack of CPAP devices made the innovation less effective than planned, especially considering the emergency context. For this reason, a retired physician, Dr. Renato Favero, supporting his colleagues within the intensive care unit, had an idea. The intuition consisted in converting full-face snorkeling masks (Easybreath model by Decathlon) into respiratory masks. His medical knowledge combined with engineering skills allowed the design of a suitable valve, later named as "Charlotte," capable of connecting to the top of the mask instead of the traditional mouthpiece.

Snorkeling masks have several advantages. First, they feature a seal that runs along the entire perimeter of the face and isolates it from the surrounding environment. They also have two different paths for the air, separating the inhalation path from the exhalation path. They exclude the ears from the treatment area, allowing a high noise reduction. They have a decent volume of air inside, which compensates for the lowering of positive pressure during the inspiratory phase. They can be sterilized. Therefore, they can easily be reused by other patients. They are comfortable to wear and allow the patient to lie supine and on both hips. The oxygen tubes are connected in the upper part and therefore do not occupy the mouth/eye area, so there is no risk that the patient moving his/her arms gets stuck with the tubes.

The multidisciplinary team had to spend much time in research and development activities before getting to the suitable Charlotte valve. After the appropriate clinical evaluations, the hospital deemed the system tested and completed with the Venturi valve suitable and functioning.

This allowed Isinnova of Cristian Fracassi to upload the Charlotte valve 3D files online, allowing anyone with a 3D printer to produce such devices.

The project quickly spread around the world. In less than a month, over 50 Italian hospitals have used snorkeling masks as ventilation devices. Over 15,000 masks have been counted throughout Italy, 150,000 in the rest of the world, with particular focus on France, Brazil, the United States, Canada, Turkey, Spain, Lebanon, Uzbekistan, and the Philippines.

14.3   CONCLUSIONS

Besides technical implications and performance of 3D-printing valves, this case study highlights relevant considerations for healthcare managers. First, the dramatic crisis and sense of urgency pushed forward by the COVID-19 pandemic demonstrated that hospitals and healthcare institutions can put into practice innovative moves that managers of these organizations believed were not possible.

However, this case study shows that the feeling "there is no other option" is not enough: other factors must be in place. In other words, the fact of being in the middle of an unprecedented pandemic is not sufficient to stimulate healthcare organizations to "explore the unexplored." This happens and—above all—leads to success only in the presence of strategic and organizational drivers of innovation.

In particular, in the case discussed, the key factor of success enabling action toward innovation again paralysis due to norms and habits is the interplay with a startup as well as the engagement of this startup in the project implementation. Interestingly, the high cognitive distance between the two parties—big versus small organization, public versus private mindset, experienced public managers versus young entrepreneurs, and so on—supported the unlocking of creativity and agility instead of creating a further barrier. In this regard, the crises played a role, supporting a different sense-making of who can really help: new players like a startup and novel patterns of collaboration. All in all, as proved in other cases, connected (Bagnoli et al., 2021a) and not connected (Bagnoli et al., 2021b) to the pandemic, paradoxes seem to be able to foster innovation and the development of new business models and solutions, which were later shared worldwide, saving the lives of thousands of COVID patients.

KEYWORDS

- **open innovation**
- **healthcare**
- **COVID-19 pandemic**
- **Venturi valves**
- **Charlotte valves**
- **3D printing**
- **ventilation devices**

REFERENCES

Albutt, K.; Luckhurst, C. M.; Alba, G. A.; El Hechi, M.; Mokhtari, A.; Breen, K.; Wing, J.; Akeju, O.; Kalva, S. P.; Mullen, J. T.; Lillemoe, K. T.; Kaafarani, H. Design and Impact of a COVID-19 Multidisciplinary Bundled Procedure Team. *Ann. Surg.* **2020,** *272* (2), e72–e73. https://doi.org/https://doi.org/10.1097/SLA.0000000000004089

Angelos, P. Surgeons, Ethics, and COVID-19: Early Lessons Learned. *J. Am. Coll. Surg.* **2020,** *230* (6), 1119–1120. https://doi.org/10.1016/j.jamcollsurg.2020.03.028

Bagnoli, C.; Dal Mas, F.; Massaro, M. The 4th Industrial Revolution: Business Models and Evidence From the Field. *Int. J. E-Serv. Mobile Appl.* **2019,** *11* (3), 34–47.

Bagnoli, C.; Dal Mas, F.; Biancuzzi, H.; Massaro, M. Business Models Beyond COVID-19. A Paradoxes Approach. *J. Bus. Models* **2021a,** Online first. https://doi.org/https://doi.org/10.5278/jbm.v9i3.6419

Bagnoli, C.; Dal Mas, F.; Lombardi, R.; Nucciarelli, A. Translating Knowledge through Business Model Tensions. A Case Study. *Int. J. Manage. Decis. Mak.* **2021b,** *20* (2), 182–197. https://doi.org/10.1504/IJMDM.2021.10033712

Barcellini, A.; Filippi, A. R.; Dal Mas, F.; Cobianchi, L.; Corvò, R.; Price, P.; Orlandi, E. To a New Normal in Radiation Oncology: Looking Back and Planning Forward. *Tumori J.* **2020,** *106* (6), 440–444. https://doi.org/10.1177/0300891620962197

Cobianchi, L.; Dal Mas, F.; Peloso, A.; Pugliese, L.; Massaro, M.; Bagnoli, C.; Angelos, P. Planning the Full Recovery Phase: An Antifragile Perspective on Surgery after COVID-19. *Ann. Surg.* **2020a,** *272* (6), e296–e299. https://doi.org/10.1097/SLA.0000000000004489

Cobianchi, L.; Dal Mas, F.; Piccolo, D.; Peloso, A.; Secundo, G.; Massaro, M.; Takeda, A.; Garcia Vazquez, A.; Verde, J. M.; Swanstrom, L. L.; Marescaux, J.; Perretta, S.; Gallix, B.; Dimarcq, J.-L.; Gimenez, M. E. Digital Transformation in Healthcare. The Challenges of Translating Knowledge in a Primary Research, Educational and Clinical Centre. In *International Business Information Management Conference (35th IBIMA)*; Soliman, K. S., Ed.; IBIMA, 2020b; pp 6877–6888.

Cobianchi, L.; Pugliese, L.; Peloso, A.; Dal Mas, F.; Angelos, P. To a New Normal: Surgery and COVID-19 during the Transition Phase. *Ann. Surg.* **2020c,** *272*, e49–e51. https://doi.org/10.1097/SLA.0000000000004083

Dal Mas, F.; Romani, G.; Modenese, M.; Lucà, R.; Manca, M. F.; Ferrara, M.; Cobianchi, L. Healthcare and Human Centered Organizational Culture in Crisis during COVID-19 Pandemic. The Italian Experience. In *Human Centered Organizational Culture Global Dimensions*; Lepeley, M. T., Morales, O., Essens, P., Beutell, N. J., Majluf, N., Eds.; Routledge: New York, 2021; pp 139–150.

Davies, G. H.; Roderick, S.; Huxtable-Thomas, L. Social Commerce Open Innovation in Healthcare Management: An Exploration from a Novel Technology Transfer Approach. *J. Strat. Mark.* **2019,** *27* (4), 356–367. https://doi.org/10.1080/0965254X.2018.1448882

Denicolai, S.; Previtali, P. Precision Medicine: Implications for Value Chains and Business Models in Life Sciences. *Technol. Forecast. Soc. Change* **2020,** *151*, 119767. https://doi.org/https://doi.org/10.1016/j.techfore.2019.119767

Denicolai, S.; Zucchella, A.; Magnani, G. Internationalization, Digitalization, and Sustainability: Are SMEs Ready? A Survey on Synergies and Substituting Effects among Growth Paths. *Technol. Forecast. Soc. Change* **2021,** *166*, 120650. https://doi.org/https://doi.org/10.1016/j.techfore.2021.120650

Derbyshire, J.; Wright, G. Preparing for the Future: Development of an "Antifragile" Methodology That Complements Scenario Planning by Omitting Causation. *Technol. Forecast. Soc. Change* **2014,** *82* (1), 215–225. https://doi.org/10.1016/j.techfore.2013.07.001

Fracassi, C. *Tutto d'un fiato*; Hoepli, 2020.

Massaro, M.; Tamburro, P.; La Torre, M.; Dal Mas, F.; Thomas, R.; Cobianchi, L.; Barach, P. Nonpharmaceutical Interventions and the Infodemic on Twitter: Lessons Learned from Italy during the COVID-19 Pandemic. *J. Med. Syst.* **2021,** *45* (50). https://doi.org/https://doi.org/10.1007/s10916-021-01726-7

Neyens, I.; Faems, D.; Sels, L. The Impact of Continuous and Discontinuous Alliance Strategies on Startup Innovation Performance. *Int. J. Technol. Manage.* **2010,** *52* (3/4), 392–410.

Peters, A. W.; Chawla, K. S.; Turnbull, Z. A. Transforming ORS into ICUs. *New Engl. J. Med.* **2020,** *382* (19), 1–2. https://doi.org/10.1056/NEJMc2010853

Pisano, G.; Sadun, R.; Zanini, M. Lessons from Italy's Response to Coronavirus. *Harvard Bus. Rev.* **2020.** https://hbr.org/2020/03/lessons-from-italys-response-to-coronavirus

Romani, G.; Dal Mas, F.; Massaro, M.; Cobianchi, L.; Modenese, M.; Barcellini, A.; Ricciardi, W.; Barach, P.; Lucà, R.; Ferrara, M. Population Health Strategies to Support Hospital and Intensive Care Unit Resiliency during the COVID-19 Pandemic: The Italian Experience. *Popul. Health Manage.* **2021,** *24* (2), 174–181. https://doi.org/0.1089/pop.2020.0255

Secundo, G.; Toma, A.; Schiuma, G.; Passiante, G. Knowledge Transfer in Open Innovation: A Classification Framework for Healthcare Ecosystems. *Bus. Process Manage. J.* **2019,** *25* (1), 144–163.

Spender, J.-C.; Corvello, V.; Grimaldi, M.; Rippa, P. Startups and Open Innovation: A Review of the Literature. *Eur. J. Innov. Manage.* **2017,** *20* (1), 4–30. https://doi.org/10.1108/EJIM-12-2015-0131

Strange, R.; Zucchella, A. Industry 4.0, Global Value Chains and International Business. *Multinatl. Bus. Rev.* **2017,** *25* (3), 174–184. https://doi.org/10.1108/MBR-05-2017-0028

Suchman, M. C. Managing Legitimacy: Strategic and Institutional Approaches. *Acad. Manage. Rev.* **1995,** *20* (3), 571–610.

Sydow, J.; Lerch, F.; Staber, U. Planning for Path Dependence? The Case of a Network in the Berlin-Brandenburg Optics Cluster. *Econ. Geogr.* **2010,** *86* (2), 173–195. https://doi.org/ https://doi.org/10.1111/j.1944-8287.2010.01067.x

Taleb, N. N. *Antifragile: Things That Gain from Disorder*; Penguin Random House LLC: New York, NY, 2012.

Tseng, J.; Roggin, K. K.; Angelos, P. Should This Operation Proceed? When Residents and Faculty Disagree during the COVID-19 Pandemic and Recovery. *Ann. Surg.* **2020,** *272* (2), e157–e158.

WHO. *Coronavirus Disease (COVID-19) Pandemic. Health Topics*, 2020a. https://www.who. int/emergencies/diseases/novel-coronavirus-2019

WHO. *WHO Director-General's Opening Remarks at the Media Briefing on COVID-19—11 March 2020*. WHO, 2020b. https://www.who.int/dg/speeches/detail/who-director-general-s-opening-remarks-at-the-media-briefing-on-covid-19---11-march-2020

CHAPTER 15

ORGANIZATIONAL CHANGE TOWARD SERVITIZATION: GUIDING MANUFACTURING FIRMS THROUGH THE DIGITAL TRANSFORMATION PROCESS

CARLO BAGNOLI, MAURIZIO MASSARO, and MATILDE MESSINA

*Department of Management, Ca' Foscari University of Venice,
Ca' Foscari University of Venice, Venice, Italy*

ABSTRACT

The current industrial scenario is soliciting firms to shift toward innovative and sustainable business frameworks. Companies are transitioning from a product-dominant to a service-oriented approach. Servitization constitutes an advanced alternative compared to traditional organizational structures. Manufacturing firms have converted their existing business models for the purpose of delivering disruptive solutions to customers. Digital technologies are crucial to enabling such business transformation. Product companies must develop proper capabilities in order to leverage the full potential of service business model innovation as well as to fulfill fluctuating customer requirements. Research has identified distinct categorizations in reference to service business models. The chapter examines six unique frameworks pertaining to a specific classification scheme. Manufacturers must embrace the opportunities that servitization offers in order to discover additional revenue streams and remain competitive.

Incorporating AI Technology in the Service Sector: Innovations in Creating Knowledge,
Improving Efficiency, and Elevating Quality of Life. Maria José Sousa, Subhendu Kumar Pani,
Francesca Dal Mas, & Sérgio Sousa (Eds.)
© 2024 Apple Academic Press, Inc. Co-published with CRC Press (Taylor & Francis)

15.1 INTRODUCTION

The current business environment requires organizations to evolve in order to survive and prosper. As a result, successful companies need to employ business model innovation to cope with changing market trends (Leker et al., 2018). The technological advancements characterizing the ongoing digital revolution enable firms to gain unique competitive advantages and contribute to blurring the boundaries between companies manufacturing products and firms providing services (Perona et al., 2017). Companies within multiple industries are incorporating services into their operations for the purpose of generating additional revenue streams as well as enhancing customer retention (Casprini, 2019). Therefore, servitization represents an innovative alternative to outdated business strategies and processes which can bring opportunities for all companies and in particular for manufacturing companies willing to disrupt their existing business models.

Although the term servitization first appeared in the literature in the 1980s, the concept of servitization remains elusive (Alvizos and Angelis, 2010). The servitization literature has evolved over the last decades, becoming more and more diverse (Raddats et al., 2019). Multiple notions have been utilized in order to deal with the present phenomenon, nonetheless, a limited number of contributions investigate service transformation in manufacturing companies (Baines et al., 2016). Furthermore, several research gaps emerge, such as the effects of the transition to a service-dominant logic (often shortened as SDL) on the business model and no models seem to describe the shift toward servitization (Martinez et al., 2010). Thus, the absence of a clear and inclusive research program creates a barrier to the implementation of the servitization solution.

In addition, research on this particular matter has proliferated in recent times (Baines et al., 2009), therefore, highlighting the need to address the numerous gaps identified in the literature. The purpose of this chapter is to consolidate current knowledge on servitization and to provide a theoretical framework in order to generate further insights on the topic, as well as to establish recommendations for future research priorities. The chapter is organized as follows. The following section aims at defining servitization. Then, its impact on the business model canvas is depicted and the process of servitization adoption across companies is illustrated through a few examples. The subsequent section outlines the fundamental competencies required to lead business transformation and the challenges that firms encounter while converting to the digital business model. The importance of the adoption of such innovation and the potential benefits deriving from its implementation are discussed in the conclusions.

15.2   DEFINING SERVITIZATION

In generic terms, servitization is conceived as a business trend adding intangible services to tangible products (Kuula et al., 2018). Nonetheless, servitization and related concepts have evolved as a result of extensive research in the field, therefore, enriching the literature with significant contributions (Kowalkowski et al., 2017).

Vandermerwe and Rada (1988) coined the term "servitization" in 1988 defining it as a movement whose characteristics included an increased offering of combinations of goods and services specifically meeting the customers' wishes and preferences. Since then, research on the topic has flourished, leading to the formulation of an abundant number of definitions highlighting different aspects connected to the concept of servitization (Velamuri et al., 2011).

Goedkoop et al. (1999) introduced the notion of "Product-Service System" (often abbreviated to PSS) in reference to the emergence of a trend enabling consumption of both products and services and defined servitization as integrated bundles of products and services both needed to meet user needs. Furthermore, integrated solutions have been recognized as environmentally sustainable alternatives compared to those offered through traditional business models (Mont, 2002). Baines et al. (2009) have described the phenomenon as an innovation promoting the change from products only to integrated product–service solutions to foster mutual value creation. Further contributors suggest that the provision of services alters product uses (Beuren et al., 2013). Recent contributions to the topic seem to converge on the fact that servitization represents a transformational process affecting manufacturing strategies (Bustinza et al., 2015) and resulting in firms shifting from a product-centric business model to a service-dominant dynamic (Benedettini et al., 2017) aimed at expanding service offerings (Benedettini and Neely, 2018). In addition, Lindhult et al. (2018) interpret servitization as a transformational challenge comprising multiple features. In particular, servitization processes require a business model transition involving the provision of customer-oriented services and outcome-based solutions (Eloranta and Turunen, 2016) and affecting all business-model-value dimensions (Ambroise et al., 2018). In addition, such business conversion implies that manufacturers generate new revenue streams through the distribution of services rather than through the exclusive sale of goods (Andrews et al., 2018). In essence, servitization models comprise technology-driven value cocreation business strategies consisting several elements, including smart-connected systems, products, and related electronic services, representing the critical factors essential to achieving long-term customer satisfaction (Zheng et al., 2018).

Regardless of opposing views, servitization is understood as a disruptive innovation delivering customer value through product–service combinations and producing effects on all business model dimensions as well as strengthening customer relationships, thus driving new revenue opportunities.

Figure 15.1 summarizes the concepts illustrated within the above paragraphs.

FIGURE 15.1   Concepts related to the construct of servitization.

15.3   SERVITIZATION BUSINESS MODELS

Servitization can be examined considering its impact on the building blocks constituting the business model canvas. The theoretical framework utilized to perform the analysis consists of the model developed by Bagnoli et al. (2018). Products, resources, internal processes, and customers represent the most significant dimensions to assess to understand the direct effects of such organizational change affecting manufacturing processes (Siagri, 2021).

Servitization identifies the approach of adding immaterial qualities to material goods, thus contributing to delivering a unique user experience. In this regard, Drucker (1986) argues that customers value services over products: specifically, value is to be attributed to the consumption of a particular good, meaning the service that the product delivers. Therefore, users are reclaiming services and products constitute the tools for delivering services.

Furthermore, servitization processes require manufacturers to develop advanced capabilities and innovative value propositions while in the process of learning to deliver services (Lusch et al., 2010; Storbacka et al., 2013). IT and finance professionals, technological competencies, and customer capabilities are essential to designing complex solutions and ensuring that customer operations are conducted in an effective manner (Huikkola et al., 2016).

Achieving value through product–service integration demands the implementation of operational processes enabling the coordination and the exploitation of adequate capabilities fundamental to driving service innovation (Baron et al., 2014). Concerning this matter, Bettencourt and Brown (2013) demonstrate that significant service innovation in manufacturing firms is the result of a deep understanding of customer value. Product companies facilitating customer involvement in service production achieve successful service innovations (Santamaria et al., 2012). Customer interaction and engagement constitute prerequisites for promoting value creation and enhancing organizational competitive advantages (Raeisi, 2017).

Servitization business models aspire to:

- integrate services, therefore enhancing traditional product functions.
- complement products through the introduction of independent services, following the implementation of digital technologies and also the exploitation of the capabilities of smart-connected products.
- replace the sale of goods with the provision of services, contributing to building effective and collaborative service design processes in order to offer personalized solutions to customers (World Economic Forum, 2015).

In recent times, scholars have investigated the servitization of manufacturing adopting a business model perspective (Adrodegari and Saccani, 2017; Dalli and Lanzara, 2011). Nonetheless, Cusumano et al. (2015) claim that the findings emerging from the research are insufficient to illustrate the unique nature of manufacturers' services. Therefore, classification schemes and categorizations concerning industrial service offerings have been generated. Although multiple ramifications seem to coexist within the same research communities, Reim et al. (2015) recognize the following established categories of product–service system business models, including product-oriented, use-oriented, and result-oriented. Additional research on the topic identified a further classification, distinguishing servitization business models in add-on hardware, add-on software, and everything-as-a-service (Bagnoli et al., 2018). Current research has contributed to developing a supplemental classification for servitization business models. Servitization can be categorized into six distinct business models which are discussed in the subsequent paragraphs.

Servitization business models include the following:

- product ownership
- product + service add-on hardware
- product + service add-on software
- product availability
- product-as-a-service
- product subscription

Below is a description of each of the aforementioned business models.

The digital era has contributed to redefining the concept of ownership applied to integrated service solutions (Tauqeer and Bang, 2018). Customers either purchase equipment and related services, or providers retain proprietorship and are in charge of their operations and maintenance (Windahl and Lakemond, 2010). Product ownership represents the first among the servitization business models. Product ownership refers to the traditional operating model involving a one-time transaction between service suppliers and customers. Manufacturers transfer product ownership to consumers in exchange for a lump-sum payment.

The servitization business model is further classified into product + service add-on hardware. The add-on hardware business model aims at providing digital-enabled solutions. Digital services represent product complements favoring performance enhancement, thus contributing to growing the business as well as generating secure revenue streams (Mathieu, 2001). Manufacturers design intangible services for the purpose of fulfilling customer requirements and improving customer outcomes (Lerch and Gotsch, 2015). Furthermore, firms develop customer capabilities for the purpose of building long-term relationships with users in order to collect data and insights as a result of interactions (Adam et al., 2018).

Product + service add-on software constitutes an additional business model involving a complete customized service solution. Servitization requires cooperation with organizational stakeholders, including providers and end customers, as consumers are fundamental to evaluating the quality of solution offerings (Beltagui, 2018). In a servitization context, customers represent the cocreators of value; therefore, product companies must integrate users into their business processes for the purpose of increasing customer involvement and fostering innovation performance (Kohtamaki et al., 2013). Moreover, technological innovation also contributes to reducing costs while optimizing service design (Hypko et al., 2010; Myrthianos et al., 2014).

Product availability consists of a further business model falling under the servitization classification scheme and establishing that digital goods are available to users as well as entailing that businesses retain ownership of the products supporting the services offered. Flexible pricing mechanisms characterize the monetization strategies adopted as consumers commit to paying depending on the utilization or performance of the product (pay-per-use agreements) (Allmendinger and Lombreglia, 2005). Dematerialization also represents a sustainable alternative encouraging firms to manufacture goods designed to last and at the same time add services in order to prolong product life, therefore, ensuring reduced material waste and environmental impact (Neely, 2009).

Product-as-a-Service (often abbreviated to PaaS) business model implies that service suppliers maintain ownership of the dematerialized product throughout its entire life cycle and transfer the digital good to customers in the form of service. The present solution is meant to be sold as a service since its inception and grants customers unlimited access to resources while charging them for a determined usage of the product or service (Probst et al., 2016). On-demand revenues are generated as service solutions are billed based on utilization or outcome.

Product subscription is the final model pertaining to the servitization categorization. Subscriptions reward firms with greater revenue growth as recurring revenue streams constitute the foundation of subscription-based businesses (Tukker, 2004). Customers are required to subscribe to a specific offering against an established periodic fee (Tauqeer and Bang, 2018). Service solutions enable firms to forge durable customer relationships and contribute to guaranteeing sustainable and predictable cash flows, thus encouraging firms to resort to cross-selling techniques for the purpose of increasing the sale of additional goods or services (Leichsenring Franco et al., 2021). Firms quit planning activities on the basis of historical data, following the introduction of subscription models as well as data collection enabling production companies to rely on forward-looking statements in order to establish future service distribution.

Figure 15.2 depicts all the aforementioned servitization business models.

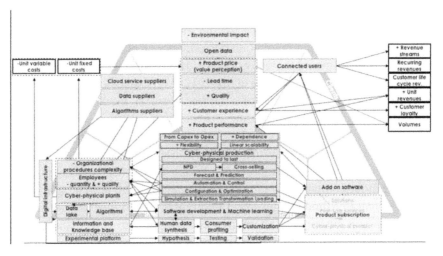

FIGURE 15.2   The servitization business model canvas.

The literature mentions a multitude of organizations introducing servitization solutions. Among the various companies operating in the service sector, Rolls-Royce is considered the most notable example of servitization business model. The leading manufacturer of aircraft engines introduced the first engine maintenance program almost five decades ago (Mo and Beckett, 2018). The British manufacturing firm delivers "power-by-the-hour" as opposed to handing over the proprietorship of the gas turbine engines to the airline firms, meaning customers are charged according to the amount of time the engine is in flight (Baines et al., 2007). Aircraft maintenance services are also provided, allowing operators of aircraft engines to forecast in a precise manner the costs associated with such mechanical intervention, therefore, avoiding the risks related to unscheduled maintenance events (Boehm and Thomas, 2013).

Over the last decades, companies within multiple industries agreed that service expansion would have represented a profitable solution to create added value for their clients and forge long-term relationships. Firms transitioned from marketing and taking care of hardware assets to offering software solutions guaranteeing the optimization of product-enabled processes

(Visintin, 2012). Examples of servitization also include the Xerox case. Most often Xerox or their local operating companies lease photocopiers. The organization does not transfer product ownership rights to the end users (Atasu, 2016). Therefore, customers are charged a fee on the service level offered. In recent times, the American corporation has migrated toward a pay-per-print model in order to charge its customers based on product utilization and began recognizing itself as an "enterprise for business processes and management" rather than a traditional photocopier manufacturer (Visintin, 2014). Xerox remains responsible for maintenance, therefore, assuring the machines are available for use. Nonetheless, as time passes, photocopiers' risk becoming obsolete and less efficient, thus, contributing to increasing total maintenance costs and forcing Xerox to substitute the machines for its customers (Johnsen et al., 2019).

15.4 OPPORTUNITIES AND CHALLENGES RELATED TO THE SERVITIZATION IMPLEMENTATION

Servitization is indeed regarded as a valuable alternative for manufacturing firms to achieve superior outcomes and performance (Wang et al., 2018). The wide offering of custom-integrated solutions contributes to creating growth opportunities as well as increasing profit (Mastrogiacomo et al., 2017). Manufacturers intend to pursue durable competitive advantage through service differentiation (Gebauer et al., 2011). Although such business model innovation implies a substantial evolution of firm capabilities (Teece, 2018), firms must adapt to evolve to survive in a continuously evolving environment and are required to invest and reconfigure internal as well as external competencies to address the changing scenario (Teece et al., 1997). Capabilities in IT management and effective exploitation of big data are crucial to developing integrated solutions (Ceci and Masini, 2011). Nonetheless, in most cases, firms are not able to generate such fundamental capabilities internally, thus requiring manufacturers to build relationships with external actors (Matthyssens and Vandenbempt, 2008). Relationship management has been identified as the principal operational characteristic of the process of augmenting the core offering (Baines and Lightfoot, 2013). Connecting with stakeholders facilitates the development and implementation of competencies enabling product-centric firms to design services and to deliver value, therefore, gaining competitive advantage (Eggert et al., 2017).

Although literature cites multiple benefits related to servitization of manufacturing, a few organizational issues threaten the successful implementation of service business models (Coreynen et al., 2017). Existing research has contributed to uncovering the impacts of the challenges concerning the implementation of service-manufacturing processes (Banerji et al., 2018). Scholars have classified servitization challenges into five distinct categories, comprising:

- the organizational structure
- the business model
- the development process
- client management
- risk management (Zhang and Banerji, 2017)

The literature review indicates that firms must overcome complex implementation challenges while undergoing a transformational shift, and such change, in turn, generates further issues within product-centric companies (Visnjic et al., 2013). The organizational culture is shifted from product-focused to service-oriented in order to sustain the strategic focus of the business (Martinez et al., 2010). This shift represents a challenge because of the influence of path dependence, meaning the traditional development path of the firm is product-oriented and this organizational feature tends to hinder the cultural change (Zarpelon Neto et al., 2015).

Service business model innovation also requires firms to recruit additional human resources (in particular service professionals), although developing a service team and achieving internal collaboration might not be immediate (Lenka et al., 2018), and to redesign the value proposition matching customer operational needs (Barnett et al., 2013).

In order to align to the business model, firms must design appropriate business processes (Alghisi and Saccani, 2015), therefore, integrating customer contributions into service development processes. Given the importance of building relationships with service consumers, scholars have advanced that servitization failure can be attributed to the complexities connected to customer knowledge transfer and integration as users might not perceive the solution as valuable enough or might not be willing to share operational data for confidential reasons (Valtakoski, 2017).

The financial consequences for developing the servitized business should also be considered, as the investment might not yield the projected returns due to the fact that the challenges can counterbalance revenues in the initial stages of the process (Benedettini et al., 2015).

15.5 CONCLUSIONS

The present chapter highlighted the relevance as well as the consequences of servitization of manufacturing in the modern business environment. A driving demand for servitization characterizes the current industrial scenario. Servitization enables manufacturers to pursue strategic differentiation via business model innovation. Findings have revealed that servitization represents a strategic choice for manufacturers in order to thrive in the digital era (Soosay et al., 2016). The growing trend toward servitization requires manufacturing firms to adhere to such organizational transformation in order to benefit from various opportunities deriving from service expansion. Valuable possibilities for growing service businesses have been identified as Chesbrough (2011) observes that the service market appears larger and more sustainable than the product market.

The chapter has illustrated multiple business model frameworks depending on specific organizational goals. The critical factors characterizing the effective implementation of servitization processes have also been clarified and include innovative guiding principles and structures capable of enabling firms to rearrange and reassign resources to enhance business model transformation as well as to leverage existing resources in order to design advanced digital products (Huikkola et al., 2016). Customer engagement is also featured among the major drivers of servitization and contributes to supporting firms in the development of solutions matching customer demands, therefore, enhancing the user experience (Beuren et al., 2013).

KEYWORDS

- **business model innovation**
- **servitization**
- **manufacturing firms**
- **digital business model**
- **technologies**
- **service transformation**
- **business model transition**

REFERENCES

Adam, M.; Strahle, J.; Freise, M. Dynamic Capabilities of Early-Stage Firms: Exploring the Business of Renting Fashion. *J. Small Bus. Strat.* **2018,** *28* (2), 49–67.

Adrodegari, F.; Saccani, N. Business Models for the Service Transformation of Industrial Firms. *Serv. Ind. J.* **2017,** *37* (1), 57–83.

Alghisi, A.; Saccani, N. Internal and External Alignment in the Servitization Journey—Overcoming the Challenges. *Prod. Plann. Cntrl.* **2015,** *26* (14–15), 1219–1232.

Allmendinger, G.; Lombreglia, R. Four Strategies for the Age of Smart Services. *Harv. Bus. Rev.* **2005,** *83,* 131–145.

Alvizos, E.; Angelis, J. What Is Servitization Anyway? In *POMS 21st Annual Conference,* 2010.

Ambroise, L.; Prim-Allaz, I.; Teyssier, C. Financial Performance of Servitized Manufacturing Firms: A Configuration Issue between Servitization Strategies and Customer-Oriented Organizational Design. *Ind. Mark. Manage.* **2018,** *71,* 54–68.

Andrews, D. D.; Dmitrijeva, J.; Bigdeli, A. Z.; Baines, T. Snakes and Ladders in Servitization: Using a Game to Capture Inhibitors and Enablers of Transformation. *Res. Technol. Manage.* **2018,** *61* (6), 37–47.

Atasu, A. *Environmentally Responsible Supply Chains*; Atasu, A. Ed.; Springer: Cham, 2016.

Bagnoli, C.; Bravin, A.; Massaro, M.; Vignotto, A. *Business Model 4.0 I modelli di business vincenti per le imprese italiane nella quarta rivoluzione industriale*; Edizioni Ca' Foscari: Venezia VE, Italy, 2018.

Baines, T. S.; Lightfoot, H. Servitization of the Manufacturing Firm: Exploring the Operations Practices and Technologies That Deliver Advanced Services. *Int. J. Oper. Prod. Manage.* **2013,** *34,* 2–35.

Baines, T. S.; Lightfoot, H. W.; Evans, S.; Neely, A.; Greenough, R.; Peppard, J.; Roy, R.; Shehab, E.; Braganza, A.; Tiwari, A.; Alcock, J. R.; Angus, J. P.; Bastl, M., Cousens, A.; Irving, P.; Johnson, M.; Kingston, J.; Lockett, H.; Martinez, V.; et al. State-of-the-Art in Product-Service Systems. *J. Eng. Manuf.* **2007,** *221* (10), 1543–1552.

Baines, T. S.; Lightfoot, H.; Benedettini, O.; Kay, J. M. The Servitization of Manufacturing: A Review of Literature and Reflection on Future Challenges. *J. Manuf. Technol. Manage.* **2009a,** *20* (5), 547–567.

Baines, T.; Lightfoot, H.; Peppard, J.; Johnson, M.; Tiwari, A.; Shehab, E.; Swink, M. Towards an Operations Strategy for Product-Centric Servitization. *Int. J. Oper. Prod. Manage.* **2009b,** *29* (5), 494–519.

Baines, T.; Bigdeli, A. Z.; Bustinza, O. F.; Guang Shi, V.; Baldwin, J.; Ridgway, K. Servitization: Revisiting the State-of-the-Art and Research Priorities. *Int. J. Oper. Prod. Manage.* **2016,** *37* (2), 256–278.

Banerji, S.; Lu, D.; Day, S. Challenges of Servitization: A Comparison Study on Manufacturers with Different Strategic Focuses. In *Proceedings of the 25th Annual EurOMA Conference,* 2018.

Barnett, N. J.; Parry, G.; Saad, M.; Newnes, L. B.; Goh, Y. M. Servitization: Is a Paradigm Shift in the Business Model and Service Enterprise Required? *Strat. Change* **2013,** *22* (3–4), 145–156.

Baron, S.; Warnaby, G.; Hunter-Jones, P. Service(s) Marketing Research: Developments and Directions. *Int. J. Manage. Rev.* **2014,** *16,* 150–171.

Beltagui, A. A Design-Thinking Perspective on Capability Development: The Case of New Product Development for a Service Business Model. *Int. J. Oper. Prod. Manage.* **2018,** *38* (4), 1041–1060.

Benedettini, O.; Neely, A. Investigating a Revised Service Transition Concept. *Serv. Bus.* **2018,** *12* (4), 701–730.

Benedettini, O.; Neely, A.; Swink, M. Why Do Servitized Firms Fail? A Risk-Based Explanation. *Int. J. Oper. Prod. Manage.* **2015,** *35* (6), 946–979.

Benedettini, O.; Swink, M.; Neely, A. Examining the Influence of Service Additions on Manufacturing Firms' Bankruptcy Likelihood. *Ind. Mark. Manage.* **2017,** *60,* 112–125.

Bettencourt, L. A.; Brown, S. W. From Goods to Great: Service Innovation in a Product-Dominant Firm. *Bus. Horiz.* **2013,** *56,* 277–283.

Beuren, F.; Ferreira, M.; Miguel, P. Product-Service Systems: A Literature Review on Integrated Products and Services. *J. Clean. Prod.* **2013,** *47,* 222–231.

Boehm, M.; Thomas, O. *Looking beyond the Rim of One's Teacup: A Multidisciplinary Literature Review of Product-Service Systems in Information Systems. Bus. Manage., Eng. Des.* **2013,** *51,* 245–260.

Bustinza, O.; Bigdeli, A.; Baines, T.; Elliot, C. Servitization and Competitive Advantage. The Importance of Organisational Structure and Value Chain Position. *Res. Technol. Manage.* **2015,** *58* (5), 53–60.

Casprini, E. *Beyond Servitization. New Managerial Challenges for Manufacturing Firms.* Wolters Kluwer Italia: Milano, Italy, 2019.

Ceci, F.; Masini, A. Balancing Specialized and Generic Capabilities in the Provision of Integrated Solutions. *Ind. Corp. Change* **2011,** *20,* 91–131.

Chesbrough, H. W. Bringing Open Innovation to Services. *MIT Sloan Manage. Rev.* **2011,** *52,* 85.

Coreynen, W.; Matthyssens, P.; van Bockhaven, W. Boosting Servitization through Digitisation: Pathways and Dynamic Resource Configurations for Manufacturers. *Ind. Mark. Manage.* **2017,** *60,* 42–53.

Cusumano, M. A.; Kahl, S. J.; Suarez, F. F. Services, Industry Evolution, and the Competitive Strategies of Product Firms. *Strat. Manage. J.* **2015,** *36,* 559–575.

Dalli, D.; Lanzara, R. *Nuovi modelli di business e creazione di valore: la scienza dei servizi.* Springer: Cham, 2011.

Drucker, P. F. *Management: Tasks, Responsibilities and Practices*; Truman Talley Books: New York, NY, 1986.

Eggert, A.; Bohm, E.; Cramer, C. Business Service Outsourcing in Manufacturing Firms: An Event Study. *J. Serv. Manage.* **2017,** *28,* 476–498.

Eloranta, V.; Turunen, T. Platforms in Service-Driven Manufacturing: Leveraging Complexity by Connecting, Sharing, and Integrating. *Ind. Mark. Manage.* **2016,** *55,* 178–186.

Gebauer, H.; Gustafsson, A.; Witell, L. Competitive Advantage through Service Differentiation by Manufacturing Companies. *J. Bus. Res.* **2011,** *64* (12), 1270–1280.

Goedkoop, M. J.; van Halen, C.; te Riele, H. R. M.; Rommens, P. J. M. *Product Service Systems, Ecological and Economic Basics,* 1999.

Huikkola, T.; Rabetino, R.; Kohtamaki, M. Resource Realignment in Servitization. *Res. Technol. Manage.* **2016,** *59* (4), 30–39.

Hypko, P.; Tilebein, M.; Gleich, R. Benefits and Uncertainties of Performance-Based Contracting in Manufacturing Industries: An Agency Theory Perspective. *J. Serv. Manage.* **2010,** *21* (4), 460–489.

Johnsen, T. E.; Howard, M.; Miemczyk, J. *Purchasing and Supply Chain Management. A Sustainability Perspective,* 2nd ed.; Routledge: Milton Park, UK, 2019.

Kohtamaki, M.; Partann, J.; Moller, K. Making a Profit with R&D Services—The Critical Role of Relational Capital. *Ind. Mark. Manage.* **2013,** *42* (1), 71–81.

Kowalkowski, C.; Gebauer, H.; Oliva, R. Service Growth in Product Firms: Past, Present, and Future. *Ind. Mark. Manage.* **2017,** *60,* 82–88.

Kuula, S.; Haapasalo, H.; Tolonen, A. Cost-Efficient Co-creation of Knowledge Intensive Business Services. *Serv. Bus.* **2018,** *12* (4), 779–808.

Leichsenring Franco, M.; Almada-Lobo, B.; Soucasaux Sousa, R. Servitization: A Service-Based Resilience Strategy for Manufacturing Firms. *INESCTEC* **2021,** *1* (2). https://science-society.inesctec.pt/index.php/inesctecesociedade/article/view/48

Leker, J.; Gelhard, C.; von Delft, S. *Business Chemistry. How to Build and Sustain Thriving Businesses in the Chemical Industry*; Leker, J., Gelhard, C., von Delft, S., Eds.; John Wiley and Sons Ltd.: New York, NY, 2018.

Lenka, S.; Parida, V.; Sjodin, D. R.; Wincent, J. Exploring the Microfoundations of Servitization: How Individual Actions overcome Organizational Resistance. *J. Bus. Res.* **2018,** *88,* 328–336.

Lerch, C.; Gotsch, M. Digitalized Product-Service Systems in Manufacturing Firms. A Case Study Analysis. *Res. Technol. Manage.* **2015,** *58* (5), 45–52.

Lindhult, E.; Chirumalla, K.; Oghazi, P.; Parida, V. Value Logics for Service Innovation: Practice-Driven Implications for Service-Dominant Logic. *Serv. Bus.* **2018,** *12,* 457–481.

Lusch, R.; Tanniru, M.; Vargo, S. L. Service, Value Networks and Learning. *J. Acad. Mark. Sci.* **2010,** *38* (1), 19–31.

Martinez, V.; Bastl, M.; Kingston, J.; Evans, S. Challenges in Transforming Manufacturing Organisations into Product-Service Providers. *J. Manuf. Technol. Manage.* **2010,** *21* (4), 449–469.

Mastrogiacomo, L.; Barravecchia, F.; Franceschini, F. A General Overview of Manufacturing Servitization in Italy. In *The 9th CIRP IPSS Conference: Circular Perspectives on Product/Service-Systems*, 2017; pp 121–126.

Mathieu, V. Product Services: From a Service Supporting the Product to a Service Supporting the Client. *J. Bus. Ind. Mark.* **2001,** *16,* 39–61.

Matthyssens, P.; Vandenbempt, K. Moving from Basic Offerings to Value-Added Solutions: Strategies, Barriers and Alignment. *Ind. Mark. Manage.* **2008,** *37,* 316–328.

Mo, J.; Beckett, R. *Engineering and Operations of System of Systems*; CRC Press: Boca Raton, FL, 2018.

Mont, O. Clarifying the Concept of Product-Service System. *J. Clean. Prod.* **2002,** *10* (3), 237–245.

Myrthianos, V.; Vendrell-Herrero, F.; Parry, G.; Bustinza, O. Firm Profitability during the Servitization Process in the Music Industry. *Strat. Change* **2014,** *23* (5–6), 317–328.

Neely, A. Exploring the Financial Consequences of the Servitization of Manufacturing. *Oper. Manage. Res.* **2009,** *1* (2), 103–118.

Perona, M.; Saccani, N.; Bacchetti, A. Research Vs. Practice on Manufacturing Firms' Servitization Strategies: A Gap Analysis and Research Agenda. *Systems* **2017,** *5* (1), 19.

Servitisation. *Pay-per-use*, 2016.

Raddats, C.; Kowalkowski, C.; Benedettini, O.; Burton, J.; Gebauer, H. Servitization: A Contemporary Thematic Review of Four Major Research Streams. *Ind. Mark. Manage.* **2019,** *83* (11), 207–223.

Raeisi, S. The Importance of Customer Engagement and Service Innovation in Value Co-creation. In *19th International Conference on Innovation, Management and Technology*, 2017.

Reim, W.; Parida, V.; Ortqvist, D. Product-Service Systems (PSS) Business Models and Tactics—A Systematic Literature Review. *J. Clean. Prod.* **2015,** *97,* 61–75.

Santamaria, L.; Nieto, M. J.; Miles, I. Service Innovation in Manufacturing Firms: Evidence from Spain. *Technovation* **2012,** *32,* 144–155.

Siagri, R. *La servitizzazione. Per un futuro senza limiti alla crescita*; Edizioni Angelo Guerini e Associati: Milan, Italy, 2021.

Soosay, C.; Nunes, B.; Bennett, D.; Sohal, A.; Jabar, J.; Winroth, M. Strategies for Sustaining Manufacturing Competitiveness: Comparative Case Studies in Australia and Sweden. *J. Manuf. Technol. Manage.* **2016,** *27* (1), 6–37.

Storbacka, K.; Nenonen, S.; Windahl, C.; Salonen, A. Solution Business Models: Transformation along Four Continua. *Ind. Mark. Manage.* **2013,** *42* (5), 705–716.

Tauqeer, M. A.; Bang, K. E. Servitization: A Model for the Transformation of Products into Services through a Utility-Driven Approach. *J. Open Innov.: Technol., Mark., Complex.* **2018,** *4* (4), 60.

Teece, D. J. Business Models and Dynamic Capabilities. *Long Range Plann.* **2018,** *51* (1), 40–49.

Teece, D. J.; Pisano, G.; Shuen, A. Dynamic Capabilities and Strategic Management. *Strat. Manage. J.* **1997,** *18* (7), 509–533.

Tukker, A. Eight Types of Product-Service Systems: Eight Ways to Sustainability? Experiences from SusProNet. *Bus. Strat. Environ.* **2004,** *13* (4), 246–260.

Valtakoski, A. Explaining Servitization Failure and Deservitization: A Knowledge-Base Perspective. *Ind. Mark. Manage.* **2017,** *60,* 138–150.

Vandermerwe, S.; Rada, J. Servitization of the Business: Adding Value by Adding Services. *Eur. Manage. J.* **1988,** *6* (4), 314–324.

Velamuri, V. K.; Neyer, A.-K.; Moeslein, K. M. Hybrid Value Creation: A Systematic Review of an Evolving Research Area. *J. Betriebswirtsch.* **2011,** *61* (1), 3–35.

Visintin, F. Providing Integrated Solutions in the Professional Printing Industry: The Case of Océ. *Comput. Ind.* **2012,** *63* (4), 379–388.

Visintin, F. Photocopier Industry: At the Forefront of Servitization. In *Servitization*; Lay, G., Ed.; Springer: Cham, 2014; pp 23–45.

Visnjic, K. I.; van Looy, B.; Neely, A. Steering Manufacturing Firms towards Service Business Model Innovation. *Calif. Manage. Rev.* **2013,** *56* (1), 100–123.

Wang, W.; Lai, K.; Shou, Y. The Impact of Servitization on Firm Performance: A Meta-analysis. *Int. J. Oper. Prod. Manage.* **2018,** *38* (7), 1562–1588.

Windahl, C.; Lakemond, N. Integrating Solutions from a Service-Centred Perspective: Applicability and Limitations in the Capital Goods Industry. *Ind. Mark. Manage.* **2010,** *39,* 1278–1290.

World Economic Forum. *Industrial Internet of Things: Unleashing the Potential of Connected Products and Services*; World Economic Forum, 2015.

Zarpelon Neto, G.; Pereira, G. M.; Borchardt, M. What Problems Manufacturing Companies Can Face When Providing Services around the World? *J. Bus. Ind. Mark.* **2015,** *30* (5), 461–471.

Zhang, W.; Banerji, S. Challenges of Servitization: A Systematic Literature Review. *Ind. Mark. Manage.* **2017,** *65,* 217–227.

Zheng, P.; Lin, T.-J.; Chen, C.-H.; Xu, X. A Systematic Design Approach for Service Innovation of Smart Product-Service Systems. *J. Clean. Prod.* **2018,** *201,* 657–667.

CHAPTER 16

BUSINESS PLANNING AND ARTIFICIAL INTELLIGENCE: OPPORTUNITIES AND CHALLENGES FOR ACCOUNTING FIRMS IN A HUMAN-CENTERED PERSPECTIVE

MAURIZIO MASSARO[1], CARLO BAGNOLI[1], ANDREA ALBARELLI[2], and FRANCESCA DAL MAS[3]

[1]*Department of Management, Ca' Foscari University of Venice, Venice, Italy*

[2]*Department of Environmental Sciences, Informatics and Statistics, Ca' Foscari University of Venice, Venice, Italy*

[3]*Lincoln International Business School, University of Lincoln, Lincoln, United Kingdom*

ABSTRACT

Accounting firms play a vital role as advisors in supporting small and medium enterprises in the development of their businesses. In some countries, accounting firms are required to go beyond their traditional auditing activity to give a "congruity evaluation" of the company's forecasted results, assuring that there are no signs of financial distress. Therefore, accounting firms are called to develop forecasts. Traditional forecasting approaches for business planning can now benefit from artificial intelligence (AI)-based solutions, which are more and more affordable and can accurately handle and process

Incorporating AI Technology in the Service Sector: Innovations in Creating Knowledge, Improving Efficiency, and Elevating Quality of Life. Maria José Sousa, Subhendu Kumar Pani, Francesca Dal Mas, & Sérgio Sousa (Eds.)
© 2024 Apple Academic Press, Inc. Co-published with CRC Press (Taylor & Francis)

vast amounts of data. Employing a human-centered perspective on AI, the chapter aims to investigate the new opportunities brought by AI for accounting firms in their forecasting and business planning activities.

16.1 INTRODUCTION

In recent years, the concept of digital transformation has gained a lot of traction (Ferreira et al., 2019). The integration of digital technologies into business operations is referred to as "digital transformation" or "digitalization" (Liu et al., 2011, p. 1728). The use of digital technologies allows products and services to be integrated across functional, organizational, and geographic boundaries (Ferreira et al., 2019). Therefore, because digital technologies have the power to disrupt the state of the art and may be utilized to promote technical development, they accelerate a major transformation in a variety of sectors (Sebastian et al., 2017). For example, the notion of "Industry 4.0" or the "smart factory" was introduced as a result of digital technology revolutionizing the way industries work (Bagnoli et al., 2019).

The increasing changing paste of the competitive landscape is making it very hard for businesses of all sizes to develop reliable predictions of financial results. Predicting future performance, such as future sales, is critical for a company's planning and strategy (Makridakis, 1996);, corporate resource allocation (Borup et al., 2006);, marketing, logistics, and supply chain management (Hyndman and Athanasopoulos, 2018). Predicting results is becoming critical, especially in the long term, where understanding future market changes is becoming difficult for several reasons, such as technology innovation, new market trends, and new business model developments. Due to its complexity, especially, small and medium enterprises (SMEs) are using external competencies to develop their expected results. Among the many consultants, accounting firms are considered the most crucial business advisors for SMEs and are often called to support the long-term plans of their clients (Massaro et al., 2015).

The overall market of professional service firms is estimated at more than 2 trillion dollars only in the United States, with accounting firms that generate more than 180 billion (Massaro et al., 2020). Interestingly, as their customers, the overall landscape of services provided by accounting firms is rapidly changing. First, technology innovation is changing the traditional way of doing business, with automation, digitalization, and new ways of permanently recording information that are transforming the accounting profession (Guthrie and Parker, 2016). Second, the legislation in several countries is asking for a new role for chartered accountants. For example, in Italy, following the European Banking Authority Guidelines on loan origination and monitoring[1] and the legislation change on financial distress and bankruptcy, chartered accountants are called to provide an independent evaluation of corporate financial information. Interestingly, while in the past this evaluation was limited to audit activity, now, accounting firms are called to give a "congruity evaluation" of the company's forecasted results. In all, accounting firms are called to assure that there are no signs of a company's financial distress.[2]

The new role assigned to accounting firms is calling to further study on how to develop reliable forecasts of companies that are facing increasing competition. The aim of this chapter is to argue how artificial intelligence (AI) can support accounting firms in developing reliable forecasts, and how accounting firms can use AI-based solutions and trust them to be even able to certify their outputs. The chapter is organized as follows. First, the next section depicts traditional approaches to forecasting. Then, an overview of the main techniques of AI can be applied for developing forecasts. The following section describes the main tools available to develop forecasts employing AI practically. A conclusion section ends the chapter.

16.2 TRADITIONAL FORECASTING APPROACHES FOR BUSINESS PLAN DEVELOPMENT

Forecasting techniques can be divided into two types: qualitative and quantitative (Hyndman and Athanasopoulos, 2018). Qualitative approaches rely heavily on subjective inputs that are often difficult to quantify (Makridakis, 1996). Quantitative approaches entail either historical data projections or the building of associative models that aim to forecast using casual (explanatory) variables. Soft data (e.g., human factors, personal opinions, hunches) can be included in the forecasting process using qualitative methodologies. Because they are difficult or impossible to quantify, those aspects are frequently overlooked or minimized when quantitative techniques are applied (Cuhls, 2003). The majority of quantitative procedures involve evaluating objective or hard data. Personal biases, which can corrupt qualitative approaches, are

---

[1]Seehttps://www.eba.europa.eu/regulation-and-policy/credit-risk/guidelines-on-loan-origination-and-monitoring

[2]See the Italian National Chartered Accounting guidelines on conformity and congruity certification on corporate financial communication (available in Italian here: https://commercialisti.it/visualizzatore-articolo?_articleId=1445298&plid=323515).

usually avoided. Thus, forecasts might be developed using one of the two approaches or a combination of the two.

In addition to the qualitative or quantitative nature, the forecasting techniques can be classified into three typologies: judgmental forecasts, time-series forecasts, and associative models (Armstrong, 2001). More precisely:

- **Judgmental forecasts.** The examination of subjective inputs received by numerous sources, including managers' and executives' expert opinions, consumer surveys and questionnaires, sales employees, and consensus panels, is used to make judgmental projections. These sources frequently offer information and insights which are unique and difficult to be found or gathered elsewhere.
- **Time-series forecasts** essentially try to extrapolate previous data into the future. These methods make use of past data, assuming that the future will rely upon what has happened before. Some approaches belonging to such methodologies only seek to spot some variations compared to what happened in the past. In contrast, other approaches try to identify specific patterns in historical sources and numbers and elaborate such patterns to be projected without fully understanding the patterns' origins and motivations.
- **Associative models** utilize equations relying on a number of variables which relations can support the identification of tentative future paths or numbers.

16.2.1 JUDGMENTAL FORECASTS

Judgmental forecasts rely purely on the judgment and opinion of the forecaster to produce forecasts. They may result in a convenient approach in several cases. For example, in case little time is available or when actions have to be taken immediately, or particularly when the political and economic scenario change, accessible data may be outdated, and more current information may not yet be accessible. Likewise, the launch of new items and the redesign of old product lines or their features (including packaging) are hampered by a lack of historical data valuable for forecasting. Generally, forecasts rely on the opinions of those using or working daily with such products or services, including managers, customers, sales staff, and other meaningful stakeholders or actors. Table 16.1 reports some of the approaches which can refer to judgmental forecasts.

TABLE 16.1   Judgmental Forecasts Approaches.

Approach	Description
Executive opinions	A joint prediction by selected executives
	Ideal for long-term planning and new product development
	Pros: Executive experts have knowledge
	Cons: Sometimes individual opinions may emerge
	Natural leaders may bias the results by convincing others toward one solution
Consumer surveys	Seeking feedback and opinions from customers using surveys
	Ideal for product development or feedback
	Pros: Customers are the ones buying products
	Cons: Building and analyzing solid and rigorous surveys needs competencies
	Results may be somehow illogic
Salesforce opinions	Seeking predictions from front-office Salesforce professionals
	Ideal for scouting customers' needs and new market trends
	Pros: Salesmen know their customers and talk to them frequently
	Cons: Biases may come from salesmen's expectation rather than customers' behavior
	Recent events may bias expectations (e.g., pessimistic views after lower sales)
	Conflicts of interest may arise
Delphi or EFTE approaches	Seeking consensus enquiring dedicated expert groups
	Ideal for assessing mixed group's opinions
	Pros: Interdisciplinary groups may be enquired
	Anonymous answers (no biases, no leadership effects, honest opinions)
	Cons: Difficult methodology to be employed in a rigorous way
	It may be difficult to involve the right experts in the panel

16.2.2   TIME-SERIES FORECASTS

A time series is a regularly spaced, time-ordered collection of data (which can happen with different frequencies, from annually to hourly). Customers' demand, earnings and profits, offers, shipping, accidents, outcomes, productivity, consumer price indexes are examples of data. Forecasting methods relying on time-series data are employed on the idea that future values of the series may largely depend on or be similar to recorded historical data and performance. When analyzing time-series data, the analyst must first determine the series' underlying dynamics. Often, simply hatching the data and visually inspecting the figure will suffice. Trends, seasonal fluctuations, cycles, or changes in respect to the average are some of the patterns that may arise. There will also be random and may be irregular variances. The methods for the analysis of the time-series data are described in Table 16.2.

TABLE 16.2   Time-Series Forecasts Approaches.

Approach	Description
Naïve methods	Based on a single previous value of a time series, like past sales according to the season
	Ideal as a starting point
	Pros: Free, quick, simple, no analysis required, easy to be understood
	Cons: Forecasts cannot represent more than a starting point
	Imprecise predictions
Techniques for averaging	Techniques which use the average to smooth down variation elements
	Changes in the average can be managed as:
	• Moving average (recent numbers matter most but equally weighted) • Weighted moving average (recent numbers matter most but not equally weighted) • Exponential smoothing (numbers are increased or decreased by a percentage)
	Ideal as a starting point
	Pros: They get more accurate as more years or time intervals are analyzed
	Cons: They do not cope with unpredictability and are based on historical data and not trends
Techniques for trend	An equation describes the trend
	Ideal as a starting point
	Pros: Trends are key elements for forecasting and strategy making
	Cons: They do not cope with unpredictability
Techniques for seasonality	Techniques which take into account seasonality within the year, months, weeks, days
	Ideal as a starting point
	Pros: Seasonality tends to be regular, so its dynamics are important to forecasting
	Cons: They do not cope with unpredictability and are based on historical data and not trends
Techniques for cycles	Techniques based on variables which may have a correlation
	Ideal as a starting point
	Pros: They are based on refined analysis
	Cons: It is difficult to identify variables which do have a correlation in a consistent way

16.2.3   ASSOCIATIVE MODELS

Associative techniques are based on the discovery of related variables that can be used to anticipate the value of the variable under assessment. The construction of an equation that describes the impacts of predictor variables is at the heart of associative approaches. Table 16.3 reports the main approaches belonging to this category.

TABLE 16.3   Associative Model Approaches.

Approach	Description
Simple linear regression	Based on the relationship between two variables
	Ideal as a starting point
	Pros: The methodology is rigorous and must meet some criteria to be considered valid
	More refined versions are possible (e.g., nonlinear regression)
	Cons: Simple linear regression can end up insufficient to address specific problems

16.3   THE OPPORTUNITIES PROVIDED BY THE IMPLEMENTATION OF AI SOLUTIONS

16.3.1   THE DEFINITION OF AI IN A HUMAN-CENTERED PERSPECTIVE

To adapt to the platform economy and uncover growth prospects in the new digital environment, businesses must employ digital technologies and platforms for data collection, integration, and usage. AI is universally recognized as a key technology to develop firms' abilities to collect, analyze, and make sense of vast amounts of data. The use of AI in forecast opens new perspectives and tools to enrich faster and more reliable forecasts.

AI has been defined in a variety of ways. The literature has defined AI as algorithms to extract knowledge (and patterns) from data, as techniques to replicate the human decision process, simulating human (or otherwise intelligent) behavior. AI applications have been used to find out optimality in a solution space, predict the status or the failure of a system, find our anomalies or defects (Dal Mas et al., 2021; Pan, 2016; Pomerol, 1997).

While many people worry that AI will replace several human roles and raise ethical concerns in its adoption, the literature has underlined how seeking the best human–machine interaction will be the best strategy for people and firms to fully enjoy the opportunities brought by new technologies (Russell et al., 2015). Moreover, AI will bring the need to develop new skills, new jobs, and new educational paths (Wilson et al., 2017).

In all, AI-based forecasts are becoming more and more common. So, on the one hand, we see an increasing need to be able to predict the future asking chartered accountants to verify the documents provided by their clients. On the other hand, even very complex AI-based solutions are becoming more affordable. However, AI forecasted models are normally developed by data scientists that have a different background compared to traditional chartered accountants. Therefore, the key question is how chartered accountants can use AI-based solutions and trust them to be even able to certify their outputs.

To understand how AI can reshape the role of chartered accountants, we need to use a human-centered classification of AI domains that sees the presence of three leading roles: the architect, the expert, and the controller.

The architect is the methodological designer who knows the inner workings of AI technologies. The architect's role is about discussing with the expert to choose the most well-suited architecture according to the system's goals and needs, understanding the details of the issue. The architect defines with the controller the assessment metrics, monitors the training model and advances of the system, the deployment and the production performances, and investigates if technical issues arise. Within this view, architects are experts of the implementation of AI solutions despite the problem addressed. Chartered accountants probably lack the expertise to become architects.

The expert knows the problem and, more importantly, the goals that the AI system should pursue. The expert has the role in discussing with the architect the various aspects of the matters, assessing that the architect understands the shades of the issues. The expert should take care of supplying examples and datasets, explaining the core features. The expert is usually responsible for the practical aspects of the deployment and assessing the system's outputs. Also in this case, the knowledge required of an expert goes beyond the ability of a chartered accountant.

The controller monitors the system, assessing the system's outputs and extracting their meaning. The controller is trained by the architect to understand the system, its eventual problems, and the tentative solutions. The controller should be able to translate the system's performance into key performance indicators for the organization, suggesting new functions and improvements and judging the system's outputs. In our understanding, here, there is the opportunity for traditional chartered accountants to get a role in this forecast revolution.

16.4 CONCLUSIONS

In concluding our chapter, we want to start from the motivations that inspired it. First, forecasting represents a growing research theme that includes several disciplines from statisticians to data scientists to accountants. Traditional approaches to forecasting could be easily covered by chartered accountants. Interestingly, nowadays, on the one side, normative evolutions are pushing chartered accountants to assure the quality of forecasts provided by their customers. On the other hand, the forecast research field is growing due to the implementation of AI-based solutions. However, AI forecasts require different competencies compared to traditional approaches, and the question becomes if there is a role for chartered accountants in this new competitive landscape to support SMEs in their forecast activities.

In all, AI forecasts require three different subjects: architect, expert, and controller. While architects require knowledge domain of the use of AI solutions (typically data scientists), experts require knowledge domain of the subject (typically sector experts) and controllers require specific knowledge on the improvement process. Here, as controller, a new opportunity emerges for chartered accountants. Thus, we believe that accounting firms can benefit from AI-based applications in various ways. AI may speed up the accounting process by creating datasets for the consultant or the entrepreneur to elaborate predictions. Employees could save time avoiding repetitive tasks and use their knowledge and skills in more value-added activities, like data analysis and performance assessment. Additionally, AI looks particularly valuable and promising when it comes to forecasting, given the ability to rely on and handle large datasets. While one single firm may not possess enough historical data to allow the algorithm to make accurate predictions, sector analysis could provide sufficient data to train AI in shaping different scenarios. AI can support the development of more accurate forecasting techniques by relying on a vast amount of data. Accounting firms can benefit from such opportunities by becoming active players in this competition as controllers of the system.

KEYWORDS

- business planning
- forecasting
- artificial Intelligence
- accounting firms
- chartered accountants
- human-centered perspective
- small and medium enterprises

REFERENCES

Armstrong, J. S. Evaluating Forecasting Methods. In *Principles of Forecasting: A Handbook for Researchers and Practitioners*; Armstrong, J., Ed.; Kluwer: New York, NY, 2001; pp 45–472.

Bagnoli, C.; Dal Mas, F.; Massaro, M. The 4th Industrial Revolution: Business Models and Evidence from the Field. *Int. J. E-Serv. Mobile Appl.* **2019,** *11* (3), 271–285. doi:10.4018/IJESMA.2019070103.

Borup, M.; Brown, N.; Konrad, K.; van Lente, H. The Sociology of Expectations in Science and Technology. *Technol. Anal. Strat. Manage.* **2006,** *18* (3–4), 285–298.

Cuhls, K. From Forecasting to Foresight Processes—New Participative Foresight Activities in Germany. *Journal of Forecasting* **2003,** *22* (23), 93–111.

Dal Mas, F.; Bagnoli, C.; Massaro, M.; Biazzo, S. Smart Technologies and New Business Models: Insights from Artificial Intelligence and Blockchain. In *Intellectual Capital, Smart Technologies and Digitalization. SIDREA Series in Accounting and Business Administration*; Chiucchi, M. S., Lombardi, R., Mancini, D., Eds.; Springer: Cham, 2021. doi:10.1007/978-3-030-80737-5_21.

Ferreira, J. J. M.; Fernandes, C. I.; Ferreira, F. A. F. To Be or Not to Be Digital, That Is the Question: Firm Innovation and Performance. *J. Bus. Res.* **2019,** *101* (November), 583–590.

Guthrie, J.; Parker, L. D. Whither the Accounting Profession, Accountants and Accounting Researchers? Commentary and Projections. *Account., Audit. Account. J.* **2016,** *29* (1), 2–10.

Hyndman, R. J.; Athanasopoulos, G. *Forecasting: Principles and Practice*; Otexts, 2018.

Liu, D. Y.; Chen, S. W.; Chou, T. C. Resource Fit in Digital Transformation: Lessons Learned from the CBC Bank Global e-Banking Project. *Manage. Decis.* **2011,** *49* (10), 1728–1742.

Makridakis, S. Forecasting: Its Role and Value for Planning and Strategy. *Int. J. Forecast.* **1996,** *12* (4), 513–537.

Massaro, M.; Dumay, J.; Bagnoli, C. Where There Is a Will There Is a Way: IC, Strategic Intent, Diversification and Firm Performance. *J. Intellect. Cap.* **2015,** *16* (3), 490–517.

Massaro, M.; Bagnoli, C.; Dal Mas, F. The Role of Human Sustainability in Professional Service Firms. Evidence from Italy. *Bus. Strat. Environ.* **2020,** *29* (6), 2668–2678. doi:10.1002/bse.2528.

Pan, Y. Heading toward Artificial Intelligence 2.0. *Engineering* **2016,** *2* (4). doi:10.1016/J. ENG.2016.04.018.

Pomerol, J.-C. Artificial Intelligence and Human Decision Making. *Eur. J. Oper. Res.* **1997,** *99* (1). doi:10.1016/S0377-2217(96)00378-5.

Russell, S.; Hauert, S.; Altman, R.; Veloso, M. Robotics: Ethics of Artificial Intelligence. *Nature* **2015,** *521* (7553), 415–418.

Sebastian, I. M.; Moloney, K. G.; Ross, J. W.; Fonstad, N. O.; Beath, C.; Mocker, M. How Big Old Companies Navigate Digital Transformation. *MIS Q. Exec.* **2017,** 16 (3), 197–213.

Wilson, H. J.; Daugherty, P. R.; Morini-Bianzino, N. The Jobs That Artificial Intelligence Will Create. *MIT Sloan Manage. Rev.* **2017,** *58* (4), 14–16.

INDEX

Milton Keynes UK
Ingram Content Group UK Ltd.
UKHW031126141024
449569UK00006B/401